THE FATE OF THIRD WORLDISM IN THE MIDDLE EAST

RADICAL HISTORIES OF
THE MIDDLE EAST

SERIES EDITORS

Dr Golnar Nikpour, Dartmouth College
Dr Mezna Qato, University of Cambridge
Dr Siavush Randjbar-Daemi, University of St Andrews
Dr Eskandar Sadeghi-Boroujerdi, University of York
Dr Omar H. AlShehabi, University of Leeds
Dr Abdel Razzaq Takriti, Rice University

OTHER TITLES IN THIS SERIES

Call to Arms: Iran's Marxist Revolutionaries by Ali Rahnema
Contested Modernity by Omar H. AlShehabi
Khalil Maleki by Homa Katouzian
A Rebel's Journey by Peyman Vahabzadeh

For more information and details of forthcoming volumes, please visit
oneworld-publications.com/series/radical-histories-of-the-middle-east

THE FATE OF THIRD WORLDISM IN THE MIDDLE EAST

Iran, Palestine and Beyond

EDITED BY
RASMUS C. ELLING
AND SUNE HAUGBOLLE

ONEWORLD
ACADEMIC

Oneworld Academic

An imprint of Oneworld Publications

Published by Oneworld Academic in 2024

ISBN 978-0-86154-728-9
eISBN 978-0-86154-729-6

Typeset by Geethik Technologies
Printed and bound in Great Britain by Clays Ltd, Elcograf S.p.A.

Oneworld Publications
10 Bloomsbury Street
London WC1B 3SR
England

Stay up to date with the latest books,
special offers, and exclusive content from
Oneworld with our newsletter

Sign up on our website
oneworld-publications.com

To the Danish Institute of Damascus,
whose generous support made
this book project possible.

Contents

Acknowledgements

This book is the result of several workshops in Copenhagen and online. We would like to acknowledge all participants, whose contribution to the debates shaped our thinking. In addition to the authors in the book, they are Leonard Michael, Mahdi Ganjavi, Marc Schade-Poulsen, William Figueroa, Sayed Ali Alavi, Shahrzad Mojab, Siarhei Bohdan, Siavush Randjbar-Daemi, Rowena Binti Abdul Razaq, and Alina Sajed. The Global Political Sociology group at Roskilde University provided useful feedback on an early draft of the introduction to the book. We would also like to thank our student assistants at the Copenhagen workshop, Samira Ebadi Tabrizi and Sol Khorshid Woloszynski Tadayoni, and the administration at Roskilde University and the University of Copenhagen. We are particularly indebted to our advisory board, Abed Takriti, Naghmeh Sohrabi, Toufoul Abou-Hodeib, and Eskandar Sadeghi-Boroujerdi, whose friendship and commitment to this project have been crucial.

Introduction

The Transformation of Third Worldism in the Middle East

Sune Haugbolle and Rasmus C. Elling

Third Worldism was the idea that revolutionary, anti-imperialist militancy in what we today term the Global South, buttressed by international solidarity, would not only lead to national liberation of oppressed peoples but also to universal emancipation. Today, such an idea might at once appear highly relevant and somewhat antiquated. International solidarity remains a key claim for social movements and political organisations fighting against capitalism, neo-imperialism, and racism across the world. The Western left at times appears torn between prioritising solidarity with oppressed people or supporting states fighting against Western hegemony – even if those states are authoritarian and oppressive. Third Worldist echoes can occasionally be heard in illiberal state rhetoric, such as when Russia's President Putin in September 2022 declared an 'anti-colonial struggle' against Western imperialism to justify his annexations in Ukraine.

Permeating these disparate examples is a sense that even though the *language* is reminiscent of Third Worldism in its 1970s heyday, the *ideology* of Third Worldism today is little more than an echo of a more powerful past when the non-Western revolutionary was considered the vanguard of a global struggle for emancipation. Lurking in this dissonance is also the gradual change to global economic and political power, which has shifted eastwards in past decades, blurring previous distinctions between the Global

South and the Global North.[1] But if Third Worldism is today an echo, how and when did it cease to be a dominant global rally cry?

The aim of this book is to revisit the time when the power of Third Worldism at once peaked *and* dramatically declined in one of the world regions where it had up until then represented a strong promise for change. The time in question spans the historical turning points of the late 1970s and early 1980s; and the region is the Middle East. Specifically, this book focuses on two struggles for national liberation and sovereignty in west Asia – namely in Palestine and Iran – that were not only pivotal to political developments in the broader region but also of great significance to a global solidarity movement.

In Iran and Palestine, opposition and liberation movements saw themselves, and were seen by supporters around the world, as holding a torch lit by the anti-colonial rebellions of the 1950s and carried through the sixties and seventies by an array of socialist and nationalist revolutions and revolutionary states, guerrilla organisations, popular uprisings, student rebellions, and activist campaigns, as well as by artistic, intellectual, and academic activism that spanned from Vietnam to Angola, from Havana to Algiers and Paris. And yet by the early 1980s, the two movements in Iran and Palestine had arguably failed to bring about the progressive visions of independence *and* freedom they had been seen by protagonists and supporters to embody. Instead, while the Iranian Revolution of 1979 had secured Iran's independence of Western powers, it had also produced an Islamic Republic with theocratic underpinnings; and by 1982, the Palestinian revolution had not only been eclipsed by civil war in Lebanon, by the Palestine Liberation Organisation's (PLO) demise as revolutionary leader, by Israeli aggression, and by intra-Arab fratricide, but also by its alliances with autocratic regimes in Syria, Iraq, and Libya.[2]

Hence, historians tell us, Third Worldism came to an end in the Middle East in or around 1979. If this is correct, then how did those championing the Third Worldist revolutions in Palestine and Iran perceive that end? This book re-examines the period leading up to two historical turning points for Iran and Palestine, namely 1979 and 1982. Specifically, the book connects micro-histories of personal, social, and political-ideological change in the

---

[1] Martin Müller, 'In Search of the Global East: Thinking between North and South', *Geopolitics* 25 (3) 2020: 734–755.
[2] Alan R. Taylor, 'The PLO in Inter-Arab Politics', *Journal of Palestine Studies* 11 (2) 1982: 70–81.

Iranian and Palestinian movements and in their transnational entanglements to the macro-history of Third Worldism as a global phenomenon. Such a connection, we argue, can help explain how long-gestating, interrelated, unresolved dilemmas and challenges for Third Worldist revolutionaries materialised in crisis in the late 1970s and early 1980s. The internal dimensions of this crisis pertained to questions about inclusivity and priorities, about theory and practice, about possibilities and limits, and about means and ends. These internal dimensions were coupled with or compounded by formidable external challenges: hostile counter-insurgency and intelligence operations, disinformation and propaganda, surveillance and infiltration, intimidation and assassinations. Looming just beyond these immediate trials was a broader change in global politics and ideology so profound that a decade later scholars would proclaim not just the end of Third Worldism but the end of the age of revolutions, or the global victory of liberalism or, indeed, 'the End of History'.[3]

To understand how the factors that together placed Third Worldism in crisis were understood at the time, the book focuses on key protagonists: roving revolutionaries, student activists, guerrilla fighters, volunteer nurses, militant intellectuals, propagandists – and the vehicles with which they transmitted and exchanged their visions and demands: manifestos and declarations, organisations and networks, delegations and missions, conferences and festivals, newspapers and periodicals, slogans and obituaries. These people, their networks, and the artefacts they left behind are brought to the centre in this book through documents from understudied archives, testimonies, and interviews in numerous languages.

Such sources for understanding the crisis of Third Worldism, we argue in this book, can help push historical research towards a more dynamic view of the role of the late 1970s and early 1980s in world history. It can also help us explain the specific circumstances of the Middle East. Hence, by juxtaposing the cases of the Iranian and Palestinian national liberation struggles, and by harnessing insights from new research, this book presents a novel reinterpretation of a seminal period in history.

The significance of this period remains undisputed, not just in relation to the Middle East but also to universal and contemporary questions about

---

[3] Robert S. Snyder, 'The End of Revolution?', *The Review of Politics* 61 (1) 1999: 5–28; Francis Fukuyama, 'The End of History?', *National Interest* (16) 1989: 3–18; B.R. Tomlinson, 'What was the Third World?', *Journal of Contemporary History* 38 (2) 2003: 307–321.

self-determination, emancipation, change, and solidarity. However, the consequences of the period under scrutiny and the tremendous changes it embodies are still open to interpretation and final verdict. This is why we insist on talking about *the fate* of Third Worldism rather than about its *end*. Aspects of Third Worldism live on today, not least in transnational solidarity movements but also in regimes that claim to represent resistance against Western hegemony.

THIRD WORLDISM

Third Worldism is used in this book as an umbrella term covering a range of related ideas and ideologies connected across time and space to national liberation movements in what was then considered 'The Third World'.[4] In the words of Robert Malley, Third Worldism was 'a political, intellectual, even artistic effort that took as its raw material an assortment of revolutionary movements and moments, wove them into a more or less intelligible whole, and gave us the tools to interpret not them alone, but also others yet to come'.[5]

This 'assortment' of revolutionary movements and states had a shared commitment to assigning agency to the non-Western world, thus continuing earlier forms of internationalism but with a less Eurocentric emphasis than classical Marxism, socialism, or liberalism. Such a vision of the future of humanity – and the future of socialism – appealed to many on the Western left. Indeed, the term *tiers-mondisme* had its roots in France.[6] Beyond the usual nationalist register, the sovereignty that Third Worldist ideologues and militants dreamed of was a radical rupture: a way to imagine and enact 'anticolonial translocal connectivity' that tied together liberation movements in a more or less cohesive project globally.[7]

---

[4] Peter Berger, 'After the Third World? History, destiny and the fate of Third Worldism', *Third World Quarterly*, 25 (1) 2004: 9–39; Rajeev Patel and Philip McMichael, 'Third Worldism and the lineages of global fascism: the regrouping of the global South in the neoliberal era', *Third World Quarterly* 25 (1) 2004: 231–254; Arif Dirlik, 'Spectres of the Third World: global modernity and the end of the three worlds', *Third World Quarterly* 25 (1) 2004: 131–148, 94–116; Robert Malley, *The Call from Algeria: Third Worldism, Revolution and the Turn to Islam* (Berkeley and Los Angeles: University of California Press, 1996).

[5] Robert Malley, 'The Third Worldist Moment', *Current History* 98 (631) 1999: 359.

[6] Andrew Nash, 'Third Worldism', *African Sociological Review* 7 (1) 2002: 94–123.

[7] Alina Sajed, 'Re-remembering Third Worldism: An Affirmative Critique of National Liberation in Algeria', *Middle East Critique* 28 (3) 2019: 243–260.

In the first period, following the Second World War – during what is often referred to as 'the Bandung Era' after the Bandung Conference in Indonesia in 1955 – leaders such as Egypt's Gamal Abdel Nasser and India's Jawaharlal Nehru championed a third way between Sino-Soviet and US hegemonies against the backdrop of the Cold War. Building on the 'Bandung spirit' of postcolonial self-determination,[8] these leaders established organisations such as the Non-Aligned Movement in 1961 on the premise that North–South divisions and conflicts mattered more than the East–West dynamics dictated by Cold War rivalry. In their Three-World model, the countries of the First World were the ones allied to the United States, whereas the Second World referred to the industrial socialist states under the influence of the Soviet Union. The Third World defined all the other countries that remained non-aligned, whether in Africa, Latin America, Oceania, or Asia. Third Worldism was, by the early 1960s, a thriving, global constellation of organisations, movements, and ideas. This division of the world was sometimes underlain by a Marxist theory of the world economy as separated into core, peripheral, and semi-peripheral countries depending on their relation to and place in global capitalism.[9]

However, Third Worldists differed significantly when it came to economic policy and strategic orientation in a Cold War world, and some of them were much more radical in speech than in action. As historians of the period have noted, these significant differences and contradictions were inherent in the very emergence of Third Worldism in the early 1950s. The political reality in development states such as Egypt, Indonesia, and Algeria commonly depended on a certain biopolitics, or form of governance of their citizens, that was 'rooted in a regime of sovereign state control, and designed to mobilise citizens in ways favourable to capital'.[10] Similarly, states committed

---

[8] See, for example, Christopher J. Lee (ed.), *Making a World After Empire: The Bandung Moment and its Political Afterlives*, 2nd edition (Athens: Ohio University Press, 2020); Luis Eslava, Michael Fakhri, Vasuki Nesiah, 'The Spirit of Bandung', in *Bandung, Global History, and International Law* (Cambridge: Cambridge University Press, 2017); Antonia Finnane and Derek McDougall, *Bandung 1955: Little Histories* (Clayton, VIC: Monash University Press, 2010), 201; Clifford Geertz, 'What was the Third World Revolution?', *Dissent* 52 (1) Winter 2005 (whole no. 218): 35–45; Adom Getachew, *Worldmaking After Empire: The Rise and Fall of Self-Determination* (Princeton: Princeton University Press, 2020).

[9] First formulated by Egyptian economist Samir Amin, world systems theory was popularised in the 1970s by Wallerstein. See Immanuel Wallerstein (ed.), *The Modern World-System in the Longue Durée* (Abingdon, Oxon and New York: Routledge, 2016).

[10] Patel and McMichael, 'Third Worldism and the lineages of global fascism...', 234.

to 'liberation' routinely restricted individual liberty. The notion, formulated by Ghana's Nkrumah and Egypt's Nasser, of a possible third way to liberation between Sino-Soviet socialism and American capitalist hegemony served as a minimal ideological glue tying quite different regimes together.

It soon turned out that many leaders were not, in fact, able or willing to adhere to strict non-alignment. Rather, they leaned or were forced by military pressure towards the Soviet Union or the People's Republic of China in the pursuit of Asian, African, Arab, or Latin American socialism. For example, Egypt's President Nasser, who was considered an important Third World leader, opposed communism domestically, but relied on Soviet military advice and support. Such ideological and strategic differences hindered total non-alignment solidarity.

Out of the general swerve towards socialist transformation came a second generation of Third Worldists championing a less nationalist and more radical and revolutionary socialist vision. Ideologically, this generation often leaned towards Maoism. The post-Bandung generation was personified in the figure of Che Guevara and associated with the idea of Tricontinentalism,[11] named after the Tricontinental Conference in Havana, Cuba in 1966, as well as with interstate-level organisations such as the Afro-Asian Peoples' Solidarity Organisation. The emergence in Cuba of a revolutionary state with internationalist ambitions created a new focal point for the increasingly fluid landscape of protests and militant 'direct action' advocated by guerrilla movements in the 1960s. The second generation was also associated with less institutionalised networks of transnational radicalism, for example in student networks.[12] Many of them turned against Soviet-led bureaucratic socialism and instead adopted less bureaucratic revolutionary ideals. A new form of global Maoism – with varying interpretations and adaptations – developed to accommodate these new energies of anti-colonial struggle and youth rebellion.[13]

This second strand of Third Worldism materialised in important iterations in the Middle East, not least in Palestine and Algeria, where Algiers became a nodal point for a transnational network of revolutionaries.[14] Key

---

[11] R. Joseph Parrot and Mark Atwood Lawrence, *The Tricontinental Revolution: Third World Radicalism and the Cold War* (Cambridge: Cambridge University Press, 2022).

[12] See, for example, Sohail Daulatzai, *Black Star, Crescent Moon: the Muslim International and Black Freedom Beyond America* (Minneapolis: University of Minnesota Press, 2012).

[13] Julia Lovell, *Maoism – A Global History* (New York: Knopf, 2019).

[14] Jeffrey James Byrne, *Mecca of Revolution: Algeria, Decolonization, and the Third World Order* (Oxford: Oxford University Press, 2016); Malley, *The Third Worldist Moment*,

thinkers like the Egyptian economist Samir Amin equipped Third Worldism with a comprehensive analysis that explained the Third World in terms of its position in the 'periphery' of the world economic system. Third Worldism also connected to so-called New Left political movements in Europe, the US and elsewhere, which increasingly displayed ideological and emotional investment in revolutionary struggle in the non-Western world.[15] Maoist ideology appealed to them because of its non-Western origins and its emphasis on bottom-up mobilisation that centred peasants as well as workers. The Little Red Book of Chairman Mao with its aphorisms and observations on rebellion thus became a manual of revolution for Middle Eastern revolutionaries as well as for middle-class Europeans, thus creating a common – albeit differently adapted – script for social transformation.[16]

Here, the historiography of Third Worldism intersects and overlaps in significant ways with literatures about what some historians call 'the long 1960s'. This generally refers to a period broader than the 1960s, spanning civil rights, anti-war, women's, and youth movements that culminated, in Europe's case, in the student uprisings of 1968. While there is disagreement on whether 1968 was a global phenomenon,[17] historians debating the period in a broader geographical perspective inevitably view 'the global 1960s' in terms of decolonisation and socialist movements for national liberation and transnational solidarity.[18] Thus, while in Europe and the US many embraced

1999; Elaine Mokhtefi, *Algiers, Third World Capital: Freedom Fighters, Revolutionaries, Black Panthers* (London: Verso, 2020).

[15] Quinn Slobodian, *Foreign Front: Third World Politics in Sixties West Germany* (Chapel Hill: Duke University Press, 2020); Guiseppe Morisini, 'The European Left and the Third World', *Contemporary Marxism* 2 1980: 67–80.

[16] Richard Wolin, *The Wind from the East: French Intellectuals, the Cultural Revolution, and the Legacy of the 1960s* (Princeton: Princeton University Press, 2018).

[17] Claudia Derichs, '1968 and the "Long 1960s": A Transregional Perspective', in *Re-Configurations: Contextualizing Transformation Processes and Lasting Crisis in the Middle East and North Africa* (New York: Springer, 2021), 105–115; Chen Jian and Martin Klimke (eds), *The Routledge Handbook of the Global Sixties: Between protest and nation-building* (London: Routledge, 2018); Samantha Christiansen and Zachary A. Scarlett (eds), *The Third World in the Global 1960s* (New York: Berghahn Books, 2013); Duco Hellema, *The Global 1970s: Radicalism, Reform, and Crisis* (London: Routledge, 2019).

[18] Odd Westad, *The Global Cold War: Third World Interventions and the Making of Our Times* (New York: Cambridge University, 2005); Jeremy Varon, *Bringing the War Home: The Weather Underground, The Red Army Faction, and Revolutionary Violence in the Sixties and Seventies* (Berkeley: University of California Press, 2004); George Katsiaficas, *The Imagination of the New Left: A Global Analysis of 1968* (London: South End Press, 1999); Abdel Razzaq Takriti, *Monsoon Revolution: Republicans, Sultans, and Empires in Oman, 1965–1976* (Oxford and New York: Oxford University Press, 2013).

feminism, ecology, and sexual minority rights, liberation groups in the Global South, faced with the brutal repression of authoritarian regimes, naturally had a more concretely militant outlook.

The Middle East certainly became a very hot zone of interaction and engagement between radical regimes, revolutionary non-state actors, and solidarity movements, all of them committed to Third Worldist anti-imperialism albeit with different means and methods. The arrival on the scene of the PLO, between its creation in 1964 and its full independence from Nasser's Egypt in 1969, gave those who advocated non-state militancy a movement to support. Student groups and particularly diasporic communities in former imperial capitals such as Paris played an important role in connecting the New Left to struggles such as those in Palestine and Iran.[19] These highly politicised students and militants shared a Marxist–Leninist and anti-imperialist inclination, but also differed widely.

Crucially, the very disparate struggles lumped together here under the umbrella of Third Worldism were often connected through the moral, economic, and logistic support of solidarity networks. This new connectivity across various geographies facilitated a political globalisation of tremendous and lasting importance. Texts by non-Western thinkers and ideologues like Frantz Fanon, Che Guevara, Ghassan Kanafani, and Mao Zedong guided political orientation and created a global 'language' of dissent. They invested their readers in a joint world-making project referred to as 'the revolution' or 'the struggle'. While different families of anti-imperialism varied in expression and focus – and in levels of freedom to organise and express themselves freely – which explains the different approaches to violent resistance – they did share the sense of being engaged in a global project that felt not only necessary but also achievable.

1979 AND THE MIDDLE EAST

Third Worldism in the Middle East manifested itself firstly through the liberation movements in Algeria, Oman, and Palestine, with the FLN in Algeria garnering global support and, after independence in 1962, making the

---

[19] Yoav Di-Capua, 'Palestine Comes to Paris: The Global Sixties and the Making of a Universal Cause', *Journal of Palestine Studies* 49 (1) 2021; Christoph Kalter, 'From global to local and back: the "Third World" concept and the new radical left in France', *Journal of Global History* 12 (1) 2017: 115–136.

capital Algiers a 'Mecca' for revolutionaries and liberation movements from places like Cuba, Angola, Eritrea, Vietnam, and Palestine.[20] Consequently, Algeria has attracted a lot of scholarly attention from historians working on Third Worldism. These scholars highlight the initial euphoria of the FLN's victory over the French colonial masters, which boosted a post-Bandung phase of more radical revolutions. They also stress the importance of Fanon as a global theorist of revolution who synthesised and universalised the experience of Algeria.

Palestine soon became equally central to these emerging international-ist co-ordinates, especially after the June 1967 war and the takeover of the Palestine Liberation Movement by guerrilla groups led by Yasser Arafat. During the 1960s and 1970s, other Arab radical regimes in Yemen, Iraq, Syria, and particularly Libya adopted a Third Worldist rhetoric, combined with elements of socialism and Arab nationalism, and generally with the backing of the Soviet Union.[21] Through the 1970s, however, it became increasingly clear that the solidarity and unity at the heart of Third Worldist rhetoric failed to match reality in these states. Furthermore, at the ideological level, socialist regionalism and Marxist internationalism were challenged by Islamic revivalist movements such as the Amal Movement in Lebanon and the Muslim Brotherhood in Egypt and Syria.

In 1979, several of these broad trends came to a head. While Egypt, the former leader of Arab nationalism and state-led socialism, further opened its economy to foreign investment and made peace with Israel, the Iranian Revolution provided political Islam with a state project. This revolution was in crucial respects rooted in a transnational radical left and while it contained overtly socialist-inspired demands,[22] it quickly led to Ayatollah Khomeini's violent purge of almost all leftist forces. Instead, the Iranian Revolution ushered in an era of resurgent Islamists making claims to state power in the country, the region, and the world.

---

[20] Jeffrey James Burne, *Mecca of Revolution: Algeria, Decolonization, and the Third World Order* (Oxford: Oxford University Press, 2016); see also: Afshin Matin-asgari, *Iranian Student Opposition to the Shah* (Costa Mesa: Mazda, 1999).

[21] Karma Nabulsi and Abdel Razzaq Takriti, The Palestinian Revolution, http://learnpalestine.politics.ox.ac.uk/, Oxford: Department of Politics and International Relations, Oxford University (2017).

[22] Eskandar Sadeghi-Boroujerdi, 'The Origins of Communist Unity: Anti-Colonialism and Revolution in Iran's Tri-Continental Moment', *British Journal of Middle Eastern Studies* 45 (5) 2018: 796–822.

In Iraq, Saddam Hussein became president in July 1979 and proceeded, a year later, to launch a devastating war with Iran that would continue until 1988. In Turkey, conservative-nationalist leader Süleyman Demirel retook the position of prime minister in the midst of political turmoil that would lead to a military coup in 1980. In Saudi Arabia, the Grand Mosque Seizure in November 1979 signalled the rise of new radical religious counter-currents in the Sunni world – a trend further propelled in the backlash to the Soviet invasion of Afghanistan in December 1979. That invasion led to almost a decade of military conflict between the Soviets and the Mujahedeen, among whom were future leaders of Jihadist terrorist groups such as al-Qaeda and ISIS. In short, while in the 1970s political opposition across the Middle East was dominated by leftist and left-leaning movements, by the beginning of the 1980s it was clear that Islamism had become a formidable if not dominant political tendency.

Indeed, when seen in retrospect, it is difficult not to view 1979 as a turning point, not just for the Middle East but for the whole world. There was Deng Xiaoping's introduction of free market policies in China from December 1978 and then the wave of socio-culturally conservative and economically neoliberal policies of UK Prime Minister Margaret Thatcher from 1979 and US President Ronald Reagan from 1981 – all of these developments marked, each in their own way, the emergence of a new politics based to varying degrees on free market capitalism, deregulation, privatisation, the undermining of collective bargaining, and attacks on welfare-state social democracy and on Keynesian economic policy.[23] In Europe, welfare state policies were further challenged by 'stagflation', poor economic performance, and high youth unemployment. The oil embargo of 1973 marked a turning point after more than a decade of growth. In most Western societies, a sense of perpetual crisis in the 1970s – summed up by the eminent historian Tony Judt as the 'the most dispiriting decade' – took hold.[24] Adding to the strangeness of the 1970s was the overlap of crisis with lingering social experimentation and rapid and wide-ranging technological advancement, which, for many people, created unease about the future and their ability to keep up with the speed of change.

---

[23] Christian Caryl, *Strange Rebels: 1979 and the Birth of the 21st century* (New York: Basic Books, 2012).
[24] Cited in Duco Hellema, 'Introduction', in Hellema (ed.), *The Global 1970s: Radicalism, Reform, and Crisis* (New York: Routledge, 2019).

Such developments in Europe and North America overlapped with those elsewhere to form a global paradigm shift. Whereas the early 1970s had been brimming with hope for 'The Third World' and the prospects of a new international economic order that would complete 'the geopolitical process of decolonisation and create a more democratic global order of truly sovereign states',[25] the early 1980s instead became dominated by the TINA doctrine, i.e. the idea that 'There Is No Alternative' to Thatcherism and Reaganomics. Meanwhile, several African, Asian, and Latin American states were forced by their failing economies to seek loans from the International Monetary Fund and the World Bank and adopt 'the Washington Consensus' of structural adjustment towards economic liberalisation that arguably involved a reinvention of neocolonial means of control, with devastating repercussions for the working class and rural poor in some countries. In sum, it is not only the change of political leadership around 1979 that signals a shift, but equally the material and cultural effects that new politics and economics had on daily life, on ideas, and on the sense of historical direction.[26]

While Washington played a long game against Soviet influence and Marxist ideas on the global stage, Khomeini's battle against socialism, atheism, and secularism was arguably different – and yet both had an impact on the global role of the revolutionary left. The new leaders of 1979 can be seen as partaking in a global conservative attempt to counter and dismantle the revolutionary rebellions of 'the long 1960s' that advocated a secular socialist way.[27] Even where these rebels had succeeded in their revolutions, repressive forces outmanoeuvred their erstwhile allies. By the early 1980s, most if not all of the states that retained a form of state socialism were ruled by autocratic regimes. In the case of Iran, Iraq, and Libya, the states co-opted the revolutionary spirit of Third Worldism, weaponising it to institutionalise authoritarian regimes. Over time, these regimes used their self-defined position as standard bearers of Third Worldism to prevent democratic reform. The co-optation of Third Worldism thus had lasting effects and continues to inform authoritarian states' claim to anti-imperialism today.

---

[25] Nils Gilman, 'The New International Economic Order: A Reintroduction', *Humanity: An International Journal of Human Rights, Humanitarianism, and Development* 6 (3) Spring 2015: 1–16.

[26] For a discussion of periodisation in global history, see Konrad Hirschler and Sarah Bowen Savant, 'Introduction – What is in a Period? Arabic Historiography and Periodization', *Der Islam* 91 (1) 2014: 6–19.

[27] Christian Caryl, *Strange Rebels: 1979 and the Birth of the 21st century* (New York: Basic Books, 2012).

BEYOND 1979

The fact that 1979 seems to embody many of the changes discussed above clearly makes it a pedagogical way to explain the fate of Third Worldism in the Middle East.[28] Indeed, the 1979 revolution in Iran is still treated in much of the broader literature on the Middle East as the breaking point between the decades dominated by secular and left-leaning ideologies and the following decades dominated by Islamism. However, a too narrow focus on 1979 as the proverbial 'sharp turning point' entails the risk of downplaying the precursors. It also affirms a traditional historiographic focus on political leadership – as opposed to social, cultural, or economic history – as the main marker of historical periods.[29] When we turn our gaze to social movements, as the authors in this book do, it becomes clear that trends manifesting themselves in 1979 had been a decade or more in the making. These trends point to an emerging social order and include authoritarian co-optation of Third Worldist anti-imperialism, splits and infights between revolutionary groups, Islamic revivalism, and the global advancement of economic liberalism.

The social order that emerged in the Middle East in the 1970s was, as the Egyptian sociologist Saad Eddin Ibrahim pointed out in an influential 1982 study, largely the product of the shift from Arab nationalist and socialist politics once embodied by Egypt's President Nasser to the 'Petro-Islam' of the Gulf states.[30] During the 1970s, this emerging Gulf power created great wealth disparity with clear social, cultural, and political ramifications: mass in-region migration, new capitalist values, and behavioural patterns linked to liberalisation alongside supposedly 'culturally authentic' identity projects propagated by authoritarian states. The Westernised capitalist turn also produced dissent, however, in the form of Islamisation, on the one hand, and the enduring attraction of revolutionary currents, on the other. If Third Worldist revolutionaries were still fighting by the mid-1970s, they were largely struggling against the current.

Due to these trends, the basic sense of historical direction arguably began to change in the late 1970s as dilemma and even defeat replaced

---

[28] D.W. Lesch, *1979: The Year That Shaped the Modern Middle East* (New York: Routledge, 1991); see also: Kim Ghattas, *Black Wave* (New York: Henry Holt, 2020).

[29] Hirschler and Bowen Savant, 'Introduction – What is in a Period?'.

[30] Saad Eddin Ibrahim, *The New Arab Social Order: A Study of the Social Impact of Oil Wealth* (Boulder, CO: Westview Press, 1982).

possibility as the primary 'structure of feeling' on the anti-imperialist left. These dilemmas partly resulted from the dynamics of the Cold War, in particular the Sino-Soviet conflict, as well as from the USA's covert and open counter-revolutionary measures and increasingly broad overtures to states and movements. They also came from internal contradictions on the left concerning the role of women, the lack of democratic organisational culture, and, more generally, a sometimes-destructive debate about the degree of economic, social, and political liberalism that the left should embrace. Another debate that was particularly heated in the Middle East, and which already created significant fissures in the mid-1970s, concerned the role of political Islam in otherwise largely secular opposition movements and organisations.

The structural change of Third Worldism played out inside and between states in the region, but it also echoed in the transnational revolutionary alliances and networks in which movements were embedded. In this way, the drift towards authoritarianism and Islamism had consequences for how the Western world viewed the rest of the world. By 1979, many Western leftists, who had generally viewed the southern political subject as inspiration for their own revolutionary ambitions in Europe and elsewhere during the Third Worldist period, became disenchanted and instead increasingly began to regard the Global South as an object in need of development and assistance.[31]

In short, it is possible to trace many of the reasons why Third Worldist movements were weakened or underwent significant changes in the latter part of the 1970s. Therefore, this book argues, the focus on 1979 also obscures the possibility that the 'breaking point' might be periodised differently. While the Iranian Revolution certainly had a major impact on the Palestinian (yet-to-be-fulfilled) revolution, there are also limits to the explanatory power of 1979. Rather, in a Palestinian historiographical lens, it is arguably 1982 that stands out as the marker of the end of an era. Following the Israeli military campaign that included full-scale bombardment of west Beirut in the summer of 1982, Arafat and the PLO were forced to leave Lebanon, ending the revolutionary stage of the Palestinian struggle, and starting a new stage that would culminate in the PLO's transformation to a state-like entity in the West Bank in the 1990s.

---

[31] Peter Berger, 'After the Third World?'; J. Garnier and Ronald S.W. Lew, 'From the Wretched of the Earth to the Defence of the West: An Essay on Left Disenchantment in France', *Socialist Register* 21 1984: n. page.

Third Worldism, as indicated above, from the beginning encompassed a statist and a non-statist project. If Iran's revolution built on earlier post-colonial liberation and state-building projects – only with a new religious colouring – the Palestinian liberation movement until 1982 embodied the spirit of guerrilla struggle. In this sense, 1982 signals a very important shift away from the broader appeal of local military mobilisation that brought initial successes in Cuba, Algeria, Vietnam, and elsewhere. Not that guerrilla activity ceased – as witnessed, for example, by the Iran-inspired and -sponsored Hizbollah movement in Lebanon, founded that year. Rather, the problem-space of Third Worldism transformed from one overwhelmingly concerned with revolution from below, and its contiguous forms of transnational networks, to one concerned with state-driven interventions.

Mirrored in this shift was the gradual decline of Marxism–Leninism as the overarching ideological framework for Third Worldist alliances and the rise of a diverse range of anti-imperialisms throughout a decade of internal splits that had begun around the 1967 war. Dominant political discourse shifted as militants began to question their tactics and commitments, from what remained of the leftist, Marxist discourse towards discourses of political Islam. As Homa Katouzian has put it, the late 1970s saw the face of resistance against imperialism change from the secular *fida'yi* to the religious *mojahed*.[32] Iran played a key role in that transition, but it also involved decades of deliberation in Arab societies. Regional tensions and fault lines meant that resistance had now acquired a wider meaning than the straightforward anti-imperialism of the 1950s and 1960s.

Lines that had begun to blur in the 1970s between former allies in the Third Worldist project became deadly in the 1980s. In fact, the most common themes in political studies of the Middle East today refer back to the conflicts of that decade: the solidification of authoritarianism, Islamism as the main oppositional camp, the decline of Arab nationalism, the bifurcation of regional politics between a normalisation camp led by Egypt and the Gulf states versus a rejection camp led by Syria and Iran, the decline of Marxism and the suppression of liberalism, and the rise of the authoritarian-neoliberal axis of power centred in the Gulf countries.

As states adopted different positions and alliances, transnational revolutionary actors were often caught between their agendas. Many militants

---

[32] Homa Katouzian, 'The Iranian Revolution at 30: The Dialectic of State and Society', *Middle East Critique* 19 (1) 2010: 35–53.

ended up on the receiving end of state repression, as they ran afoul of the official positions of authoritarian regimes. For their part, the regimes of leaders like Ruhollah Khomeini, Saddam Hussein, Hafez al-Assad, and Muammar Gaddafi sought to monopolise and instrumentalise the anti-imperialist struggle in this new age. Conflicts such as the Iran–Iraq War and the Lebanese civil war pitted them against each other, and at the same time exacerbated state repression across the region. The competition for hegemony and ownership of the Third Worldist mantle meant that authoritarian states took a firmer grip on their control over cultural expression, sidelining, exiling, incarcerating, and killing dissidents. This meant that by the mid-1980s, the dominant expression of Third Worldism in the region was no longer organically produced material from social movements, dissident intellectuals, and artists, but rather regime-sponsored propaganda.[33]

CONTRIBUTIONS, METHODOLOGY, AND THEORY

The aim of this book is to show how revolutionary groups and milieus experienced and negotiated the watershed moment before the new order of the 1980s settled. While historians have written detailed accounts of the emergence of Third Worldism in its heyday of the 1950s, 1960s, and 1970s, no one has really explained *why* Third Worldism declined or ended. This book makes four related proposals for resolving this question. First, that the most instructive answers can be found in the Third Worldist revolutionaries' own words and deeds; second, that analytical explanations must be rooted in the study of a longer history of gradual change, which in turn challenges the historiographical privileging of 1979 as a 'breaking point'; third, that a dual focus on Iran and Palestine as two cases and two causes with global ramifications can help bring about a more nuanced and comprehensive account of the fate of Third Worldism in the Middle East; and fourth that such research is of direct benefit to a global history of revolution and solidarity beyond the Middle East.

Regarding the book's first contribution, we have been inspired by histories of periodic shifts that allow for both large-scale structural analysis of, for example, geopolitics and ideology and for granular analysis of social

---

[33] See, for example, Amir Moosavi and Narges Bajoghli (eds), *Debating the Iran-Iraq War in Contemporary Iran* (London: Routledge, 2018).

transformations.[34] International and diplomatic history, for example, might render the reasons for political mobilisation as primarily a game of elite actors, thus obfuscating the deeper roles of non-elites and social movements, where fundamental negotiations of values, norms, and ideological direction often take place. Hence, this book joins a recurring trend in history in which focus is shifted from the macro-scale of 'big politics', 'big men', and grand narratives to the meso- or micro-scale of personal and interpersonal experience in collectives. Instead of the focus on geopolitics, states, and state leaders typical of the literature that associates fundamental change with 1979,[35] the focus shift to a smaller scale allows this book to dissect the internal contradictions and splits in the Third Worldist movement.

The focus on key actors in the movement, we argue, can open our eyes to new, surprising, and often contradictory dimensions of ideological formation, forms of mobilisation and organisation, political sensibilities, and subjectivities inside and between the movements and networks connecting militants across the region and globally. For example, recent research[36] has shown the importance of recognising authoritarian, regressive, nationalist, localist, and so-called nativist currents in global and transnational settings as being on a par with those normally favoured by scholars, i.e. internationalist solidarity. Hence, by connecting international relations to social and militant movements and to gradual social change, we hope to shine a light on such seeming contradictions.

Answering big sociological questions about the world and the region four decades ago through 'small' histories[37] of Third Worldism is only possible by pushing methodological boundaries. It has required all the authors in this book to cross-read between historical sources – such as written and visual material and oral history – and knowledge production from the time before and after 1979/1982. Historical sociology involves a quest for new archives that can challenge (or confirm) established foci and narratives

[34] Peter Stearns, 'Toward a Wider Vision: Trends in Social History', in Michael Kammen (ed.), *The Past before Us: Contemporary Historical Writing in the United States* (Ithaca, NY: Cornell University Press, 1980), 224.

[35] Hamit Bozarslan, 'Revisiting the Middle East's 1979', *Economy and Society* 41 (4) 2014: 558–567; Christian Caryl, *Strange Rebels: 1979 and the Birth of the 21st Century* (New York: Basic Books, 2014); David W. Leasch, *1979: The Year that Shaped the Modern Middle East* (New York: Routledge, 2018).

[36] See, for example, David Motadel, 'Global Authoritarian Movement and the Revolt Against Empire', *The American Historical Review* 124 (3) 2019: 843–877.

[37] Naghmeh Sohrabi, 'Where the Small Things Are: Thoughts on Writing Revolutions and their Histories', *Jadaliyya*, 21 May 2020, https://www.jadaliyya.com/Details/41154.

about the period. Hence, this book brings various ongoing excavations of new archives and materials into dialogue. We believe that these sources fill gaps but have the potential to also provide a narrative that is largely lacking.

The second main contribution of this book lies in its emphasis on the gradual nature of change in the late 1970s and the early 1980s, during which the internal contradictions of and external challenges to Third Worldism crystallised. Instead of the spectacularising focus on 1979, we consider longer historical perspectives with an appreciation of the contingency of local events with global and regional processes. We are not the first to highlight this gradual transition as opposed to what we could call 'the 1979 paradigm' in Iranian, Middle Eastern, and global history. Even in Iranian studies, where attention to 1979 may be understandable given the defining nature of the revolution, the paradigm is being challenged. In path-breaking research like the NYU-based project *Global 1979: Geographies and Histories of the Iranian Revolution*, and the resultant edited volume, scholars have argued that the political struggles associated with 1979 should be *decentred*: that the revolution should be placed within genealogies that do not dictate linearity in causation; and that the revolution should be understood as a way of imagining *the world* rather than (only) the nation. Indeed, cutting-edge Middle East history projects have shown that 1979 can only be analysed properly in a longer perspective[38] and in a broader, indeed global, context that releases the narrative from the confines of national history.[39]

This book further develops this 'global but grounded' approach, which reconfigures historical 'turning points' as gradual transformations crystallising around 1979 and 1982. Indeed, as studies of the change from communism to democracy in Eastern Europe after 1989 have shown, ideological transition rarely happens in a condensed period but is more likely to be effected over a decade or more of cultural and political changes.[40] Hence, the book shows that 1979 was not a *birth moment* either of Islamisation or

---

[38] A notable example that this book draws on is the online collection of essays *The 1979 Moment in the Middle East*: https://trafo.hypotheses.org/category/the-1979-moment-in-the-middle-east.

[39] 'Revolution in Iran 1978–1979: Assessments and Reassessments upon the Fortieth Anniversary', seminar with Drs Touraj Atabaki, Stephanie Cronin, and Siavush Randjbar-Daemi, chaired by Dr Eskandar Sadeghi-Boroujerdi, Middle East Centre (St Anthony's College, Oxford University), 2019. Recording available at: https://podcasts.ox.ac.uk/revolution-iran-1978-1979-assessments-and-reassessments-upon-fortieth-anniversary.

[40] Ghia Nodia, 'How Different are Postcommunist transitions?', *Journal of Democracy* 7 (4) 1996: 14–29.

of authoritarian politics in the Middle East; nor was it necessarily a *death moment* of Third Worldism in the Middle East.

The third major contribution of this book lies in the methodological, theoretical, and historiographical challenge of juxtaposing two cases of Third Worldism that are often mentioned together in the existing literature but rarely if ever studied closely together. The point with placing Iran and Palestine into dialogue is not to reify or pass an essentialist judgement on the nature and fate of '*Middle Eastern* Third Worldism'. It is rather a methodological challenge designed to tease out new findings that are relevant both to the two countries' histories as well as to a comparative discussion about Third Worldism regionally and globally. The substantial differences between the two cases of Iran and Palestine highlight commonalities and divergences, and thus open a conversation about an analytical object that is avowedly transnational and yet tangibly anchored on national, regional, and local scales. Indeed, the historiographic discussion about how to study a transnational phenomenon such as Third Worldism is as much about methodology as it is about theory.

By extension, a fourth contribution we hope this book will provide is to nuance our understanding of revolutions as a global phenomenon. This, we argue, requires historians to take globality down to the analytical scale of collective and individual trajectories, and thus to engage with how historical change was experienced, analysed, and lived. In this respect, the book is in dialogue with a field of scholarship that since the 1990s has made the case for approaching the history of revolutions through a framework of connected, or crossed, histories (*histoires croisées*). As expressions of the globalisation of the field of history and concerted attempts to overcome the limitations of conventional nation-state histories, new historians of revolution – such as Houri Berberian in her *Roving Revolutionaries*[41] about the interconnected revolutions in Russia, Iran, and the Ottoman Empire in the early 1900s – tend to follow the cue of Micol Seigel and go 'beyond comparison'. This approach, Seigel writes, allows the historian to 'illuminate the complex, global networks of power-inflected relations that enmesh our world, including those connections generated by the academic engagement and observation'.[42] Our aim with studying the revolutions of

[41] Houri Berberian, *Roving Revolutionaries: Armenians and the Connected Revolutions in the Russian, Iranian, and Ottoman Worlds* (Berkeley: University of California Press, 2019).
[42] Micol Seigel, 'Beyond Compare: Comparative Method after the Transnational Turn', *Radical History Review* 91 (Winter 2005): 78.

Iran and Palestine together as a methodological challenge is to go beyond merely comparing and contrasting the two parallel cases and instead to highlight the 'enmeshment' of the world in and through the cases of Iran and Palestine.

THEMES OF THE BOOK

This book is the result of a research project that engaged Middle East-focused historians working on social and revolutionary movements, guerrilla groups and militias, solidarity networks and activism, intellectuals and ideologues, and cultural production. In a series of workshops, we invited them to reflect on a set of overlapping questions and themes that were meant to unpack the year 1979 as a turning point for Third Worldism.

As our conversations progressed, we realised that we had to decentre 1979 and rather see it as part of a continuum of around a decade. Here, 1982 emerged as an equally crucial median for the historical forces that together undid the second phase of Third Worldism. During the 1970s, the Palestinian liberation movement had gained such a central and iconic role for anti-imperialism, that the PLO's demise in Lebanon's civil war and the end of its revolutionary period had to be engaged with. This is how 1979 and 1982 became the two pivots of the book's analysis. The themes we initially suggested to our contributors related to broad propositions about the transformations that the world and the region underwent. We were inspired by the workshop participants and other scholars whose work is currently reshaping our view of the period.

The first theme concerned the dilemma of *nationalism*. We asked if nationalist registers of liberation clashed with (Marxist) notions of internationalism, and if so, how questions of nationhood and self-determination or particularist or even chauvinist tendencies were resolved. Similarly, we asked how issues pertaining to the mobilisation of a popular movement – including the bridging of class, generational, socio-cultural, or geographic divides – impacted on the power or viability of Third Worldism as a movement, and which role theory played in hampering or impeding intersectional activism. Some of these questions are addressed by Rasmus Elling and Jahangir Mahmoudi in their chapter on the radical left in Iran and its uneasy relationship with the Kurdish national liberation struggle during the 1979 revolution. In this case, questions of majority and minority ethnicity and nationalism to some extent undermined the solidarity between oppressed peoples prescribed by Third Worldism.

A related theme was that of internal diversity and the gender blind-spot – a topic which has been addressed in research on leftist, Islamist, and anti-imperialist movements during the long 1960s and beyond[43] – but still warrants further questioning. Did Third Worldist movements fail to embrace gender equality in practice and thought? Did critiques and experiences from below reverberate, or were they effectively shut down? These questions are addressed by Marral Shamshiri in her chapter about the gendered politics surrounding the death of female transnational revolutionaries of a Third Worldist cause.

Another overall question related to the study of the micro-practices of infighting, sectarianism, and splits in Third Worldist movements. Did such fragmentation undermine the aspirations of a movement that was formally internationalist and universalist? On the Palestinian side, fighting in the Lebanese civil war certainly altered political positions and world-views. As the chapter by Nathaniel George shows, the late 1970s was a time of internal splits and reorientations among ordinary *fida'yin*. At the same time, the Palestinian internationalism that had expanded through solidarity networks in the early 1970s no longer enjoyed a free and open space in Beirut, as Klaudia Wieser shows in her chapter about the PLO Research Centre. Ideological fragmentation, therefore, was not just a result of deliberation in the PLO leadership in reaction to regional splits. It also emerged as emotional, individual reactions to personal experiences in the Lebanese civil war.

However, two chapters of the book indicate that the focus on fragmenta-tion might also hamper an understanding of both continuity and the forg-ing of new bonds. In her chapter on Cuban–Palestinian solidarity, Sorcha Thomson shows that even though official state–quasi state relations could make transnational bonds prone to instability, the solidarity forged between actors and activists often developed into deep friendships. Conversely,

---

[43] See, for example, Hanan Hammad, 'Arwa Salih's "The Premature": Gendering the History of the Egyptian Left', *Arab Studies Journal* 24 (1) 2016: 118–142; Haideh Moghissi, *Populism and Feminism in Iran: Women's Struggle in a Male-Defined Revolutionary Movement* (London: Macmillan, 1994); Parvin Paidar, *Women and the Political Process in Twentieth Century Iran* (Cambridge: Cambridge University Press, 1995); Hammed Shahidian, 'The Iranian Left and the "Woman Question", in the Revolution of 1978–79', *International Political Science Abstract* 44 (6) 1994: 697; Janet Afary, *Sexual Politics in Iran* (Cambridge: Cambridge University Press, 2009).

Simon Wolfgang Fuchs, in his chapter on the Islamic Republic of Iran's 'revolution export' to African and Asian countries, shows that even though this endeavour took place simultaneously with an Islamist expropriation of a previously left-dominated Third Worldism, it nonetheless constituted a vigorous and, to some extent, successful 'afterlife' of revolutionary solidarity across the Global South.

In other realms, the afterlife of revolution primarily manifested itself as regret and self-critique. Memory sharing by the left became a major theme in the historiography of the period after the end of the Cold War, when some former militants wrote mea culpa memoirs of their experiences. We invited reflection on whether the style and practice of self-critique, including in debates over the legitimate use of violence, impacted Third Worldist and New Left movements already during the period. As Sune Haugbolle shows in his contribution, some Marxist–Leninists began to perceive their ideological framework as insufficient for creating the necessary 'Mass Line' to mobilise the broad population. Even before the Iranian revolution, Palestinian Maoists turned to Islamist thought to seek an alternative. This transformation became much more prevalent and visible in the early 1980s with the formation of Islamist resistance groups in Palestine and Lebanon.

There is little in terms of mea culpa to be found in the object of study in the chapter by Nasser Mohajer and Eskandar Sadeghi-Boroujerdi. Here, the focus is on a key translator of Third Worldist ideas from around the world into the Persian language and into Iranian political discourse, namely Manuchehr Hezarkhani. The chapter uses critically contextualised biography to show how the fate of one person can exemplify the contradictory trajectories in and around Third Worldism, that in this case brought an internationalist student activist through revolution, political defeat, exile – and then unfaltering, unrepentant support for a faction that degenerated into an isolationist personality cult. With Hezarkhani's fate in focus, the chapter raises broader questions about the relationship between praxis, concrete political decisions, and manoeuvring through turbulent times.

A further theme pertained to global institutions: How did the relationship between formal organisations championing Third Worldism (e.g. NAM, OSPAAAL, AAPSO) and the New Left movements on the ground impact the gradual demise of Third Worldism? And related to this, how did revolutionary movements such as the PLO react to changing registers of solidarity? Here, the chapter by Pelle Valentin Olsen on Norwegian Palestine activists and their medical aid programmes in Lebanon is instructive. Olsen shows how these activists, hailing from solidarity movements founded around 1970 and active in Lebanon throughout the decade, gradually embraced humanitarian aid. However, contrary to existing scholarship, Olsen argues that this transformation did not de-politicise solidarity activists. Rather, he finds a remarkable continuity between the early 1970s and the 1980s in terms of the political commitment of solidarity activists.

While the focus of the book is often bottom-up, the larger geopolitical landscape is of course never distant. Thomson's chapter on the Cuban state's politics of solidarity with Palestine has already been mentioned, as has Fuchs' chapter on the Iranian state's outreach abroad. In Ataie's chapter on the Gathering of Liberation Movements in Tehran in 1980 we see how the question of alliance with or resistance to the Soviet Union – on the background of the Soviet invasion of Afghanistan – became a crucial driver of the division between Islamists and secular/leftist forces of Third Worldism during the tumultuous process of turning a revolution into a state apparatus. The final result of this process is foreshadowed in the material under investigation in Alemzadeh's chapter, namely the discursive transformation of Palestine solidarity in Iran after 1979 as expressed in a key newspaper published by what would soon become the sole, ruling faction. In this fashion, Alemzadeh documents the subtle but foundational changes in Third Worldism between its revolutionary phase and its post-revolution state phase.

To summarise, the chapters aim to answer several overlapping questions that are not easy to divide neatly. For the same reason, we have not imposed a chronological order on the chapters. In keeping with the global-historical ambition behind the book, we have instead ordered chapters according to the scales or levels that they are addressing in their key foci. In Part One, we have three chapters dealing with the directly transnational and international scale of Third Worldism: Cuban–Palestinian solidarity, Norwegian–Palestinian solidarity, and Iranian–African/Asian outreach. In Part Two, there are four chapters dealing explicitly with an intra-regional scale: Iranian engagement in Dhufar, Middle Eastern representatives in Tehran, a Lebanese revolutionary whose life was entangled with Palestine, and Iranian views of Palestine. And then, finally, in Part Three, four chapters zoom in on the intra-national and sub-national scale: one on the role of an Iranian activist in bringing Third Worldist ideas to Iran, one on relations between the majority and the minority in the midst of a revolution, one on the intellectual labour of a Palestinian political centre, and one on Palestinians between Lebanon and Palestine.

We hope that together these in-depth studies can give a stronger impression of what the rallying cry of Third Worldism sounded like. And why its echoes remain important.

PART ONE

THIRD WORLDISM AND THE WORLD

1

DEMYSTIFYING THIRD WORLD SOLIDARITY

Cuba and the Palestinian Revolution in the Seventies

Sorcha Thomson

International solidarity and the politics of Third Worldism have been funda-mental to the Cuban revolutionary project. In the 1970s, Cuban state solidarity was explicitly internationalist, and it intended to 'export revolution' to the world by supporting fraternal struggles for national liberation.[1] Due to its successful armed struggle (1953–1959) and continued defiance against US imperialism, the post-1959 country became an inspiration to anti-colonial and leftist movements around the world. As the seat of the Tricontinental movement after 1966, Cuba represented a militant strand of anti-imperialism within the broader landscape of Third Worldism. The Palestinian Liberation Organisation (PLO), and the *fida'yin* at its helm after 1968/1969, held a special place in Cuba's Tricontinental vision, presented across Cuban publications as a fraternal revolutionary force on the frontlines of global anti-imperial struggle.

Part of the mission of the Tricontinental Conference in 1966 and the Havana-based Organisation of Solidarity with the Peoples of Africa, Asia, and Latin America (OSPAAAL) it created was to elaborate diverse historical

---

[1] Jorge I. Domínguez, *To Make a World Safe for Revolution: Cuba's Foreign Policy* (Boston: Harvard University Press, 1989), 127; Margaret Randall, *Exporting Revolution: Cuba's Global Solidarity* (Durham: Duke University Press, 2017).

experiences into a general line of thought and action.[2] Across OSPAAAL platforms, in its publications, statements, artwork, and events, was a remarkable integration of distinct anti-colonial, anti-racist, and anti-imperial struggles into a common language and imagery of revolutionary solidarity. In the case of Palestine, this contributed to the positioning of Palestinian national liberation as a central Third Worldist cause in the aftermath of the 1967 Arab–Israeli War, when Palestinian organisations were provided with a Tricontinental platform to communicate their strategic and ideological positions to a broad international audience.[3]

As much as the Tricontinental archive remains a rich and yet to be fully explored source of material about the connections established between revolutionary states, national liberation movements, and left groups of the 1960s and 1970s, it is necessary to critically interrogate the rhetoric of transcontinental cohesion within it, especially if we want to better understand what was lost of that world, and what might remain. In line with the enquiry of this book, this chapter looks to the transformations of Third Worldism through the lens of the Cuban–Palestinian fraternal relationship between 1973 and 1983. To demystify this relationship, it is necessary to move beyond hagiographical interpretations of Third Worldism shaped by lament and nostalgia for a lost imagined unity, or by a narrow focus on factionalism and internal divisions as a sign of terminal weakness.

To do so we must begin with the recognition that the transnational movement of revolutionary solidarity with Palestine that emanated from Cuba is separate but connected to the formal positions of the Cuban state.[4] One

[2] Amilcar Cabral, 'The Weapon of Theory', Address delivered to the first Tricontinental Conference of the Peoples of Asia, Africa and Latin America, January 1966. https://www.marxists.org/subject/africa/cabral/1966/weapon-theory.htm.

[3] Nate George, 'In The Hour of Arab Revolution: Tricontinental and the Question of Palestine' (Houston: Rice University, 2015); Fernando Camacho Padilla and Jessica Stites Mor, 'Presence and visibility in Cuban anticolonial solidarity: Palestine in OSPAAAL's photography and poster art', in *Palestine in the World: International Solidarity with the Palestinian Liberation Movement*, eds Sorcha Thomson and Pelle Valentin Olsen (London: I.B. Tauris, 2023); Anna Bernard, 'Palestinian voices in the Tricontinental: Revolutionary journalism and the literary history of Palestine solidarity', in *Palestine in the World*.

[4] On the relationship between the Cuban state and OSPAAAL, see Anne Garland Mahler, *From the Tricontinental to the Global South: Race, Radicalism, and Transnational Solidarity* (Durham: Duke University Press, 2018), 7; Jessica Stites Mor, 'Rendering Armed Struggle: OSPAAAL, Cuban Poster Art, and South-South Solidarity at the United Nations', *Jahrbuch für Geschichte Lateinamerikas/Anuario de Historia de América Latina*

of the defining features of solidarity in the seventies was the relationship between transnational movements and Third Worldist states, like Cuba, that participated in an infrastructure through which connections of anti-imperial internationalism could take place.[5] Distinguishing and viewing state and transnational solidarities in relation to one another can serve to illuminate various of the factors often cited as characteristic of the decline of Third Worldism, including the NGOisation of solidarity at the expense of state-sponsored and movement networks, and the turning of postcolonial nations towards neoliberal state-building at the expense of transnational liberation ideals. Rather than seeking another causal explanation for the decline of Third Worldism, this chapter makes the methodological point that state and transnational solidarities must be looked at in tandem as a starting point from which to assess the transformation of the Cuban–Palestinian Third World relationship across the seventies and beyond.

Student activities in Cuba are a fruitful source for investigating these transformations, as they in many ways existed between state and transnational spheres. They were closely connected to the positions and priorities of the government, and they generated transnational journeys and lasting friendships and solidarities among participants. Today, the granting of scholarships to Palestinians to study in Cuba remains an important expression of Cuba's solidarity with the Palestinian people and an avenue for Palestinian activism in Cuba. Rather than viewing Cuba as an anomalous location from which to assess the fate of Third Worldism, its continued existence as a socialist revolutionary state defiantly at odds with the changes that accompanied the end of that era, this chapter views Third Worldism in Cuba as part of a global political culture whose transformations were more gradual, relational, and continuous than a list of causal factors or landmark moments can define. By tracing the inception of the scholarship tradition to the seventies, I want to demystify the fraternal Third Worldist relationship, showing that it was not an imagined ideal connection of a unified revolutionary era. Rather, it was the product of political relations between groups, institutions, and movements, and so subject to the changing internal dynamics, external pressures, and structural realities they faced. These political relationships produced forms of interaction, through which political imaginations were

---

56 (2019): 42–65, and *South-South Solidarity and the Latin American Left* (Madison: University of Wisconsin Press, 2022), 51.

[5] Stites Mor, *South-South Solidarity and the Latin American Left*, 18.

exchanged and expanded, and which shaped transnational lines of solidarity beyond the shifting dynamics of state–quasi state relations.

ARCHIVES OF SOLIDARITY WITHIN AND BEYOND THE STATE

Because of the global reach of the Palestinian movement, traces of its activities and ideas can be found in state archives, personal archives of activists, extant archives of local movements, institutional archives of international organisations, and in various forms of print and visual culture in different parts of the world. Recent work has shown that while they are unable to replace what was lost, stolen, or destroyed in the Israeli looting of Palestinian institutions, these archives can help to mitigate the scattered and precarious nature of the Palestinian archive.[6] However, there is a danger in relying on accessible public statements and curated public activities of solidarity, which can tell a story of unity and transnational cohesion at the expense of the contentious politics that were ever-present.

While it is true that the vast archive of global history is not primarily held in official buildings or documented on letter-headed paper, the fact that access to state archives remains in many places all but impossible means that gaining access to such 'conventional' archives – even when fragmentary – can offer up important findings in tandem with other sources.[7] In Cuba, the intelligence archives, the armed forces archives, and the central committee archives of the Cuban Communist Party (CCP) remain classified.[8] Other institutions such as the Institute of Friendship with the Peoples (ICAP), established in 1961 and responsible for non-governmental solidarity relations, hold a wealth of material about Cuban connections with the world that has not yet been processed into an accessible archival collection.[9] The

---

[6] Sorcha Thomson, Pelle Valentin Olsen, and Sune Haugbolle, 'Palestine Solidarity Conferences in the Global Sixties', *Journal of Palestine Studies* 51:1 (2022), 27–49.

[7] Sara Honarmand Ebrahimi and Ismay Milford, 'Roundtable: the archives of global history in a time of international immobility', *Historical Research* 95:270 (2022), 586–597.

[8] Piero Gleijeses, 'Inside the Closed Cuban Archives', Sources and Methods: History and Public Policy Program, Wilson Center, 31 July 2017, https://www.wilsoncenter.org/blog-post/inside-the-closed-cuban-archives.

[9] Author interview with Elizabeth Ribalta (Northern European Officer for ICAP), Havana, January 2022.

MINREX archive, which has been opened selectively, houses documents related to Cuba's bilateral international relations, and therefore makes it possible to ascertain a key part of the Cuban state's official, behind-the-scenes perspective on important events.[10] Without a formal declassification process, the granting and scope of access remains unpredictable. Researchers are not allowed to access entire collections for reasons of national security or in cases where there is information about a friendly leader or movement regarding delicate internal problems in their own country. Just as there must be caution when reading the public archives of solidarity, relying on the limited availability of internal state archives also presents only a partial story.

Visiting the MINREX archives between 2020 and 2022, I consulted material on Palestine in the 1970s, including minutes from meetings with Palestinian delegations, internal Cuban reports on the Palestinian movement, and material received from Palestinian groups (sometimes via Arab embassies in Havana or Cuban representatives in Beirut, Baghdad, and Pyongyang). As with all archives, the material is fragmented, incomplete, and in many cases raises more questions than it answers. But when read alongside other materials and secondary literature, these MINREX records offer an important insight into the internal considerations of the Cuban state regarding relations with the Palestinian movement, and the operation of Third World state solidarity in the seventies. This chapter connects the fragmented material available in the MINREX archives with more heterogenous archival material, including documents from the Palestine Mission in Havana,[11] materials relating to student solidarity activities from the José Martí National Library in Havana, Cuban and Palestinian publications, and interviews conducted between 2020 and 2022 with Cuban and Palestinian cadres active in international work in the seventies. From these combined sources, it is possible to tell a history of the fraternal Cuban–Palestinian relationship in the seventies that avoids only seeing factionalism or alternatively sliding into nostalgia for the unity of a lost Third World project.

---

[10] Blanca Mar León, 'Revolutionary Diplomacy and the Third World', in *Towards a Global History of Latin America's Revolutionary Left*, eds Tanya Harmer and Alberto Martín Álvarez (Gainesville: University Press of Florida, 2021), 69.

[11] Scanned documents in Arabic from the PLO Mission in Havana were generously shared with me by Fadi Kafeety.

SUPPORTING THE PLO: FROM STATE POLICY TO STUDENT NETWORKS

Charting the evolving dynamics of the Cuban–Palestinian relationship shows how the formalisation of student networks was a direct consequence of Cuban state policy in relation to geopolitical and internal Palestinian developments. Though the majority of Afro-Asian countries and the USSR broke off diplomatic relations with Israel after the 1967 Arab–Israeli War, and a revolutionary discourse of solidarity emanated from Cuba through OSPAAAL and other institutions, it was not until 1973 that Cuba broke off diplomatic relations with Israel, and only in 1975 that a representative PLO office was first established on the island.[12] This is not to deny the longer history of Cuban support for the Palestinian cause: its delegation (the only Latin American country to do so) voted against the 1947 UN partition plan;[13] meetings had taken place between Cuban representatives and Palestinian resistance groups in the 1960s; military training links with *fida'yin* groups had existed since at least 1968;[14] artists, filmmakers, and writers travelled between the regions;[15] Cuban media elevated Palestinian perspectives across Latin America and beyond; and joint communiqués called for the establishment of a Palestinian homeland and for the recognition of Palestinian national rights.[16]

All these factors played an important role in mobilising solidarity for and on behalf of the Palestinian movement. But until 1973 Cuba maintained a dual policy of recognition of Israel and defence of the Palestinian position, at odds with the position of OSPAAAL which called for a cultural, economic, and political boycott of Israel in 1966.[17] Salah Khalaf (Abu Iyad) recalled in the memoirs of his trip to Cuba in 1970 how Castro spoke frankly to him about the limitations of Cuba's ability to offer its full public backing to the Palestinian struggle. Despite considering Israel a tool of US imperialism,

---

[12] Domínguez, *To Make a World Safe for Revolution*, 130.

[13] Ernesto Gómez Abascal, *Palestina ¿Crucificada la justicia?: historia de un angriento conflict* (Havana: Editora Politica, 2004), 2nd ed., 2004, 46–49.

[14] Domingo Amuchastegui, 'Cuba in the Middle East: A Brief Chronology', Institute for Cuban and Cuban-American Studies (Miami: University of Miami, July 1999), https://2009-2017.state.gov/p/wha/ci/cu/14745.htm.

[15] 'Revolution and the Issue of Art', *al-Hadaf*, no. 27, vol. 1, 31 January 1970, 10 (Uri Davis Collection, University of Exeter).

[16] David Fernández, *Cuba's Foreign Policy in the Middle East* (Boulder: Westview Press 1998), 71.

[17] Fernández, *Cuba's Foreign Policy in the Middle East*, 39.

'Cuba had relations with influential Jewish business circles for its foreign trade, he explained, and still maintained diplomatic ties with Israel which he didn't want to compromise' – and so he wanted to avoid 'strong language' in the joint communiqué released after the meeting.[18] It was the same attitude that Abu Iyad had encountered on an earlier trip to North Vietnam, where the Worker's Party Politburo had preferred to use 'moderate, even vague terms, so as not to offend American Jews, many of whom were active in the anti-war movement'.[19] Such exchanges provided a valuable lesson for the Palestinians on the politics of international solidarity with their cause.

There are multiple explanations for why Cuba broke off relations with Israel in 1973 and strengthened its relations with the Palestine Liberation Organisation (PLO). Some explanations describe the stages of Cuban foreign policy as it evolved from 1959, in which 1973–1975 marks not just a turning point in relations with Palestine but also in Cuba's status, ability, and willingness to intervene in the Third World.[20] These explanations highlight the role of closer Soviet–Cuba ties and the recognition that co-operation in the international arena could be mutually beneficial.[21] The MINREX files do show that closer relations between the PLO and the socialist camp were an important consideration for Cuba, with the establishment of PLO offices in Moscow and Belgrade viewed as a precedent for the Cuban office.[22] Other explanations highlight pressure from within the Non-Aligned Movement (NAM) and the Arab states, to the effect that relations with Israel were no longer compatible with Cuba's position in the NAM.[23] MINREX documents likewise confirm that the recognition of the PLO as the sole legitimate representative of the Palestinian people in Algiers (Arab Summit Conference, November 1973) and Lahore (Second Islamic Summit Conference, February 1974) was considered to have 'completely modified the situation in the region for the Palestinian resistance'.[24] Jamil Musab Mahmoud has also highlighted the regional Latin American context of support for Israel, and

[18] Abu Iyad with Eric Rouleau, trans. Linda Butler Koseoglu, *My Home, My Land: A Narrative of the Palestinian Struggle* (New York: Times Books, 1981), 71.

[19] Abu Iyad, *My Home, My Land*, 70.

[20] Fernández, *Cuba's Foreign Policy in the Middle East*, 11.

[21] Fernández, *Cuba's Foreign Policy in the Middle East*, 12.

[22] *PALESTINE 1976, ORDINARIO*. Sobre el problema palestina, 2.11.1974, MINREX-Palestina, Havana.

[23] Camacho Padilla and Stites Mor, 'Visibility and imagery in Cuban anticolonial solidarity with Palestine', 172.

[24] *PALESTINE 1976, ORDINARIO*. Sobre el problema palestina, 2.11.1974.

Cuba's place as the first country in the region to break its ties in a move against the consensus of the Americas.[25]

In addition to these regional and geopolitical explanations, a prominent question in the communications of the Cuban foreign ministry was on the status of unity and factionalism within the Palestinian movement. Cuba was conscious that divisions among allies could awaken differences within the Cuban foreign policy apparatus and that factionalism abroad may translate into factionalism at home.[26] The satisfactory unity of the Palestinian movement was emphasised by PLO delegations to Cuba in their meetings with Cuban officials and OSPAAAL in the early seventies,[27] but factionalism was viewed by MINREX as among the factors 'conspiring to limit the role of the organisation as a regional and international force': the 'more than ten guerrilla organisations' and 'the ideological differences and "fractionation" of the movement in numerous organisations, motivating rivalries among them, lacking co-ordination and application of different military and political tactics despite having the same strategic objectives'.[28]

The revision of the Palestinian strategy in 1974, considering an impending negotiated settlement of the Arab–Israeli conflict, to implicitly accept a Palestinian state that need not include the entirety of historic Palestine,[29] exacerbated divisions within the Palestinian movement between a rejectionist

---

[25] Jamil Musab Mahmoud, 'Amrika al-latiniya wa al-yasar: al-Ibti'ad 'an al-jar al-amriki iqtirab min falastin', *Journal of Palestine Studies* 79 (2009).

[26] This has been shown to be the case in relations with South Yemen, where following the early 1970s decision to cultivate such relations, personnel of both MINREX and the Armed Revolutionary Forces (FAR) worked to establish relations with their South Yemeni counterparts. By 1978, when faced with factionalism within the Yemeni government, the Cubans found themselves faced with the dilemma of whom to support. The embassy staff (under the direction of Osmani Cienfuegos) sided with the more moderate group, and the FAR mission (headed by Carlos Rafael Rodriguez) allied themselves with the more pro-Soviet. The final decision as to which group should be supported came from Castro, who decided in favour of the pro-Soviet faction backed by the FAR. Cienfuegos lost his position as regional chargé d'affaires, apparently replaced by Rodriguez, in a move that reflected a closer alignment with Moscow (Fernández, *Cuba's Foreign Policy in the Middle East*, 23).

[27] 641.1 Palestina. Reunion del Departamento Politico-Economico, Enero 12 1971, 10.35AM. Invitados: Delegacion de Palestina – Shafiq al Hout and Majed Abu Sharar. MINREX-Palestine, Havana.

[28] *PALESTINE 1976, ORDINARIO*. Sobre el problema palestina, 2.11.1974.

[29] Palestinian National Council, 'Political Programme Adopted by the Twelfth Session of the Palestinian National Council', Cairo, 8 June 1974, *Filastin al-Thawra* (Beirut, 12 June 1974), translated by *The Palestinian Revolution*, 2016. http://learnpalestine.politics.ox.ac.uk (5.3.2018).

front that opposed the strategy and the groups who had promoted and accepted it. These dynamics were closely monitored by the Cuban state, particularly through its embassy in Beirut. The Cuban ministry followed the consensus of the socialist bloc and the NAM in favouring the new position, considered to be 'realistic on the part of the PLO' and contributing 'in a special way to the strengthening of the Palestinian cause in the international arena'.[30] As a result of the new position of the PLO, an anonymous report written for the Vice-Minister concludes that 'given the prospect that the PLO requests approval from our government and party for the opening of an office in Havana, we understand that, for the reasons stated, our country must accede to that request as one of the forms of expression of our militant support to the Palestinian cause'.[31] The report also indicates a preference for Fatah – described in it as 'the most significant organisation' – and the Democratic Front for the Liberation of Palestine (DFLP) – described as 'following a scientific socialism', rather than what it calls the 'most radical sectors opposed to any kind of dialogue' (including the Popular Front for the Liberation of Palestine (PFLP) – described in one word as 'Maoist'). The report further takes the view that the 'position of these radical groups cannot seriously influence the evolution of the conflict'. The report notes that Cuba's position 'would be interpreted by most radical organisations as a decision by Cuba against the divergent currents within the resistance ... [redacted]'. The redacted information stops short of indicating more on the potential effects of this position on relations with the rejectionist organisations.

Such internal communications were the prelude to Arafat's visit to Cuba after his landmark 14 November 1974 UN speech.[32] The choice of Havana as the first stop after the speech was a political statement, and not without contention. As Arafat explained to the CCP Central Committee on 15 November, in a meeting attended by the Soviet representative in Havana, some Arab countries had asked him not to travel to Cuba, but he wanted to extend his stay from two days to five days as a sign of his commitment.[33] During the trip, as well as appearances at schools, in public squares, and at press conferences in which the leaders exchanged revolutionary gifts and

---

[30] *PALESTINE 1976, ORDINARIO.* Sobre el problema palestina, 2.11.1974.
[31] *PALESTINE 1976, ORDINARIO.* Sobre el problema palestina, 2.11.1974.
[32] *Granma,* 15–19 November 1974.
[33] Letter. Urgente. Republica de Cuba. Viceministro Primero de Relaciones Exteriores, VMP/S/005, 16 November 1974.

greetings,[34] official conversations began between the CCP and the PLO in which Cuba reiterated its 'militant solidarity with the Palestinian people and opposition to all attempts to liquidate the Palestinian movement'.[35] A joint communiqué was published as an outcome of the visit which agreed to, among other things, the establishment of a PLO representative office in Havana.[36] Khader Mansour became the first PLO representative on the island. The establishment of this permanent office gave the PLO the opportunity to participate in official activities, press conferences, seminars, and international events, as well as to meet with other solidarity groups and liberation leaders represented in Havana, particularly from Latin America and the Caribbean.[37]

One of the direct outcomes of these significant diplomatic developments was the programme of Cuban scholarships for Palestinian students. Records from the Palestine Mission in Havana show that the first cohort of students arrived in 1975, the same year that the PLO office was opened. These state-sponsored scholarships built upon a longer tradition of student activism and educational networks in Palestinian, Cuban, and broader Third Worldist contexts.[38] Palestinian and Cuban students had also collaborated before, in international forums since at least 1966 when the General Union of Palestinian Students (GUPS) attended the Latin American conference of students in Havana and published a joint statement with the Cuban Federation of University Students (FEU).[39] But the scholarship programme represented a large increase in the number who were able to travel and take up opportunities for interaction and exchange. By 1980, there were 277 Palestinian students enrolled in different schools across the country, ranging from fifth year to first year, in medicine courses as well as in engineering,

---

[34] 'Llego a Cuba Yasser Arafat; fue recibido en el aeropuerto por el comanandante Jefe Fidel Castro', *Granma*, 15 November 1974, 3.

[35] 'Inician conversaciones oficiales la organización para la liberación de palestina y el Partido comunista de Cuba', *Granma*, 16 November 1974.

[36] 'Comunicado Conjuncto Cubano-Palestino', *Granma*, 19 November 1974.

[37] Delegacion de la Organización de Liberación Palestina sostuvo encuentro con el Comite Chileno de Solidaridad, *Granma*, 19 November 1974.

[38] Yezid Sayigh, *Armed Struggle and the Search for State: The Palestinian National Movement, 1949–1993* (Oxford: Oxford University Press, 1997), 102. On the transnational significance of the GUPS and student networks, see Mjriam Abu Samra, 'The Palestinian Student Movement 1948–1982: A Study of Popular Organisation and Transnational Mobilisation', PhD dissertation, University of Oxford, 2020.

[39] *Al-kitab al-sanawi al-qadia al-falistiniya al-'am 1966* [The Yearbook of the Palestinian Cause Year 1966] (Beirut: Institute of Palestine Studies, 1967), 106–109.

mechanics, history, philosophy, sports, and other disciplines. Alongside their studies, they were given intensive language training in Spanish and lessons on the history and theory of Marxism–Leninism in a first preparatory year.[40] The scholarship provided all necessities – including personal clothes, bed sheets, laundry, three meals a day, and a personal stipend.[41]

Students were invited not through the PLO but through party affiliations, and so the reception and numbers of the Palestinian students can be seen as a lens into the relations between the Cuban government and the different Palestinian groups. After 1983, Cuba – having tried and failed to reconcile the different Palestinian faction leaders in the Middle East and in Havana[42] – had a preference for the Marxist–Leninist PFLP and the DFLP, evident in the distribution of the Palestinians who received scholarships to study in Cuba (mostly from the PFLP).[43] Yet in 1980 the majority were members of Fatah, followed in number by the DFLP, and then the PFLP,[44] mirroring Cuba's policy preference for the groups behind the revised strategic programme in the PLO.

These scholarships were closely tied to the positions and preferences of the Cuban government and the dynamics of their relationship with the PLO and the various parties within it. Beyond offering an important alternative insight into the strategic-political preferences of the Cuban government in relation to the different Palestinian parties when state materials remained scarce, analysing student activities can reveal different layers to the dynamics of Third Worldism in the seventies: the celebrations of solidarity, friendship, exchanges of knowledge, and emotional responses that took place at the same time as state–quasi state relations were concerned with critical factional tensions and external pressures.

---

[40] Author interview with Basil Ismael Salem, Havana, February 2022.

[41] Author interview with Basil Ismael Salem, Havana, February 2022.

[42] David Fernández, *Cuba's Foreign Policy in the Middle East* (Boulder: Westview Press 1998), 72–73.

[43] Camacho Padilla and Stites Mor, 'Visibility and imagery in Cuban anticolonial solidarity with Palestine', 174.

[44] According to the list of the names of those studying in Cuba sent by the PLO office in Havana to the PLO Political Department on 20 November 1980 – Imad Jadaa, Misión de la Organización para la Liberación de Palestina, Havana, Cuba. 'Qa'imat bi asma' al-tulab al-filastiniyin al-darisin fi kuba ma' tawzia'ha hasab al-munazamat', 1980.

STATE-SPONSORED STUDENTS AND TRANSNATIONAL SOLIDARITIES

During their studies, Palestinian students in Cuba participated in a political culture of revolutionary solidarity that over a decade of internationalist foreign policy had created on the island. An example of this was the 1978 XI International Union of Students (IUS) and World Federation of Democratic Youth (WFDY) Festival of Youth and Students, held in Havana between 28 July and 5 August, where some 20,000 delegates from more than 140 countries travelled to take part.[45] The Soviet-backed IUS had provided an important space for Third World student connections since 1956, including Cuban and Palestinian student groups who had both attended the IUS Executive Committee meeting in Tunis in February 1960.[46] Its co-sponsored World Youth Festivals were a significant feature in the student calendar; the previous event in East Germany in 1973 had welcomed Arafat alongside international revolutionary figures such as Angela Davis to voice their calls for anti-imperialist solidarity. In 1978, 150 Palestinians (one third of whom were women) travelled as GUPS delegates from Beirut to Havana. The Palestinian delegation was made up of members of different resistance organisations and headed by PFLP member and student leader Taysir Quba'a and Abu Sakhr (a member of the Fatah Revolutionary Council).[47]

In the preparations for the festival, Cuban officials remained critically aware of the crisis of factionalism unfolding in the Palestinian movement. In a communication dated '2 June 1978 Year of the XI Festival', the Cuban ambassador in Lebanon, Alberto Velazco, reported on a meeting that had taken place with Abu Abbas, head of the Palestine Liberation Front (PLF), a splinter group from the PFLP-GC led by Ahmed Jibril, itself a split from the PFLP. The meeting is described as having taken place in the spirit of 'continuing the line of work of extending the relations of our embassy with all the different Palestinian organisations'. The reported interview with Abu Abbas describes PFLP-GC 'direct military actions against us [PLF] to destroy our forces'. Also attached is a document, described by Abu Abbas

---

[45] 'Eleventh International Youth Festival, Cuba 1978', *PLO Information Bulletin*, vol. 4, no. 14, 15 August 1978, 6.

[46] Abu Samra, 'The Palestinian Student Movement 1948–1982', 193; Philip G. Altbach, 'The International Student Movement', *Journal of Contemporary History* 5:1 (1970), 171–172.

[47] 'Todo listo en Panama para transportar a La Habana a delegados latinoamericanos', *Granma*, vol. 14, no. 171, 20 July 1978.

as 'seriously dangerous' and said to be circulating in the Fatah Central Committee, about a joint DFLP and PFLP five-point memorandum accusing Fatah of 'not seriously trying to seek the unification of the official and popular Arab progressive forces within the framework of a united front hostile to a capitulation arrangement'.[48] As with other official Cuban documents held in MINREX, the text cuts off at the point of 'our own [Cuban] opinions on this level'. The reporting of the meeting to the highest levels of the foreign ministry demonstrates how such factional developments were considered an important concern and so were closely followed by Cuban officials stationed in Arab countries.

However, in the public materials and popular activities of the XI Festival these divisions are largely invisible. The Palestinian delegation engaged in meetings with Cuban institutions, such as OSPAAAL, and interviews about the movement were published in the *Tricontinental* magazine as a result, with no mention of factional crisis.[49] Cuban newspapers educated their readers in advance about the visiting delegations, including the role of the GUPS as a unifying student body.[50] The PLO office in Havana and the National Palestinian Preparatory Committee published booklets (in English and Spanish) covering the longer history of the Palestinian struggle, for distribution at the festival.[51] Public engagement with the cause was encouraged, through a Cuban–Arab Friendship Association 'Solidarity with the Palestinian People' song writing competition, advertised in a national newspaper, of which the winner would have the opportunity to record and perform their song.[52] The festival adopted methods for political communication that were well established within the canon of anti-imperialist praxis, such as the 'Youth Accuses Imperialism International Tribunal'.[53] The

---

[48] Entrevista con el compañero Abou Abbas Jefe del Frente Nacional para la Liberación De Palestina; Comando General, Embajada de Cuba, Libanon, 2 June 1978, MINREX-Libano, Havana.

[49] Programa Cronológico de Actividades del XI Festival, edited by the Centre for Translation, Interpretation and Reproduction, XI World Festival of Youth and Students, José Martí National Library, Havana, 301.431 FES P 1978.

[50] See the magazines *Juventud Rebelde* and *La Bohemia*, July 1978.

[51] 'The Palestinian Revolution, 14 Years of Continuous Struggle', *The National Palestinian Preparatory Committee for the 11th World Festival of Youth & Students, Cuba 1978*, F.956.94.Nat.P.1978, José Martí National Library, Havana.

[52] Concurso de solidaridad con el pueblo palestino, *Granma*, vol. 14, no. 124, 26 May 1978.

[53] Umberto Tulli, 'Wielding the human rights weapon against the American empire: the second Russell Tribunal and human rights in transatlantic relations', *Journal of Transatlantic Studies*, 19 (2021), 215–237, 1–2.

National Preparatory Committee of Palestine headed the list of those who provided accusatory statements to the tribunal and, following a hearing of the statements, US imperialism was declared 'morally and materially guilty' of 'forcibly maintaining the colonial status of the peoples of Palestine'.[54] In all these public activities, critique of internal division is absent and the collective Palestinian peoples' liberation struggle is foregrounded as the basis for a universal solidarity.[55]

Eman Morsi has argued that the linguistic barriers and top-down centralised control of such activities made it very difficult, if not impossible, for any lateral grassroots interactions to take place.[56] While in some ways channels of communication were highly orchestrated in line with official objectives, exchanges took place in ways that did not necessarily follow a strict party line. Dancing, eating, singing, and celebrating were a major part of the programme alongside the formal meetings. Communication between participants was also facilitated by volunteer student translators. Miriam Mujica, who was studying history in Damascus at the time of the event, remembers how she and other Cubans studying abroad came back to the country to assist in the festival, with tasks including translating between delegations and partnering with individuals to guide them in the country.[57] The Palestinian *kufiyya*, which by the late 1970s had emerged as part of the transnational solidarity visual repertoire, circulated as a symbol and a clothing item.[58] Images from the event show the ubiquity of the item, draped across the shoulders of medal-adorned Vietnamese revolutionaries, and worn by students with their festival T-shirts and even as a sarong at the beach.[59]

For the Palestinian students living in Cuba, the experience of the political culture of internationalism and opportunities for political education extended beyond the festival. Basil Ismael Salem, a Palestinian from the

---

[54] 'Final Declaration of the Youth Accuses Imperialism International Tribunal, 11th World Festival and Youth and Students, For Anti-Imperialist Solidarity, Peace, and Friendship', International Union of Students Collection, 5 August 1978, IISH, Amsterdam.
[55] Front Cover, *PLO Bulletin*, vol. 4, no. 14, 15 August 1978; 'Palestina y Cuba', PLO Unified Information Office, The Palestine Poster Project Archives, *c.*1985.
[56] Eman Morsi, 'Cuba in Arabic and the Limits of Third World Solidarity', *The Global South* 13:1 (Spring 2019), 174.
[57] Author interview with Miriam Mujica, Havana, February 2022.
[58] 'Cuba '78 World Students Conference', *Filastin Al Thawra*, no. 20, 4 September 1978.
[59] XI Festival Cuba 78, Comite Organizador Cuba 78 XI Festival Mundial de la Juventud y Los Estudiantes, Editorial de Ciencias Sociales, 1984, José Martí National Library, Havana, 301.431 FES O 1985.

Gaza Strip, was among one of the early groups of Palestinians to study in Cuba, arriving in 1979 to study mechanics in Santa Clara, a city around three hundred kilometres from Havana. Applications for scholarships were delivered to the Cuban embassy in Beirut, from where they were distributed among the different resistance organisations. In 1979, the PFLP – of which he was a member – received ten scholarships, and he was chosen to go, based on his academic performance and his political commitment. The Political Department of the Front gave the selected students an intensive preparation course, which included 'essential information like who is Fidel, who is Guevara, how did the Cuban revolution happen'.[60] Also in the preparations were lessons in why the Palestinian revolution and the PFLP were sending young people to study there, with the implication that on their return to the Middle East they would contribute to the revolution as instructors, engineers, and doctors in the camps.

In Cuba, the students often acted as political representatives of their movement and participated in the reception events of visiting Palestinian delegations and in international events. In this way, they formally represented their parties. Alongside participation in meetings with visiting delegations, Salem explained how the main way of maintaining communication with party developments was through issues of the PFLP's weekly newspaper *Al Hadaf*, which was sent from Beirut and would take three months to arrive in Havana. In my interview with Salem, he did not mention the divisions that existed between the different students in those days, nor did he view himself then as solely a part of the PFLP cadre, but rather as an international representative of the Palestinian cause. He described an atmosphere of internationalism and friendship, and the opportunities these provided for building solidarity with other students:

In Santa Clara we had students from Laos, Cambodia, Vietnam, Afghanistan, Lebanon, Yemen, Syria ... I learnt the history of Puerto Rico, of Guatemala, El Salvador, Nicaragua, and Chile. And they learnt about Palestine. Together we discovered the connections between our peoples, and the connections of friendship between the students developed into political connections ... Many of the students were sent here through revolutionary parties, parties which were interested not

---

[60] Author interview with Basil Ismael Salem, Havana, February 2022.

just in the revolution in their own country but in the international revolution. So, for us it was a space of exchange and learning.[61]

These exchanges created long-lasting friendships, between students from different parts of the world and between the Palestinians who shared in this enriching experience.

These friendships and the students' lives were never far from the political-military developments of the Palestinian movement. During the visit of Khalil al-Wazir to Havana in November 1980, the military leader asked that the Cuban authorities agree to freeze Palestinian studies for one year, so that students could be recalled for military service in the escalating crisis in Lebanon.[62] As Pelle Valentin Olsen shows in this collection, the reception and service of medical volunteers was an important avenue and source of international and Third World solidarity in the 1970s. Although Cuba never did send any official Cuban medical delegations to serve in Lebanon, as it did in Yemen, Dhufar, Algeria, Angola and elsewhere during the 1960s and 1970s, it did provide material support to the Palestinian Red Crescent (PRC). A NAM delegation led by the Cuban president of MINREX, Carlos Lechuga (and including representatives from Afghanistan, DPRK, India, Jamaica, and Yugoslavia) was invited by the PLO to Lebanon in August 1981, where they met with Dr Fathi Arafat, president of the PRC, and visited several PRC-run hospitals. As well as highlighting the need for more specialist personnel, the PRC requested a list of essential equipment including ambulances, blood bags, antibiotics, and respirators, which the NAM delegation agreed to help supply.[63]

People's lives and experiences were tied to these political developments. A significant number of Palestinians trained as doctors by the Cuban system did return to become *médicos-guerrilleros* with the resistance movement. The concept of the *médico-guerrillero* was part of the lexicon of the Cuban revolution, most famously embodied by Che Guevara,[64] but also by the

---

[61] Author interview with Basil Ismael Salem, Havana, February 2022.

[62] Imad Jadaa, 1980 Report from the OLP Mission in Havana to Head of Political Department, Misión de la Organización Para La Liberación de Palestina, Havana, Cuba.

[63] Informe de La Misión del Buro de Coordinación de los Países No Alineados Sobre Su Visita a el Líbano en Agosto de 1981, OLP 624, Palestine 1980–1982 S/F, MINREX, Havana.

[64] For the origins of Guevara's concept of the 'revolutionary doctor', see his thesis 'On Revolutionary Medicine', 16 August 1960. *Obra Revolucionaria*, Ano 1960, no. 24. https://www.marxists.org/archive/guevara/1960/08/19.htm.

thousands of doctors who had been trained to understand their service to the health of the people as a revolutionary act.[65] It was in this tradition that the Palestinians were trained, and the training travelled with those who returned to the Middle East.

The experience of returning to Lebanon and joining the resistance as a *médico-guerrillero* was described by a Palestinian doctor writing in *La Bohemia*, a widely circulated Havana-based Spanish-language cultural and political magazine published under various editors since 1908. The magazine is known for its role in providing a space for radical critique within Cuba across various stages of its history, and in forging a regional political culture of anti-imperialism and anti-dictatorship.[66] The doctor's account gives a sense of the way in which a transnational history was embedded in the psyche of these young Palestinians, who had travelled thousands of miles to study in a country whose revolutionary icons they had learned about since youth before returning to offer their services to the struggle for the liberation of their homeland, as the liberation movement faced its greatest attack in 1982. The testimony, written in the first person, with the inclusion of dialogue and personal reflection, is more in line with the Latin American literary form of the *testimonio* than the humanitarian-style testimony which equates the storytelling process with a victim narrative. As Anna Bernard has shown, this *testimonio* had been used in the *Tricontinental* magazine to serve an organisational purpose, as an account of collective struggle, narrated by one of the participants on behalf of the movement.[67]

The *testimonio* in *La Bohemia* describes the experience of the doctor – Walid – arriving in Damascus on 20 June 1982 before being driven to the Beqaa valley in Lebanon. While driving, he thinks back to a few days before, in Havana, when he was absorbed in his final exams, and then had to leave behind his girlfriend and the Cuban friends who had helped him complete his studies.[68] Arriving at his destination, he is surprised to hear a familiar voice speak to him in Spanish, the voice of a close friend from Havana who has also returned to offer his medical skills to the movement: it was 'Nael', whom he had met in Havana in 1975 at the outset of their

[65] For the testimonies of the international journeys of these *médicos-guerrilleros*, see Médicos guerrilleros testimonios/compilación por Nydia Sarabia (Havana: Consejo nacional de sociedades científicas del ministerio de salud pública, 1982).

[66] Richard Denis, Una Revista al Sevicio de la Nación: Bohemia and the Evolution of Cuban Journalism (1908–1960), PhD thesis, University of Florida, 7–8.

[67] Anna Bernard, 'Palestinian voices in the Tricontinental', 208.

[68] 'Ida Sin Vuelta', *La Bohemia*, vol. 75, no. 26, 1 July 1983, 76.

studies. They exchanged warm greetings and memories of Havana before being sent to separate places to continue their adaptation into their 'new life as a médico-guerrillero'.[69] After days of heavy bombardment, operating in terrible conditions – 'blood everywhere, just a lot of blood and mud' – Walid meets another friend from his studies in Cuba, Kassem, who invites him to meet the director of the hospital. It is here that the news is delivered of how Nael was killed by a shell the previous day. Walid remembers their times in Cuba together, their first difficulties with the Spanish language, the schools they attended, their enthusiasm for the marches and parades celebrating Cuban history.

They discuss plans to send Nael's body to his family, but Kassem tells Walid that Nael was an orphan, so he didn't have any parents. They will try to send his body to his sister in Palestine, via Syria, and – 'if the Zionists don't allow it'[70] – he will be buried in Jordan. Walid exclaims: 'Ah Kassem, none of us know where we are going to live. If we live, we do not know where we are going to die. If we die, who knows where we will be buried? I have come to hate that Arab world which sees us die with such indifference'.[71] He finishes his account with an impassioned condemnation of the horrors of war, which conveys a sense of the pressures of optimism upon the younger members of the *thawra* generation in the face of the incessant brutality and loss of life that accompanied the revolutionary defeat.

> Nael fell, and many other Naels will fall. The blockade on Beirut continues, Palestine is vilified, and the war continues, until one day we arrive to victory.
>
> I hate the planes that kill!
>
> I hate the tanks and the cannons that assassinate!
>
> I hate the ambulances with their sirens announcing injuries and death!
>
> I hate to see a child injured!

---

[69] 'Ida Sin Vuelta', 77.

[70] 'Ida Sin Vuelta', 77.

[71] 'Ida Sin Vuelta', 78.

Oh war! How I hate you!

But for peace, for my Palestine, I am obliged to say: *viva la guerra* [long live the war]![72]

More than a purely personal expression of grief, the author's conclusion indicates the mounting pressures on the coherence of what Laleh Khalili calls the 'heroic liberationist discourse' that had so powerfully motivated a sense of shared optimism among the disparate revolutionary movements of the 1960s and 1970s. We can see the moment when a possible future was, or was felt to be, lost; and when the pressures of revolutionary optimism began to feel unbearable in the face of such loss. The pressures upon maintaining revolutionary optimism, however, are not enough to cause the writer to break with the refrain of the necessity of continued struggle – 'until one day we arrive to victory'.[73] But the ending of his 1983 *testimonio*, published after the evacuation of the PLO leadership from Beirut and the collapse of the movement's infrastructures in Lebanon, does bring to mind the growing distance between on the one hand the official conclusions of PLO tracts as they entered into the 1980s, when the declarations issued were still expressed in the language of revolution, and on the other hand personal criticisms and popular doubt in a climate of lost leadership and unity. The title of the piece too is laden with meaning – 'Ida Sin Vuelta' [literally: going without return] can either refer to a literal or metaphorical one-way journey (referring possibly to the journey of Walid or Nael from which neither will be able to 'go back') or it can also be read as a meditation on the unrealised state of the ongoing Palestinian struggle for the return to their homeland.

CONCLUSION

By 5 October 1979, shortly after the XI Festival, the CCP made the decision that 'all Palestinians in Cuba' (namely the representatives of Fatah, the DFLP, and the PFLP) would now be dealt with through the office of the PLO (staffed and led by Fatah). According to a report sent by Imad Jadaa, director of the PLO Office, to the PLO Political Department in Beirut, the

---

[72] 'Ida Sin Vuelta', 79.
[73] 'Ida Sin Vuelta', 79.

representatives of the DFLP and the PFLP contested this decision, but the Cubans refused their request for the opening of alternative official offices.[74] PFLP and DFLP representatives continued to operate on the island, receiving visitors, and maintaining friendly relations with Cuban officials, but also at times angering the PLO office when Palestinian visitors to the island co-ordinated with one of the front offices instead of with the PLO. On 6 October 1981, following the visit of a Palestinian delegation to Havana led by senior PLO official Farouq Qaddoumi, a CCP–PLO co-operation agreement was signed that upgraded the status of the PLO office in Havana to that of a diplomatic mission in line with the Vienna Convention on Diplomatic Relations. It included the clause that 'official relations between the CCP and the Palestinian resistance will be conducted through the PLO'.[75] Diplomatic relations between Fatah and Cuba were formally closer than ever. The 1982 war and its aftermath changed things: any remaining sense of Palestinian unity under Fatah's leadership was lost, and Cuba – evident in the ranking of the officials who welcomed visiting delegations and the distribution of scholarships – began to focus more on the Marxist–Leninist factions of the Palestinian movement.[76]

As Karma Nabulsi has written, among the achievements – and subsequent losses – of the Palestinian revolution was its ability to bring representation and unity to the Palestinian people.[77] This chapter has shown how the principle of unity was also fundamental to the fraternal Third World solidarity that was established with the movement in the seventies. However, a discourse of shared experience and a common enemy – the basis of the fraternal Cuban–Palestinian relationship – was not enough to determine how such solidarity relations would develop.[78] As the Cuban foreign ministry archives show, questions of factionalism – who legitimately represented the Palestinian movement and its strategic interests – were ever-present in the bilateral relations between the PLO and Cuba, and played an important

---

[74] 'Al-'ilaqat al-filastiniya al-kubiya' [Palestinian–Cuban Relations], Misión de la Organización Para La Liberación de Palestina, Havana, Cuba, 5 September 1979.

[75] 'Al-bayan al-kubi al-filastini al-mushtarak', Misión de la Organización Para La Liberación de Palestina, Havana, Cuba. Cooperation Agreement Between the Cuban Communist Party and the PLO, 6 October 1981.

[76] Camacho Padilla and Stites Mor, 'Visibility and imagery in Cuban anticolonial solidarity with Palestine', 174.

[77] Karma Nabulsi, 'Lament for the Revolution', London Review of Books, vol. 32, no. 20–21, October 2010. https://www.lrb.co.uk/the-paper/v32/n20/karma-nabulsi/diary.

[78] Reem Abou-El-Fadl, 'Building Egypt's Afro-Asian Hub: Infrastructures of Solidarity and the 1957 Cairo Conference', Journal of World History 30:1–2 (2019): 157–192.

role in determining the nature and extent of Cuban support for the various Palestinian organisations. At the same time, and made visible when we look beyond the official records of ministry archives, the revolutionary state played a central role in mobilising support for Palestine that transcended factional concerns: from the curated encounters of the youth and student festival to the more granular, everyday encounters, as in the post-classroom conversations of scholarship students, talking of home, family, politics, and international revolution.

What kind of story can we tell about transformations of Third Worldism in the seventies and beyond? Different types of sources – from previously unutilised state archives to interviews with the people who took part – allow for a more complicated story than one of increasing connection and com- mitment to a shared cause expressed in the official rhetoric of Third World solidarity, or only of factionalism, fractures, and insurmountable divides. Internal struggles, splits and disagreements were present throughout the seventies and translated into the international relations of the movement, and there also existed a shared language and project, communicated and mobilised through state-supported infrastructures but not tied to state–quasi state relations, which facilitated and sustained enduring transnational soli- darity between movements and peoples. Recognising the entangled nature of state and transnational solidarities within the Third World project of the seventies does not make it easier to pass a final judgement on when or how the era of Third Worldism might have ended, but it is a necessary step towards a demystification of the fraternal relations upon which it was based.

2

NURSING THE REVOLUTION

Norwegian Medical Support in Lebanon as Solidarity, 1976–1983

Pelle Valentin Olsen

One late evening in the early autumn of 1976, Eldbjørg Holte, a young Norwegian assistant nurse, was woken by her friend Trond Linstad, a medical doctor and fellow member of the Norwegian Palestine Committee (PalKom). Linstad suggested that they travel to Lebanon to provide medical solidarity to the Palestinian revolution. Holte immediately agreed and after making the necessary arrangements, the two began their journey to Lebanon a couple of days later as PalKom's first medical team. Prior to their departure, PalKom had been collecting donations, medicine and medical supplies and equipment, which the Iraqi embassy in Stockholm had promised to send to Lebanon. As the Beirut airport was closed after heavy bombardment in the summer of 1976 and Lebanon was generally closed off to foreigners, with the help of Palestinians living in Norway who were well connected to groups within Fatah, Linstad and Holte travelled to Lebanon via Copenhagen, Baghdad, Cairo, and Cyprus. After spending three weeks in a hotel in Baghdad, they joined three hundred Iraqis and Palestinians on their way to join the Palestinian revolution as fighters. Since the Syrian border was closed after Syria had entered the Lebanese civil war (1975–1990) on the side of Christian forces earlier in 1976, they first flew from Baghdad to Cairo. Then, after making their way to Alexandria, they boarded a boat that took them to the Lebanese coastal town of Saida via Cyprus, alongside the three hundred fighters, ten tons of ammunition, and other military and medical equipment. In Saida, they were welcomed by Fathi Arafat, Yasser Arafat's brother and head of the Palestinian Red Crescent Society (PRCS), which had been founded in 1968 in Jordan.

From Saida, the two young Norwegians went to Beirut, where they worked at the Nazareth children's hospital treating and tending to child survivors of the massacre of the Tall al-Za'atar refugee camp carried out by Lebanese Christian militias earlier that year. Later, they worked at the Nasser hospital close to the Burj al-Barajneh camp, where they mostly treated wounded Palestinian fighters. Holte and Linstad returned to Norway after three months.[1] As members of PalKom's first medical team in Lebanon, they were responding to a direct call for medical support by Fathi Arafat and Khalil al-Wazir (Abu Jihad), one of the founders of Fatah and the military leader of the PLO (Palestine Liberation Organisation), after the outbreak of the Lebanese civil war in 1975 and the 1976 siege and massacre of the Tall al-Za'atar refugee camp.[2] Relying on activists to organise donation campaigns and using their informal recruitment networks at hospitals across Norway, throughout the 1970s and early 1980s, PalKom continued to send medical teams to Lebanon, where they worked under the protection of the PLO and within the institutions and organisations of the PRCS. For members of PalKom, medical support, which had been a cornerstone of the committee's solidarity work since 1976, was part and parcel of their political commitment to and support for the Palestinian revolution and the PLO. However, after the Israeli invasion and siege of Beirut in 1982, the expulsion of the PLO, the increase of Christian Phalangist power, and the election of Maronite leader Amin Gemayel to president (1982–1988), it became practically impossible for political organisations and people who had worked with the Palestinians to obtain visas to Lebanon. As a result,

---

[1] Interview with Eldbjørg Holte, Oslo, 23 November 2021. See also 'Jeg har faktisk håp om at det en dag blir fred i Palestina' [I actually believe that there will one day be peace in Palestine], interview with Eldbjørg Holte, *Fritt Palestina*, 2, 2019, 43–45; *For PLO i Libanon: Brev fra Palestina Komiteens Helseteam 1979–78* [For the PLO in Lebanon: Letters from the Palestine Committee's Medical Teams 1976–78] (Oslo: Palestinakomiteen, 1980), 11, Arbeiderbevegelsens Arkiv og Bibliotek (The Labour Movement's Archive and Library), Oslo, Norway (henceforth ARBARK).

[2] Interview with Eldbjørg Holte, Oslo, 23 November 2021; interview with Ebba Wergeland, Oslo, 18 November 2021; Erik Fosse, *Med Livet I Hendene* [With Life in My Hands] (Oslo: Gyldendal, 2013), 30.

PalKom decided to separate the medical work from its political activities and official support for the PLO. In 1983, members of PalKom established the Norwegian Aid Committee (NORWAC) as an independent and non-political humanitarian aid organisation.

Following recent work that looks to micro-level changes in transnational networks of activists and revolutionaries as indicative of larger global trends and transitions,[3] by focusing on medical support organised by PalKom this chapter examines the overlooked, but expansive, geography and history of medicine and medical support as a transnational act and unit of Third Worldism and solidarity. In tandem, it traces the transition to new modes of solidarity in the 1980s when several Palestine solidarity movements in the Global North shifted part of their focus to humanitarian aid and human rights advocacy. More specifically, focusing on PalKom, this chapter examines the transition from explicitly political medical support to humanitarian aid. Through a micro-history of PalKom's medical support, understood as a material practice of solidarity, the following sections challenge the notion that the transformation of solidarity in the 1980s was necessarily a straightforward acceptance of the new politics of humanitarianism and de-radicalisation. The Norwegian case suggests that the transformation outlined above was gradual, contested, and material in nature rather than necessarily ideological. The transition from PalKom to NORWAC, this chapter argues, was one of necessity and occurred only after 1982 when the military option for liberation was defeated (see Sune Haugbolle's chapter in this book), when the PLO and PRCS infrastructure was destroyed, and when it became impossible for most solidarity activists to obtain visas to Lebanon. In other words, the decision to form a humanitarian aid organisation was a strategic acceptance of changing material realities, immobility, and new power dynamics in Lebanon, meant to secure the continuation of medical support to a people in crisis and under attack.

However, while the process was not straightforward, the creation of NORWAC in 1983 did eventually result in an increased focus on humanitarianism and professionalism. This was a departure from the earlier period

---

[3] Mezna Qato, 'Forms of Retrieval: Social Scale, Citation, and the Archive of the Palestinian Left', *International Journal of Middle East Studies* 51, 2 (2019): 312–315; Naghmeh Sohrabi, 'Where the Small Things Are: Thoughts on Writing Revolutions and their Histories', *Jadaliyya*, 21 May 2020, https://www.jadaliyya.com/Details/41154; Sune Haugbolle, 'Entanglement, Global History, and the Arab Left', *International Journal of Middle Eastern Studies* 51, 2 (2019): 301–304.

when medical support, as a radical political act of solidarity, was seen as the most important aspect of PalKom's work. While the new institutional frameworks did not deliberately seek to limit solidarity, beginning in the 1980s they gradually resulted in a separation of the medical support from the radical political context in which it had emerged. On the material level, however, and in the modes of practice and organisation, continuity rather than a complete rupture characterised NORWAC's early history. For example, while no official ties existed between PalKom and NORWAC, the people involved in the two organisations were for many years the same group of activists who used the same recruitment networks and continued their political and ideological support for the Palestinians and their struggle through other venues.

Like the other contributions in this book, this chapter revisits the period of the late 1970s and early 1980s to investigate the changing contours of Third Worldism in the Middle East. Rather than rupture, sudden transformation, and depoliticisation, this chapter highlights continuity and gradual transformation as it traces the transnational scale of Third Worldism through the committed lives of Norwegian solidarity activists and their Palestinian partners.

MEDICAL SUPPORT AS A FORGOTTEN INFRASTRUCTURE OF REVOLUTION

It is generally accepted that a transformative shift in the political framework of solidarity occurred with the transition into the 1980s. During the earlier period, referred to by some as the 'global sixties', solidarity was driven by a sense of collective struggle, anti-imperialism, opposition to global capitalism, injustice, and racism led by national liberation movements, starting in the 1950s during the period of decolonisation, and the global New Left.[4] In the 1980s, international solidarity changed when the Global South, including Palestine, came to be viewed through a framework of

---

[4] See, for example, Zeina Maasri, Cathy Bergen, and Francesca Burke, eds, *Transnational Solidarity: Anticolonialism in the Global Sixties* (Manchester: Manchester University Press, 2022); Samantha Christiansen and Zachary A. Scarlett, eds, *The Third World in the Global 1960s* (New York: Berghahn Books, 2013); Chen Jian, Martin Klimke, Masha Kirasirova, Mary Nolan, Marilyn Young, Joanna Waley-Cohen, eds, *The Routledge Handbook of the Global Sixties: Between Protest and Nation-Building* (London: Routledge, 2018).

humanitarianism, victimhood, and development, rather than as a source of revolutionary inspiration. These changes, all part of the decline of the Third World project, had profound consequences for anti-colonial politics and national liberation struggles. For Palestinians, the destruction of a representative national liberation structure after the 1982 Israeli invasion forced the PLO to leave Beirut, and the creation of the Palestinian Authority (PA) in the 1990s with the Oslo Agreement resulted in the separation of the liberation struggle from meaningful political representation. Changes since Oslo have had clear effects on the framing of international solidarity with the Palestinian people, with Palestinians increasingly understood by international organisations through a lens of neoliberal models of conflict, development, and humanitarian aid.[5]

The topic of medical support as a form of solidarity has received limited scholarly attention, perhaps as a result of the way in which it largely became part of, and was discredited by, the transition to humanitarianism and aid of the 1980s and 1990s. Except for a recent MA thesis written at the University of Oslo, Norwegian medical support has not been explored.[6] Using the example of PalKom, this chapter re-situates medical support, as a form of solidarity, within the context of radical and politically motivated support for the Palestinian revolution in which it originated. Since medicine and medical support are often framed and understood, from a contemporary

[5] Linda Tabar, 'From Third World internationalism to "the internationals": the transformation of solidarity with Palestine', *Third World Quarterly* 38, 2 (2017): 414–435; Laleh Khalili, *Heroes and Martyrs of Palestine: The Politics of National Commemoration* (Cambridge: Cambridge University Press, 2007); Toufic Haddad, *Palestine Ltd.: Neoliberalism and Nationalism in the Occupied Territory* (Bloomsbury: I.B. Tauris, 2018); Ilana Feldman, *Life Lived in Relief – Humanitarian Predicaments and Palestinian Refugee Politics* (Berkeley: University of California Press, 2018). For more on the history of the Palestinian experience in Lebanon, including the history of Palestinians as refugees and recipients of humanitarian aid, see, for example, Rosemary Sayigh, *Too Many Enemies: The Palestinian Experience in Lebanon* (London: Zed Books, 1994); Diana Allan, *Refugees of the Revolution: Experiences in Palestinian Exile* (Stanford: Stanford University Press, 2014); Julie Peteet, *Landscape of Hope and Despair: Palestinian Refugee Camps* (Philadelphia: University of Pennsylvania Press, 2005).

[6] Lærke Ajaaja Madsen Otzen, 'Fra Oslo til Beirut og tilbage' [From Oslo to Beirut and Back], MA Thesis, Oslo University, 2022, 44–100. Three other MA theses, also written in Norwegian, have explored the history of official Norwegian aid to Lebanon: Endre Stangeby, 'Samarbeid i Strid. Norsk hjelpearbeid under borgerkrigen i Libanon', MA Thesis, Oslo University 2017; Mathias Skovli Pettersen, 'Nødhjelp by Proxy. Det norske utenriksdepartements nødhjelpspolitikk overfor Libanon, 1975–1982', MA Thesis, Oslo University 2016; Jostein Peter Eikrem, 'En ubetydeleg bidragsytar? Norsk bistand til palestinske flyktningar, 1967–1993', MA Thesis, Oslo University 2011.

perspective, as non-political, the ways in which they assisted and nursed the Palestinian struggle are partially hidden and obscured. Writing against the erasure of the multiple forms of medical support, care, nursing, and healing that were integral to the Palestinian and other revolutions and their infrastructures is an important task. Many of the doctors, nurses, and other medical professionals working in Lebanon, Palestinian as well as foreign, were active in radical and revolutionary politics as part of or in addition to their medical work. Because of the masculine frame through which the period, and revolution more generally, is remembered, celebrated, and idealised, the fact that many medical workers and volunteers were women has pushed this form of solidarity to the margins of the historical narrative of the period. As Marral Shamshiri points out in her chapter in this volume, due to the gendered hierarchy of roles in the often hypermasculine setting of revolution, the work of women, including teaching, care work, medical work, and nursing, has often been considered secondary and 'behind the front'. 'Writing revolutions as if women mattered', Naghmeh Sohrabi has recently argued, requires us to change the analytical focus 'away from revolution as *intellectual work* (primarily located in the imaginings of revolutionary strategists and theoreticians) to revolution as *political work* (primarily located in action and in the streets)'.[7] Writing revolutions in this way, as if women mattered, according to Sohrabi, can expand the history of revolution beyond ideology and theory and modify what counts as revolutionary history.[8] Writing the history of medical work as a radical and revolutionary practice of solidarity, as this chapter shows, does both.

A small, albeit not insignificant, part of the medical work was carried out by foreign activists and volunteers, including the many Norwegians who travelled to Lebanon in the late 1970s and early 1980s. To study these practices of solidarity, we must pay attention to their materiality. For example, while the medical teams sent by PalKom provided both material and moral support, they were completely dependent on and worked within Palestinian institutions such as the PRCS. They needed both the support and approval of Palestinian organisations and individuals to secure visas, build clinics, and organise travel. The same institutions provided translators, transportation, security, and food and shelter. Finally, focusing on medical support adds a new dimension that is both material and imaginary to recent studies

---

[7] Naghmeh Sohrabi, 'Writing Revolution as if Women Mattered', *Comparative Studies of South Asia, Africa and the Middle East* 42, 2 (2022): 546.

[8] Ibid., 547.

exploring state-driven, diplomatic, cultural, and artistic forms and venues of solidarity.[9] Focusing on medical support offers a window into some of the infrastructures and political economies of solidarity, including the distribution of finance, funding structures, and the exchange of non-military equipment and supplies that have, until now, remained largely hidden.

PALESTINE SOLIDARITY IN NORWAY

Back in Norway, before joining PalKom's first medical team, Eldbjørg Holte was already active in leftist politics. She became a member of PalKom in 1971, a year after it had been established by young activists with strong ties to the Maoist Norwegian Workers' Communist Party, or AKP (m-l). While PalKom was not officially affiliated with one particular Norwegian political party, many of the early members, as mentioned above, identified as Maoists and some were members of the AKP (m-l). As a result, members of PalKom were in close contact with Maoist factions within the PLO.[10] As pointed out by scholars such as Mjriam Abu Samra, student groups and Palestinian diasporic communities in imperial capitals played a key role in the early years of Palestine solidarity outside of the Middle East.[11]

---

[9] Paul Thomas Chamberlin, *The Global Offensive: The United States, the Palestine Liberation Organization, and the Making of the Post-Cold War Order* (Oxford: Oxford University Press, 2012); Dina Matar, 'PLO Cultural Activism: Mediating Liberation Aesthetics in Revolutionary Contexts', *Comparative Studies of South Asia, Africa and the Middle East* 38, 2 (2018): 354–364; Kristine Khouri and Rasha Salti, eds, *Past Disquiet: Artists, International Solidarity, and Museums in Exile* (Chicago: University of Chicago Press, 2018); Nadia Yaqub, *Palestinian Cinema in the Days of Revolution* (Austin: University of Texas Press, 2018); Zeina Maasri, *Cosmopolitan Radicalism: The Visual Politics of Beirut's Global Sixties* (Cambridge: Cambridge University Press, 2020); Shahab Ahmad, 'The Poetics of Solidarity: Palestine in Modern Urdu Poetry', *Alif: Journal of Comparative Poetics* 18 (1998): 29–64; see also Maha Nassar, '"My Struggle Embraces Every Struggle": Palestinians in Israel and Solidarity with Afro-Asian Liberation Movements', *Arab Studies Journal* 22, 1 (2014): 74–101; Michael R. Fischbach, *Black Power and Palestine: Transnational Countries of Color* (Stanford: Stanford University Press, 2018); Joseph Ben Prestel, 'Heidelberg, Beirut, und die "Dritte Welt": Palästinensische Gruppen in der Bundesrepublik Deutschland (1956–1972)', Zeithistorische Forschungen/*Studies in Contemporary History* 3 (2019): 442–466; Naghmeh Sohrabi, 'Remembering the Palestine Group: Global Activism, Friendship, and the Iranian Revolution', *International Journal of Middle East Studies* 51 (2019): 281–300.

[10] Interview with Ebba Wergeland, Oslo, 18 November 2021.

[11] Mjriam Abu Samra, 'The Palestinian Student Movement 1948–1982: A Study of Popular Organisation and Transnational Mobilisation', PhD dissertation, University of Oxford, 2020.

In Norway as well, during the late 1960s and early 1970s, solidarity with Palestine emerged out of New Left and student milieus and movements. A small number of committed activists set up Arbeidsgruppen for et Fritt Palestina (Working Group for a Free Palestine) in 1969. After participating in the Second World Conference for Palestine, organised in Amman in September 1970 by the GUPS (General Union of Palestinian Students), the Working Group officially founded PalKom. The committee quickly began publishing the monthly journal *Fritt Palestina* (*Free Palestine*) and setting up local branches and reading groups all over Norway, participating in public debate and inviting Palestinian representatives to Norway.[12]

As we will see in the following section, after 1976 medical support quickly became the flagship operation of PalKom. However, while the number of Norwegians who travelled to Lebanon to provide medical support makes the case of Norway stand out,[13] it is important to point out that they were part of a much larger international phenomenon of medical solidarity practised by states, organisations, and individuals from across the globe. For example, Cuban solidarity, the topic of Sorcha Thomson's chapter in this book, consisted of medical missions and the education of doctors through scholarships.[14] In Lebanon, PalKom's medical teams worked alongside Soviet, East German, Bulgarian, Arab, Pakistani, Bangladeshi, Indian, US, and Canadian missions, as well as those of many other nationalities. Similarly, while PalKom's medical solidarity work did not begin until 1976, there exists a much longer history of medical solidarity and internationalism. PalKom drew inspiration from some of these older traditions. In fact, according to Erik Fosse, a young Norwegian surgeon who joined PalKom's third medical team in 1979, the model on which PalKom's medical support was based was the work of Norwegian volunteers during the Spanish civil war in the

[12] Sigvart Fredriksen, 'Discovering Palestine: How Norwegian Solidarity with Palestine Emerged in the Transnational 1960s', MA Thesis, Oslo University, 2020.
[13] Egil Fossum, *Palestine Volunteers: Glimpses of Solidarity Work with the Palestinians* (Nicosia: P. & P. Intertype, 1986), 86.
[14] See, for example, John M. Kirk and H. Michael Erisman, *Cuban Medical Internationalism: Origins, Evolution, and Goals* (London: Palgrave Macmillan, 2009); Piero Gleijeses, 'Cuba's First Venture in Africa: Algeria, 1961–1965', *Journal of Latin American Studies* 28, 1 (1996): 159–195. For personal accounts see Chris Giannou, *Besieged: A Doctor's Story of Life and Death in Beirut* (London: Bloomsbury, 1991); Youssif Iraki, *The Diary of a Doctor in Tel Al-Zaatar, a Palestinian Refugee Camp in Lebanon* (Beirut: Democratic Front for the Liberation of Palestine, 2016); Swee Chai Ang, *From Beirut to Jerusalem: A Woman Doctor with the Palestinians* (London: Collins, 1989).

1930s.[15] Palestinafronten (the Palestine Front), another Norwegian Palestine solidarity group, which split from PalKom in 1976 after disagreements over the role of the Soviet Union, also sent medical teams to Lebanon. The ideological splits that occurred throughout the 1970s in Norway mirrored splits in the wider project of Third Worldism and in Palestine solidarity movements globally.

'IF THE PLO BELIEVES THAT WE CAN BE USEFUL THEN IT IS OUR DUTY TO GO': MEDICAL SUPPORT AS SOLIDARITY, 1976–1983

This section examines the politically committed forms of medical support practised by PalKom beginning in 1976. Before the arrival of the first medical team, an article in *Fritt Palestina* explained to readers, 'If the PLO believes that we can be useful then it is our duty to go.'[16] As we will see, this sense of duty and the placing of decision-making with the PLO and the PRCS characterised most of PalKom's medical support. Moreover, it was the integration into PRCS infrastructure that made PalKom's medical support possible and effective. According to one Norwegian volunteer, 'Without the PRCS we are nothing.'[17] Once in Lebanon, PalKom's medical teams worked closely with the PRCS and it was the PRCS who decided where in Lebanon the Norwegians were needed.[18] The first medical teams worked across Lebanon, but in October of 1978 PalKom began working permanently at a clinic in the village of Kfair in southern Lebanon, as well as in the Palestinian camp of Rashidiyya, where Swedish Palestine solidarity activists

---

[15] Fosse, *Med Livet I Hendene*, 30.

[16] *Fritt Palestina*, 'Solidaritet Norge-Palestina!', 1976, 6, 1.

[17] Fossum, *Palestine Volunteers*, 10.

[18] For detailed studies of the history and organisational structure of the PRCS, including the location of clinics and hospitals, and the number of foreign doctors working within the organisation, see ʿAbd al-ʿAziz al-Labadi, 'al-Hilal al-Ahmar al-Filastini', *Shuʾun Filastiniyya* 86, 1979, 144–150; ʿAbd al-ʿAziz al-Labadi, *Jamaʿiyyat al-Hilal al-Ahmar al-Filastini* (Amman: Sanabil, 1986); Fathi Arafat, *al-Sihha wa al-Harb* (Beirut: Jamaʿiyyat al-Hilal al-Ahmar al-Filastini, 1980); Ahmad Omar Shahin, 'Jamaʿiyyat al-Hilal al-Ahmar al-Filastini', *Samid* 79, February 1989, 50–66; Fathiyya al-Saʿudi, *Ahwal al-Filastiniyin al-Sihhiyya fi Lubnan* (Beirut: al-muʾassasa al-ʿarabiyya lil-dirasat wa al-nashr, 1979); Asʿad Hamuri, 'al-Hilal al-Ahmar al-Filastini', *Shuʾun Filastiniyya* 41–42, 1975, 539–545; Fossum, *Palestine Volunteers*, 58–62.

had their base.[19] Around 1980, PalKom began sending medical teams to the West Bank and Gaza. A couple of years later, they began staffing the PRCS nursing school in Cairo with teachers and instructors.[20] In 1981, PalKom moved its medical work to one of the PRCS's clinics in the Burj al-Shamali camp in southern Lebanon. The fact that the new clinic was located inside a camp allowed the Norwegians working there to get closer to the PLO and PRCS infrastructure, including educational, health, and political organisations, as all of the PLO's different branches were represented in the camp. The Norwegians also established close connections and friendships with camp residents and fighters, who would often be transferred to the clinic after surgery at a bigger hospital.[21] At the same time, the medical work was expanded and PalKom began sending physiotherapists and dentists in addition to doctors and nurses. PalKom also began sending more specialised teams consisting of surgeons and anaesthesiologists in the immediate aftermath of several extremely lethal and devastating Israeli attacks in 1981. These more specialised teams were active throughout the attack and siege of Beirut in 1982, operating mostly in west Beirut and northern Lebanon.[22]

As mentioned at the beginning of this chapter, Holte and Linstad made up PalKom's first medical team in Lebanon. In Norway, Holte worked in an intensive care unit at Ullevål Hospital. Linstad had already worked with the PFLP (Popular Front for the Liberation of Palestine) and other Palestinian organisations as a doctor in Jordan during the events of Black September, when Palestinian organisations fought the Jordanian army. Until he was expelled in 1971, Linstad worked alongside Cuban and other foreign doctors, caring for Palestinian fighters and civilians. In 1973, he worked as a doctor in Lebanon. He was the driving force behind PalKom's medical support initiative.[23] When they arrived in Lebanon, Holte and Linstad had with them medicine to the value of 20,000 NOK (3,846 USD) and an

[19] For PLO i Libanon, 5.
[20] 'Sykepleierskole i Kairo' [Nursing School in Cairo], ARBARK, Palestinakomiteen, Da-SAKSARKIV, DA-L0013; 'Informasjonsmappe for heleseteamarbeidere i Libanon' [Information folder for medical team workers in Lebanon], PalKom, Oslo, Synne Holan's personal archive.
[21] Fritt Palestina 4, 1980, 15.
[22] 'Informasjonsmappe for heleseteamarbeidere i Libanon'. For an excellent analysis of the transition to specialised medical teams, see Otzen, 'Fra Oslo til Beirut og tilbage', 36–44.
[23] Interview with Eldbjørg Holte, Oslo, 23 November 2021. For more on foreign medical workers in Jordan before, during, and after Black September, see Fossum, Palestine Volunteers, 16–18, 26–27.

additional 150,000 NOK (27,272 USD) in cash to support their medical work.[24] Responding to a direct appeal from the Palestinians, before sending the first medical team to Lebanon, PalKom organised a large donation campaign drawing on activists from local branches all over Norway. The money and medicine that Holte and Linstad took with them had been collected during the 1976 donation campaign, 'Solidaritet Norge-Palestina' (Solidarity Norway–Palestine). PalKom's campaign was political from the very beginning and the committee actively distanced its work from that of humanitarian organisations:

> We won't send the money to the Red Cross or other purely humanitarian organisations who are unwilling to make up their minds about who is the oppressed and who is the oppressor, who attacks and who is the attacked.[25]

In their internal communications as well as in their publications, PalKom continuously stressed the differences between solidarity and humanitarian work:

> PalKom has always distinguished between solidarity and humanitarian work. We send medical teams, not because Palestine can be liberated through medical aid, but because we want to take part in the struggle, show our support, and stand with the Palestinians. We are happy to make ourselves useful through medical support, but the future of the Palestinians will not be found through the distribution of aid by professional humanitarian aid workers. What the Palestinians need is support for their liberation struggle.[26]

In an article published in *Fritt Palestina*, Bjørg Kvamme Wendelborg, a nurse specialising in emergency medicine and member of PalKom's 1977 third medical team, similarly stressed that although the medical support was important, 'it is only through armed struggle that the situation will change ... The Palestinian people are engaged in a just fight against imperialism, fascism and Zionism' and they 'make up the frontline in this fight globally'. Wendelborg added that PalKom wanted to help 'by taking part in the medical

[24] *For PLO i Libanon*, 11.
[25] *Fritt Palestina*, 'Solidaritet Norge-Palestina!', 1976, 6, 2.
[26] 'Informasjonsmappe for heleseteamarbeidere i Libanon'.

work which is a part of the liberation struggle'.[27] Before leaving Lebanon, Wendelborg was interviewed by *Majalla* (Magazine), a monthly Arabic-language magazine published by the PRCS. *Majalla* regularly published reports and articles about and interviews with Norwegian and other foreign medical workers in Lebanon.[28] Wendelborg was interviewed in a special issue dedicated to women working for the PRCS and spoke at length about the importance of solidarity between Norwegian and Palestinian women as well as the importance of Palestinian women joining the struggle, both as workers and mothers of fighters.[29]

Another important aspect often highlighted by PalKom was the fact that their medical teams, which most often worked for three months at a time, did not receive salaries. The medical work was financed entirely through donations and the activists worked for free 'out of a political conviction that the Palestinian struggle is just'.[30] Synne Holan, a politically active Maoist and one of the founders of the AKP (m-l), first went to Lebanon with PalKom in 1983. Holan, who was a midwife by training, later worked with NORWAC in northern Lebanon and between 1984 and 1986 taught at the PRCS nursing school in Cairo. Holan describes how she saw her work with PalKom as part of a larger movement attempting to radically change the world. For Holan, being part of this movement and showing '*ekte solidaritet*' (real solidarity) necessitated 'a willingness to sacrifice'. As part of this, not receiving a salary was an ideological decision and part of being 'a radical human'. Holan worked for free and recalls how she and her fellow activists actually looked down on nurses and doctors working for larger international organisations that paid salaries.[31] While it was certainly easier for Norwegians, compared to solidarity activists from poorer countries, to work without salaries, forgoing pay was seen as a necessary sacrifice.

In addition to relying on the political commitment and conviction of its members, PalKom also stressed that its work was supported financially

---

[27] 'Konkret støtter til frigjøringsbevægelsen' [Concrete support for the liberation movement], *Fritt Palestina* 1, 1977, 1.

[28] See, for example, the long interview with Japanese nurse Mariko Nakato, who joined the Palestinian revolution as a nurse in 1971: *Majalla* 3, November 1974, 17–19. In March of 1978, *Majalla* published a long article and interview with members of the Swedish medical team: *Majalla*, 54–55, March 1978, 14–15.

[29] *Majalla* 32, April 1977, 21–23.

[30] 'Informasjonsmappe for heleseteamarbeidere i Libanon'; Fosse, *Med Livet I Hendene*, 30.

[31] Interview with Synne Holan, Oslo, 20 November 2021.

almost entirely by 'individuals and labour unions. While we have received limited [Norwegian] state funding for specific tasks, that can never be the main source for financing our work.'[32] PalKom financed most of its medical work through the collection of donations on streets and squares across Norway, a membership organisation called Helseteamvenner (Friends of the Medical Teams), which published its own quarterly magazine, *Nytt fra Helseteamene* (Medical Team News), and donations from labour unions. This allowed PalKom to be independent of external funding and political pressure. Collecting money from members, the Norwegian public, and labour unions represented a new strategy for PalKom's solidarity work and offered non-members an opportunity to actively support the Palestinians financially. Through its donation campaigns, PalKom was successful in mobilising support from and radicalising a part of the Norwegian labour movement, which had historically supported Israel. In its magazine, PalKom announced that the campaign 'would not stop before Palestine is fully liberated'.[33] The medical teams became one of the most important aspects of PalKom's solidarity work between 1976 and 1983. Similar donation campaigns took place in neighbouring Sweden and Denmark around the same time,[34] but PalKom was the first group in Scandinavia, and perhaps in northern Europe, to organise its own medical teams as part of its solidarity with the Palestinian revolution. A folder prepared by PalKom and handed out to medical team members emphasised that its solidarity was based on a shared sense of struggle: 'We support a people in struggle, not a suffering people. We support them not because we pity them, but because their cause is just.'[35]

PalKom described its medical work as 'a concrete expression of solidarity through which the Palestinians learn that they have friends everywhere'.[36] At the same time, however, providing medical support as a form of solidarity was never seen as a unidirectional transaction and the members of PalKom, who were critical of the official policies of the Norwegian government beyond Palestine, saw the Palestinians and their struggle as role models:

---

[32] 'Informasjonsmappe for heleseteamarbeidere i Libanon'.
[33] *Fritt Palestina*, 'Solidaritet Norge-Palestina!', 1976, 6, 2.
[34] *Medlemsblad*, 'Skandinavisk Konferanse om Palestinaarbeidet', 1976, 2.
[35] 'Informasjonsmappe for heleseteamarbeidere i Libanon'.
[36] Ibid.

We use the term solidarity when we talk about the medical work. This is essential for us. Solidarity is about equality. The medical work is not a one-way street – something that we give to the Palestinians. The Palestinians fight for justice ... and there are many of us who see them as a tremendous driving force and inspiration in the fight against the imperialist system that oppresses people all over the world.[37]

Most of the Norwegians who travelled to Lebanon to show solidarity with the Palestinians through medical work were recruited by word of mouth. PalKom had an extensive network of hospitals across Norway, which made it easy to recruit medical workers. The first medical teams consisted of people who were already active in PalKom or in Maoist circles in Norway. Others were recruited among feminist and other New Left groups or through the many letters and articles published in Norwegian newspapers by PalKom members.[38] In his memoir, Erik Fosse describes how he became involved in the medical work in Lebanon after reading several articles and letters published by PalKom's medical teams in the Norwegian newspaper *Klassekampen* (The Class Struggle) throughout 1978. In 1983, Fosse became one of the founders of NORWAC.[39]

Some were passive supporters of PalKom's work for years before becoming actively involved. Helga Hvidsten, a Norwegian physiotherapist, became a member of PalKom after meeting a medical team member who had recently returned from Beirut. After donating to the medical work for years, she went to Beirut in 1980.[40] While most of the medical teams consisted of young people, PalKom also sent older nurses and doctors who had experience working with older medical equipment, which was still in use in Lebanon.[41] According to Eldbjørg Holte, for PalKom members and non-members alike, the experience of providing medical support in Lebanon often led to politicisation and radicalisation. Holte describes how many of the medical team members realised that while they could not significantly change the medical realities in Lebanon, there was an equally important fight awaiting in Norway.[42] Ulla Andersen, head of PalKom's medical committee in 1980,

37 Ibid.
38 *Fritt Palestina*, 5, 1978.
39 Fosse, *Med Livet I Hendene*, 28–31, 77.
40 Helga Hvidsten, 'I kommiteen tjeneste' [In the service of the committee], *Fritt Palestina* 2, 2019, 36.
41 Interview with Synne Holan, Oslo, 20 November 2021.
42 Interview with Eldbjørg Holte, Oslo, 23 November 2021.

described her time in Lebanon as a 'school in solidarity' in an article in *Fritt Palestina*: 'When I first went to Lebanon, I thought a lot about suffering and misery, but what characterises the Palestinians is their fighting spirit. This is contagious and has made us enthusiastic about the solidarity work here in Norway. This is also why so many of us become Palestine activists when we return.'[43]

Statements and slogans like the ones mentioned above take up significant space in PalKom's publications. Such slogans often hide as much as they reveal because they gloss over obstacles, differently situated experiences, and the obvious limitations of imagining Norwegians and Palestinians as taking part in a shared struggle. In an article published in *Aktivisten* (The Activist), the internal monthly magazine of the Oslo branch of PalKom, the author reminded fellow members of their duties: 'are you tired and worn out? Do you feel a need to focus more on yourself and your needs? Do you feel a need to meditate, work out, and visit the gym? OK, but don't let the self-centredness go too far. Remember that the solidarity work that we do means a lot to the Palestinians.'[44] Judging from the number of articles published about Norwegian solidarity in Palestinian publications, the work of PalKom was appreciated and seen as both important and necessary. Already in 1977, a year after PalKom had sent its first medical team to Lebanon, Yasser Arafat praised their efforts in an interview in *Fritt Palestina*. 'PalKom's medical teams have contributed with important medical aid and have taught the Palestinian people that they have close friends all over the world.'[45] In September 1981, *Majalla* published a long article about Norwegian medical support. The article opens with the following sentence: 'The snows of the Scandinavian countries do not prevent them from clearly hearing the call of the PRCS ... The Norwegian mission was among the first international medical missions to arrive in Lebanon to rescue the victims of the Zionist barbarity committed against civilians.'[46] The article then describes the conditions under which Norwegian and PRCS medical staff had to work during the constant Israeli bombardments of southern Lebanon and asks: 'what makes a medical team from Norway, a country that has forgotten all

---

[43] 'Et helseteam til PLO – En skole i Solidaritet' [Medical team to PLO – A school of solidarity], *Fritt Palestina* 1, 1980, 19.
[44] 'En trend i tiden?' [A New Trend?], *Aktivisten – Internblad for Oslo-PalKom* [The Activist – internal magazine of the Olso PalKom], 20 December 1983, ARBAK.
[45] *Fritt Palestina* 5, 1977, 1.
[46] 'al-ba'tha al-tibbiyya al-nurwijiyya' [The Norwegian Medical Mission], *Majalla* 85, September 1981, 120.

about the horrors of war, travel to Lebanon?' The answer to the question is provided by an unnamed Norwegian doctor interviewed in the article. In addition to praising the work of the PRCS and their hospitals under extremely difficult conditions, the doctor states that, 'We are convinced that you are fighting for your right to return to your land, which has been occupied by the Zionists. We consider your cause to be our cause.'[47] *Shu'un Filastiniyya* (Palestinian Affairs), an intellectual and cultural magazine launched in 1971 and published quarterly in Beirut by the PLO's Palestine Research Centre, also published several articles on the topic of Norwegian medical support. In an article about the history of the Norwegian solidarity movement, including a very detailed report about the political landscape in Norway, written after a visit by a delegation from the Palestinian women's movement to Oslo on International Women's Day, Salwa al-'Amd describes how PalKom, in addition to their successful medical support, had managed to change public opinion on Palestine in Norway.[48]

Articles such as these suggest that inviting and enlisting international volunteers was a political decision that brought both moral and material support and visibility to the Palestinian revolution. While the PRCS had to provide organisational resources, translators, food, and shelter, the Norwegians brought medicine, medical equipment, and professional medical workers. This added to the capacity of Palestinian medical institutions and allowed Palestinian and Lebanese medical workers to focus their efforts elsewhere. Just as importantly, however, Norwegian medical support furthered the visibility of the Palestinian struggle. Like Ulla Andersen, after returning from Lebanon many medical team workers committed themselves to giving lectures and talks all over Norway, organising donation campaigns, writing articles and op-eds, and bringing attention to the Palestinian cause in other ways. Members of one of the 1978 medical teams also translated Palestinian children's books into Norwegian.[49] PalKom was very clear about the necessity of also working on the home front:

> Medical work for the PLO is important at home as well. People who have been to Lebanon give lectures, take part in meetings, and talk

[47] Ibid., 122.
[48] Salwa al-'Amd, 'al-Quwa al-Siasiyya al-Nurwijiyya wa harakat al-Tadamun ma' kifah al-sha'b al-filastini, *Shu'un Filastiniyya* 114, 1981, 140–145.
[49] Interview with Eldbjørg Holte, Oslo, 23 November 2021; Rolv Rynning Hanssen, 'Tilbakke til 70–tallet' [Back to the 1970s], *Fritt Palestina* 2, 2019, 26.

to friends and family after they return ... and win support for and
solidarity with the Palestinian liberation struggle in Norway ... We
believe that the medical work has had an enormous effect on changing public opinion in Norway.[50]

Returning medical team workers, many of whom had witnessed Israeli
bombardments and other attacks on Palestinian and Lebanese civilians
first-hand, reported their experiences back to the Norwegian public through
their writings and lectures in order 'to make the Palestinian cause known in
Norway and to make more people at home understand that the Palestinian
struggle, under the leadership of the PLO, is just and deserving of our
support'.[51] In 1982, *Fritt Palestina* published several excerpts from the
diaries of Norwegian and other foreign medical workers, who had spent
several days in a makeshift bomb shelter in a Palestinian camp in southern
Lebanon during a period of extremely intense and indiscriminate Israeli
attacks. One medical worker described how 'we force each other to eat a
little, drink tea with loads of sugar, but the only things that help me are the
cigarettes.'[52] For some of the Norwegian medical workers, including Ebba
Wergeland, the home front was where the real battle was waged. Wergeland
graduated with a degree in occupational medicine in 1970 and later received
a doctorate in the same field. After her graduation, she cancelled a sched-
uled exchange in the US in protest over the war in Vietnam and instead
went to Algeria, where she volunteered at a medical clinic. Before joining
PalKom, she had been active in Maoist circles as well as in protests against
the war in Vietnam. She was a regular member of PalKom until 1977, when
she was recruited to take part in the second medical team. She stayed in
Lebanon for almost a year and worked both in Saida and in Bint Jebail in
southern Lebanon. Wergeland describes that although she saw the medical
work as a concrete way of showing support for the Palestinians that was
inseparable from other forms of solidarity, the most important task was
to change Norwegian public opinion. According to Wergeland, changing
public opinion and putting pressure on Israel would potentially be more
effective than sending nurses, doctors, and medicine.[53] For some of the
Norwegians in Lebanon, showing support by simply being present and using

---

[50] 'Informasjonsmappe for heleseteamarbeidere i Libanon'.
[51] *For PLO i Libanon*, 6.
[52] *Fritt Palestina* 2, 1982, 7–9.
[53] Interview with Ebba Wergeland, Oslo, 18 November 2021.

their experiences to translate and produce knowledge about the Palestinian revolution and change public opinion in Norway after they returned, was as important as providing medical aid. In this sense, medical solidarity was about much more than providing care and aid. While the institutional frameworks changed with the transition from PalKom to NORWAC, the commitment of the people involved did not.

FROM MEDICAL SUPPORT TO HUMANITARIAN AID

This section examines the period after the 1982 Israeli invasion and the transition from PalKom to NORWAC. Throughout the second half of the 1970s, PalKom's medical teams built up important experience and skills. However, already in 1981, when Israel intensified its bombardments and attacks, more specialised doctors, surgeons, and nurses trained to handle the new situation were needed. As a result, and after another direct request from the PLO and the PRCS, PalKom began recruiting more widely in order to be able to send crisis teams to Lebanon. Unlike the medical teams which mostly worked at clinics, the crisis teams were sent to hospitals in west Beirut and southern Lebanon. According to Otzen, PalKom's crisis teams represented a more targeted medical professionalism and specialisation and can be seen as the first move towards a more humanitarian agenda.[54] Predicting that a siege of Beirut would soon begin, ten days after the Israeli invasion of Lebanon in June 1982 PalKom sent a crisis team to Beirut. While some of PalKom's medical teams were evacuated in 1982, during most of that year they had medical workers in Beirut throughout most of the siege.[55]

While the PRCS was the best organised and funded and provided the most health services, many other Palestinian organisations had their own medical sections, including the PFLP, DFLP (Democratic Front for the Liberation of Palestine), PFLP-GC (Popular Front for the Liberation of Palestine – General Command), ALF (Arab Liberation Front), PLF (Palestine Liberation Front), PPSF (Palestinian Popular Struggle Front), al-Saʿiqa and others.[56] As argued by Mona Yonis, the services provided by these organisations were indispensable for Palestinians living in Lebanon,

---

[54] Otzen, 'Fra Oslo til Beirut og tilbage', 35–37.
[55] Fosse, *Med Livet is Hendene*, 73–87.
[56] Mona Yonis, 'L'invasion du Liban et la situation sanitaire des Palestiniens', *Revue d'études Palestiniennes* 8 (1983): 40.

as well as for many Lebanese citizens. Therefore, 1982 and the evacuation of the PLO and other Palestinian organisations, including their medical services, had disastrous consequences. Before 1982, the PRCS had more than thirty clinics and hospitals in Lebanon. After 1982, most of this medical infrastructure was left in ruins. The results were directly and immediately felt by the Palestinians in Lebanon who had relied on these services. At the same time, the destruction of medical and resistance infrastructure also had global ramifications affecting practices of solidarity, as it made the crossing of Lebanon's borders much more difficult. These borders, which had previously been crossed by Norwegian and other solidarity activists with relative ease, suddenly became impenetrable due to the difficulty of obtaining visas, preventing the delivery of both moral and material medical support.

After the siege ended in August, PalKom's medical infrastructure, including its clinics, had been destroyed and the PRCS, on whose infrastructure and assistance they had relied, were forced to relocate to Cairo. Most of the PRCS archive, which had been stored at the 'Akka Hospital in Beirut, was also destroyed. PalKom continued to send medical and crisis teams throughout the autumn of 1982, but with increasing difficulties. The new political landscape, created by the expulsion of the PLO, the Israeli occupation of the south, and the increase of Christian Phalangist power, meant that for the Lebanese authorities PalKom was seen as too political and too pro-Palestinian and therefore no longer welcome. The internal power dynamics of post-1982 Lebanon are analysed in more detail by Nathaniel George in this volume. In October of 1982, PalKom's co-ordinator in Beirut, Norwegian nurse Sissel Skipperud, tried to secure visas through Lebanese aid organisations with connections to the Lebanese Communist Party, but without success. At the same time, the Norwegians in Beirut reported that they were under increasing surveillance by Lebanese security.[57] It was in this context that the idea of forming a new humanitarian organisation with a less political profile and with no official links to PalKom took form. While many members of PalKom were hesitant to channel their activism and solidarity into a non-political humanitarian organisation, NORWAC was formally established in 1983.[58]

Sissel Skipperud, who was still a member of PalKom, became NORWAC's first co-ordinator in Lebanon. In early May of 1983, however, she was

---

[57] Fosse, *Med Livet is Hendene*, 100.
[58] Ibid., 103.

arrested by Lebanese security due to her connections to PalKom and Palestinians in Lebanon. After being interrogated for two days, Skipperud was put on a plane to Amman where she was picked up by Jordanian security and later allowed to leave the country. PRCS staff and several foreign medical volunteers were harassed and even killed during and after the Israeli invasion.[59] After Skipperud's expulsion, it was decided that a new NORWAC leadership was needed. The organisation's first president was surgeon Mads Gilbert, who had already worked with several medical and crisis teams in 1981 and 1982 but was not an official member of PalKom.[60] Nurse Kirsti Owe and midwife Synne Holan became the first Norwegian NORWAC representatives in Lebanon after Skipperud's expulsion. At the same time, NORWAC began working with the Lebanese communist Sa'ad family and the Ma'ruf Sa'ad Foundation which ran schools, clinics, summer camps, and a kindergarten in southern Lebanon.[61] In 1984–1985, NORWAC began operating all over Lebanon, often using funds from Palestinian organisations, but under their own name.[62]

Many former medical team members agree that the transition from PalKom to NORWAC was in many ways little more than a technicality or a formality, at least during the first few years of NORWAC's existence. Similarly, most agree that it was not so much a rupture as a gradual transition, since most of the people involved remained the same.[63] Wergeland too suggests that the transition to NORWAC was one of necessity and pragmatism that occurred when PalKom members were either expelled from Lebanon or refused visas. NORWAC was created by members of PalKom and even if the new organisation could not officially show its politics, it took over PalKom's contacts in Lebanon and continued to provide medical support to many of the same people. While no official ties existed between PalKom and NORWAC, the people involved in the two organisations were, for many years, the same and PalKom continued its political and ideological support for the Palestinians and their struggle through other venues. In addition, for several years after the creation of NORWAC, PalKom continued

59 Fossum, *Palestine Volunteers*, 61.
60 Fosse, *Med Livet is Hendene*, 107.
61 Interview with Mona Sa'ad, Beirut, 12 April 2022; Otzen, 'Fra Oslo til Beirut og tilbage', 51–52.
62 Fosse, *Med Livet is Hendene*, 104–105.
63 Interview with Synne Holan, Oslo, 20 November 2021.

to clandestinely send medical and crisis teams, including surgeons and anaesthesiologists, to Palestinian camps in northern Lebanon via Cyprus.[64]

However, unlike PalKom, which had funded its work through donations and membership fees, NORWAC applied for funding from NORAD (Norwegian Agency for Development Co-operation), which was part of the Norwegian foreign ministry, and other official bodies. Throughout the mid- and late 1980s, however, PalKom remained important as a funder of NORWAC's projects and also assisted with their implementation and execution.[65] As argued above, in the early years of NORWAC's existence, members saw the new organisation as a necessary but pro-forma cover for PalKom that allowed them to secure visas and continue their work. While the former activists all agree on this interpretation of events, NORWAC increasingly became a strictly humanitarian organisation; it began recruiting medical workers from outside of activist circles, toned down the political slogans used by PalKom, and did not openly and publicly support the PLO, armed struggle, and other Palestinian resistance and liberation organisations.[66] This transition, however, only happened gradually and not in the first years after NORWAC's creation. The transition was far from clear-cut and continuities on the material level persisted. Similarly, the modes of practice and organisation did not change significantly. With time, however, in the late 1980s and early 1990s, as NORWAC expanded its recruitment base, the medical teams began including people who were not necessarily politically active or committed to the Palestinian cause as activists. While the core of the activists remained the same, the new recruitment base was larger and less ideological. This allowed NORWAC to continue and expand its important medical work. At the same time, however, several of the new recruits who volunteered their time and labour only stayed for brief periods of time and were less likely to continue working towards creating solidarity with the Palestinians once back in Norway. In contrast, PalKom's medical teams often stayed in Lebanon for long periods of time. This allowed for the creation of strong bonds of friendship and solidarity with the Palestinians. Some of this was undoubtedly lost after 1982 when the kind of politically motivated medical support and solidary practised by PalKom became difficult.

---

[64] Fosse, *Med Livet I Hendene*, 130–131.
[65] Otzen, 'Fra Oslo til Beirut og tilbage', 55.
[66] Ibid., 55–57.

CONCLUSION

Today, NORWAC's website states that the organisation 'adheres to the main principles of humanitarianism and medical ethics, in particular the principles of impartiality'.[67] Such a statement contradicts PalKom's medical support as it was practised before the creation of NORWAC in 1983 and for several years after that. While the new institutional frameworks did not deliberately seek to limit solidarity, with time they effectively and officially separated medical support from the radical political context in which it emerged in the middle of the 1970s. However, as this chapter has demonstrated, although the institutional frameworks changed with the transition from PalKom to NORWAC, the commitment of the people involved did not. Moreover, this chapter challenged the notion that the transformation of solidarity in the 1980s was necessarily a straightforward move to humanitarianism and deradicalisation. The Norwegian case shows that the transformation outlined above was gradual, contested, and pragmatic. The transition from PalKom to NORWAC was one of necessity and occurred only when it became impossible for Norwegian solidarity activists to obtain visas to Lebanon. In other words, the decision to form a humanitarian aid organisation was a strategic acceptance of changing realities and power dynamics in Lebanon, meant to secure the continuation of medical assistance to a people in struggle and under attack. Through this micro-history of Norwegian medical support in Lebanon, we can begin to understand some of the gradual changes and new forms of mobilisation and organisation, as well as the novel political sensibilities and subjectivities that were created as both the New Left in the West and the project of Third Worldism changed course. Last but not least, it shows that changing notions of solidarity, including material forms of solidarity such as medical support, were determined as much by pragmatic questions of mobility and borders as by philosophical and ideological debates.

---

[67] NORWAC, 'About Us', https://www.norwac.no/about-us/, accessed 3 November 2021.

3

SEARCHING FOR FRIENDS ACROSS THE GLOBAL SOUTH

Classified Documents, Iran, and the Export of the Revolution in 1983

Simon Wolfgang Fuchs

In this chapter, I make use of a batch of classified Iranian documents to revisit the question of how the Islamic Republic reached out to the Global South in the early 1980s. I argue that Iran's export of the revolution in the form of several delegations traversing countries from Gabon to Malaysia was not only ad-hoc and improvised but also affected by the serious tension of navigating pan-Islamic solidarity and Third Worldism. At a time when left- ist Iranian groups involved with the revolution of 1978–1979 had become marginalised and eliminated, the 'travelling revolutionaries' in Iran's delega- tions still tried to play the card of international anti-imperialist solidarity.[1] In 1983, however, they had come to feel much more at home in a specific Islamic idiom. In making these arguments, the chapter intervenes in two debates. First, it ties in with major themes of this volume, adding weight to the observation that the period of the early 1980s was a crucial turning point for Third Worldism as a result of conservative counter-revolutions and co-optation. By reading untapped archives, my contribution provides

---

[1] On the fate of the communist Tudeh Party after the revolution, see Asghar Schirazi, *Modernität und gestörte Wahrnehmung. Eine Fallstudie über die Tudeh-Partei des Iran und ihr Verhältnis zur Demokratie* (Hamburg: Deutsches Orient Institut, 2003), 119–133.

insights into how far-flung global connections were negotiated in several local settings.

Second, the arguments presented here challenge conventional narratives of how quickly the initial Islamist, and even Third Worldist, fascination with the Iranian Revolution supposedly soured. The year 1983 was arguably the last heyday of behaving in a truly disruptive manner on the world stage in Iran before, in 1984, Iran increasingly resorted to a 'conciliatory open-door foreign policy'.[2] This did not mean, however, that factional conflict over the nature of Iran's relations with the outside world was over. The 'traditional right', who emphasised the primacy of the 'religiosity of the Islamic Republic' and an 'extensive role for the clergy' in running the country, while down-playing the republican dimensions of the regime, never wholeheartedly endorsed confrontation or the 'export of the revolution'.[3] The 'Islamic Left', influential until the death of Khomeini in 1989, by contrast, perceived 'the populist and revolutionary dimensions of the state to be equally important if not more vital than its religiosity'.[4] This meant upholding 'the highly celebrated slogan of the Iranian revolution: "death to America"'.[5]

The rivalry between these two camps had clear implications for Iran's foreign policy. As the documents treated in this chapter will show, members of the Iranian delegations were highly self-critical and aware of their attempted tightrope in negotiating various forms of solidarity. Their reflections from 1983 display the many 'aspirational geographies and universalisms' the Iranian Revolution of 1978–1979 was bound up with.[6] The uprising and revolution clearly emboldened and inspired Sunni Islamists from North Africa to South Asia.[7] The influential Pakistani thinker Abu 'l-A'la Mawdudi (d.1979), for example, called on Muslims everywhere to support

---

[2] R.K. Ramazani, *Independence Without Freedom. Iran's Foreign Policy* (Charlottesville, VA: University of Virginia Press, 2013), 120; Eric Lob, 'The Islamic Republic of Iran's Foreign Policy and Construction Jihad's Developmental Activities in Sub-Saharan Africa', *IJMES* vol. 48, no. 2 (2016): 314.

[3] Mehdi Moslem, *Factional Politics in Post-Khomeini Iran* (Syracuse, NY: Syracuse University Press, 2002), 99–101, 110.

[4] Ibid., 111–112. See also Eskandar Sadeghi-Boroujerdi, *Revolution and Its Discontents: Political Thought and Reform in Iran* (Cambridge: Cambridge University Press, 2019), 136–186.

[5] Moslem, *Factional Politics*, 124.

[6] Arang Keshavarzian, 'Globalizing the Iranian Revolution: A Multiscalar History', in *Global 1979. Geographies and Histories of the Iranian Revolution*, ed. Arang Keshavarzian and Ali Mirsepassi (Cambridge: Cambridge University Press, 2021), 53.

[7] 'Al-Ma'rifa yurashshih al-Khumayni li-nayl ja'iza al-Malik Faysal al-'alamiyya', *al-Ma'rifa* vol. 5, no. 9 (1979): 9.

the revolution shortly before his death in September 1979. His party, the Jamaat-e-Islami, emphasised its affinities with revolutionary Iran due to a common dedication to establishing God's sovereignty on earth.[8] Sunni and Shi'i Lebanese clerics alike embraced the 'Khomeinist script', which 'exalted the virtues of clerical political engagement, assertiveness, agitation, and leadership, which Khomeini exemplified'.[9] Crucially, also beyond the boundaries of a purely Islamic framing, Tehran emerged for a brief moment in 1979, and before the definitive Islamist turn of 1981, as a utopian global capital for some (European) leftist thinkers and liberation movements from the Global South.[10] By hosting international congresses and defying the existing Cold War order, as the chapter by Ataie in this volume discusses in detail, Iran aimed at claiming the mantle of Third Worldism and putting into practice its avowed goal of 'exporting the revolution'.[11]

Yet existing scholarship displays only a vague understanding of how Tehran went about forging these linkages across the Global South. This chapter foregrounds one crucial element of the Iranian outreach, the Unit for Islamic Liberation Movements (UILM) (*Vahed-e nahzat-ha-ye azadibakhsh-e eslami*), discussed in more depth in the next section. The Unit is often mentioned in the literature but its precise activities, organisational setup, and split into two entities throughout the 1980s remain unexplored.[12] By using a hitherto untapped archive of formerly classified, internal documents held at the National Library of Iran, this chapter shines a light on how a

---

[8] Simon W. Fuchs, 'A Direct Flight to Revolution: Maududi, Divine Sovereignty, and the 1979-Moment in Iran', *Journal of the Royal Asiatic Society* vol. 32, no. 2 (2022): 333–354.

[9] Mohammad Ataie, 'Exporting the Iranian Revolution: Ecumenical Clerics in Lebanon', *International Journal of Middle East Studies* vol. 53, no. 4 (2021): 3. See also Raphaël Lefèvre, *Jihad in the City. Militant Islam and Contentious Politics in Tripoli* (Cambridge: Cambridge University Press, 2021).

[10] Claudia Castiglioni, '"Anti-Imperialism of Fools"? The European Intellectual Left and the Iranian Revolution', in *The Age of Aryamehr: Late Pahlavi Iran and Its Global Entanglements*, ed. Roham Alvandi (Chicago, IL: The Gingko Library, 2018); Simon W. Fuchs, 'Tehran's Open Horizon. Lebanese Views on the Iranian Revolution of 1979', Rosa Luxemburg Stiftung, https://www.rosalux.de/en/publication/id/41232/tehrans-open-horizon (accessed 20 June 2023).

[11] Ruhollah Khomeini, *Sodour-e enqelab az didgah-e emam Khomeini* (Tehran: Pazhoheshkadeh-e emam Khomeini va enqelab-e eslami, 2008), 33.

[12] Examples of the lack of details in discussing the Unit include Fred Halliday, 'Iranian Foreign Policy Since 1979: Internationalism and Nationalism in the Islamic Revolution', in *Shi'ism and Social Protest*, ed. Juan R. Cole (New Haven, CT: Yale University Press, 1986), 103; Afshon Ostovar, *Vanguard of the Imam: Religion, Politics, and Iran's Revolutionary Guards* (New York, NY: Oxford University Press, 2016), 112; and Lob, 'The Islamic Republic of Iran's Foreign Policy', 316.

new reincarnation of the Unit sent out delegations across the Global South in February 1983 to test Iran's standing. Individual and often contradictory reports filed by its members give us a sense of how the lived experience of reaching out to the Third World played out on the ground. As my analysis will show, this is a story of difficulties in reconciling Third Worldism and ecumenism with Shi'i commitments, logistical missteps, and the continuing appeal of the revolution in the Global South.

THE MYSTERIOUS UNIT (OR UNITS?) FOR (ISLAMIC) LIBERATION MOVEMENTS

The Unit for Liberation Movements, initially without the 'Islamic' qualifier, emerged out of the revolutionary chaos as part of the Islamic Revolutionary Guard Corps (IRGC). While scholars have highlighted the Unit's involvement in Lebanon,[13] the general consensus is that the 'branch faded with time'.[14] The relative dearth of clarity has to do with the fact that several of its leading figures were later sidelined or faced an even worse fate under the Islamic Republic.

The Unit's most senior supporter was Ayatollah Hossein-Ali Montazeri (d.2009), originally a close confidant of Khomeini and his designated successor, who was later put under house arrest. Since the 1970s, Montazeri had developed a notable interest in pursuing the cause of 'anti-imperialism' and considered the Iranian Revolution as a gift to oppressed people everywhere, a goal he was willing to facilitate with money and resources.[15] His eldest son, Mohammad Montazeri, had established close personal contacts during the 1970s with Islamist movements in Pakistan, Afghanistan, Lebanon, and the Arab Gulf states to propagate his vision of a 'global Islam' (*eslam-e jahani*) and of Islam as liberation. He strove to bring about an 'Oppressed International' and considered the revolution as an incubator for a global wave of uprisings. Mohammad Montazeri made some headway in organising conferences and establishing various journals but was killed in the June 1981

[13] Mohammad Ataie, 'Revolutionary Iran's 1979 Endeavor in Lebanon', *Middle East Policy* vol. 20, no. 2 (2013): 143–144.

[14] Maryam Alemzadeh, 'Revolutionaries for Life: The IRGC and the Global Guerrilla Movement', in *Global 1979*, eds Keshavarzian and Mirsepassi, 208.

[15] Sussan Siavoshi, *Montazeri. The Life and Thought of Iran's Revolutionary Ayatollah* (Cambridge: Cambridge University Press, 2017), 124.

bombing of the Islamic Republican Party's meeting in Tehran.[16] Finally, the somewhat enigmatic but important figure Mehdi Hashemi (d.1987) was executed by Iranian authorities for 'treason' in 1987. Hashemi was a close friend of Mohammad Montazeri and displayed a profound interest in how colonised people could assert themselves against the superpowers.[17] While the Iranian parliament officially recognised the Unit for Liberation Movements in November 1982, Hashemi, with the public approval of Ayatollah Montazeri, 'removed his organisation from the Pasdaran [IRGC] and transformed it into an independent institution with its base in Qom'.[18] Hashemi's independent stance led to an explicit rebuke from Khomeini, who in 1986 ordered that 'all the activities in the name of support to so-called liberation organisations must stop and all those involved in this matter condemned'.[19]

The disappearance of the three men from the centres of power in Iran, partly as a result of bitter factional struggles, means that reliable documents on the UILM are hard to come by and research on this issue by Iranian colleagues remains restricted to this day.[20] What adds to the prevailing confusion is that by 1983, as substantiated by the classified documents, a new Unit of Islamic Liberation Movement had been established, this time under the control of the Ministry of Islamic Guidance (*Vezarat-e ershad*).[21] The existence of this second Unit calls into question existing accounts, such as Shireen Hunter's claim about a single 'Bureau of World Liberation Movements' existing next to the Ministry of Islamic Guidance under the supervision of Mehdi Hashemi, which was supposedly closed in 1985.[22] The second Unit was, however, not explicitly set up as a rival organisation

---

[16] Timothy Nunan, '"Doomed to Good Relations": The USSR, the Islamic Republic of Iran, and Anti-Imperialism in the 1980s', *Journal of Cold War Studies* vol. 24, no. 1 (2022): 47–50. See also Vahed-e nahzat-ha-ye azadibakhsh-e eslami-ye sepah-e pasdaran, ed., *Nahzat-ha-ye azadibakhsh-i jahani dar gozargah-e enqelabi-ye eslam*, 1982.

[17] Ulrich von Schwerin, 'Mehdi Hashemi and the Iran-Contra-Affair', *British Journal of Middle Eastern Studies* vol. 42, no. 4 (2015): 520–537.

[18] Ibid., 527.

[19] Quoted in Sadeghi-Boroujerdi, *Revolution and Its Discontents*, 153.

[20] For a detailed account of the falling out between Ayatollahs Montazeri and Khomeini, in which the Mehdi Hashemi affair played an important role, see ibid., 150–160.

[21] I am grateful to Mohammad Ataie for this observation. Ulrich von Schwerin holds that the original organisation was already called the 'Office for Islamic Liberation Movements'. See von Schwerin, 'Mehdi Hashemi', 525. The 1982 publication of the Pasdaran mentioned in fn. 15 seems to support von Schwerin's view.

[22] Shireen Hunter, 'Iran and the Spread of Revolutionary Islam', *Third World Quarterly* vol. 10, no. 2 (1988): 743.

to Mehdi Hashemi's activities. This can be demonstrated by the fact that Hossein-Ali Montazeri met all delegations before their travels.[23] His advice and framing of the mission was frequently picked up in the reports and he is mentioned as the single most important source of guidance and inspiration.[24] Montazeri opined that the delegations should socialise with local Muslims during Friday prayers and focus on respected and 'loved' leaders, including *ulama* and students of the religious sciences.[25]

Having already touched upon the archive I use for this article, the next section will spell out in more detail the character of the documents in question.

CLASSIFIED DOCUMENTS: A WINDOW INTO IRANIAN OUTREACH EFFORTS

During my fieldwork in Iran in September 2019, I came across several hundred pages of Persian documents labelled 'top secret' (*kheili mahramaneh*) in the National Library of Iran.[26] These open an unprecedented window into Iran's early efforts of reaching out to both Muslims and non-Muslim groups and individuals in the Global South. The files document how the UILM sent out several delegations in conjunction with the fourth anniversary of the revolution in February 1983. These groups travelled to Lebanon, Syria, Pakistan, Bangladesh, Malaysia, Nigeria, Sierra Leone, Gabon, Ivory Coast, Kenya, Tanzania, and Madagascar. What makes the documents particularly intriguing is the composition of these delegations. They usually consisted of a senior Shiʿi cleric, a representative of the Ministry of Islamic Guidance, an official from the Ministry of Foreign Affairs, a Sunni cleric, and a translator, as well as a journalist and photographer. These men usually filed individual and very frank accounts of their travels, of the problems they faced, and whom they met. The stated goal in collecting such individual reports was to equip future propagandists with as many detailed insights into the socio-economic and political conditions of the destination countries as possible,

---

[23] Vahed-e nahzat-ha-ye azadibakhsh-e eslami, ed., *Safarnameh-ye daheh-ye fajr, sal-e 1361. Shomareh-ye 5. Shamel-e keshvar: Pakestan*, 1983, 9.

[24] See, for instance, Seyyed Reza Taqva, 'Gozaresh-e safar-e Hojjat al-Islam Seyyed Reza Taqva', in *Safarnameh-ye Pakestan*, 15–16.

[25] Ibid.

[26] Unfortunately, I have no further information as to how the documents found their way into the library, and when or by whom they were deposited.

to make sure that they could turn this information into a 'pounding weapon' (*salahi kubandeh*) against rival 'systems built on polytheism and unbelief'.[27]

An illustrative example is from the delegation to sub-Saharan Africa. It was headed by Ayatollah Ebrahim Amini (d.2020),[28] whose website still displays images of the travels without, however, spelling out the actual purpose of these visits.[29] Amini was accompanied by the then junior cleric Hojjat al-Islam Seyyed Mohammad Hosseini Shahroudi (b.1958),[30] a Sunni representative called Mawlana Abd al-Razzaq, an employee of the Ministry of Foreign Affairs, a translator, and a journalist who also doubled as a photographer. They began their journey on 4 February 1983 and spent nineteen days in Nigeria, five days in Ivory Coast, five days in Sierra Leone, and six days in Gabon.[31]

Another example is the group travelling to Lebanon and Syria under the supervision of Hojjat al-Islam Fazel Harandi (d.2006).[32] Along with him came Seyyed Mohammad Kiyavash, a deputy for Ahvaz,[33] Mahmud Hashemi Bahramani as political adviser from the Ministry of Foreign Affairs, Mowlana Jalal al-Din Talebi, a Sunni Turkmen cleric, Hasan Khamiyar from the Ministry of Islamic Guidance as translator, as well as photographer Masud Bahmanpur.[34] Bahmanpur was a member of the Organisation for Islamic Propagation (*Sazman-e tablighat-e eslami*), 'the country's most prominent organisation for the promotion of the regime'.[35]

In order to establish and deepen ties, sustain themselves, and wield a budget for discretionary distribution, the delegations received between

---

[27] Vāhed-e hay'at-ha-ye a'zami-ye setad-e khareji-ye daheh-ye fajr, 'Wal-fajr wa-layal 'ashr', in *Safarnameh-ye Pakestan*, 7.

[28] Ebrahim Amini, 'Zendegi-ye siyasi', http://www.ibrahimamini.com/fa/node/10 (accessed 12 October 2022).

[29] Compare, for instance, 'Nayjeriyeh', http://www.ibrahimamini.com/fa/node/1025 (accessed 12 October 2022).

[30] 'Zendeginameh-ye nemayandeh-ye vali-ye faqih dar ostan-e Kordestan', *Mehr News*, https://tinyurl.com/2p8tjfcd (accessed 12 October 2022).

[31] Vahed-e nahzat-ha-ye azadibakhsh-e eslami, ed., *Safarnameh-ye daheh-ye fajr, sal-e 1361. Shomareh-ye 2. Shamel-e keshvar-ha: Nayjeriyeh, Sira Le'un, Gabon*, 1983, 4.

[32] 'Murur bar zendeginameh-ye Ayatollah Fazel Harandi be bahaneh-ye nohomin salgerd-e ertehal', *Esfahan Sharq*, https://tinyurl.com/yckn6sf8 (accessed 12 October 2022).

[33] 'Seyyed Mohammad Kiyavash', Markaz-e pazhuhesh-ha-ye majles-e showra-ye eslami, https://rc.majlis.ir/fa/parliament_member/show/762752 (accessed 15 August 2022).

[34] Vahed-e nahzat-ha-ye azadibakhsh-e eslami, ed., *Safarnameh-ye daheh-ye fajr, sal-e 1361. Shomareh-ye 4. Shamel-e Keshvar-ha: Lobnan, Suriyeh*, 1983, 4.

[35] Narges Bajoghli, *Iran Reframed: Anxieties of Power in the Islamic Republic* (Palo Alto, CA: Stanford University Press, 2019), 61.

15,000 and 25,000 USD in cash. They were supposed to proselytise among revivalist movements while paying particular attention to the 'downtrodden', i.e. the *mostaz'afin* and the *mahrumin*.[36] The thinking that lay behind the geographical spread of such outreach activities was that revolutionary leadership, if restricted to a particular geographic location only, could easily be eliminated. This danger could be avoided if liberation movements were all brought together under the umbrella of Iranian guidance on a global level (*dar sath-e jahani*).[37] Pursuing such international work was risky and not necessarily in line with the official foreign policy of the Islamic Republic. The documents betray the conviction that Iran could not rely on official channels alone to get her message across. Since such diplomatic routes were constrained in their efforts of making the revolution known, parallel scholarly and religious bodies needed to be activated.[38] This thinking also reflected the fluid character of the UILM. Even though it was perhaps no longer under the control of Mehdi Hashemi, it was still an organisation that could not be easily placed within Iran's contentious factional politics.

The documents and the arguments I present in this chapter should be read against the backdrop of the existing literature, which displays an interesting tension regarding the evaluation of Iran's revolutionary global reach. Most of this literature points out the failure of these endeavours and highlights instead how pragmatic considerations of overcoming international isolation and re-establishing economic ties with Western Europe and neighbours such as Turkey and Pakistan became Iran's main concern during the early 1980s.[39] The reason for Iran's new flexibility was that the country quickly became bogged down by the disastrous war with Iraq, which also made most Arab states in the region side with Saddam Hussein, the only significant exceptions being Syria, Libya, and Lebanon.[40] Iran unsuccessfully pushed back against Iraq in the context of the Non-Aligned Movement but had no other choice than to procure weapons from 'Godless leftists' such

---

[36] Taqva, 'Gozaresh-e safar', 18. For a similar statement, see Vahed-e nahzat-ha-ye azadibakhsh-e eslami-ye sepah-e pasdaran, 'Pishgoftar', in *Nahzat-ha-ye azadibakhsh-e jahani*, 14–15.

[37] Ibid., 16.

[38] Taqva, 'Gozaresh-e safar', 24.

[39] Ramazani, *Independence without Freedom*, 102–106; Alex Vatanka, *The Battle of the Ayatollahs in Iran. The United States, Foreign Policy, and Political Rivalry since 1979* (London: I.B. Tauris, 2021), 55–56.

[40] David Menashri, 'Khomeini's Vision: Nationalism or World Order?', in *The Iranian Revolution and the Muslim World*, ed. David Menashri (Boulder, CO: Westview Press, 1990), 47.

as China, North Korea, and the Soviet Union.[41] Additionally, conventional wisdom holds that Sunni thinkers and groups distanced themselves from Iran at an early stage. They were not fooled by the seemingly ecumenical façade the Iranians tried to erect but called the revolution out for being a Shi'i attempt at world domination.[42] The material that I draw on provides us with an opportunity to ask a different set of questions that transcend primarily geopolitical or economic concerns. The Iranian effort towards finding like-minded friends across Asia and beyond was indeed hampered by the realities of war and infighting. It was chaotic in its execution. Yet in 1983 various audiences across the Global South were still able to see their aspirations and hopes reflected in the Islamic Republic.

THE AD-HOC CHARACTER OF ORGANISING (AND RELATED SELF-CRITICISM)

When we study the reports closely, the ad-hoc character of many of the arrangements is striking. Here is the example of Nigeria:

After arriving in Lagos, the Iranian delegation resorted to several random mosque visits in the vicinity of the embassy for noon and evening prayers. They achieved nothing more than exchanging pleasantries with the Friday prayer leader, who did not even invite them inside his house.[43] It was the Iranian ambassador who suggested that the south of the country was probably not the most suitable region for outreach activities, due to its Christian majority. They should instead fly to northern Nigeria. The diplomat casually brushed aside concerns about lacking authorisation from the Nigerian authorities: 'If you ask for permission, you won't get it. Simply go and do your work.' When Amini, the delegation leader, asked whether it was not advisable to at least announce that a delegation had come from Iran on the revolution's anniversary, the ambassador simply replied: 'That's not necessary' (*lazem nist*).[44] Later on, this carelessness, criticised in the report by

---

[41] A.W. Singham and Shirley Hune, *Non-Alignment in an Age of Alignments* (London: Zed Books, 1986), 237–240; Vatanka, *The Battle of the Ayatollahs*, 63.

[42] Vali Nasr, *The Shia Revival: How Conflicts within Islam Will Shape the Future* (New York, NY: Norton, 2006), 173–174.

[43] Ebrahim Amini, 'Gozaresh-e safar-e hojjat-ol-eslam va-l-moslemin aqa-ye Ebrahim Amini sarparast-e hay'at-e a'zami be keshvar-e Nayjeriyeh', in *Safarnameh-ye Nayjeriyeh, Sira Le'un, Gabon*, 10.

[44] Ibid., 11.

Amini, proved highly detrimental to the further course of the visit. The delegation was briefly detained in the city of Sokoto, their luggage was searched, and they were banned from delivering any further lectures.[45] Christian Nigerian security officials enquired about each of their contacts and who had helped the Iranians in facilitating their stay.[46] The delegation was told that Iran's influence as an Islamic country was not in Nigeria's interest. Their (Muslim) superior later took a slightly different line. He promised that Iran was surely welcome to build mosques and provide support with the propagation of religion – he only needed them to tell him who in Nigeria had helped organise their outreach programme.[47] At the end, a secret police officer returned with them to Lagos, where the Iranian ambassador had to get involved to secure their release from detention after two days.[48] Amini was particularly outraged. He insisted during the interrogation that his expectation had been to come to a friendly country (*keshvar-e dust*) with the goal of strengthening peaceful relations and spreading Islam. Such an attitude was reflected in all the lectures they gave, he claimed. After all, he was a religious scholar yet had been treated like a criminal. They did, however, have some success on their mission, particularly among Nigerian students, who had welcomed the Iranians in Kano, organised lectures at several universities, and introduced them to Iran-friendly university teachers in several cities, some aspects of which I will discuss in more detail shortly.

The delegation to Pakistan similarly complained about a lack of adequate preparation. The Iranians had not been given any suitable briefing before their departure. The consulate in Karachi turned out to be 'useless' and could not even provide them with a basic introduction to the country's society.[49] Their 'translator' spoke no Urdu and only a little English. He had mainly been taken on board because he was supposed to provide intelligence for the Revolutionary Guards.[50] The situation was not significantly brighter in Malaysia. Some members of the delegation were not allowed to travel, and the remaining members complained that no one had explained to them the cultural and political background of Malaysia. It soon became apparent that their camera and video equipment was not up to the task: their designated

---

[45] Ibid., 14.
[46] Ibid., 21.
[47] Ibid.
[48] Ibid., 22.
[49] 'Majmuʿeh-ye gozareshat-e aʿza-ye hayʾat-e Pakestan', in *Safarnameh-ye Pakestan*, 29.
[50] Ibid., 33.

photographer was forced to spend his first day in Kuala Lumpur looking for a flashgun, appropriate filters, and another camera. Since this was his first trip outside of Iran, he needed help from other members of the delegation to navigate this foreign environment.[51] Even more troubling was the fact that the propaganda material brought from Iran was often defective, too. The delegation to Bangladesh lacked effective visual materials such as films or slides, its photographer Amir-'Ali Javariyan argued. An unforgivable mistake, since in the 'third world' people supposedly did not always follow the latest news very closely; hence inspiring films could have made a real difference. The same applied to Iranians back home: without high quality equipment, there was no way to document the outreach work and to introduce compatriots to the situation of Muslims abroad. No lessons had been learned from the revolution itself, according to Javariyan: 'Images played an outsize role in the revolution in terms of covering the regime of the Shah with shame and images acted as a witness to all that had happened.'[52]

Misgivings such as these abound in the files. The Pakistani delegation did not have appropriate Urdu material to distribute but rather was left with brochures in Arabic, English, and French.[53] There were also reservations about 'outdated' books. It was simply not enough to reprint once again the writings by Shahid Beheshti or Ali Shari'ati. Their experiences did not necessarily resonate outside of Iran since they 'have no connection to the situation today'.[54] During a stopover in Italy, Iranian students whom they met in Rome emphasised that Italians were underwhelmed by Iranian public relations efforts. The distribution of a magazine with Khomeini on the cover might be appropriate in Iran but not in Europe, the students argued. Rather, Islam should be spread in more comprehensive terms. This meant covering artistic and cultural aspects and organising conferences at universities or hosting seminars for intellectuals and students. If there was a budget, Iran should deliver content to local radio and TV stations. For Amini at least, such suggestions were novel territory: he indicated in his report that the Ministry of Islamic Guidance should carefully take note of

---

[51] Jalal al-Din Farsi, 'Gozaresh-e safar-e hay'at-e tablighi-ye daheh-ye fajr be keshvar-ha-ye Maleyzi', in *Safarnameh-ye daheh-ye fajr, sal-e 1361. Shomareh-ye 6. Shamel-e keshvar: Maleyzi*, ed. Vahed-e nahzat-ha-ye azadibakhsh-e eslami, 1983, 5–6.

[52] Amir-'Ali Javariyan, 'Gozaresh-e khabarnegar va 'akkas va filmbardar-e daheh-ye fajr sal-e 1361', in *Safarnameh-ye daheh-ye fajr, sal-e 1361. Shomarah-ye 1. Shamel-e keshvar: Bangladesh*, ed. Vahed-e nahzat-ha-ye azadibakhsh-e eslami, 1983, 47.

[53] 'Majmu'eh-ye gozareshat-e a'za-ye hay'at-e Pakestan', 31–32.

[54] Amini, 'Gozaresh-e safar', 10.

this.[55] The delegation travelling to Lebanon blamed their inability to secure interviews with the country's quality newspapers on the 'weakness of the foreign propaganda of the Islamic Republic' (*za'f-e tablighat-e khareji-ye jomhuri-ye eslami*). This problem manifested itself also in places such as Kuwait and France. Consequently, foreign journalists 'everywhere' were not ready to accept Iranian invitations for conducting an interview.[56] A Nigerian student in Kano whom they met at the city's airport put it bluntly: this convert to Islam confessed that he was not really into the available Iranian literature since it only contained blood and war – two topics which he greatly despised. Amini once again noted that the Ministry of Islamic Guidance should 'take note of this attitude'.[57]

Several delegations insisted that the lack of carefully planned outreach was no light matter. Without any knowledge of the local needs of a society or its 'special psychology' (*ravanshenasi-ye khass*), superficial propagation (*tabligh*) could cause a lot of harm. Explaining all aspects of the revolution in condensed form without knowing a particular target country 'will not only have no benefit but will also have negative consequences'.[58] Future delegations should be properly trained by, for example, choosing fitting reading material about the countries to be visited at least four to six months prior to departure.[59] In fact, the entire concept of parachuting in should be rethought:

> If we go to a particular *madrasa* for one occasion, what can really come out of it? We should live together and talk for about a week, then religious students could become familiar with us, and we could truly understand the problems they face.[60]

More intensive contact would enable the Iranians to comprehend unfamiliar living conditions, which would then have a tremendous impact on the effectiveness of *tabligh*.[61] Revolutionary fervour was not enough for navigating

---

55 Ibid., 9.
56 Hasan Khamiyar, 'Gozaresh-e safar-e hay'at-e a'zami-ye Lobnan', in *Safarnameh-ye Lobnan, Suriyeh*, 48.
57 Amini, 'Gozaresh-e safar', 10.
58 'Abd al-Hossein Mo'azzi, 'Noqat-e mosbat va manfi-ye safar', in *Safarnameh-ye Bangladesh*, 17.
59 Ibid.
60 Ibid., 20.
61 Ibid.

foreign territory. In the future, delegations should closely collaborate with people who had actually travelled abroad and were familiar with the lie of the land, the report recommended.[62] This way, language barriers that had significantly impeded the delegations could also be overcome. The current state was untenable. When an Iranian cleric gave a speech in Persian, it first had to get translated into English and once more into Bengali: 'How can we get in touch with the people there? Reaching them via two intermediary stages is really difficult. When we talk for forty-five minutes, in reality, we have only talked for fifteen minutes, the rest is merely translation!'[63]

CLARIFYING THE MISSION: THE TENSION BETWEEN SPREADING ISLAM AND THIRD WORLD SOLIDARITY

When we consult Iranian Islamist authors from the 1980s, it seems as if they 'could embrace contradictory concepts of world order' and were in a position to easily reconcile the idea of the *umma* – the Islamic world community of believers – with Third Worldism.[64] Upon closer inspection of the reports, however, severe disagreements about the core meaning of exporting the revolution become palpable. Hojjat al-Islam Mo'azzi, who was a member of the delegation to Bangladesh, questioned, for instance, whether it was wise to travel abroad in conjunction with the anniversary of the revolution. The timing, he argued, only heightened tensions and let the mission descend into a shouting match and lots of misunderstandings.[65] He urged his fellow countrymen to revisit the scope of their outreach, a suggestion that touched on the heart of the matter as to whether the revolution had appeal beyond a narrow Shiʿi base. Iranians faced some stark choices. Was the purpose of the delegations to address Sunni–Shiʿi questions? Or human questions (*masaʾel-e ensani*)?

> Or shall we talk about the peculiarity (*khosusiyyat*) of Islam in comparison with Marxism and the hypocrite movement of Saudi Arabia? As a response they say that the inhabitants of our border regions are

---

[62] Ibid., 21.
[63] Ibid.
[64] Timothy Nunan, '"Neither East nor West," Neither Liberal nor Illiberal? Iranian Islamist Internationalism in the 1980s', *Journal of World History* vol. 31, no. 1 (2020): 57.
[65] Moʿazzi, 'Noqat-e mosbat va manfi-ye safar', 19.

all majority Sunni and that we wage a war in Azerbaijan, Kurdistan, Sistan and Baluchistan. They accuse us of being a Sunni-killing movement (*harakat-e sonni-kosh*). We also get asked why Sunnis have no mosque.[66]

The reports give us a sense of the struggle to justify the actions of the Iranian state while still displaying commitment to fostering ecumenical ties, and, to a lesser extent, to reaching out beyond the *umma* in order to propagate a non-religious form of Third Worldism. There were a few situations when such a reconciliation appeared to be still within reach. Fazel Harandi, who led the delegation to Lebanon, put it in the following way during a meeting with the Association of Muslim *Ulama* in Lebanon (*Tajammu' al-'ulama' al-muslimin fi Lubnan*), an organisation that was explicitly focused on Sunni–Shi'i unity:[67]

> We have tried to send delegations to countries of the Third World, among these are also Islamic countries. We're trying step by step to strengthen our ties with the oppressed (*mustaz'afin*). In the past, our delegations travelled to Europe or to communist countries. This is no longer the case.[68]

When the Iranians met Syrian parliamentarians, there was no mention in the reports of whether exporting the Islamic part of the revolution played any role in their discussions. Rather, the debates revolved around strategies for increasing agricultural production and the benefits of rural co-operatives. Was it advisable that the village community or rather the state owned the fields? What could be learned from recent organisational approaches in Czechoslovakia, where the state was preparing the way for a gradual transition to private ownership? Harandi elaborated on the problem 'that if we are handing over lands to private property owners, they only work for their own advantage'.[69] In Sierra Leone, the Iranians also discussed the issue when visiting the Ministry of Public Welfare. Ebrahim Amini offered the observation that the appearance of the ministry itself provided, in a nutshell, a good sense of how imperialism ruins a country: the reception room was

---

[66] Ibid.
[67] For more details, see Ataie, 'Exporting the Iranian Revolution'.
[68] Khamiyar, 'Gozaresh-e safar', 47.
[69] Ibid., 66.

no bigger than four square metres and equipped with only one worn-out chair and a telephone but neither air conditioning nor a fan.[70] The delegation explained to the minister that Iran pursued the policy of friendship with the Third World (*jahan-e sevvom*) and that the latter could be liberated from the 'clutch of imperialism' (*changal-e este'mar*).[71] The minister reacted warmly and, in turn, outlined his own very personal encounter with Iran, identifying himself as an early supporter of the revolution. He had spent time in Germany and had even participated in student demonstrations against the Shah. During one of these episodes, he had been injured and was forced to spend a week in bed: 'Afterwards, I have supported you everywhere!' The minister tied this confession to the current oil crisis which affected Sierra Leone. He expressed his gratitude to Iran for selling oil on advantageous terms: 'A true friend is someone who helps a friend who is in dire straits' (*dar mowqe'-e gereftari*).[72]

This last remark touched upon a delicate point which speaks to Iran's transition from a revolutionary movement to a (post-revolutionary) state: can 'true' (Third World) solidarity be established and bought through financial contributions? The delegations often felt that ulterior monetary motivations lurked in the background and that they were being manipulated. In the reports, we find suggestions that the Iranians should fundamentally rethink the way money is distributed. So far, according to Mo'azzi, when speaking of the delegation to Bangladesh, people would assume 'that we are only spending money and leave. We give the impression that problems can be solved with dollars.' The current approach, he wrote, supposedly raised the expectation that it made sense to simply wait for yet another delegation, be it from Saudi Arabia or elsewhere, that would hand over even more cash. Instead of throwing foreign currency at the issue, Iran should face the really hard question: 'how can we square the guardianship of the jurisprudent (*velayat-e faqih*) with Sunni beliefs'?[73]

The shadow of Saudi Arabia and its activities loomed over the delegations. The Iranians were constantly on the lookout for potential trouble and

---

[70] Ebrahim Amini, 'Gozaresh-e safar-e hay'at-e a'zami-ye jumhuri-ye eslami be-monasebat-e daheh-ye fajr be keshvar-e Sira Le'un', in *Safarnameh-ye Nayjeriyeh, Sira Le'un, Gabon*, 37.

[71] Ibid.

[72] Ibid.

[73] Mo'azzi, 'Noqat-e mosbat va manfi-ye safar', 20.

duly noted all signs of Saudi influence.[74] The Supreme Islamic Council in Sierra Leone claimed that the Saudis had already contributed 10,000 USD for their work to foster Muslim unity and to strengthen the Islamic response to Christian missionary efforts. Consequently, the Iranian delegates became immediately reluctant when asked for an additional contribution. They could only discern a picture of King Fahd ibn ʿAbd al-ʿAziz Al Saʿud (d.2005) in the office but no sign of Khomeini. Even though the Supreme Islamic Council claimed that they had in the past collaborated with the Revolutionary Guards to organise a Hajj seminar, the visitors noted that Iranian organisations should not have any further dealings with the Council.[75] In the context of Malaysia, we find conflicting advice. Jalal al-Din Farsi, the leader of the delegation, argued that both the Foreign Ministry and the Ministry of Islamic Guidance should set up a special budget catering to the material needs of Malaysian Muslims in order to combat the effectiveness of Saudi Arabia and Iraq spreading their influence there.[76] In his report, the photographer Parviz Safari however begged to differ: if Iran really wanted to extend its call to all the corners of the earth and would continue to spend so much money on welfare projects, this propagation needed to have a real effect and should make people familiar with the revolution.[77]

The delegates betrayed their own biases and reservations about engaging with the real existing Third World. The accounts are replete with shock and disbelief when being confronted with the extensive poverty and low standards of education prevalent among Iran's new allies. These included the scandalous living conditions in the displacement camps for Pakistanis in Bangladesh, as the delegation leader Mohammad Yazdi detailed. True, the Iranians were greeted with shouts of *takbir* and lots of joy. Participants read out a special poem and expressed their demand: 'May Khomeini come to our aid!' When the delegates waded deeper into the camps, however, they were surrounded by a foul-smelling morass. The dwellings were nothing

---

[74] ʿAbbas Shirazi, 'Gozaresh-e mashruh-e hayʾat-e aʿzami-ye be keshvar-ha-ye Kenya, Tanzaniya, Madagaskar', in Vahed-e nahzat-ha-ye azadibakhsh-e eslami, ed., *Safarnameh-ye daheh-ye fajr, sal-e 1361. Shomareh-ye 3. Shamel-e keshvar-ha: Kenya, Tanzaniya, Madagaskar,* 1983, 6.

[75] Amini, 'Gozaresh-e safar be keshvar-e Sira Leʾun', 42.

[76] Farsi, 'Gozaresh-e safar', 14. On Farsi, who 'had turned by the 1970s into a highly committed Islamist "ideological entrepreneur" seeking to spread a militant breed of Shia Islam' and fled the Shah's Iran for Lebanon, see Lefèvre, *Jihad in the City,* 176.

[77] Parviz Safari, 'Gozaresh az safar-e hayʾat daheh-ye fajr beh keshvar-e Maleyzi', in *Safarnameh-ye Maleyzi,* 19.

more than dark caves, 'in which not even animals could have lived'. One such cave contained a woman with her children, who were naked with the exception of a loin cloth. The only source of light consisted of an oil-burning wick which exuded suffocating smoke. The woman cooked potatoes on firewood and distributed these among their children: 'a pen does not have the power to describe their life as life', Yazdi noted.[78]

In a survey of the religious schools of Pakistan, the Iranian observers noticed that the low income level of the country meant that most *madrasas*, unlike those in Iran, did not even have the 'most basic necessities'. Students had to sit on damp dirt floors. Instead of writing paper, they resorted to wooden boards for their writing exercises. Even mosques had no carpets but only dried grass.[79] This pertained to Shi'i establishments located in 'filthy' neighbourhoods as well. The Iranians connected this palpable poverty to people's level of knowledge, which was 'very low' (*kheyli pa'in*).[80] Similar observations were made in Kenya.[81] All of this demonstrates not only the middle-class background of the delegation leaders, but their difficulties in transcending their worldview shaped in the religious environment of the *howzeh*.

These observations demonstrate that it was definitely one thing to extol Iran's unwavering international solidarity in writing and in speeches, but quite another to experience the mechanics of such outreach efforts first-hand. Instead of finding eager takers of their revolutionary offerings, the delegation members encountered the messiness of competing interests, financial demands, and doubts about the reliability of alleged friends.

CHALLENGES TO A SUPPOSEDLY UNIVERSAL MESSAGE

Neither the conventional logic of the emerging new Iranian nation-state nor Iran's Shi'i character was ever far from the discussions between delegates and locals, despite the expectation that their conversations were suppos-edly steeped in revolutionary solidarity. As the Malaysian delegation put it, they refrained from meeting officials in the country due to 'the special situation of the Islamic forces in Malaysia and the strong plea (*sala-ye hadid*)

---

[78] Muhammad Yazdi, 'Gozaresh-e safar-e hay'at', *Safarnameh-ye Bangladesh*, 8.
[79] Taqva, 'Gozaresh-e safar', 17.
[80] 'Majmu'eh-ye gozareshat-e a'za-ye hay'at-e Pakestan', 28.
[81] Shirazi, 'Gozaresh-e mashruh-e hay'at-e a'zami', 10–11.

of the [Iranian] ambassador'. They mostly engaged with *ulama*, Islamic organisations, and students. The only 'officially sanctioned' visits were to an orphanage and a rehabilitation centre.[82] 'Abd al-Hossein Mo'azzi complained that in Bangladesh members of the group were primarily perceived as representatives of the new regime. They were forced to constantly justify Iranian policies and felt unfairly treated. Pakistan, he argued, was a military dictatorship but passed as a perfectly Islamic country, while Iran was measured more harshly.[83]

The delegations were keenly aware of how tricky it was to reach out to Sunni audiences at this particular time. I have already touched upon the stated difficulty they had with handling questions about the revolution's supposed anti-Sunni bias. In their reports, the delegates repeatedly detailed their difficulties regarding how they should square the issue of *velayat-e faqih* with Sunni beliefs. The groups took issue in this regard with the limited role of the Sunni scholars that accompanied them. These men had no real responsibility beyond a decorative one ('*alem-e sonni bara-ye dekor ast*) and were there for 'documentary reasons' only.[84] The documents also give a sense that the delegations delivered differing messages in Sunni and Shi'i settings. In Nairobi, the speech in the Sunni mosque was focused on Muslim unity. In front of Shi'i audiences in the city, by contrast, open discussions on revolutionary details were held, such as the fate of Mohammad Kazem Shariatmadari (d.1986) and how he was stripped of his position as a Grand Ayatollah (*cheguneh az marja'iyyat khal' shod*), or the Iranian ban on the broadcasting of some music tapes.[85] Global Shi'i networks clearly facilitated outreach activities, the Bilal Muslim Mission in Kenya being a good example.[86] Yet, the Iranians repeatedly found these local Shi'is and their traditional leadership 'too integrated' into local societies and lacking revolutionary fervour.[87] Lebanon with its Shi'i community constituted a special case.[88] The deep impact of Iran became especially visible in Baalbek, which the reports labelled as 'headquarters of the Imam' (*maqarr-e emam*) and the 'biggest city

---

[82] Farsi, 'Gozaresh-e safar-e hay'at', 5.

[83] Mo'azzi, 'Noqat-e mosbat va manfi-ye safar', 19.

[84] Ibid., 22.

[85] Shirazi, 'Gozaresh-e mashruh-e hay'at-e a'zami', 15–16.

[86] Ibid., 7.

[87] Ibid., 15; Taqva, 'Gozaresh-e safar', 18. For the context of Pakistan compare also Simon Wolfgang Fuchs, *In a Pure Muslim Land. Shi'ism Between Pakistan and the Middle East* (Chapel Hill, NC: University of North Carolina Press, 2019).

[88] Hasan Khamiyar, 'Gozaresh-e safar', 33.

of the Islamic Revolution'. There, Iranian propaganda had clearly taken root. Between twenty thousand and thirty thousand people reportedly attended the celebrations on the occasion of the revolution's fourth anniversary, with Shiʿi *ulama* walking in the first row and armed veiled women being visible, too.[89] Basiji committees had been formed by members of the Islamic Amal with a joint Iranian–Lebanese leadership and several branches active on the village level.[90] In summary, then, the promotion of (Islamic) Iranian Third Worldism in the early 1980s was deeply affected by the transition towards a revolutionary state in a context of other nation-states.

THE UNEXPECTED JOY OF FINDING ALLIES

So far, I have discussed in detail the self-made logistical troubles and the cultural challenges each delegation confronted in 1983. While the revolution had lost some of its early lustre and faced plenty of criticism, this should not distract us from the fact that the delegations also recorded noticeable excitement about the Iranian message in early 1983. Three groups stand out in particular: university students, Palestinians, and a significant number of Sunni *ulama*. The analysis now turns to each of these groups.

Students

The reports claim that Iranians could still rely on widespread appeal among students. In northern Nigeria, they were able to build on the good offices of activists who had been dismissed from the university for publicly supporting the revolution. Hearing about their arrival, the Nigerians visited them at their hotel and put together a programme which also introduced them to Sunni *ulama* and university teachers.[91] Several of the latter had clear Islamist leanings, which they foregrounded by displaying images of Hasan al-Banna and Khomeini in their offices.[92] In Kano, for instance, they were visited by Professor Abd al-Rahman Tayyib, who had been to Iran before and after the revolution. During their hour-long conversation,

---

[89] Seyyed Mohammad Kiyavash, 'Gozaresh-e safar be Lobnan', in *Safarnameh-ye Lobnan, Suriyeh*, 10.

[90] Ibid., 11.

[91] Amini, 'Gozaresh-e safar', 11.

[92] Ibid., 12–13.

Tayyib acknowledged the revolution as Islamic and underlined that his most recent trip had convinced him that Iran had been transformed into a country where the impact of Islam was 'visible everywhere'.[93] This encounter led to a speaking engagement at the University of Kano on Friday evening, which was interrupted several times by eager students shouting *takbir*.[94] The delegation often attracted hundreds of listeners, as in the case of Ahmadu Bello University in Zaria, where students expressed their denunciation of both Saddam Hussein and the US and engaged in a ninety-minute discussion after the end of the lecture.[95]

These Q & A sessions would raise hard-hitting questions, for example at the Polytechnical University of Kaduna where students enquired about Khomeini's position on the four rightly guided caliphs and whether the underlying reason for the war between Iran and Iraq was religious, political, or economic. They wanted to know why the Iranians did not simply end the war and whether the Iranian Revolution was in fact a Shi'i revolution and not an Islamic one, as was claimed.[96] Further, would only Shi'is reach paradise? They pressed the delegation to clarify whether Shi'is in Iran cursed the first Umayyad caliph Mu'awiya, and why the Islamic Republic supported Syria even though the country clamped down on the Muslim Brotherhood. [97] This frankness, as reported by Amini, did not mean enmity. As the delegations saw it, students were still a crucial constituency for the Iranians' message. A case in point was Ibrahim Yaqoub Zakzaky, an almost legendary student activist and former vice president of the Muslim Students' Society of Nigeria. His outspoken support for Iran and an Islamic revolution in Nigeria had landed him in trouble with the law. By the time the delegation arrived, he had already served three years of a four-year term.[98] Zakzaky later travelled to Iran, converted, and became a Shi'i *'alim* and leader of the Islamic Movement in Nigeria.[99]

In the context of Malaysia, university students were supposedly responsible for buying up Iranian publications and diligently copying thousands

[93] Ibid., 12.

[94] Ibid., 13–14.

[95] Ibid., 15–16.

[96] Ibid., 18.

[97] Ibid., 13–14.

[98] Ibid., 16–17.

[99] For more background on Zakzaky and his movement, see Toyin Falola, *Violence in Nigeria: The Crisis of Religious Politics and Secular Ideologies* (Rochester, NY: University of Rochester Press, 2000), 195–200.

of cassettes. They shared them among themselves, sent them to the villages, and listened to Iranian messages in cars.[100] In Bangladesh, students from an organisation called Hezbollah waved flags together with workers from another Islamic association, and they had practised praise poems in Persian.[101] The Iranians soon realised, once more, that many of their most ardent supporters were terribly poor. Several Bangladeshi students were unable to come up with the necessary public transport fare to return to their residences after meeting the delegation,[102] and their level of Islamic awareness was not always to the Iranians' liking. In short, their indigenous supporters were not yet the 'human material' they needed. Amini suggested that their conceptualisation of Iran needed to be drastically improved by setting up a radio station and distributing newspapers and magazines. The current system of infrequent shipments of printed matter by the Iranian embassy was clearly insufficient.[103]

Palestinians

As already discussed, Lebanon formed perhaps the most important foreign theatre for the Revolutionary Guards. These efforts among Lebanese Shi'is since 1979 brought together 'a collection of like-minded militants and low-level clergy in the establishment of a pro-Khomeini Lebanese Shiite resistance – a movement that eventually coalesced into the Hezbollah organisation'.[104] Iranian delegation members highlighted the strong presence of the Revolutionary Guards in the Beqaa Valley in particular.[105] Yet, the delegation also made a dedicated effort to expand the Iranian base by reaching out to Palestinians in Beirut. According to their reporting, they were welcomed in the camps of Sabra and Shatila in Beirut with the slogan 'Long live Khomeini'. The Iranian promise to devote special attention to the question of Palestine and to work for its liberation seemingly had not yet lost its appeal. They were eager to include anecdotes in their travelogues to underline this experience. Seyyed Mohammad Kiyavash, for instance, narrated how they asked an eight-year-old boy in southern Beirut whether

[100] Farsi, 'Gozaresh-e safar', 13.
[101] Yazdi, 'Gozaresh-e safar-e hay'at', 9.
[102] Baharlu, 'Gozaresh-e motarjem-e hay'at', in *Safarnameh-ye Maleyzi*, 34.
[103] Amini, 'Gozaresh-e safar', 16.
[104] Ostovar, *Vanguard of the Imam*, 114.
[105] Kiyavash, 'Gozaresh-e safar beh Lobnan', 9–10.

he knew Khomeini. The boy reportedly answered with full conviction: 'Yes, I do!' When probing him to see how profound his knowledge was, the boy gazed out onto the Mediterranean where five warships of the US navy were anchored. The Iranians perceived him 'lost in trance, like a mystic who intended to express his love for God', when he replied: 'I know him in the same way as these waves know the ocean.'[106] Similar experiences in the Gaza hospital were in store for the delegation, where Khomeini was repeatedly praised as the only hope for the Palestinian cause.[107] The Iranians found it easy to relate to the Palestinians since they could build sympathies by drawing on their own wartime suffering.[108]

Sunni ulama

Throughout their travels, the delegations were able to call on various types of Sunni *ulama*, many of whom had close personal experiences of Iran. Take the example of the well-connected Senegalese Tijani Sufi Muhammad Mansur Sy, whom the Iranians met in Gabon. Sy was the son of Abd al-ʿAziz Sy (1904–1997), the caliph of the Tivaouane branch of the Tijaniyya order.[109] According to Amini's report, Sy openly shared how he had prayed for counsel (*estekhareh*) after the victory of the revolution and had received the answer that journeying to Tehran would be to the advantage of Islam. During his time in Iran, he became aware of three aspects that all resembled a miracle for him. First, the Iranian nation was in the hands of Khomeini. It obeyed him in a way that reminded Sy of the Prophet's own time, which should be understood as 'divine confirmation' (*taʾid-e elahi*). Second, he noted the strong commitment of the Iranian people in terms of self-sacrifice (*janbazi*) and defence of Islam. Third, there was the spiritual strength and faith of Khomeini, who single-handedly challenged both East and West. It was clear to Sy that Khomeini had received a gift resembling divine inspiration (*shabih-e elham*). Khomeini was in contact with the hidden world: 'If the people of the world would recognise him as the Imam and if they would acknowledge his right, I would be convinced that the exile of Islam

---

[106] Ibid., 7.

[107] Khamiyar, 'Gozaresh-e safar-e hayʾat', 39.

[108] Ibid. On the complex and shifting Shiʿi–Palestinian relations in southern Beirut during the 1970s and 1980s, see Rosemary Sayigh, *Too Many Enemies: The Palestinian Experience in Lebanon* (London: Zed Books, 1994), 221–223.

[109] Mara A. Leichtman, *Shiʿi Cosmopolitanisms in Africa: Lebanese Migration and Religious Conversion in Senegal* (Bloomington, IN: Indiana University Press, 2015), 99.

(*ghorbat-e eslam*) would come to an end and religion would rise.' God, in Sy's perception, had prepared this moment and Khomeini was a foretaste of the coming *mahdi*.[110] During one night in Iran, Sy had suddenly woken up and could clearly perceive Khomeini's power and spiritual exaltedness (*qodrat va 'azimat-e ruhi*), his peerless deeds, and how he partook in the essence of the Prophets.[111] Sy realised in that moment that he had, in fact, only come to Iran to see the Imam.[112] In the view of the Senegalese Sufi, God had intended to let Islam 'rise again from Iran' (*az Iran tolu' konad*) and be spread on a global scale. 'I talk and I write about what I have seen in Iran and understood there. I distribute this message not in order to please you but for the sake of pleasing God.'[113]

This reported encounter was a highlight that gave the Iranian delegation a much-needed psychological boost in their otherwise chaotic outreach activities. Amini was strongly impressed and insisted that Iran should try to utilise the services of Sy.[114] Yet, it is important to underline that the Sufi's emphatic condonement of Iran was no outlier or isolated incident in 1983. Especially in Gabon the Iranian delegation members saw many developments that gave them hope. As they put it, they seemed to have arrived exactly at the right time. The mighty Hassan II Mosque, funded by Morocco, had just opened. It provided an ideal platform for the delegates to speak about the revolution and the importance which Iran attached to Friday prayers.[115] Afterwards, *ulama*, including the Friday Imam and religious people, along with ten recent returnees from Iran, assembled for the celebration of the revolution. Hajj Ibrahim Khalil, who was responsible for Islamic propaganda on Gabon radio and television, freely talked about his experience in Iran. He lauded the atmosphere and emphasised that he had been able to speak to a large number of Iranians, who had all been pleased with the state of their revolution.[116] In Bangladesh, the Iranians could clearly identify their Sunni allies, such as the Deobandi scholar Maulana Mohammadullah (d.1987), known as Hafezzi Huzur, who had publicly

---

[110] Ebrahim Amini, 'Gozaresh az safar-e hay'at be keshvar-e Gabon', in *Safarnameh-ye Nayjeriyeh, Sira Le'un, Gabon*, 48–49.
[111] Ibid., 49.
[112] Ibid.
[113] Ibid.
[114] Ibid., 50.
[115] Ibid.
[116] Ibid., 51.

denounced Iraq and the Baʿth regime after being invited to Baghdad.[117] The Pakistani Islamist party Jamaat-e-Islami was seen as being a big help in the further development (*roshd*) of the revolution. The delegation suggested expanding on the good relations with them by co-operating with activities in Iran's cultural centres and TV programming.[118] In Lebanon, the group noticed that the Sunnis of the Beqaa valley already proceeded 'on the path of the revolution'. Muhammad ʿAli al-Rifaʿi, the Friday Imam of Baalbek, for example, praised Khomeini as a 'giant and hero of Islam'.[119]

Does this show of support amount to more than mere sloganeering? Did some of these individuals rise to positions of influence and power in their respective domestic contexts? How do we make sense of the reports that I have presented on the previous pages? The conclusion will try to shed some light on these tricky questions.

CONCLUSION

There is no doubt that by 1983 the revolution had suffered from infighting, the Khomeinists' violent purge of all non-Khomeinist forces, a horrible war, and the killing of some of its most important ideologues. Iran's image as a liberating force for Muslims and non-Muslims alike had been seriously tainted. The Unit of Islamic Liberation Movements, established under the control of the Ministry of Islamic Guidance, and strategically guided by Hossein-Ali Montazeri, had to learn about this changed global landscape the hard way. Its delegations, despatched abroad in 1983 ahead of the revolution's fourth anniversary, were quickly confronted with the implications of the Islamic Republic's fading Third Worldist credentials. Iranian emissaries tried hard, and in many instances unsuccessfully, to reconcile the official ecumenical message with their own Shiʿi commitments. To make things worse, the missions were undermined in various local settings by a number of logistical missteps, ranging from insufficient

---

[117] Vahed-e nahzat-ha-ye azadibakhsh-e eslami, *Safarnameh-ye Bangladesh*, 29. On Huzur, see Ali Riaz and Kh. Ali Ar Raji, 'Who are the Islamists?', in *Political Islam and Governance in Bangladesh*, ed. Ali Riaz and C. Christine Fair (London: Routledge, 2010), 46–70.

[118] 'Majmuʿeh-ye gozareshat-e aʿzaye hayʾat-e Pakestan', 31–33.

[119] Hasan Khamiyar, 'Gozaresh-e safar-e hayʾat-e aʿzami-yi Loban', in *Safarnameh-ye Lobnan Suriyeh*, 56.

planning to unhelpful outreach material. Exporting the revolution became to a large part lost in translation.

Delegation members consequently were anxious that any form of pro-Iranian attitude was just a ruse to obtain financial support. Yet, what the detailed reports also demonstrate is that, at least in Islamist circles, there was still palpable excitement. Iran trying to make friends even in Sunni settings was not as outlandish a task as it appears in today's sectarianised Islamic world (with notable exceptions like Palestinian Hamas). As the reports claim, Iran still counted as a Third Worldist and Islamic answer for university students, religious scholars, and Palestinians in many parts of the Global South. This experience led to serious reflections on what audiences from sub-Saharan Africa to Southeast Asia saw in Iran's anti-imperialist project.

An important manifestation of this phenomenon is the Nigerian student activist turned preacher and Shiʿi convert Ibrahim Zakzaky. Shortly after 1979 he started to demand that Nigeria become like Iran and publicly expressed his rejection of the Nigerian constitution as being directed against the Quran and Islam. By 1989, Zakzaky had already spent eight years in jail. After each release, thousands of his supporters waited for him at the gates.[120] In fact, Zakzaky managed to closely direct his movement while behind bars. He regularly instigated riots and violence against opponents and representatives of the state throughout the 1990s in ways that made provincial governors and Nigerian state authorities look helpless.[121] Zakzaky has arguably become Iran's 'most valuable and important "proxy" in Western Africa' with a 'state inside a state like in Lebanon'.[122] In order to render such links durable, Iran often had to make them appear religious-sectarian so they would fit the context in question.

Unfortunately, the material does not allow us to get a sense of how or whether the various suggestions filed by the unit were incorporated into future outreach programmes. Since there are no comparable, accessible reports for the later 1980s, it is difficult to assess the afterlives of the 1983 delegations. Future scholarship could compare how the political shifts of 1984 played out in terms of the contacts established by the delegations.

---

[120] Falola, *Violence in Nigeria*, 196.
[121] Ibid., 198–203.
[122] Sohail Wahed, 'Exporting the Revolution to Africa: The Nigerian Experience', in *Law, Religion and Human Flourishing in Africa*, ed. M.C. Green (Stellenbosch: African Sun Media, 2019), 159.

Who was later welcome in Tehran? Which organisations and figures fell by the wayside? Did the eventual fading of the UILM affect subsequent outreach programmes? In all events, the classified delegation reports give us an unprecedented window into the difficulties of reconciling the logic of a revolutionary state bogged down by war, with outreach activities that were ostensibly Shi'i but meant to transcend this narrow religious focus at the same time.

PART TWO

THIRD WORLDISM AND THE REGION

4

THE GENDERED POLITICS
OF DEAD BODIES

Obituaries, Revolutionaries, and Martyrs Between the Iranian, Palestinian, and Dhufar Revolutions

Marral Shamshiri

'Dead people belong to the live people who claim them most obsessively.'

JAMES ELLROY[1]

'Where there is collective memory there is also organised forgetting.'

BRIDGET FOWLER[2]

In an obituary published by an Iranian front organisation operating from exile in the Middle East in 1975, Rafat Afraz, an Iranian woman who joined the Dhufar Revolution earlier that year, was remembered for fighting in the People's Liberation Army in Dhufar. Published shortly after her death in *Bakhtar-e Emruz*, a publication of the Organisations of the National Front Abroad, it described her as a 'comrade' who had been sent by the organisation to serve alongside her Omani 'brothers' against 'imperialism and reaction'.[3] Born into a middle-class family in the city of Jahrom, Afraz

---

[1] James Ellroy, cited in Katherine Verdery, *The Political Lives of Dead Bodies: Reburial and Postsocialist Change* (New York: Columbia University Press, 2000), 24.
[2] Bridget Fowler, 'Mapping the Obituary: Notes towards a Bourdieusian Interpretation', *The Sociological Review* 52, no. 2 (2004): 149.
[3] *Bakhtar-e Emruz*, no. 69, November–December 1975.

became a schoolteacher and moved to Tehran, where she joined the revolutionary anti-imperialist Islamist-Left organisation the People's Mojahedin Organisation of Iran (*Sazman-e mojahedin-e khalq-e Iran*, or Mojahedin) in 1970/1971. In commemorating her short life, the obituary stated that she had been sent to Oman as the organisation was strengthening its ties with revolutionary groups in the region. For several months, it noted, in the most difficult conditions, Afraz continued the struggle in the 'People's Liberation Army of Oman led by the Popular Front for the Liberation of Oman' until she reached 'martyrdom' from an illness.[4] Months later, in January 1976, the Palestine Liberation Organisation's (PLO) weekly magazine *Filastin al-Thawra* published an Arabic translation of part of her obituary, the words 'shahida [martyr] Rafat Afraz' inscribed beneath her photograph.[5]

In this chapter, I use obituaries to explore questions of gender and revolution. Taking the example of Rafat Afraz's death, I trace the revolutionary obituary as a transnational object of Third Worldist revolution, following its production, circulation, and reception. I explore how, as the obituary reveals connections between Iranian and Arab movements, it opens questions concerning gender, women, and revolutionary culture more broadly. The chapter argues that contrary to the constructed image of the militant revolutionary woman, the gendered political work Iranian women engaged in at the site of the Dhufar Revolution was omitted in narratives of martyrdom which made political claims on dead women's bodies. The first section looks at the revolutionary obituary as a historical source and transnational object. Its circulation between Iranian and Arab revolutionary movements maps the networks of Iranian revolutionaries who fought in the Middle East. The second section closely follows the travelling obituary of one woman, Rafat Afraz, across South–South networks and student metropolitan centres. It shows how competing narratives of martyrdom were constructed about women's revolutionary lives and political roles among Iranian political organisations. The third section goes beyond narratives of martyrdom by exploring the experiences of Rafat Afraz and revolutionary Iranian women in Dhufar, showing that there was a gendered division of labour which was erased in narratives of women's armed political participation as circulated through the obituary. Finally, the fourth section explores how dead Iranian

---

4 Ibid.
5 *Filastin al-Thawra*, no. 174, 18 January 1976.

women's bodies have become sites of political contestation when claimed in state-funded historiographical debate within Iran.

شهادت رفیق رفعت افراز در ظفار

'The Martyrdom of Comrade Rafat Afraz in Dhufar'. Photo of Rafat Afraz in her obituary in Bakhtar-e Emruz, *no. 69, November–December 1975.*

THIRD WORLDIST MATERIAL CULTURE: THE REVOLUTIONARY OBITUARY AS TRAVELLING OBJECT AND HISTORICAL SOURCE

Among the material cultures of revolutions, in other words the objects and material things produced, circulated, and consumed in times of political transformation, the revolutionary obituary might seem an unusual item. These relatively short tributes were scattered across militant Third Worldist revolutionary periodicals and pamphlets in memory of the lives lost in the armed struggle of the 1960s and 1970s. For clandestine revolutionary movements in the Middle East, death – conceived and narrated as martyrdom – typically meant that the observation of secrecy was no longer a necessity concerning the role and involvement of an individual in underground political activities. Much beyond a mere public distribution of grief, the revolutionary obituary was the place where this information was made visible for the first time. For the movement and organisation that the individual was a part of, the obituary was a display of sacrifice and tragedy, collective and organised memory, heroic and often hyperbolic rhetoric, and an opportunity for political mobilisation as it travelled across radical networks and geographies through pamphlets and publications.[6]

Read alongside other sources, the obituary reveals important biographical details about the lives of the Iranian revolutionaries who joined revolutionary movements in the Middle East in the 1960s and 1970s. Iraj Sepehri, for example, established relations between the Marxist Organisation of the People's Fada'i Guerrillas (*Sazman-e cherik-ha-ye fada'i-ye khalq*, or Fada'iyan) and the Popular Front for the Liberation of Palestine – General Command (PFLP-GC). He was remembered in the Marxist Fada'iyan periodical, *Nabard-e Khalq*, for his involvement in the Palestinian ranks.[7] The obituary revealed that Sepehri had commanded a group in the Golan Heights. Referred to by his Palestinian comrades as Abu Sa'id-e Irani, Sepehri was given the rank of captain, an honour for a non-Palestinian.[8] His brother Farhad Sepehri joined the ranks of the Dhufar Revolution and was said to have died in combat in 1974. He was commemorated and presented as a hero (*qahreman*), the Fada'iyan's first martyr 'in the way of an internationalist goal of serving the fighting peoples of the world', as he was the first to be martyred in a revolutionary front outside of Iran.[9] Accounts of armed militancy and sacrifice underpinned these obituaries, highlighting a global shared struggle against imperialism on multiple fronts, and revealing the role of Iranians in networks abroad.

More than a repository of archival and biographical information for clandestine Iranian revolutionary movements, the obituary was a transnational object which travelled across and contributed to 'insurgent geographies of connection' between Third Worldist revolutionary movements.[10]

---

[6] I draw on sociologist Bridget Fowler's reading in Bridget Fowler, *The Obituary as Collective Memory* (London: Routledge, 2007), 25–40. Most obituary studies including hers focus on the newspaper obituary: Mushira Eid, *The World of Obituaries: Gender Across Cultures and Over Time* (Detroit: Wayne University Press, 2002); Hussein A.H. Omar, '"Snatched by Destiny's Hand": Obituaries and the Making of Class in Modern Egypt', *History Compass* 15, no. 6 (2017): 1–12. In discussing Dhufari revolutionary culture, Takriti notes that obituaries of 'sister revolutions' were 'laden with political meaning and anti-colonial sympathies, promptly published whenever a major international revolutionary figure died', Abdel Razzaq Takriti, *Monsoon Revolution: Republicans, Sultans, and Empires in Oman 1965–1976* (Oxford: Oxford University Press, 2013), 237.

[7] *Nabard-e Khalq*, no. 3, May–June 1974; see Iraj Sepehri, *Az jebheh-ye nabard-e Felestin: Khaterat-e rafiq kargar-e fada'i shahid Iraj Sepehri* (Tehran: OIPFG Publications, 1974).

[8] *Nabard-e Khalq*, no. 3, May–June 1974.

[9] *Nabard-e Khalq*, no. 4, July–August 1974, 73–74; *Bakhtar-e Emruz*, no. 59, October–November 1974.

[10] David Featherstone, *Solidarity: Hidden Histories and Geographies of Internationalism* (London: Zed books, 2012), 62.

Following the execution of Ali Akbar Safa'i-Farahani, a prominent Iranian Marxist guerrilla who had trained with Palestinian groups in the late 1960s, on 16 March 1971 by the Pahlavi regime, Fatah published an article commemorating his life in its periodical *Fatah*. The obituary 'Iran, al-aghwar wa bil'aks' [Iran, the Jordan Valley, and back] was translated into Persian and published in the Iranian periodical *Bakhtar-e Emruz*.[11] Safa'i-Farahani earned the joint title of 'Martyr [*shahid*] of the Palestinian Revolution and Iranian Revolution', in a joint statement published by Fatah and the Organisations of the National Front Abroad.[12]

Similarly, following the death of Iranian Mojahedin fighter Reza Rezai in a siege and shoot-out with SAVAK security forces in Iran in 1973, obituaries circulated across both Iranian and Arab networks. A prominent revolutionary leader of the Mojahedin, Rezai was a fugitive who escaped prison and avoided the mass 1972 trials of his organisation's membership.[13] His 'martyrdom' was covered extensively in Palestinian outlets including the PLO's news agency Wafa, Palestinian radio, and its magazine *Filastin al-Thawra*.[14] They revealed that Rezai left his university studies to join the Palestinian revolution, where he undertook military training in Jordan and fought against Jordanian forces during Black September in 1970. He was recognised by the PLO in *Filastin al-Thawra* as a fighter, defender, and martyr of the Palestinian revolution.[15] Indeed, Rezai was one of dozens of members of the Mojahedin who trained in Palestinian camps in the 1970s.

As obituaries travelled and were received, they wedded these Third Worldist revolutions together. The circulation revealed connections on material and emotional levels: the commitment to and co-construction of a shared political horizon, and cross-border communication networks. The obituary and its movement revealed for the first time the broader network to which these Iranians belonged. Like their obituaries, these shared fighters had once traversed national borders.

---

[11] It was translated by Torab Haghshenas, a central member of the People's Mojahedin Organisation of Iran in charge of foreign relations in the Middle East. Torab Haghshenas, *Az Feyzieh ta Peykar: Khaterat va neveshteh-ha* [From Feyzieh to Peykar, Memories and Writings] (Frankfurt: Andeesheh va Peykar Publications, 2020), 213.

[12] *Bakhtar-e Emruz*, no. 14, July 1971.

[13] See Ervand Abrahamian, *Radical Islam: The Iranian Mojahedin* (London: I.B. Tauris, 1989), 126–144.

[14] *Bakhtar-e Emruz*, no. 45, August 1973; *Payam-e Mojahed*, no. 12, May–June 1973.

[15] *Filastin al-Thawra*, no. 49, 1973; *Filastin al-Thawra*, no. 59, 1973.

MILITANT WOMEN: TRACING THE OBITUARY
OF RAFAT AFRAZ

Iranian women were part of these revolutionary networks in the Middle East. Rafat Afraz, a Mojahedin revolutionary, was one of several militant Iranian women who engaged in clandestine political activities across the region, who both took part in and died in the Dhufar Revolution. She likely died from malaria, on 30 August 1975.[16] As detailed in the opening of this chapter, Rafat Afraz's obituary was first published shortly after her death in 1975. The obituary and photograph originated in *Nashriyeh-ye Khabari-ye Sazman-e Mojahedin-e Khalq-e Iran* (The Newsletter of the People's Mojahedin Organisation of Iran), a publication of the Mojahedin abroad, and was reprinted in *Bakhtar-e Emruz*.[17] Her death and subsequent martyrdom were not limited to the Iranian and Dhufari revolutionary movements, but the Palestinian revolution too. In January 1976, in the (PLO) weekly magazine *Filastin al-Thawra*, an Arabic translation of the same obituary and her photograph were published in part, alongside an article condemning the Iranian regime's death sentence for ten Iranian *munadhileen* (fighters), all members of the Mojahedin.[18]

Afraz's obituary in *Filastin al-Thawra* stated that it was taken from the periodical *Iran al-Thawra*, an Arabic-language counterpart to *Bakhtar-e Emruz* published by the Organisations of the National Front Abroad.[19] In death, similar to the early Marxist Fada'i Ali Akbar Safai Farahani, and Mojahed Reza Rezai, Afraz was recognised as a martyr by the Palestinian revolution – the highest honour for any revolutionary of her time; a rare one too for a non-Palestinian. Unlike those of the Iranians mentioned above, Afraz's obituary did not mention if she had fought or trained in the Palestinian revolution. Yet it could in fact be assumed that this qualifying link was made, as she had had a short round of military training in Palestinian camps in Damascus in 1973.[20]

---

[16] According to her first obituary; 28 August 1975 according to the later obituary from Peykar.

[17] *Nashriyeh-ye Khabari-ye Sazman-e Mojahedin-e Khalq-e Iran*, Supplement, no. 17, September– October 1975.

[18] *Filastin al-Thawra*, no. 174, 18 January 1976.

[19] Eskandar Sadeghi-Boroujerdi, 'The origins of Communist Unity: anti-colonialism and revolution in Iran's tri-continental moment', *British Journal of Middle Eastern Studies* 45, no. 5 (2018): 796–822.

[20] Mohsen Nejat-Hosseini, *Bar faraz-e Khalij-e Fars* (London: Farsibook, 2013), 348–350.

Laleh Khalili has shown that the heroic *fida'yi* figure of the 1960s and 1970s emerged in the Palestinian revolution for the mobilisation of support. In the liberation movements of Third Worldist struggle, discourses of martyrdom emphasised a hypermasculine narrative of heroism in relation to the dead bodies of men and women. The defeat and loss of a revolutionary fighter was reclaimed as a strength of the movement through the self-sacrificing martyr, yet the revolutionary was foremost a national hero.[21] The interesting aspect of Afraz's commemoration as a martyr by the PLO, like Safai Farahani and Rezai before her, was the PLO's recognition of these figures as transnational heroes. The part of Afraz's obituary that was reprinted was her photograph and the section on her membership of the Mojahedin and role in the People's Liberation Army of the Popular Front for the Liberation of Oman (PFLO). As the obituary was reproduced by the PLO, the biographical aspects of her personal life were removed, and her militant heroism and transnational revolutionary affiliations celebrated. It was therefore not just the discourse of martyrdom that was a transnational phenomenon among liberation movements, but the recognition of the transnational martyrs themselves. Shared heroes and martyrs could, in this sense, evidence the wide support and shared struggles of connected movements for liberation, gaining symbolic capital to further mobilise their supporters.

The circulation of Afraz's obituary went beyond revolutionary circles across South–South locations and to the metropolitan centres also constituted in these Third Worldist networks. Traversing linguistic and geographic borders once again, the 1975 obituary of Afraz travelled to Europe and North America through materials published by the Confederation of Iranian Students – National Union (CISNU). In February 1976, the same obituary and photograph appeared in *Peyman*, the central defence journal of CISNU.[22] It was positioned next to a military update from units of the 'People's Liberation Army' in Dhufar, which extensively listed operational gains, casualties, and military updates over two pages, reproduced from the translated version or summarised from the original in the PFLO's publications *Sawt al-Thawra* or *9 Yunyu*. Read together, it would have been understood that Rafat died fighting heroically alongside the PFLO.

CISNU was an early supporter of the Dhufar Revolution and had close links to the PFLO. With an unrivalled international network of affiliated

[21] Laleh Khalili, *Heroes and Martyrs of Palestine: The Politics of National Commemoration* (Cambridge: Cambridge University Press), 133.
[22] *Peyman*, no. 68, February–March 1354, February 1976, 2–3.

student groups across Europe, the US, and parts of Asia, the reach of this publication, read by the thousands of Iranian students abroad, was significant. In another information booklet on 'The Revolution in Oman', collated and published by the Iranian Students' Association of the United States (ISAUS), the US chapter of CISNU, a few lines on Afraz's deployment and martyrdom in Dhufar accompanied her photograph, amidst several articles on the history and politics of Oman, translated excerpts of Fred Halliday's *Arabia Without Sultans*, and messages of Iranian solidarity with the revolution. Noticeable absences in these outputs were the two Iranian revolutionary men who died in Dhufar, the aforementioned Farhad Sepehri and Fada'i Mohammad Ali Khosravi Ardebili. The two men had, like Rafat Afraz, died fighting with the PFLO, yet it was the photograph of the revolutionary woman which was reproduced.

The image and narrative of Afraz's martyrdom in circulation, reproduced and canonised across Iranian and Arab political organisations and student networks, was one of heroism and militancy. The obituary projected normative ideals onto her dead body: she was an example of the close relations between the Iranian and Arab organisations in the region, who had been sent by the Mojahedin to support her 'Omani brothers'; she symbolised the shared fight against imperialism and reaction in the region; and as a woman, she was an ostensible equal to men in fighting in the People's Liberation Army. If the intended impact of claiming Afraz as a martyr was political mobilisation, it was probably successful in inspiring supporters and women. As Zohra Khayam, a former ISAUS student member explained to scholar Manijeh Nasrabadi, 'We all wanted to prove that women could do anything that men can do. When it came to armed struggle in Oman, we were automatically siding with women who took arms. Or with the Palestinian movement. Leila Khaled – she was one of the female symbols of Palestinian struggle ... [there was] a window of opportunity for us to learn about other women and how they have participated in the struggle. It was really inspiring for us.'[23] As Arielle Gordon has argued, the figure of the 'female fighter' was one visual idiom among many, such as the clenched fist, the V-sign, and the carnation-laden gun

---

[23] Manijeh Nasrabadi, '"Women Can Do Anything Men Can Do": Gender and the Affects of Solidarity in the U.S. Iranian Student Movement, 1961–1979', *Women's Studies Quarterly* 42, no. 3/4 (2014): 140–141.

in the cultural inventory of the global 1960s revolution.[24] In death, Afraz became one such fighter.

Yet competing claims to Afraz's body emerged thereafter. In contrast to her first obituary, which travelled across Arab and student networks and which implied that 'comrade' Rafat Afraz had fought in the People's Liberation Army, another obituary published almost immediately afterwards sought to remember Rafat not as a comrade but as a 'sister', with an explicit claim to her legacy as a devout Muslim.[25] *Payam-e Mojahed* was a publication of the religious Liberation Movement of Iran, which had connections to the Mojahedin.[26] In December 1975/January 1976, an article commemorated the 'martyrdom of sister mojahed Rafat Afraz'.[27] It stated that Afraz, who had helped the revolutionaries in Dhufar, had been martyred, with no explanation as to the cause of her death. What followed was a short obituary written by a friend, together with a poem that she had sent to her friend. The first part of the obituary written by the unnamed friend was written in a conventional form; her life was observed and celebrated, from her role as breadwinner of the family after her father's death, to her education, her role as a teacher at Refah girls' school, and her deep political convictions against injustice. Her political convictions were seen through the lens of Islamist justice, from the references to the *chador* (hijab) that she 'always wore', her consistent alignment of views with an Islamic frame of mind, and her belief in God, 'the masses', and the evolutionary path of humans towards freedom. Her actions were 'a torch for her friends and her fellow Muslim fighters'.[28] The obituary carried an infusion of revolutionary Islamist and socialist imagery into the discourse of liberation and justice.[29]

The poem accompanying this obituary was printed in Rafat's own handwriting as an 'indicator of her ideology and beliefs'.[30] Titled 'Mosalmani keh bayad bud' [The Muslim one ought to be], it was about achieving justice

[24] Arielle Gordon, 'From Guerrilla Girls to Zainabs: Reassessing the Figure of the "Militant Woman" in the Iranian Revolution', *Journal of Middle East Women's Studies* 17, no. 1 (2021): 64–95.

[25] *Payam-e Mojahed*, no. 37, December 1975/January 1976.

[26] H.E. Chehabi, *Iranian Politics and Religious Modernism: The Liberation Movement of Iran under the Shah and Khomeini* (Ithaca: Cornell University Press, 1990).

[27] *Payam-e Mojahed*, no. 37, December 1975/January 1976, 4.

[28] Ibid.

[29] This language resonates with the revolutionary Islamism of the Muslim Mojahedin and the Islamic liberation theology of Ali Shariʻati: see Ali Rahnema, *An Islamic Utopian: A Political Biography of Ali Shariʻati* (London: I.B. Tauris, 1998).

[30] *Payam-e Mojahed*, no. 37, December 1975/January 1976, 4.

in an Islamic sense, and was imbued with vivid references to overcoming oppression, obtaining revenge for the dispossession of innocent people, and the eager desire to demand and reach justice.[31] In particular, it outlined Muslim duty towards the struggle of the Palestinian people at the hands of the Israeli 'occupiers'. By appending this handwritten poem to the obituary as evidence, which it stated had recently been sent to her friend, a claim of legitimacy was made over Rafat Afraz's life and death through this close association. It is plausible that as someone with strong convictions, she was a devoted Muslim as much as she later developed impassioned Marxist tendencies. Afraz's death, moreover, came at a time of internal crisis and turmoil in the Mojahedin, as the organisation had recently declared the ideological split from Marxism in 1975. Taking the poem at face value (not knowing its author, nor the date when it was written), it is at the least clear that claiming religiosity (or refuting her Marxism) made her body a site of political contestation in a turbulent period following the Mojahedin's violent ideological split in 1975 between its Marxist and Islamist members, as the former distanced themselves from Islam.[32]

The commemoration of Rafat Afraz as a martyr continued to circulate in the collective memory of her political organisation. On the first anniversary of her death in 1976, her organisation, now the Mojahedin (Marxist–Leninist) published a five-page 'biography' of Afraz. This biography gave shape to Rafat's life story, her upbringing and early political consciousness, her passion for teaching and for the works of activist and writer Samad Behrangi, and her entry into the Mojahedin organisation. It stated that in her organisational mission to Dhufar to serve the people of Oman, she carried out revolutionary duties for her organisation and for her Dhufari comrades. Here too, an excerpt of her handwritten notes was printed on the final page.[33] In 1978, the organisation published a short obituary of Afraz again, in *Iran al-Jamahir*, an Arabic-language newspaper published abroad by the Mojahedin (Marxist–Leninist), in which a short article and a photograph remembered her participation in 'the struggle in the ranks of the PFLO' as an expression of the struggling Iranian people's solidarity with Oman.[34] Afraz – named publicly here with her *nom de guerre*, 'Comrade Seddiqeh', as though this intimate detail could be shared in the safety of a

[31] Ibid.
[32] Abrahamian, *Radical Islam*.
[33] *Mojahed*, no. 6, July–August 1976.
[34] *Iran al-Jamahir*, no. 3, February 1978.

different language – was remembered as a martyr of both the Iranian and Omani revolutions.

Adding to the contestation over whether she was a 'comrade' or a 'sister', this time after the 1979 Iranian Revolution, yet another obituary was published in 1979 by comrades who claimed to know Afraz, in *Peykar*, a publication of the organisation of the same name that emerged from the reorganisation of the Mojahedin (Marxist–Leninist). Here, she was again a 'comrade', and handwritten evidence in the form of her daily notes while serving in Dhufar was again appended. While it could not possibly be known whether Afraz would have joined Peykar, the organisation claimed her. Critically, unlike her previous obituaries and organisational biography, this obituary revealed for the first time that Rafat Afraz had been sent to Dhufar 'to serve in a medical team'.[35] She was sent alongside her sister, Doctor Mahbubeh Afraz, who died in December 1978 and whose own obituary in the same *Peykar* issue presented details of her transnational clandestine activities publicly for the first time: Rafat Afraz had *not* picked up arms to fight alongside her Omani brothers, as previous obituaries had implied. Her revolutionary work had been medical care work, mostly with women, what her comrades would later describe as revolutionary activities behind the front (*posht-e jebheh*) – so why had this detail about her role been omitted in early commemorations of her martyrdom, and was she a comrade or a sister?

GENDER AND REVOLUTION: IRANIAN REVOLUTIONARIES IN THE DHUFAR REVOLUTION

The changes, silences, and contestations in the narratives of Rafat Afraz's martyrdom, which have been rendered visible through a close reading of the obituary, provide an invitation to explore what it meant to take part in the Dhufar Revolution as a woman. If Rafat Afraz had not been a combatant alongside fighters in the People's Liberation Army, as her original 1975 obituary in circulation had suggested, what had her medical role involved? The obituaries of both Rafat Afraz and her sister Mahbubeh Afraz, published in *Peykar* in 1979, offered a shred of new information. Daily notes written by the Afraz sisters while in Dhufar were published in a memoir in 2015,

---

[35] *Peykar*, no. 19, 3 September 1979.

presenting a fuller picture of their political activities.[36] Here, it became clear that Rafat Afraz spent her time in the Dhufar Revolution as a nurse. With the publication of this memoir, the former eulogies of martyrdom no longer narrated these women's lives: their diaries did.

On 15 June 1975, Mahbubeh and Rafat Afraz arrived at the Al-Shahida Fatima Ghanana Hospital in al-Ghaydah, a coastal town in the sixth province of the PDRY approximately seventy miles from the border with Oman. Revolutionaries in the west of Dhufar would retreat to the mountainous terrain between Dhufar and the al-Ghaydah area, beyond the fighting. The makeshift clinic was named after a female martyr and established on 26 July 1974 with Cuban aid. Permanent Cuban medics assisted wounded revolutionaries and provided training courses in the PDRY.[37] The sisters' organisation, the Mojahedin (Marxist–Leninist), sent them to Dhufar: Mahbubeh Afraz as a doctor, who was the youngest woman to graduate medical school, the School of Medicine at the University of Tehran, at the age of twenty-three with a dissertation on ectopic pregnancy;[38] and Rafat Afraz, twelve years older, who was sent as a nurse.

Mahbubeh wrote about their various activities in the hospital outside of clinic hours, such as nursing and caring for patients, sorting medical supplies and donations from abroad, and carrying out home visits to women and children, including a home for the wives and widows of fighters and martyrs, and their children.[39] As a medical volunteer based in al-Ghaydah, and later in the Al-Shahid Habkook Hospital in Hawf, Rafat Afraz assisted with wounded patients, cooked, cleaned, nursed, provided mothers with food for their infants, and supported women and children. While they were not combatants, the political work the sisters engaged in was primarily care work. In the context of revolution and armed struggle– as in other armed liberation movements, such as those in Zimbabwe, Mozambique, or Eritrea – women were often combatants, but the gendered division of labour was still

---

[36] Mahbubeh Afraz and Rafat Afraz, ed. Torab Haghshenas, *Hamrah ba enqelabiyun-e Omani: Yaddasht-ha-ye jang-e Zofar* [Alongside the Omani Revolutionaries: Notes from the Dhufar War] (Frankfurt: Andeesheh va Peykar Publications, 2015). Academic work on the Afraz sisters includes: Naghmeh Sohrabi, 'Where the Small Things Are: Thoughts on Writing Revolutions and their Histories', *Jadaliyya*, 21 May 2020; Shahrzad Mojab, 'Women and revolution in the Middle East', in Suad Joseph and Zeina Zaatari, eds, *Handbook on Women in the Middle East* (New York: Routledge, 2022).

[37] Takriti, *Monsoon Revolution*, 303.

[38] *Ettela'at*, Tuesday 5 September, 1967; Sohrabi, 'Small Things'.

[39] Afraz, 81–82.

reproduced.[40] Another pair of Iranian sisters who spent time in Dhufar were Pouran and Hayedeh Bazargan, who were not combatants. Pouran is said to have spent some time in the Dhufar Revolution as a teacher, and later worked at the Palestinian Red Crescent Hospital in Damascus and in the Sabra camp in Beirut. Her sister, Hayedeh, worked in Aden, PDRY, in radio and media work, in Gaza Hospital in Beirut, and in the Sabra and Shatila refugee camps.[41]

Rafat and Mahbubeh Afraz were among a number of Iranians who joined the revolution in Dhufar. As clandestine revolutionaries navigating political repression and state surveillance in 1970s Pahlavi Iran, despite the material dangers of complicated border-crossings (and notwithstanding the dangers of engaging in any meaningful political opposition in Iran), some twenty Iranians travelled to Dhufar to engage with the revolution in some capacity – as medical volunteers, for military training, in joint media and radio collaborations with the PFLO, in solidarity, for cover and for their own oppositional political activities against the Shah's regime. This seemingly small number is significant in proportion to the number of members these clandestine organisations had at the time, particularly as several of these individuals (men) were central committee cadres. Half of them were women: Rafat Afraz and Mahbubeh Afraz, Hayedeh Bazargan and Pouran Bazargan, and Jaleh and Parvin (*noms de guerre*) were all members of the Mojahedin; one woman (not named) was from the Fada'iyan; two women (not named) were from the so-called Star Group, operating under the front organisation the Organisations of the National Front Abroad, and from the Organisation of Communist Revolutionaries, a group formed by students in California, a woman named Farah Ebrahimi undertook a short solidarity visit.[42] While Iranian men are said to have taken up arms with the PFLO (those named being Farhad Sepehri, Mohammad Ali Khosravi Ardebili, and Hemad Sheibani), this seemingly counters the PFLO's policy that non-Omanis could not volunteer in the revolution as fighters.[43] Taqi Shamkhi, the first Iranian

---

[40] See, for example, Maria Mies, *Patriarchy and Accumulation on a World Scale: Women in the International Division of Labour* (London: Zed Books, 1986), 195.

[41] Pouran Bazargan, 'Khatereh-ye man az mosharekat-e zanan dar bakhsi az jonbesh-e mosallahane-ye do dahe-ye 1340 va 50', available online: http://www.peykarandeesh. org/article/Pouran-Bazargan.html.

[42] Meeting with Parviz Shokat, 18 November 2021. See Farah Ebrahimi's daughter's memoir, Neda Toloui-Semnani, *They Said They Wanted Revolution: A Memoir of My Parents* (New York: Little A, 2022).

[43] Conversation with former PFLOAG committee member Abdulnabi Alekry, 13 January 2022.

to join the Dhufar Revolution from the (Muslim) Mojahedin, was also said to have trained with the Dhufaris.[44] Other Mojahedin members in Dhufar were Mojtaba Taleghani, Naser and Vahidi, and three men from the Star Group.[45]

Placing the sisters' roles beside the political work of their male counterparts in the Dhufar Revolution and broader clandestine Middle East operations – military training, diplomatic liaison roles, radio broadcasts and media work – the gendered and hierarchical nature of these roles becomes apparent: men did not engage in care work. Of course, roles at the site of revolution were not exclusively gendered – the Cuban Doctors' Front medical team which was based at the Martyr Fatima Ghanana hospital consisted of both men and women, while Iranian women are said to have taken part in media and radio work. Yet in comparing Rafat Afraz's care work in the revolution with the image that circulated in her obituary – a combatant fighting alongside her Omani brothers – the tensions between revolutionary propaganda and reality become abundantly clear. In martyrdom, Rafat Afraz's revolutionary role had been stretched to construct an image of the heroic woman fighter, who was no different to her male comrades. In this regard, she was no different to the short-haired Dhufari girl with a Kalashnikov on her back whose image adorned revolutionary periodicals and pamphlets and inspired activists across the world. The imagery of militancy that travelled through her obituary was underpinned by a hypermasculine narrative in which women's gendered revolutionary practices were erased. She was remembered as a combatant who had picked up arms alongside her brothers and not for the political medical work she engaged in. Rafat, as a militant woman, was portrayed as equal to men in being a combatant. Yet this image reflected not only women having to adjust to masculinist modes of revolutionary subjectivity but also a neglect of the gendered division of labour, and the inevitably gendered and hierarchical political work.

Despite the evident importance of this political work, there is, in the daily writings of Mahbubeh Afraz, a strong distinction between work that was 'behind the front/*posht-e jebheh*' – medical work – and fighting on the frontline, the latter clearly valorised as the main site of revolution. Her diaries note several examples of protest and frustration with the activities she was asked to engage in. On one occasion, Mahbubeh Afraz asked why she and Rafat were placed in al-Ghaydah with the Cuban doctors while the hospital in

---

[44] Taqi Shamkhi, *Hamrah ba enqelabiyun-e Zofar* [Alongside the Dhufari Revolutionaries] (Tehran: Samadiyeh, 2021).

[45] Naser and Vahidi *noms de guerre*.

Hawf – a Yemeni town connected to the Oman border and a base for another hospital – did not have a single doctor. The response was that those in Hawf knew the mountains and were familiar with the environment, and that as women they would not be able to cope with the conditions there.[46] At the end of 1975 and near the end of the war (Mahbubeh Afraz having finally been sent to the inhospitable mountains), Hawf was bombarded with airstrikes, and Mahbubeh Afraz was asked to return to the hospital in al-Ghaydah to support the Cuban doctors. Her response had been, 'I will go wherever you wish to place me, but please do not think that I have come here to serve only behind the front.'[47] Her comrade replied, 'Aren't you being bombed now? Right now this is a military region, it is no different to the centre [battlefront]!'[48]

In the obituary written for Rafat Afraz in 1979 by *Peykar*, her role was described as being in a 'medical team in the liberation war front'.[49] The emphasis here on being on the war 'front' is interesting given that the experience of these women was that their roles were 'behind the front/ *posht-e jebheh*', in contrast to the real revolutionary work in combat on the 'front'. These women were prevented from participating as combatants despite the organisation claiming Rafat's armed participation. As already mentioned, Rafat Afraz had received a short round (less than a day) of military training in a Fatah camp in Damascus in October 1973.[50] A closer look at the sources reveals, however, that the main intention of her trip was not military training but the delivery of a message.[51] Mohsen Nejat-Hosseini, a Mojahedin cadre in charge of training militants in Palestinian camps in the Middle East during that time, confirmed that her trip to Damascus was not primarily for military training but to deliver a message, and the organisation apparently decided that she could acquire basic military familiarity with arms while she was there.[52]

In addition, Mojahedin sources have suggested that the main reason why the Afraz sisters were sent to Dhufar was to escape SAVAK infiltration of the Refah school in Tehran. The school was under the administration of Pouran Bazargan and Rafat Afraz, who maintained a clandestine Mojahedin network through the school including communication and printing activities for

[46] Afraz, *Hamrah*, 82–84.
[47] Afraz, *Hamrah*, 204.
[48] Ibid.
[49] *Peykar*, no. 19, 3 September 1979.
[50] Nejat-Hosseini, *Bar Faraz*, 348–350.
[51] Haghshenas, *Peykar*, 788.
[52] Author's interview with Mohsen Nejat-Hosseini, 18 August 2022.

the Mojahedin. In February 1975, Fatemeh Amini, a teacher at Refah, was arrested, imprisoned, and interrogated by SAVAK about the Mojahedin's clandestine operations. Amini, who had become a Marxist during the Mojahedin's split, refused to give any information away, which led to her death in a prison cell in August 1975, having been tortured by the police.[53] The arrest of Fatemeh Amini sent tremors through the organisation as it was feared that SAVAK would infiltrate the Mojahedin network at Refah – and it was thus necessary to send the women associated with the network abroad. In this context, as Mohsen Nejat-Hosseini explained, the Afraz sisters needed to leave Iran urgently, but where would they go? There were not any roles for them to fulfil in the Mojahedin's operational political network in the Middle East (because they were women), so the organisation sent them 'behind the front/*posht-e jebheh*', to volunteer in Dhufar.[54]

The extent to which the armed militant woman had been internalised as the real revolutionary subject is retrospectively understood by Torab Haghshenas, a colleague and a central member of the People's Mojahedin Organisation of Iran, who writes that the Mojahedin had, prior to her arrival in Dhufar, suggested to Mahbubeh that she should distance herself from clandestine work and open a clinic. While initially agreeing, she decided against it as she felt it would mean that 'she was not capable or worthy of revolutionary struggle'.[55] Haghshenas continues, 'those days, the youth's romanticised passion for revolution could not be easily fulfilled'.[56] This point, while somewhat condescending, is interesting in Mahbubeh Afraz's example given that so many notable (armed) revolutionaries and socialists of the twentieth century worked as doctors, such as Che Guevara, Beatriz Allende, and George Habash. But it was also the same imagery and creation of the sacrificial guerrilla fighter, which Haghshenas and his comrades constructed through the narrative of martyrdom in Rafat's obituary, that inspired young revolutionaries like Mahbubeh, whose primary focus in the age of decolonisation and liberation struggles was not on social transformation as political and revolutionary change, but on armed action as revolutionary practice.

---

[53] Abrahamian, *Radical Islam*, 147.
[54] Author's interview with Mohsen Nejat-Hosseini, 18 August 2022.
[55] Haghshenas, *Hamrah*, 3.
[56] Ibid.

THE POLITICAL LIVES OF DEAD BODIES: 1979 AND THE END OF THIRD WORLDISM

The life of Rafat Afraz became a matter of speculation among competing Iranian political groups following her death in 1975. In addition, with the death of her sister Mahbubeh Afraz, the legacies of both sisters became a subject of historiographical debate in post-revolutionary Iran. In the literature produced inside Iran on the Mojahedin, there are two issues concerning the lives of each Afraz sister. What remains at stake is not a set of questions around the identities and lives of these women, but rather the attempt by competing political groups, and the state, to claim an authoritative narrative on ideological grounds. The anthropologist Katherine Verdery has shown how 'dead bodies' take on political lives, due to their most important properties of ambiguity and polysemy.[57] She writes that in contrast to the living body, which is capable of producing complex and ambiguous behaviours, the dead body presents multiple personal histories depending on various aspects of the dead person's life, and thus identification with their life story can be made from multiple possible vantage points – one life story is presented as the one single significance of a single body.[58] The narratives about Rafat's life, indeed whether she was a sister or a comrade, flatten any such complexities and seek singular authoritative claims.

The continued controversy over whether Rafat Afraz was a Muslim or a Marxist resurfaces in two state-funded studies on the Mojahedin published in Tehran in 2006/2007 by the Political Studies and Research Institute (PSRI) and 2019 by the Islamic Revolution Documentation Centre (IRDC). Both works reconstruct the same narrative and use exactly the same sources, in more or less the same order.[59] First they bring up the matter of suspicious death and suicide. Rafat Afraz's early involvement in the Mojahedin is mentioned, followed by the argument that in the process of the organisation's

---

[57] While Verdery writes about elite dead bodies in the former Soviet Union and Eastern European context, I extend this thinking to the non-elite, subaltern figure; here, how state-funded institutions with political power produce narratives of the dead body.

[58] Verdery, *Political Lives*, 28–29.

[59] PSRI, *Sazman-e mojahedin-e khalq: peyda'i ta farjam (1344–1384)*, vol. 2 (Tehran: Moasese-ye motale'at va pajouheshha-ye siyasi [Political Studies and Research Institute], 1385/2006–7), 174–180; Ahmadreza Karimi, *Taqi Shahram: be ravayet-e asnad* [Taqi Shahram: according to the documents] (Tehran: Markaz-e Asnad-e Enqelab-e Eslami [Islamic Revolution Documentation Centre], 1398/2019), 165–171.

ideological split from Marxism, Rafat Afraz showed resistance.[60] According to the PSRI text, evidence from Marxist forces outside the country demonstrates her resistance during the ideological split, which resulted in her being sent to Dhufar under the pretence of joining the PFLO. No such evidence is cited. However, both studies cite an interrogation transcript of Mohammad Hassan Ebrari Jahromi (whom Rafat Afraz had married within the organisation), stating that Rafat, as a zealous Muslim, could not accept Marxism, and as the organisation could not influence her easily, they effectively sent her to Dhufar. The source cited is the SAVAK file on Jahromi, with no question as to the dubiousness of such a source, the nature and implications of an interrogation, or indeed the date of the interrogation. The PSRI has routinely used unreliable SAVAK material, often fabricated or otherwise gathered under torturous conditions, as objective historical evidence.

In addition, both texts cite the forced confessions of three former members of the Mojahedin – Fariborz Labafinejad, Sadegh Kordahmadi, and Zahra Najafi – which were publicly staged and broadcast in the media in 1977 to denounce their former 'terrorist' activities and seek repentance.[61] A headline on the front page of the daily newspaper, *Ettela'at*, read, 'The girl who criticised the group was sent to Dhufar and was killed there'.[62] In the published transcript of the confession, Labafinejad insinuated that like the violent killing of Majid Sharif-Vaghefi – the Mojahedin member who was murdered by the organisation for opposing the ideological change to Marxism – he knew of many others, such as 'the girl who was sent to Dhufar' for opposing the new aims of the organisation.[63] He stated that as her criticisms were dangerous for the organisation, the leadership decided to send her to Dhufar when the guerrillas there requested support. Realising that she did not have the necessary experience, the group had said 'even better!!', and two weeks later she was dead.[64] The confession, seemingly scripted, contradicts the timeline and notebooks of the sisters, as well as accounts from other revolutionaries Rafat crossed paths with in Dhufar and Aden.[65]

---

[60] PSRI, *Sazman-e mojahedin-e khalq*, 173; Ahmadreza Karimi, *Taqi Shahram*, 165.
[61] *Ettela'at*, 'Ma be dar o divar sho'ar-ha-ye zedd-e dowlati mineveshtim' [We would write anti-government slogans on the walls], 6 February 1977.
[62] *Ettela'at*, 6 February 1977, 18.
[63] Ibid.
[64] Ibid.
[65] Afraz and Afraz, *Hamrah*; see also Haghshenas, *Feyzieh*; Hasan Masali, *Negareshi be gozashteh va ayandeh: panjah sal-e mobarezeh dar rah-e azadi*, vol. 1 (Wiesbaden, 2013), 398; Shamkhi, *Hamrah ba enqelabiyun-e Zofar*.

The confession is again assumed to be a reliable source which implies that Rafat Afraz was, if not murdered by the organisation, likely sent to Dhufar for her Islamic criticism of the Marxist Mojahedin.[66]

In Rafat Afraz's notes, published in 2015, her handwriting was again reproduced as evidence, alongside two typed-out accounts from her note-book. In the first, her Marxist tendencies were evident in statements on the school textbooks used in Aden: 'The contents of the book are not indica-tive of Marxist revolutionary country and culture...'[67] In the second, she wrote about her encounter with a Marxist Fada'i comrade, Mohammad Ali Khosravi Ardebili, whom she had met in Dhufar before he died.[68] These accounts demonstrate her convictions at a particular moment prior to death, and connections to other Iranian Marxist groups in Dhufar. Yet, the 2015 memoir contains only two notebook accounts from her – curiously both concerning only the above-mentioned Marxist tendencies – as a supple-ment to the main body of text, which consists of the extensive writings of her sister Mahbubeh.

In November or December 1978, Mahbubeh Afraz died in Paris. After the Dhufar Revolution, she was in Aden working on the Mojahedin's radio broadcasts before moving to Paris. Her 1979 obituary published in *Peykar* stated that it had been read out from the radio station in Aden in November/December 1978.[69] Naghmeh Sohrabi has written about the competing Marxist/Islamist narratives concerning the death of Mahbubeh Afraz. Sohrabi contrasts the narrative of Mahbubeh Afraz's husband and former Marxist comrades – that she died by suicide – with the account by Marzieh Hadidchi, an Islamist revolutionary in Khomeini's circles, who speculated that she had been killed by the Marxist Mojahedin.[70] The PSRI and IRDC studies offer additional information on these narratives. Both refer to the same three perspectives on the suspicion around her death: 1) that of the third sister, Behjat Afraz, whose account contains the suspicion that the organisation Peykar killed her, while she was pregnant, after learning that she had attended a sermon by Khomeini in Paris and sought to talk to him; 2) that of her organisational husband (a practice of inter-organisational marriage) Mohammad Yazdanian who stated in his confessions that she

---

[66] PSRI, *Sazman-e mojahedin-e khalq*, 175; Ahmadreza Karimi, *Taqi Shahram*, 166.

[67] Afraz, *Hamrah*, 257–258.

[68] Afraz, *Hamrah*, 256.

[69] Peykar, no. 19, 3 September 1979.

[70] Sohrabi, 'Small Things'.

had committed suicide; and 3) that of Taqi Shahram, the member most associated with the Marxist Mojahedin, who claimed that she had been told to get an abortion by Yazdanian, and had instead committed suicide.[71] Both the PSRI and the IRDC texts are in agreement that it is most likely that Mahbubeh Afraz committed suicide because of mental illness and problems with her partner – which the recollections of Torab Haghshenas, her Marxist comrade, also indicate.[72]

With Mahbubeh Afraz's notebooks, there is no doubt about her Marxist convictions, but without a coroner's report the exact cause of her death remains unknown, though it seems unlikely that her own organisation killed her. Whether Rafat Afraz was a Muslim, a Marxist, or likely both, remains more open to interpretation. It is significant, as Naghmeh Sohrabi writes, that Rafat Afraz's body lies somewhere on the border between Yemen and Oman, materially reflecting an important moment of connection in the twentieth-century history of revolutions.[73] Crucially, an underlying thread of anti-communism and anti-guerrilla counter-insurgency has informed both the Pahlavi regime's and the Islamic Republic of Iran's preferred narratives about her life, and about the Mojahedin, to delegitimise their political opponents. Four decades on from the death of these sisters, their complicated revolutionary paths, identities, and activities continue to unsettle and provoke claims to singular, authoritative narratives.

CONCLUSION

This chapter was primarily concerned with the gendered revolutionary politics of Third Worldist movements in the Middle East. The revolutionary obituary was an important form of material culture that had currency and meaning in the era of national liberation and decolonisation. Its movement across Iranian and Arab publications, through Persian and Arabic archives, shows that the obituary was a transnational object that revealed the networks of Iranians fighting in the Middle East. For clandestine Iranian

---

[71] PSRI, *Sazman-e mojahedin-e khalq*, 178–179; Ahmadreza Karimi, *Taqi Shahram*, 167–169; Behjat Afraz supported the Islamic Republic of Iran and is known for her work with prisoners of war during the Iran–Iraq War. She died in 2019. See Behjat Afraz, *Khaterat-e khanum Behjat Afraz* [Memoirs of Behjat Afraz] (Tehran: Islamic Revolution Documentation Centre, 2008/9).

[72] Haghshenas, *Hamrah*, 7–8; Haghshenas, *Peykar*, 790–791.

[73] Sohrabi, 'Small Things'.

organisations, the obituary was not only important in making information about dead members public for the first time, but it was also the only form of commemoration possible given the political conditions of being underground. Methodologically then, the obituary is an important historical source, albeit with limits.

A critical reading shows how the obituary constructed gendered imagery and narratives, and how the woman's body was a site of political contestation. I have closely traced the obituary of Rafat Afraz to explore questions of gender and revolution. The narrative first produced in the construction of a heroic image after her death, the circulation of this image in different periodicals across languages and across borders, and its reception in student networks, reveals the workings of masculinity and femininity in the construction of the iconic image of the revolutionary woman of the 1960s and 1970s. The imagery produced in the obituary subsumed her gendered revolutionary practice as a nurse, presenting her as an equal combatant and, disregarding the gendered division of labour, valorising the hypermasculine discourse of armed struggle. Yet, the care work of the nurse was as revolutionary as armed combat, without which the revolution would not have been sustained.

The example of Rafat Afraz's first obituary, which was subsequently reproduced, had currency in Marxist circles for its projection and ideals of the leftist revolutionary woman. This case is uniquely interesting given that Rafat and Mahbubeh Afraz were part of the Mojahedin, a revolutionary organisation that bridged both Marxism and Islamism. The sisters appear to have been part of the Marxist faction, which split from the Mojahedin in 1975. In the tense factional climate following the split, the dead body became a site and target of political contestation, with both the Marxist and Islamist factions projecting claims onto Rafat Afraz's body. Further research should look at the ideals and images constructed around Islamist women martyrs in comparison to those of leftist women.

Through the examples of Rafat Afraz, and by extension the death of Mahbubeh Afraz, women's dead bodies have been used by political groupings and indeed the state to construct authoritative historical truths, based on singular political narratives that flatten the complexities of these women and their political identities and activities. At the same time, the practices and collective memory of repressed political organisations cannot be equated with the outputs of state-funded studies aimed at delegitimising the former. The sisters' examples additionally show that in contrast to the complicated figure of the revolutionary militant woman which was once part of the repertoire of global 1960s iconography with universal meaning and claims,[74] the figure of the contested revolutionary woman in the aftermath of 1979 in Iran became constricted within an Islamist frame, foreclosing the once internationalist, Marxist universe of the revolutionary Third World.

---

[74] Gordon, 'Guerrilla Girls'.

I would like to thank Toufoul Abou-Hodeib, Maryam Alemzadeh, Sune Haugbolle, Siavush Randjbar-Daemi, Sara Salem, Sorcha Thomson, and especially Rasmus Christian Elling for their helpful feedback and/or comments on earlier drafts of this chapter. I am grateful to the workshop participants for also engaging with this work.

5

BROTHERS, COMRADES, AND THE QUEST FOR THE ISLAMIST INTERNATIONAL

The First Gathering of Liberation Movements in Revolutionary Iran

Mohammad Ataie

In January 1980, a few weeks into the seizure of the US embassy in Tehran, activists from liberation movements across the world convened in Tehran. The students who had stormed the US embassy compound in Tehran, known as the Muslim Student Followers of Imam's Line, organised the so-called 'Gathering of International Liberation Movements' to flaunt transnational solidarity around the embassy occupation and condemn the role of the US in Iran.[1] 'Given the international propaganda against the students ... we wanted to influence the international public opinion and forge bonds with the revolutionary forces', recalls Mohsen Mirdamadi, a leading member of the Imam's Line Students.[2] The gathering marked the first convention of liberation movements in revolutionary Iran, signalling to the world the revolution's turn away from what could be called the Iran-first stance of the interim government under Prime Minister Mehdi Bazargan, towards 'revolution export' (*sodur-e enqelab*). Bazargan, who pursued a strictly

---

[1] *Gerdehama'i-ye jonbesh-ha-ye azadibaksh.*
[2] Mohsen Mirdamadi, author's interview (Tehran, Iran, 12 May 2019).

Iran-focused foreign policy and rejected hosting liberation movements in Iran, had just resigned in protest against the embassy occupation in November 1979. The internationalists, who had clashed with Bazargan over the question of 'revolution export', played a central role in organising the conference. Mohammad Montazeri, a cleric and leading advocate of an Islamist international, who during exile in the 1970s had built a transnational network, was key in bringing delegations to Tehran.[3] 'We helped with invitations from Lebanon, Eritrea, Egypt, and so on,' recounts an associate of Montazeri. 'We had made these links from Lebanon and through Fatah. Some [of the invitees] also were Mohammad [Montazeri's] and Abu Sharif's friends from Europe.'[4]

A few weeks earlier, before the Gathering of International Liberation Movements, Montazeri had attended the 'Conference in Solidarity with the Arab People and Their Central Issue, Palestine' in the Portuguese capital, Lisbon.[5] This turned out to be an opportunity to discuss the idea of gathering the leaders of liberation movements in Tehran. Around seven hundred delegates from more than one hundred countries participated in the Lisbon Conference, which coincided with the seizure of the US embassy in Tehran.[6] In his remarks at the event, Montazeri declared Iran's solidarity with liberation movements across the globe and spoke about developments in Iran. Many international activists told him that they were eager to visit Khomeini and even suggested that Tehran should host the next 'Conference in Solidarity with the Arab People'.[7] Upon his return to Iran, Montazeri wrote a letter to Ayatollah Khomeini and proposed inviting 'Muslim and non-Muslim scholars to Iran for solidarity, intellectual collaboration, and co-operation'. He urged Khomeini to take practical steps for 'consolidating

---

[3] Montazeri had forged a diverse range of relationships and connections to Third Worldist movements, liberation fighters, and clerics with the PLO and the pro-al-Shirazi Message Movement at the core of this network.

[4] Anonymous, author's interview by Skype (Madison, US – Dubai, UAE, 12 May 2018). Abu Sharif was the sobriquet of Abbas Aqa-Zamani, from the time when he resided in Bourj al-Barajneh camp in the southern suburbs of Beirut between 1970 and 1979. After 1979, Aqa-Zamani became a co-founder and commander of the IRGC.

[5] *Enqelab-e Eslami*, 14 Aban 1358/7 November 1979. Montazeri attended the 2–6 November conference with five Iranian associates.

[6] 'World conference in solidarity with Arab People – Lisbon Declaration, Letter from Lebanon', 28 November 1979, https://www.un.org/unispal/document/auto-insert-189811/.

[7] See Montazeri's letter to Khomeini in Anonymous, *Farzand-e eslam va qor'an* [The Scion of Islam and Quran], vol. 1 (Tehran: Vahed-e Farhangi-ye Bonyad-e Shahid, 1362/1983), 306 and 312.

the downtrodden front' and suggested convening international conferences in Tehran with the participation of 'the liberation movements from Asia, Africa, Latin America, and the Native Americans and Black Americans in the United States'.[8]

Mohammad Montazeri's ID badge from the Lisbon conference
(source: private collection).

Back in Tehran, when Iranian students expressed their interest in holding such a gathering, Montazeri contacted the activists he had met in Lisbon to invite them to the conference.[9] He also talked to the Palestinian ambassador, Hani al-Hassan, and the Libyan envoy, Sa'ad Mujbir, about bringing in liberation movements and arranged for the invitation of a number of delegates, including the leftist Revolutionary Option in Morocco, the Popular Front for the Liberation of Oman, and the Eritrean Liberation Front.[10]

By focusing on this gathering, its global make-up, and the debates and controversies among its participants, the present study seeks to show how pro-Khomeini revolutionaries had been inspired and influenced by the circulation of transnational ideas and people of the 1970s. It sheds light on the importance of the transnational networks and relationships that pro-Khomeini revolutionaries had forged before 1979, primarily with the Palestinian Fatah and the clerical network of Al-Harika al-Risaliyya (henceforth the Message Movement), in order to organise the conference

---

[8] Anonymous, *Farzand-e eslam va qor'an*, vol. 1, 307–308.
[9] Anonymous, *Farzand-e eslam va qor'an*, vol. 1, 285.
[10] Al-Ikhtiyar al-Thuri fi al-Maghrib, al-Jabha al-Sha'biya li-Tahrir 'Uman, and Jabhat al-Tahrir al-Iritria. Anonymous, author's interview by Skype (Madison, US – Dubai, UAE, 12 May 2018).

*Poster advertising the gathering (source: Middle Eastern Posters
Collection, Box 2, Poster 49, Hanna Holborn Gray Special
Collections Research Center, University of Chicago Library).*

and export the revolution.[11] This chapter asks why the issue of 'West and
East imperialism' and inter-Arab politics became divisive in the conference, foreshadowing future tensions between Tehran and an array of Third
Worldist and Islamist movements that were not in line with the global
ambitions of Khomeini's Iran.[12] Why did Khomeini's Iran and left-wing anti-

---

[11] Al-Harika al-Risaliyya, also known as the Messengers' Vanguard (Harika al-Tala'i'
al-Risaliyyin) was established in Karbala in the second half of the 1960s and became an
influential transnational Shi'i movement after the 1978–1979 revolution. It was also known
as the Marja'iyya Movement. See Laurence Louër, *Transnational Shia Politics: Religious and
Political Networks in the Gulf* (New York, NY: Columbia University Press, 2008), 88–99.
[12] I use the term 'Islamist' in reference to those who 'attempt to articulate a political
order based around Islam', without the intention to ignore their ideological and political
diversity. This definition is informed by Peter G. Mandaville, *Transnational Muslim
Politics: Reimagining the Umma* (London: Routledge, 2003), 55.

imperialist movements, especially the PLO, begin to diverge immediately after the victory of the revolution? How did the disputes among delegates over Shiʿi Amal's position in Lebanon serve as a signal of coming tensions in Khomeini's relationship with a range of Shiʿi and Sunni movements and clerics across the region? How did Khomeini's Iran come to respond to momentous questions that divided the conference over the pan-Islamist, Third Worldist, pro-Soviet, and pan-Arab leanings of the participants? By answering these questions, the present study shows that what transpired in the conference informed and influenced the course of Khomeini's Iran's solidarity with Palestine – and the Islamic Republic's relationship with left-wing and Islamist liberation movements. The chapter furthermore offers insight into the decline in Third World solidarity since the mid-1970s and the transformation of the Third Worldist revolutionary project from leftist liberation to Islamism.[13]

SOLIDARITY GATHERING OF BROTHERS AND COMRADES IN TEHRAN

On 3 January 1980, as the revolution was nearing its first anniversary, the Gathering of International Liberation Movements kicked off at Hotel Qods in Tehran.[14] It was a fraught time, with the revolution fractured from within and with spiking tensions with the United States and the Soviet Union.[15] In December 1979, the Soviet army had launched an invasion of Afghanistan.

---

[13] See Paul Thomas Chamberlin, 'The PLO and the Limits of Secular Revolution, 1975–1982', in *The Tricontinental Revolution: Third World Radicalism and the Cold War*, eds R. Joseph Parrott and Mark Atwood Lawrence (Cambridge: Cambridge University Press, 2022), 101–102. This chapter seeks to contribute to the scholarship on the shift from secular Third Worldism to Islamism. See Raphaël Lefèvre, *Jihad in the City: Militant Islam and Contentious Politics in Tripoli* (Cambridge: Cambridge University Press, 2021); Manfred Sing, 'Brothers in Arms: How Palestinian Maoists Turned Jihadists', *Die Welt des Islams* 51, no. 1 (2011): 1–44; Timothy Nunan, '"Neither East Nor West," Neither Liberal Nor Illiberal? Iranian Islamist Internationalism in the 1980s', *Journal of World History* 31, no. 1 (2020): 43–77.

[14] *Payam-e enqelab*, no. 2, 2 Esfand 1358/21 February 1980, 12.

[15] Although Iranian guerrilla groups, such as the *Sazman-e cherik-ha-ye fadaʾi-ye khalq* and the *Sazman-e mojahedin-e khalq-e Iran*, had strong ties with the PLO and Fatah, they were not extended an invitation to the gathering. This reveals a widening rift between pro-Khomeini revolutionaries and these left-wing movements after 1979. See Seyyed Ali Alavi, *Iran and Palestine: Past, Present, Future* (London: Routledge, 2019), 9–20. See also Elling and Mahmoudi's chapter in this volume.

Earlier, in November 1979, the occupation of the Grand Mosque of Mecca and the eruption of popular uprisings against Al Saud seemed to foreshadow a coming Islamic revolution on the Arabian Peninsula. In Iraq, Saddam Hussein had elevated himself to president in July 1979 and was intent on wiping out clerical activism and crushing mass protests that had been flaring up across the country since the victory of the revolution in Iran. Similarly, Syria was in the grip of growing popular dissent against Assad and a militant campaign by the Muslim Brotherhood, who aspired to an Islamic revolution akin to the one Khomeini had led against the Shah. Lebanon, still in shock from political and religious leader Seyyed Musa al-Sadr's disappearance in September 1978, saw clashes between the Syria-backed Amal Movement and the PLO and its leftist allies in the south of the country and in Beirut. Meanwhile, following the 1978 Camp David Accords, Sadat's Egypt was slipping further away from a Soviet embrace. These crucial events in 1979, with the 1978–1979 revolution at their heart, ushered in a new era in the Middle East.[16] The year 1979 marked the end of the heyday of Marxist liberation movements in the world, pivoting the locus of revolutionary power from Third Worldism to Islamist transnationalism.[17] It also marked a confounding turn for the PLO and liberation movements that had thrived in the era of secular and left-wing transnationalism.[18] They came to Tehran with the hope of solidarity against US imperialism and the Israeli occupation. By contrast, for their Iranian hosts, the gathering was a response to a global counter-revolution, led by both Eastern (Soviet) and Western imperialism. The Soviet invasion of Afghanistan reinforced their perception that both East and West imperialists sought to surround and confine the Islamic Revolution within the borders of Iran. 'We would perish if we did not act the same way that imperialism functions across the globe,' proclaimed Mohammad Montazeri.[19] Solidarity and co-operation with anti-colonial and anti-imperial movements and activists across the Global South was central to this vision of transnationalism that sought to counter both US and Soviet imperialism.[20] The week-long conference signalled this global

---

[16] On the year 1979 as a main watershed in modern Middle East history, see David W. Lesch, *1979: The Year That Shaped the Modern Middle East* (Boulder, CO: Westview Press, 2001).

[17] On the shift from left-wing radicals to religious leaders after 1979, see Chamberlin, 'The PLO and the Limits of Secular Revolution', 100.

[18] See Sune Haugbolle's chapter in this volume.

[19] *Payam-e enqelab*, no. 27, 9 Esfand 1359/28 February 1981, 43.

[20] Anonymous, author's interview (Tehran, Iran, 26 October 2016).

aspiration as an occasion for creating a united front of the downtrodden, exchanging ideas, and sharing experience among the liberation movements.[21]

The organisers sent invitations to fifteen groups that all had Marxist leanings (with the exception of the Movement of the Deprived, which represented the Shi'i community in Lebanon).[22] Several Islamic groups and activists from Afghanistan, Iraq, and Saudi Arabia, who had not been initially among the invitees, were later added to the list.[23] Outwardly, the organisers were hosting groups which were, according to one of the students, 'anti-imperialist, popular (*mardomi*), and independent from world powers'.[24] But in fact, some of these movements, like the Polisario Front or the Palestinian Fatah, had strong ties with the Eastern Bloc.

At the conference, the delegates were seated below large photos of the leaders of the revolution: Ali Shari'ati, Ayatollah Khomeini, Ayatollah Taleqani, and Ayatollah Montazeri. Palestinians, in fact Arafat's men, had a prominent presence in the conference. The organisers put Khalil al-Wazir, known as Abu Jihad, in charge of managing the meetings. Flanked by Seyyed Mohammad Musavi-Kho'einiha, the leader of the radical students occupying the US embassy, and Abbas Aqa-Zamani, who had worked with the PLO in Lebanon and Syria, Abu Jihad opened his speech by praising the organisers and describing the gathering as an important opportunity to network with liberation movements.[25]

Both Khomeini and Montazeri sent messages to the conference. This was a rare consensus on backing for liberation movements between Montazeri, a fierce internationalist, and Khomeini who, throughout the 1980s, would demonstrate far less enthusiasm for revolution export. The latter's message consisted of general praise for the liberation movements, urging the downtrodden across the globe to end the 'sinful' tolerance of suppression and revolt against their rulers.[26] Ayatollah Montazeri sent a longer message,

---

[21] *Sobh-e Azadegan*, 16 Dey 1358/6 January 1980.
[22] Harikat al-Mahrumin, established by Seyyed Musa al-Sadr in 1974. The Marxist-leaning movements were the PLO, the Eritrean Liberation Front, the Popular Front for the Liberation of Oman, the Movement of the Canary Islands, the Movement of Uruguay, the Salvadoran Movement, the Montoneros, Revolutionary Option in Morocco, and the American Indian Movement.
[23] Daneshjuyan-e Mosalman-e Payrow-e Khatt-e Emam, *Nokhostin gerdehama'i-ye jonbesh-ha-ye azadibakhsh dar jomhuri-ye eslami-ye Iran* [The First Gathering of Liberation Movements in the Islamic Republic of Iran] (n.p., n.d.), 6–9.
[24] *Sobh-e Azadegan*, 10 Dey 1358/31 December 1979.
[25] *Ettela'at*, 20 Dey 1358/10 January 1980.
[26] *Sobh-e Azadegan*, 16 Dey 1358/6 January 1980.

which displayed a heartfelt and keen interest in the gathering, describing liberation movements as 'the vanguard and strong arms of downtrodden nations'.[27] He pledged to the participants that if they relied on God and the power of the masses, 'our clamorous revolution is ready to share all its experiences and achievements with you'.[28] Striking a similar note, the message of the Muslim Student Followers of the Imam's Line to the conference emphasised the role of *ulama* in the victory of the Islamic Revolution, which had its roots in the Tobacco protest movement against British colonialism and Mohammad Mosaddeq's 'national revolution'. The Islamic Revolution, the students' message added, succeeded under the leadership of the 'progressive clergy' and through the unification of the religious and political leadership.[29]

In addition to the Palestinians and the Lebanese, the meeting in Tehran brought together activists from Afghanistan, Bahrain, Iraq, Oman, and Saudi Arabia. The Moro National Liberation Front, which struggled for the independence of Muslim Bangsamoro natives in the southern Philippines, also attended.[30] It seems that Libyans initially facilitated the internationalists' contact with the Front, as its leader Nur Misuari was in touch with Mohammad Montazeri during the revolutionary upheavals in Iran.[31]

From the Americas, several activists were present whose name plates read: the Movement of Uruguay, the Salvadoran Movement, and the Montoneros, a left-wing Peronist guerrilla group in Argentina.[32] From the United States, John Thomas and Russell C. Means, both leading figures in the American

---

[27] *Sobh-e Azadegan*, 22 Dey 1358/12 January 1980; Mustafa Izadi, *Gozari bar zendegi-ye faqih-e 'aliqadr Ayatollah Montazeri* [Ayatollah Montazeri: A Review of the Life of the Distinguished *Faqih*] (Tehran: Sorush, 1362/1983), 361.

[28] *Sobh-e Azadegan*, 22 Dey 1358/12 January 1980; Izadi, *Gozari bar zendegi-ye faqih-e 'aliqadr*, 361.

[29] Daneshjuyan-e Mosalman, *Nokhostin gerdehama'i-ye*, 18–19.

[30] *Enqelab-e Eslami*, 10 Dey 1358/31 December 1979.

[31] Anonymous, *Farzand-e eslam va qor'an* [The Scion of Islam and Quran], vol. 2 (Tehran: Vahed-e Farhangi-ye Bonyad-e Shahid, 1362/1983), 921. In his speech at the June 1982 Liberation Movements Conference in Tehran, Nur Misuari stated that Mohammad Montazeri was the link between his movement and Iran. See Vahed-e nehzat-ha-ye azadibakhsh-e eslam-e Sepah-e Pasdaran, *Nehzat-ha-ye azadibakhsh dar gozargah-e enqelab-e eslami* [Liberation Movements at the Crossing of the Islamic Revolution] (Tehran: Chapkhaneh-ye daftar-e entesharat-e sazman-e enerzhi-ye atomi-ye Iran, 1361/1982), 127.

[32] Movimiento Peronista Montonero.

Indian Movement, represented Native Americans at the event.[33] While in Tehran, Thomas and Means managed to visit the US embassy. There, Thomas told a crowd of reporters and people that 'I stand here as evidence of the oppression, injustice, and genocide ... of the United States against my people.'[34] They also met the hostage American diplomats who asked them to hand-carry letters to their families back in the United States.[35]

Abu Jihad, Seyyed Ali Khamenei, and the Libyan envoy, Sa'ad Mujbir, at the gathering (source: Danishjuyan-e Musalman-e Payruv-e Khat-e Imam, Nukhustin Girdihamai-ye).

From Africa, the Eritrean Liberation Front, which had waged a war of independence against Ethiopia since 1961, was invited to the gathering. The initial contacts between the Front leadership, including Ahmad Mohammad Naser, and the anti-Shah opposition took place at Palestinian refugee camps

---

[33] John Thomas and Russell C. Means were both Indigenous Oklahomans. Thomas represented an international Indigenous organisation connected to the American Indian Movement (AIM), famous for its occupation of a federal building in Washington DC. Means, who was an outspoken Indian rights activist founded AIM in 1968 and was the organiser of numerous protests against the US government's treatment of Native Americans. John T. Truden, '"You're in apple land but you are a lemon": Connection, Collaboration, and Division in Early '70s Indian Country', *Online Journal of Rural Research & Policy* 15, no. 3 (2020).

[34] Truden, '"You're in apple land but you are a lemon"'.

[35] John K. Cooley, 'American Indian brings message: "No Shah, no hostages"', *The Christian Science Monitor*, 21 January 1980, https://www.csmonitor.com/1980/0121/012160.html.

in Syria and Lebanon, where they all gathered for guerrilla training.[36] Other Front members, such as Isma'il 'Ali Ahmad, had cultivated a relationship with Mohammad Montazeri in Europe and discussed possible ways of co-operating.[37] The Iranian internationalists and the Eritrean activists became so close that in July 1977 the Front's representatives attended the fortieth-day memorial ceremony of Ali Shari'ati in Beirut.[38] The conference saw the participation of representatives from other African movements, including the Movement of the Canary Islands (MPAIAC), advocating for independence from Spain, the Popular Democratic Front in Egypt, the Polisario Front fighting for the rights of the indigenous people of Western Sahara, and the Revolutionary Option in Morocco.[39] The representatives of the Revolutionary Option – followers of Mahdi Bin Barka, the disappeared opponent of King Hassan II – met Mohammad Montazeri during the Solidarity Conference in Lisbon, expressing interest in co-operation with the Islamic Revolution.[40] In Tehran they declared that 'the only genuine popular opposition' to King Hassan II is the Islamic Movement in Morocco, and added that because of the Islamic Revolution in Iran, the Islamists had gained widespread popularity in Morocco, especially among students, artisans, and intellectuals.[41] Similarly, the Polisario Front struggled against King Hassan II. But during the gathering of liberation movements, disagreement surfaced between the

---

[36] John Markakis, *National and class conflict in the Horn of Africa* (Cambridge: Cambridge University Press, 1987), 139.

[37] 'Mosahebeh ba Esm'ail 'Ali Ahmad az enqelab-e eslami-ye Eritriyeh: Navar-e mizegerd-e nehzat-ha-ye azadibaksh, bashgah-e sherkat-e naft, navar-e 1 va 2' [Interview with Ism'ail 'Ali Ahmad from the Eritrean Islamic Revolution, the cassette of The Liberation Movements' Roundtable, Oil Company Club, Cassettes 1 and 2], audio recording from private collection, Isfahan, 8 Tir 1364/29 June 1985 (Qom, Iran).

[38] 'Bozorgdashte-e doktur 'Ali Shari'ati dar Bayrut: Chehelomin ruz-e dar-gozasht' [Commemorating Dr Ali Shari'ati in Beirut: The Fortieth Day], from: http://40.drshariati.org.

[39] Polisario stands for the Popular Front for the Liberation of Saguia el-Hamra and Río de Oro.

[40] *Payam-e Shahid*, no. 8, 20 Mordad 1358/11 August 1979.

[41] *Al-Shahid*, no. 47, 10 January 1980. After the death of Mohammad Montazeri in 1981, the Moroccan opposition maintained ties with Seyyed Mehdi Hashemi. For example, he invited a delegation of Moroccan Islamists, headed by a certain man called Faqih, to a gathering in Isfahan to celebrate the birthday of the Shi'i Twelfth Imam and the Global Day of the Downtrodden. Seyyid Mehdi Hashemi, 'Tavallod-e emam-e zaman' [The Birthday of Imam of the Age], audio recording from private collection, Isfahan, n.d. (Qom, Iran).

two groups as the Moroccan opposition was outspoken against Polisario's struggle for the independence of Western Sahara.[42]

Among the delegates in the room, the ones that captured everyone's attention were the Saudi opposition members, sitting with thick black sunglasses and their faces shrouded by chequered kaffiyehs to hide their identity from the Saudi authorities back home. They were members of the Islamic Revolutionary Organisation of the Arabian Peninsula, a branch of the Message Movement. This transnational movement had its origin in Karbala under the leadership of Seyyed Mohammad Taqi al-Mudarrisi and Seyyed Hadi al-Mudarrisi.[43] Addressing the conference, the representative of the organisation spoke about Al Saud's violent crackdown on recent mass protests in the Kingdom and called for an Islamic revolution in the Arabian Peninsula.

The conference took place around the same time that two major events in Saudi Arabia shook the Kingdom to its core: the occupation of the Grand Mosque of Mecca, the most sacred site in Islam, by a Salafist-millenarian group of armed men on 20 November 1979;[44] and, five days later, the eruption of popular uprisings in the Eastern Province, which came to be known as the Muharram Uprising. These two events were not linked, except that their timing was right in the middle of dramatic developments in Iran.[45]

---

[42] *Al-Shahid*, no. 48, 10 September 1980. With revolutionary Iran's intention to roll back the Shah's close friendship with King Hassan II and the Pahlavis' recognition of Rabat's claim over Western Sahara, in February 1980 Tehran officially recognised Polisario and elevated the front's liaison office to the Embassy of the Democratic Republic of Western Sahara. IRGC's mouthpiece praised the move, describing it as 'expanding ties with the oppressed masses'. *Payam-e Enqelab*, no. 10, 8 Tir 1359/29 June 1980, 11.

[43] Munazama al-Thawra al-Islamiyya fi al-Jazira al-'Arabiyya. The al-Mudarrisis became friendly with Mohammad Montazeri during his exile years in Iraq, Kuwait, and Bahrain. The spiritual leader of the movement was Ayatollah Seyyed Mohammad Shirazi, who had a noticeable following in Iraq and the Persian Gulf region. See Toby Matthiesen, *The Other Saudis: Shiism, Dissent and Sectarianism* (New York, NY: Cambridge University Press, 2014), 91–104; Louër, *Transnational Shi'a Politics*, 88–99.

[44] A group of approximately three hundred armed insurrectionists led by Juhayman al-Utaybi stormed and seized control of the Grand Mosque. These 'rejectionist Islamists' questioned the Islamic credentials of the ruling family and its ties with the West. See Pascal Menoret, 'Fighting for the Holy Mosque: The 1979 Mecca Insurgency', in *Treading on Hallowed Ground: Counterinsurgency Operations in Sacred Spaces*, eds C. Christine Fair and Sumit Ganguly (Oxford: Oxford University Press, 2008); Thomas Hegghammer and Stephane Lacroix, 'Rejectionist Islamism in Saudi Arabia: The Story of Juhayman al-Utaybi Revisited', *International Journal of Middle East Studies* 39 (2007): 117.

[45] See Matthiesen, *The Other Saudis*, 103; Bernard Haykel, Thomas Hegghammer, Stephane Lacroix (eds), *Saudi Arabia in Transition: Insights on Social, Political, Economic and Religious Change* (New York, NY: Cambridge University Press, 2015), 112.

While the Message Movement praised the occupation of the Grand Mosque as the 'Sanctuary Revolution' (*Thawrat al-Haram*) and sought to co-opt the event as part of an Islamic awakening in the Arabian Peninsula against the Al Saud and its American patron, they did play a central role in the uprising in the Eastern Province.[46] On 26 November, in the midst of the shocking turmoil in Mecca, thousands took to the streets of Qatif and other cities and towns in the predominantly Shi'ite-populated Eastern Province, the heart of the Kingdom's oil production, to protest the government's discrimination and show support for the revolution in Iran. Women and men, some of whom raised pictures of Khomeini, marched in the streets of Qatif, al-'Awamiyya, and other towns and villages of the Eastern Province chanting 'O Hossein, your revolution is a guide for the world' and 'Neither Sunni nor Shi'ite; revolution, the Islamic revolution'.[47] The protestors also shouted anti-US slogans in sympathy with the seizure of the US embassy in Tehran, demanding the boycott of oil sales to the United States, much of which was supplied from nearby oil fields.[48] In the ensuing bloody crackdown, many of the agitators and activists as well as ordinary people were arrested and jailed by the Saudi security forces or went into hiding. Others, such as Sheikh Hasan al-Safar, Tofiq al-Sayf, and Baqir al-Nimir fled the Kingdom and took refuge in Iran.[49] Indeed, al-Safar and al-Sayf were among the invitees to the gathering of the liberation movements in Tehran.[50] At the conference, al-Sayf, whose face was shrouded by a kaffiyeh, accused the Al Saud of serving US interests.[51] When the international delegations travelled to Mashhad, a holy city in north-east Iran, the Message Movement activists covered the walls in the neighbourhoods surrounding the Shrine of Imam Reza with posters that showed the al-Aqsa Mosque in Jerusalem and the

---

[46] For example, see *al-Shahid*, no. 52, 22 December 1980, 26; *al-Thura al-Islamiyya*, no 39, Shawal 1403/July–August 1983.

[47] 'Adil al-Labad, *Al-Inqilab: Bai' al-Wahm 'ala al-Dhat* [The Revolution: The Selling of the Illusion to the Self] (Beirut: Dar al-jamal lil-tab'a wa al-nashr, 1430/2009), 36.

[48] Hassan Mousa al-Saffar, *Al-Madhab wa al-Watan* [Religion and Homeland] (Beirut: al-Mouasisa al-'arabiyya lil-dirasat, 2006), 178–179; Badr al-Ibrahim and Muhammad al-Sadiq, *al-Hirak al-Shi'i fi al-Saudiyya: Tasyis al-Madhab wa-Madhhabat al-Siyasa* [Shi'i Movement in Saudi Arabia: The Politicisation of Sect and the Sectarianisation of Politics] (Beirut: al-Shabaka al-'Arabiyya li-l-Abhath wa-l-Nashr, 2013), 104.

[49] Louër, *Transnational Shi'a Politics*, 161.

[50] Sadiq al-Ibadi, author's interview (Tehran, Iran, 12 October 2019).

[51] Daneshjuyan-e mosalman, *Nokhostin gerdehama'i-ye*, 52–53.

Kaaba in Mecca locked in chains. The posters read 'The emancipation for the two *qiblas* of Muslims'.[52]

This panoply of revolutionaries, liberation movements, clerics, activists, and fighters from Asia, Africa, and Latin America thus convened at the conference to demonstrate transnational solidarity with the revolution in Iran and work towards a united front of the downtrodden from all corners of the globe. However, the occasion took a contentious turn over diverging anti-imperialist visions of the pro-Soviet participants and Islamist delegates and over inter-Arab politics and the Lebanese civil war.

CONFLICTING ANTI-IMPERIALIST VISIONS

The first conference of liberation movements does not stand out merely for inaugurating similar future gatherings in Khomeini's Iran.[53] While drawing on Third Worldist, leftist, and Islamist solidarity networks and connections of the global 1970s, the resources, logistical help, and presence of which were crucial in putting together the conference, it also became an early site of tensions between the anti-imperialist visions of Islamist participants and delegates with a pro-Soviet position. Hence, while the conference was inspired by the capture of the US embassy and aimed at showcasing the US 'crimes' in Iran, serious disagreements began to surface among these participants over the Soviet invasion of Afghanistan.

Some of the invited Third Worldist movements, like the Palestinian Fatah, had strong ties with the Eastern Bloc. The only imperialist, in their eyes, was the United States. 'We gathered here with other combatants,

---

[52] Vahid Muzhdeh, author's interview (Kabul, Afghanistan, 24 October 2008). According to Muzhdeh, an Afghan author and journalist who was present in the gathering of the liberation movements in Mashhad, the participants also visited the shrine of Imam Reza and attended the Friday Prayer there. Some conservative visitors at the shrine were angry that non-Muslims were allowed to hear the sermon.

[53] A few examples are the August 1980 'Congress for the Emancipation of Jerusalem' (Kongereh-ye azadi-ye Quds), the June 1982 'Conference of Liberation Movements' in Tehran; the June 1985 'Meeting of Liberation Movements' in Isfahan (Neshast-e nehzat-ha-ye azadibaksh, bashgah-e sherkat-e naft); the 1978 'Conference of the Liberation movements and Hezbollah Cells in the Islamic world' (Mu'tamar Harikat al-Taharur wa Khalaya Hizbullah) and a series of conferences and seminars under the title of 'Islamic Thoughts' (*Konferans-e andisheh-ha-ye eslami/Mu'tamar al-Fikr al-Islami*) and the 'Global Assembly of 'Ulama' and Friday Prayer Leaders' (*Kongereh-ye jahani-ye a'emeh-ye jome'eh va jama'at/Al-Mu'tamar al-'Alami li-A'imat al-Jum'a wa-l-Jama'at*).

the tortured, and free people of the world to tell the Islamic Revolution of Iran that we are in your fight against American imperialism,' proclaimed the Fatah representative on behalf of the PLO at the conference.[54] This position sparked an argument with Afghani and Eritrean participants, who were locked in a bitter confrontation with the Soviet Union: the former at war with the advancing Soviet army in Afghanistan and the latter in the throes of its war of independence against Soviet-backed Ethiopia.[55] One Afghan representative criticised anyone leaning on *either* superpower for the purpose of a liberation struggle, stating that 'the Soviet Union and its mercenaries have committed in Afghanistan the same atrocities the US and its mercenaries [have done] in Iran and Palestine.'[56]

In the days leading up to the gathering, Soviet troops had mounted an invasion of Afghanistan. This lent irony to an anti-US imperialism conference that was supposed to take place in the shadow of the US embassy siege. In their remarks, Afghan Mujahedeen delegates called for a clear condemnation of the Soviet Union, whose tanks had just rolled into Kabul in December 1979. However, delegations with strong ties to Moscow did not want to put the Soviet Union on a par with the United States. This created an awkward situation when Fatah, the Popular Front for the Liberation of Oman (PFLO), and the Polisario Front baulked at condemning the Soviet invasion of Afghanistan. Fighting two enemies, the Marxist Omani delegate averred, would not be wise. Referring to the PFLO's war against Sultan Qaboos Bin Saʻid, the ruler of Oman, the delegate added that the struggle against US imperialism was already too much of a burden for the movement.[57] Pro-Soviet delegates even attempted to dissuade the representative of the Islamic Movement of Afghanistan from speaking about the Soviet invasion.[58]

Indeed, Fatah clearly valued its relationship with the Soviet Union. Palestinians feared that tensions between the Soviets and the Iranians would embroil the PLO in yet another international dilemma, namely, choosing between two friends. They insisted that Moscow and Tehran hammer out their differences since, according to the PLO ambassador Hani al-Hasan, 'friction between Iran and the Soviet Union won't be in the

---

[54] Danishjuyan-e Musalman, *Nukhustin Girdihamai-ye*, 23.
[55] *Sobh-e Azadegan*, 10 Dey 1358/31 December 1979.
[56] Danishjuyan-e Musalman, *Nukhustin Girdihamai-ye*, 33.
[57] *Al-Shahid*, no. 33, 16 January 1980.
[58] *Al-Shahid*, no. 33, 16 January 1980.

interest of the Palestinian cause'.[59] During the conference, Fatah, PFLO, and the Polisario Front pushed back against any suggestion to mention the Soviet Union's imperialism and its invasion of Afghanistan in the final statement. In response, the Islamist groups from Afghanistan, Bahrain, the Arabian Peninsula, Iraq, Lebanon, and Morocco, along with the Moro National Liberation Front and the American Indian Movement, signed a secondary statement. 'We the undersigned,' read the statement, 'strongly and unequivocally condemn the military occupation of Afghanistan by the Social imperialism of the Soviet.'[60] The Soviet invasion of Afghanistan not only spilled into the conference agenda, but also cast a heavy shadow on Arafat's relationship with Khomeini, who advocated for a transnationalism formulated on the principles of 'Neither East, nor West'.

FATAH CONFRONTS ARAB DISSIDENTS

No less controversial than Soviet imperialism among the conference participants was inter-Arab politics. In particular, Fatah's friendly ties with Arab regimes spurred a vituperative backlash among Iraqi and Saudi activists. The disagreements started during the first day of the conference. When delegates had to vote for the conference board, participants chose Iranian student leader Seyyed Mohammad Musavi-Kho'einiha as chairman, and Abu Jihad as first secretary. Kho'einiha proposed that the second secretary should be a member of the anti-Saudi regime delegation, specifically the Islamic Revolutionary Organisation of the Arabian Peninsula. While the Lebanese and Iraqi delegations, both linked to the Message Movement transnational network, were in favour of this proposal, the Fatah delegation expressed strong opposition. Abu Jihad suggested that the second secretary had to be a member of the Omani Liberation Front. The Lebanese delegation dismissed the idea and proposed a vote on the issue. But Fatah threatened that it would withdraw altogether from the conference board if anyone from the anti-Saudi opposition was admitted to it.

Although, during his first visit to Tehran, Arafat had gushed about the unity of the Iranian and Palestinian revolutions (see the chapter by Sune Haugbolle in this book), he could not afford to realign away from his

---

[59] *Sobh-e Azadegan*, 14 Esfand 1358/4 March 1980.
[60] Daneshjuyan-e mosalman, *Nokhostin gerdehama'i-ye*, 149.

long-time Arab supporters, such as Saudi Arabia and Iraq. At the gathering, a Fatah member defended the movement's position concerning the Saudi activists with reference to 'the PLO's interests in Saudi Arabia, where forty thousand Palestinians live'.[61] During the conference, Abu Jihad also showed reservations towards the Iraqi and Bahraini oppositions.[62] The Message Movement leaders, already in a life and death struggle with the Saudi and Iraqi regimes, were unhappy to see that Palestinians put their ties with Arab regimes above comradeship with fellow liberation movements. As a member of the Message Movement recounts, Seyyed Hadi al-Mudarrisi and Sheikh Hasan al-Safar, who led the anti-Saudi opposition, 'knew that Abu Jihad's stance was because of the close relationship between Fatah and the Saudi government'.[63]

The following week, *al-Shahid* – an Arabic bimonthly associated with the Message Movement – ran a piece castigating Fatah's 'astonishing position' at the gathering. 'With such a mentality,' *al-Shahid* wondered, 'how can a liberation movement succeed in its struggle against Zionists?'[64] The piece took aim at Fatah's relationship with the Saudi government, asking 'why should any genuine revolutionary movement refrain from condemning a reactionary pro-American regime that suppresses the downtrodden people in Saudi Arabia?'[65] Abu Jihad's response during the conference was that '[w]e think that the members of the board should be from movements with an extensive revolutionary background and old ties with other global liberation movements.'[66]

Later, a dozen Message Movement activists congregated outside the hotel where Yasser Arafat resided during one of his visits to Tehran. They welcomed the PLO chief with shouts of 'Neither East, nor West, the Islamic Republic'.[67] 'When we entered the hotel and walked into the elevator,' an

---

[61] *Al-Shahid*, no. 33, 16 January 1980.
[62] Anonymous, author's interview by Skype (Madison, US – Dubai, UAE, 12 May 2018).
[63] Anonymous, author's interview by Skype (Madison, US – Dubai, UAE, 12 May 2018).
[64] *Al-Shahid*, no. 33, 16 January 1980. *Al-Shahid* was launched in January 1978 and was initially published under the name of *The Islamic Movement in Iran* (*al-Harika al-Islamiyya fi Iran*). The content, which included news from inside Iran, Khomeini's speeches, and analysis by activists like the Mudarrisis and Muhammad Montazeri, was produced and put together in Kuwait, published in Beirut, and distributed from London. After publishing about fifteen issues, the journal established itself inside Iran and was named *al-Shahid*. Sahib Shushtarizadeh, author's interview (Tehran, Iran, 9 March 2022).
[65] *Al-Shahid*, no. 33, 16 January 1980.
[66] *Ettela'at*, 20 Dey 1358/ 10 January 1980.
[67] *Na sharqi na gharbi, jomhuri-ye islami.*

IRGC officer in charge of protecting the PLO leader recalls, 'Arafat asked me, "Why are they doing this?" I said, "They are denouncing your relationship with Saudi Arabia and Iraq." Hani Hassan said that "this is the revolution! Everyone can express his opinion freely."'[68]

The Fatah position, however, was by no means a surprise to the Message Movement leaders. Indeed, a few years earlier members of the movement had established ties with the PLO, through Mohammad Montazeri and Abbas Aqa-Zamani in Syria and Lebanon, in order to receive military training at Palestinian refugee camps. They had to register for training as Iranian citizens, because the PLO's stated policy was one of non-interference in the internal affairs of Arab countries. Fatah did not want to trouble its relationship with Arab capitals by embracing and training opposition movements in the camps.[69] Thus, with Mohammad Montazeri's assistance, the Message Movement activists registered as Iranians from Khuzestan, a south-western province of Iran with a substantial Arab population.[70]

Despite Arafat's warm relationship with Iranian revolutionaries, the PLO's stance concerning Afghanistan and various Arab regimes raised eyebrows in Tehran. When Abu Jihad visited Khomeini in Qom, the Ayatollah chided him for the PLO's silence about the Soviet invasion of Afghanistan.[71] The troubles in the Arafat–Iran relationship had started even before the beginning of the Iraq–Iran War and the formation of the Syria–Iran partnership, which later overshadowed Khomeini–Arafat relations.[72] These two consequential developments would upend the friendship between Arafat and the Islamic Republic.[73]

---

[68] Anonymous, author's interview by Skype (Madison, US – Dubai, UAE, 12 May 2018). The officer was also a member of the Message Movement.

[69] Al-Shahid, no. 43, 16 July 1982.

[70] Not all the Message Movement activists knew Persian, which sometimes, according to one of them, landed the activists in trouble when encountering people who spoke the language. Al-Shahid, no. 43, 16 July 1982.

[71] Mohammad Sadeq al-Husayni, author's interview (Tehran, Iran, 1 July 2009).

[72] See Maryam Alemzadeh's analysis in this volume.

[73] As Sune Haugbolle's chapter in this volume highlights, Palestinian nationalism and statist ambitions were influential within the PLO. This was partly behind the tensions between the PLO and revolutionary Iran. Despite Arafat's refusal to side with Iran in the aftermath of the Iraqi invasion, the Islamic Republic hoped that it would eventually bring Arafat into its transnational orbit. For example, in May 1982 Mohtashami met Arafat in Damascus and proposed establishing a joint bank account to finance Fatah operations against Israel. In Mohtashami's telling, Arafat turned out to be only interested in receiving money and not undertaking a serious fight against Israel. Arafat also insisted on Iran changing course in the war with Iraq and ending it quickly. Although this became

LEBANON AND SOLIDARITY WITH THE PLO

Lebanon, a country violently riven at the time by sectarian conflict and a deep divide over the PLO, was another contentious issue among the conference participants. However, this time Fatah and its Lebanese leftist allies found common cause with Iranian internationalists in their efforts to bolster 'the Palestinian revolution' against right-wing forces in Lebanon. Both Fatah and their Iranian friends were also distrustful of the Shi'i Amal Movement, which had backed the 1976 Syrian intervention in Lebanon to prevent the defeat of the Maronite-dominated Lebanese Front.[74] The conference marked an opportunity for Arafat to enhance his position in Lebanon and for the Iranian internationalists to discredit pro-Amal factions in Tehran, which added further intrigue to the proceedings.

For a long time, Lebanon had been a cause of acrimony in the anti-Shah movement. This partly went back to the simmering tensions between pro-Khomeini revolutionaries and Seyyed Musa al-Sadr in the 1960s and 1970s over al-Sadr's connections with the Shah, and al-Sadr's increasingly precarious relationship with 'the Palestinian revolution' in Lebanon.[75] While al-Sadr expressed sympathy for Palestinian resistance, he did not want Palestinian *fida'yin* to open a front in the south against Israel and expose the Lebanese in that region to Israel's so-called retaliatory attacks. Al-Sadr accused the Palestinians of creating anarchy in the south, and over time the Amal movement, established by al-Sadr in 1975, became the umbrella for opposition against Palestinian activities.[76] This soured the relationship between al-Sadr and many Khomeini followers, especially Mohammad Montazeri, Abbas Aqa-Zamani, Jalaleddin Farsi, and Ali Akbar Mohtashemi, who came to embrace Palestinians as their allies after 1979. Pro-Sadr forces, who believed that Palestinians were stirring things up between Amal and Iran, backed

---

the last meeting between Mohtashami and Arafat, Fatah's ties with Iran and Hezbollah continued in the subsequent years. Seyyid Ali Akbar Mohtashami, author's interview (Tehran, Iran, 17 July 2010).

[74] Augustus Richard Norton, *Amal and the Shia: struggle for the soul of Lebanon* (Austin, TX: University of Texas Press, 1987), 48; Patrick Seale, *Asad: The Struggle for the Middle East* (Berkeley: University of California Press, 1995), 283–288.

[75] On al-Sadr's relations with the Shah, see Arash Reisinezhad, *The Shah of Iran, the Iraqi Kurds, and the Lebanese Shia* (Cham, Switzerland: Palgrave Macmillan, 2019), 98–103, 305–308; Abbas William Samii, 'The Shah's Lebanon Policy: The Role of SAVAK', *Middle Eastern Studies* 33, no. 1 (1997): 72–74; Norton, *Amal and the Shia*, 41.

[76] Fouad Ajami, *Vanished Imam: Musa al-Sadr and the Shi'a of Lebanon* (Ithaca, NY: Cornell University Press, 1992), 178.

the Bazargan government. As Rubab al-Sadr, who briefly succeeded Musa al-Sadr as the head of Amal, put it, 'after Imam Musa al-Sadr, Palestinians, and in fact Fatah, began propaganda and slander against Amal'.[77] In particular, al-Sadr's acolytes deemed the Palestinian embassy in Tehran and its ambassador Hani al-Hassan to be in collusion with anti-Amal Iranians to undermine the movement.[78] Mistrust and rage were in full flow when shortly after the revolution Libyan officials – who were responsible for the disappearance of al-Sadr – came to Iran while Mohammad Montazeri recruited Iranian volunteers in November–December 1979 for despatch to southern Lebanon in support of the Palestinian *fida'yin*. Since the Bazargan government, particularly its foreign minister Ibrahim Yazdi and defence minister Mustafa Chamran, opposed any relationship with Libya and sided with Amal, the internationalists' relationship with Amal grew even stormier.

Against this intense backdrop, the internationalists extended invitations to several Islamist and pan-Arab factions and activists from Lebanon. Pro-Sadr individuals were also invited under the title of the Movement of Deprived. They arrived at a difficult moment, when Amal suffered a major blow from the resignation of Bazargan in November 1979. An Amal politburo member lamented that they subsequently paid dearly for their relationship with liberals and the Iran Freedom Movement,[79] whose members controlled the Bazargan government: 'They [pro-Palestinian Iranians] believed that we were part of the Iran Freedom Movement. We were saying that our relationship with the Iran Freedom Movement did not mean that we are against other factions in Iran. We, as Amal, can represent Iran in the Arab world.'[80]

At the conference, young and fervent members of the Committees of National Islamic Action (which comprised Lebanese activists who took part in the resistance against the Israeli invasion) and the Islamic Committees in Support of the Islamic Revolution (which were formed by activists in Lebanon shortly before the fall of the Shah), sat in the room next to the representative of the Lebanese National Movement – all of them hostile to Amal back home.[81] Hence, the conference was an important occasion for the

---

[77] Rubab al-Sadr, author's interview (al-Dahiya al-Janubiya, Lebanon, 22 April 2010).
[78] 'Aatif 'Aoun, author's interview (al-Zahrani, Lebanon, 4 November 2009).
[79] Nehzat-e azadi-ye Iran.
[80] 'Aatif 'Aoun, author's interview (al-Zahrani, Lebanon, 4 November 2009).
[81] The Arabic names of the three entities were: Lijan al-'Amal al-Watani al-Islami, al-Lijan al-Islamiyya al-Muthanida le-l-Thoura al-Islamiyya fi Iran, and al-Harika al-Wataniyya al-Lubnaniyya. A number of future leaders of Hizbollah, such as Mohammad al-Burjawi and Mohammad Fenesih were members of the Committees of National Islamic Action.

Iranian internationalists to show solidarity with the pro-Palestinian forces in Lebanon. Collaborating with Fatah throughout the conference, they aimed to marginalise the pro-Sadr delegation and elevate opponents of Amal, including radical Shiʻi activists. This led to an argument between pro-Sadr attendees and the Iranian internationalists, as well as their Lebanese and Palestinian friends, regarding the representation of the Lebanese Shiʻites at the conference. The pro-Sadr participants insisted that due to the leading role they asserted al-Sadr had played in the victory of the revolution, they were the true representatives of the Lebanese Shiʻites – and hence demanded an exclusive place above other Lebanese delegates.

The anti-Amal Lebanese Shiʻites who came to the conference had begun activism in the mid-1970s, around the time Amal was established by al-Sadr to become the political arm of the disadvantaged Shiʻi community in the sectarian political order of Lebanon. But these Shiʻi young people, many of them in their twenties and influenced by Marxist ideas, preferred to associate themselves with leftist factions that rivalled al-Sadr.[82] One of these Shiʻite activists was Seyyed Hani Fahs, a young cleric from the southern village of Jebchit, where he grew up among the poor Shiʻite tobacco farmers and suffered Israeli atrocities committed against the Palestinian refugees and southern villagers. Before 1979, Fahs formed a group of young activists and worked with the PLO and anti-Shah dissidents in Lebanon and Iraq.[83] 'I and other pious youth wanted to put forward a different example, which would carry the agony of the poor on its shoulder. But it would not be part of the left. It was neither Marxist nor rightist,' Fahs states, in order to explain why he never joined pro-Sadr organisations. 'We sat, talked, debated, and concluded that we needed to be protected by a force. In Fatah, we found a good ground on which to achieve our goals. We established ties with

---

According to al-Khazem, a young pro-Khomeini Shiʻi cleric at the time, other Shiʻi groups that participated in the conference were: al-Lujna al-islamiyya fi-l Uzaʻi or al-Lujna al-islamiyya fi Masjid Zeynul ʻAbiddin fi-l Ghubayri, and al-Lujna al-islamiyya fi Hay al-Selum. Seyyed Hani Fahs, author's interview (al-Dahiya al-Janubiya, Lebanon, 1 May 2010); Sheikh ʻAli al-Khazem, author's interview (al-Dahiya al-Janubiya, Lebanon, 23 July 2010); Sheikh ʻAfif Nablusi, author's interview (Sidon, Lebanon, 22 July 2009).
[82] See Asʻad Abu-Khalil, 'Shiites and Palestinians Underlying Causes of the Amal-Palestinian Conflict', in *Amal and the Palestinians: Understanding the Battle of the Camps*, eds Elaine Catherine Hagopian, Naseer Hasan Aruri, and Asad AbuKhalil (Belmont, MA: Association of Arab-American University Graduates, 1985), 9–10.
[83] This group was the Committees of National Islamic Action, Lijan al-'Amal al-Watani al-Islami.

Arafat and Abu Jihad.'[84] After the revolution, Fahs moved to Qom and Tehran and became involved with internationalists' efforts to promote the Islamic Revolution in the region. Although Fahs did not participate in the Liberation Movement's gathering in Tehran, some of his associates, including Ja'far Shu'ayb and Sheikh Ali Khazim, attended the conference. They would later become part of the Iranian endeavour to spread the revolution to Lebanon, leading to the formation of Hizbollah in 1982.

Tensions among the Lebanese participants came to a head over the question of who should address the conference on Lebanon's behalf. Not Amal, the Iranian internationalists insisted. 'We believed that Amal did not represent the Shi'ites of Lebanon and that it only represented itself,' says Salman Safavi, an associate of Mohammad Montazeri, who was present at the meetings. '[But] it called itself the representative of the entire Lebanese Shi'ites.'[85] The dispute, as Sheikh Ali Khazim recalls, split the conference. 'On one hand, there were Amal and conservative clergy and their Iranian supporters who insisted that the movement delivers the main speech on behalf of Lebanon, and on the other hand, there were Lebanese radical Islamic groups along with the National Movement who were resolute in not giving this advantage to Amal.'[86] The Palestinian delegation backed the anti-Amal side and tried to give pro-PLO Lebanese the upper hand.

Finally, participants reached an agreement that one representative from Amal and one from the other side would give two separate speeches on behalf of Lebanon.[87] Therefore, young activists like Sheikh Ali Khazim and Jihad al-Husseini, who represented the Committees of National Islamic Action in Lebanon, were invited to the podium to speak about the situation and their activities in Lebanon.[88] This was a symbolic setback for Amal, which insisted that it had to be the main ally and sole bridge between Tehran and the Lebanese Shi'ites. When the Muslim Student Followers of the Imam's

[84] Seyyed Hani Fahs, author's interview (al-Dahiya al-Janubiya, Lebanon, 1 May 2010). On the relationship between Lebanese and Palestinian student activists and young intellectuals and their ties with Fatah, see: Lefèvre, *Jihad in the City*, 170–175.
[85] Salman Safavi, author's interview (Tehran, Iran, 17 July 2010). In 1976, Salman, the brother of the former IRGC commander Rahim Safavi, joined Mohammad Montazeri's network in Syria and Lebanon to receive military training at Fatah bases.
[86] Sheikh 'Ali al-Khazem, author's interview (al-Dahiya al-Janubiya, Lebanon, 19 June 2010).
[87] At the meeting, Ghada Jabber, Mustafa Chamran's wife, spoke on behalf of the Amal movement.
[88] Sheikh 'Ali al-Khazem, author's interview (al-Dahiya al-Janubiya, Lebanon, 19 June 2010); *Al-Shahid*, no. 38, 9 April 1980, 28.

Line published a booklet containing the speeches of participants, the only remark that referred to Lebanon was from a representative whose title read 'the South Lebanon movement'.[89] In narrating the struggle of the land of Jabal 'Amil in southern Lebanon, he praised the Palestinian revolution, without mentioning al-Sadr or the Amal movement.

Besides the question of Soviet imperialism and Fatah's relationship with Arab regimes, the position of Shi'i Amal became divisive during the gathering. The rancorous arguments about Amal and the representation of Lebanon prefigured later tensions in the relationship of Khomeini's Iran with some established and influential Shi'i and Sunni movements and clerics elsewhere. For example, the Muslim Brotherhood, the Supreme Islamic Shi'i Council in Lebanon, al-Da'wa, and the Islamic Movement of Afghanistan came to find themselves in ideological and political tensions with Khomeini's Iran. They were viewed in Tehran as nationalists, distant from the cause of Palestine, having shady dealings with the US, and, most importantly, not in line with the *vali-ye faqih*, Iran's leader.[90]

CONCLUSION

The Gathering of International Liberation Movements ended on 9 January 1980, with a closing statement that condemned US imperialism as the 'foremost enemy of the downtrodden nations in the world'.[91] It also underscored the unique status of Yasser Arafat by declaring full support for the armed struggle of the Palestinian people under the leadership of the PLO. The conference was the product of the pan-Islamic, anti-imperialist, and Third Worldist solidarities and connections of the global 1970s that the anti-Shah movement had forged, especially with Fatah and the Message Movement. All the same, it was also the site of contradictions among the

---

[89] See Daneshjuyan-e mosalman, *Nokhostin gerdehama'i-ye*, 66–73.

[90] The Islamic Movement of Afghanistan (harkat-e eslam-ye Afghanistan), led by Asif Muhseni. On such tensions in the context of Afghanistan, Pakistan, Iraq, and Lebanon see Anonymous, *Farzand-e eslam va qor'an*, vol. 1, 514–515; Simon Wolfgang Fuchs, 'Third Wave Shi'ism: Sayyid 'Arif Husain al-Husaini and the Impact of the Iranian Revolution in Pakistan', *Journal of the Royal Asiatic Society* 24, no. 3. (2014): 493–510; 'Ali al-Mo'min, *Jadaliyat al-Da'wa* [The Controversies of al-Da'wa] (Beirut: Dar al-Rawafid, 2017), 211–271; Faleh Jabar, *The Shi'ite Movement in Iraq* (London: Saqi, 2003), 225–263; Mohammad Ataie, 'Exporting the Iranian Revolution: Ecumenical Clerics in Lebanon', *International Journal of Middle East Studies* 53, no. 4 (2021): 672–690.

[91] *Al-Shahid*, no. 34, 30 January 1980.

varying ideological and political leanings that these Islamist brothers and leftist comrades envisioned. The Soviet invasion of Afghanistan catalysed their ideological and strategic divergence and elicited sharp disagreements in the conference between two different visions of anti-imperialism.[92] Despite the pounding insistence of Afghan and Message Movement activists on the condemnation of Soviet imperialism, the statement left out the Soviet invasion of Afghanistan, only stating that '[w]e will fight America in a united front and stand firmly against imperialism, Zionism, racism, and fascism.'[93]

It is true that Fatah leaders walked away from the conference with an endorsement for Arafat's leadership, Fatah's position in the Lebanese civil war, and a concession to the PLO's view of the Soviet Union. But the debates and dismay at the gathering revealed the limits of brotherhood between Islamists and pro-Soviet liberation movements. As such, it was an early indication of the Islamic Revolution's drift to a transnationalism away from left-wing Third Worldism.[94]

The pan-Islamic solidarity that internationalists espoused was not devoid of tensions either. These tensions, which surfaced over Amal in the conference, soon became a confounding issue in Iran's pursuit of its particular vision of transnationalism. By elevating the doctrine of 'Neither East, nor West' to the centre of its transnationalism, the revolution began charting a different path towards what the internationalists called the Islamist International (*baynolmellal-e eslami*). As the export of the revolution evolved from an amorphous idea into a pan-Islamic strategy within the IRGC, it steadily moved towards primarily Islamist forces, which were, at least outwardly, independent from the influence of either superpower. In the words of Seyyed Mehdi Hashemi, who emerged as the head of the Islamic Liberation Movements Unit in the IRGC (1980–1982), 'the priority' shifted to locating and backing 'genuine Islamic forces'.[95] This transpired through either promoting pro-Khomeini Islamists wherever they had already existed, for example in Lebanon, or cultivating Islamic alternatives to the existing left-wing liberation movements, which was the case in Palestine. Gradually, by

---

[92] On the collision of the Soviet and Islamic visions over Afghanistan, see Nunan, '"Neither East Nor West," Neither Liberal Nor Illiberal? Iranian Islamist Internationalism in the 1980s', 43–77.

[93] *Sobh-e Azadegan*, 24 Dey 1358/14 January 1980; *al-Shahid*, no. 34, 30 January 1980.

[94] See Simon Wolfgang Fuchs' analysis in this volume.

[95] Seyyed Mehdi Hashemi, 'Enqelab-e bayn-ol-mellal-e eslami, jalaseh-ye 14' [The International Islamic Revolution, Session 14], audio recording from private collection (n.p., *c*.1983–1984).

the mid-1980s, Islamists inside and outside the occupied territories replaced the left-leaning Fatah in Iran's Palestinian strategy. Hence, when in June 1982 the Islamic Liberation Movements Unit convened the largest gathering of international liberation movements in Tehran, instead of Arafat's men the Palestinian representatives invited were the clerics and leftists-turned-Islamists, who became the original core of the Islamic Jihad in Palestine.[96]

---

[96] Among them were the Palestinian thinker Monir Shafiq, a former Maoist who defected Fatah, Ibrahim Ghunayim, and Salim al-Lababidi, who were two Palestinian sheikhs in Lebanon, and Bashir Naf'i, a close associate of Fathi al-Shiqaqi, the founder of the Islamic Jihad in Palestine. On the Maoists in Fatah who turned Islamist under the influence of the Islamic Revolution, see Sing, 'Brothers in Arms: How Palestinian Maoists Turned Jihadists', 1–44.

I am grateful for the invaluable comments and incisive feedback from Rasmus Christian Elling and Sune Haugbolle. I thank all the participants for their thoughtful discussions during the two workshops that served as the basis of this book. I am especially indebted to Toufoul Abou-Hodeib, Ali Alavi, Maryam Alemzadeh, Simon Wolfgang Fuchs, and Naghmeh Sohrabi for their illuminating feedback. I also would like to thank Ervand Abrahamian, Jennifer Heuer, Monika Ringer, and Mary C. Wilson who read the earlier draft of this paper and offered invaluable comments. This paper was supported by the Marvin Ogilvie Memorial Award for Foreign Language Study and the Henry Luce Foundation through the 'Re-assessing the Impact of the 1979 Iranian Revolution on Sunni Islamism' Project.

6

ABU JUBRAN AND JABAL ʿAMIL BETWEEN THE PALESTINIAN AND IRANIAN REVOLUTIONS

Nathaniel George

Jabal ʿAmil, Lebanon's mountainous, underdeveloped southern periphery bordering the colonised Palestinian Galilee, is an ideal location from which to consider the crossing currents of the Palestinian and Iranian revolutions internationally. Historically the region was remote from central or even provincial authority, whether from the Ottoman Sublime Porte, or Paris or Beirut during the mandate. Before the Nakba, Jabal ʿAmil's cultivation, kinship, and employment were directed more towards the cities of northern Galilee such as Safad, Haifa, and ʿAkka than to Sidon or Beirut. Beginning in the 1930s, Arab anti-colonial militants prized its rugged terrain as a strategically favourable location from which to mobilise anti-colonial armed struggle, situated as it was on high ground overlooking Zionist settlements.[1] Secondly, its peripheral location and social status combined with its character as one of the historic centres of Lebanon's Shiʿi community. Demographically large yet underrepresented in parliament, cabinet, and public employment, the marginalised status of the Shiʿi in the Beirut-focused sectarian capitalist regime conditioned Jabal ʿAmil into a historic reservoir

I would like to thank Husayn, Farah, and Gebran Baʿlbaki for their generosity in hosting us and sharing their stories. The chapter has benefited from the support of Fawwaz Traboulsi and the incisive comments from Raed Charaf, Abdel Razzaq Takriti, Sune Haugbolle, Susann Kassem, and the participants in the seminar.
[1] Rula Jurdi Abisaab and Malek Abisaab, *The Shiʿites of Lebanon: Modernism, Communism, and Hizbullah's Islamists* (Syracuse, NY: Syracuse University Press, 2014); Laila Parsons, *The Commander: Fawzi al-Qawuqji and the Fight for Arab Independence, 1914–1948* (London: Saqi, 2017).

of political opposition. The area gained particular geopolitical importance in the 1970s, when it became the sole operational front of the Palestinian revolution and armed struggle following the expulsion of the PLO from Jordan in 1970–1971 and the cessation of active hostilities between the Arab states and Israel in the aftermath of the October 1973 war.

Along with Iran and Palestine, southern Lebanon became an important site of struggle in the transition between secular, nationalist, and socialist modes of Third World anti-colonialism and revolutionary international-ism and the rise of Islamic revolutionary politics. In this context, the main expression of secular Third Worldism was the Lebanese National Movement (LNM), the broad front organisation of the multi- and anti-sec-tarian Lebanese left, which was tightly aligned with the Palestine Liberation Organisation (PLO) from the late 1960s through the mid-1980s. Together, they became known as the Joint Forces (*al-Quwwat al-Mushtaraka*) during the 1975–1990 war in Lebanon. If Islamic political movements were marginal in 1970, they came to represent the primary vehicle of organised, ideological opposition by the end of the Cold War and the Lebanese civil war in 1990. How and why this process unfolded remains a topic of perennial interest.[2] A prevalent view – held by many Orientalists and Islamists alike – sees this as the natural and inevitable outcome of Muslims shedding the influence of foreign ideologies and reconnecting with their alleged authentic religious subjectivities.[3] More specialist works often lay the blame narrowly on the alleged disorganisation and malpractice of the Joint Forces, characterising

---

[2] Examples include Manfred Sing, 'Brothers in Arms: How Palestinian Maoists Turned Jihadists', *Die Welt Des Islams* 51 (2011): 1–44; Nicolas Dot-Pouillard and Eugénie Rébillard, 'The Intellectual, the Militant, the Prisoner and the Partisan: The Genesis of the Islamic Jihad Movement in Palestine (1974–1988)', *Muslim World* 103, no. 1 (2013): 161–180; Abisaab and Abisaab, *Shi'ites of Lebanon*; Rula Jurdi Abisaab, 'Sayyid Musa Al-Sadr, the Lebanese State, and the Left', *Journal of Shi'a Islamic Studies* 8, no. 2 (2015): 131–157; Jihane Sfeir, 'The Disenchantment of the Left: Two Memories of the Palestinian Struggle', *TRAFO – Blog for Transregional Research* (blog), 5 June 2018, https://trafo.hypotheses.org/9905; Paul Thomas Chamberlin, 'The PLO and the Limits of Secular Revolution, 1975–1982', in *The Tricontinental Revolution: Third World Radicalism and the Cold War*, ed. R. Joseph Parrott and Mark Atwood Lawrence (Cambridge: Cambridge University Press, 2022).

[3] If Edward Said's criticism of Orientalism has achieved hegemony in academia, the 'Return of Islam' thesis, pioneered by Bernard Lewis, can still be readily found in Western media and more scholarly works. For a paradigmatic case that comes from a liberal internationalist angle as opposed to the rather more influential works by conservative imperial hawks such as Lewis or Samuel Huntington, see Alastair Crooke, *Resistance: The Essence of the Islamist Revolution* (London: Pluto, 2009).

their policies as ineffectual, if not 'callous, arrogant, and short-sighted'.[4] That Israel's brutal 1982 invasion prompted the ejection of the overwhelming bulk of the Palestinian revolution's political and military presence in Lebanon has tended to reinforce the assumption that its experience was primarily one of failure and false promises. It is also evident that the fortunes of the principal parties of the LNM, the Lebanese Communist Party (LCP), and the Organisation of Communist Action in Lebanon (OCAL), declined considerably in the wake of the PLO withdrawal. Yet each of these narratives is analytically lacking and empirically deficient.

Buried under the condescension of the larger defeats is an underappreciated history of significant achievements and continuous struggle against overwhelming power. If the Joint Forces' capabilities were so ineffectual, why did their formidable adversaries – principally Israel, the counter-revolutionary Lebanese Front coalition, the US, and their allies – exert so much blood and treasure to eradicate them through invasions and operations large and small? Why did Syria, a state that also claimed anti-colonial Arab commitments, as well as its allies continuously attempt to gain control over the Joint Forces and their constituency? Seizing upon the possibilities and contradictions of their 1960s conjuncture, rank-and-file secular Arab nationalists, socialists, and communists launched the resistance at a time when expressly Islamic political activists were largely disengaged from anti-colonial activity. By mobilisation as well as by example, their many militants inculcated a popular culture and institutional infrastructure of anti-colonial consciousness and resistance. In the 1970s and 1980s, the Joint Forces frustrated multiple attempts to establish Lebanese counter-revolutionary sovereignty, whether via partition or centralisation; or impose Israeli hegemony over the state in general, and the south in particular. The liberation of south Lebanon from Israeli occupation in May 2000 – spearheaded and maintained

---

[4] Augustus Richard Norton, *Amal and the Shiʿa: Struggle for the Soul of Lebanon* (Austin, TX: University of Texas Press, 1987), 50. On the one hand, Rashid Khalidi blames the LNM for having 'dragged [the PLO] into local quarrels'. This omits how the adversaries of the PLO (and the LNM) also 'dragged' it into Lebanese political disputes. Indeed, the LF used the PLO presence as justification not to accept internal political reforms. On the other hand, Khalidi chastises the LNM–PLO mobilisation as the cause of the LF's intensive armament and mobilisation. Clearly, mobilising for Lebanese political transformation and Palestinian liberation were goals that would inevitably provoke resistance from local, regional, and imperial powers. Rashid Khalidi, *Under Siege: PLO Decisionmaking During the 1982 War* (New York, NY: Columbia University Press, 2014 [1986]), 20.

by Hizbollah – was a decades-long process that witnessed successive waves of organising efforts that have yet to be convincingly parsed.

But an analysis of the overall performance and positions of the LNM and the PLO in the south is beyond the scope of this chapter. Instead, it draws on micro-historical approaches to challenge a clear-cut declension narrative of the Joint Forces by revisiting a largely repressed history of victory and contestation.[5] It examines the trajectory of the Lebanese left primarily through a series of oral history interviews Susann Kassem and I conducted in rural south Lebanon with Husayn Ba'lbaki – also known by his patronymic, Abu Jubran – a long-time, influential, southern Lebanese communist partisan. Alongside the interviews with Ba'lbaki, the chapter draws from recently published memoirs of other participants. These include accounts by two of his closest Palestinian comrades in the late 1970s, Mu'in al-Tahir and Shafiq al-Ghabra, influential fighters and leaders in Fatah's Student Battalion (al-Katiba al-Tullabiyya, see Sune Haugbolle's chapter in this volume). The Fatah Student Battalion played a major role in the Palestinian revolution and Lebanese civil war, and during their time in Jabal 'Amil they changed their name to the Jarmaq Battalion, a tribute to the mountain in Palestinian Galilee they often gazed upon from their field.

This focus on political practitioners complements the recent wave of anglophone research on the twentieth-century Arab left, which has thus far focused considerably on the history of its professional intellectual component.[6] This focus is understandable given that the available written

---

[5] Another recent micro-history of an LNM partisan is Dylan Baun, 'Claiming an Individual: Party, Family and the Politics of Memorialization in the Lebanese Civil War', *Middle East Critique* 30, no. 4 (2021): 353–371.

[6] Some of these texts include Laure Guirguis, ed., *The Arab Lefts: Histories and Legacies 1950s–1970s* (Edinburgh: Edinburgh University Press, 2020); Fadi A. Bardawil, *Revolution and Disenchantment: Arab Marxism and the Binds of Emancipation* (Durham, NC: Duke University Press, 2020); Hicham Safieddine, 'Mahdi Amel: On Colonialism, Sectarianism and Hegemony', *Middle East Critique* 30, no. 1 (2021): 41–56; Ahmad Agbaria, 'Dār Al-Talī'ah and the Question of Arab Authenticity in the 1960s', *Journal of Arabic Literature* 52, no. 1 (2021): 228–253; Ahmad Agbaria, 'From Translation to Critique: The Formation of the New Arab Left in Beirut 1960s', *Global Intellectual History* 7, no. 3 (2020): 593–610; Zeina Maasri, *Cosmopolitan Radicalism: The Visual Politics of Beirut's Global Sixties* (Cambridge: Cambridge University Press, 2020); Michaelle Browers, 'Beginnings, Continuities and Revivals: An Inventory of the New Arab Left and an Ongoing Arab Left Tradition', *Middle East Critique* 30, no. 1 (2021): 25–40; Ilham Khuri-Makdisi, *The Eastern Mediterranean and the Making of Global Radicalism, 1860–1914* (Berkeley, CA: University of California Press, 2010). Important contributions

sources tend to be produced by professional intellectual circles, states, and empires. Moreover, historians have only recently begun to tap the voluminous sources of the period. Yet the history of southern Lebanese political subjectivities is difficult to narrate from these types of archives. Professional intellectuals were but one collective group among many others that came together to create a broad-based coalition for change, such as urban workers, peasants, students, trade unionists, guerrilla fighters, politicians, and party cadres. These made up the bulk of the social base of the LNM–PLO alliance. Therefore, oral histories and memoirs of committed participants and villagers who were the subjects and objects of various political projects need to be collected, carefully contextualised, and juxtaposed with policy records, print media, and memoirs.[7] The steadily advancing age of this generation makes the necessity of such investigations even more pressing. Conscious of the distortions of hindsight, the chapter balances retrospective personal accounts with consideration of long-term, impersonal social and political structures, individual and popular agency, and specific historical conjunctures in order to avoid essentialised sectarian, narrow nationalist (whether Lebanese or Palestinian), Zionist, or imperialist readings. The dead-end debate on whether exclusively internal or external factors condition Arab social relations needs to be transcended.[8] As Karl Marx succinctly wrote some 170 years earlier: 'men make their own history, but they do not make it just as they please.'[9]

---

beyond intellectual history are Abdel Razzaq Takriti, *Monsoon Revolution: Republicans, Sultans, and Empires in Oman, 1965–1976* (Oxford: Oxford University Press, 2013); Abdel Razzaq Takriti, 'Political Praxis in the Gulf: Ahmad al-Khatib and the Movement of Arab Nationalists, 1948–1969', in *Arabic Thought Against the Authoritarian Age: Towards an Intellectual History of the Present*, eds Jens Hanssen and Max Weiss (Cambridge: Cambridge University Press, 2018), 86–112.

[7] Pioneering contributions to Palestinian and Lebanese oral history include Rosemary Sayigh, *The Palestinians: From Peasants to Revolutionaries* (London: Zed, 2007 [1979]); Rosemary Sayigh, *Too Many Enemies: The Palestinian Experience in Lebanon* (London: Zed, 1994); Karma Nabulsi and Abdel Razzaq Takriti, 'The Palestinian Revolution', 2016, http://learnpalestine.politics.ox.ac.uk/; American University of Beirut, 'Palestinian Oral History Archive', 2019, https://libraries.aub.edu.lb/poha/.

[8] For an example of such internally focused 'anti-anti-imperialism', see Bardawil, *Revolution and Disenchantment*.

[9] Karl Marx, 'The Eighteenth Brumaire of Louis Bonaparte', in *Collected Works of Marx and Engels: 1851–53*, by Karl Marx and Friedrich Engels, vol. 11 (London: Lawrence & Wishart, 1979 [1852]), 103.

THE STORY OF ABU JUBRAN

Husayn Baʿlbaki was born circa 1931 in ʿAytarun, a southern border village overlooking the Palestinian Galilee. His father made a comfortable living for the family working as a camel porter, smuggling goods between British Palestine and French Lebanon, evading customs.[10] His mother was thoroughly preoccupied with domestic social reproduction. The Baʿlbakis' world was shaped, on the one hand, by the arbitrary power of the local notables, the zuʿamaʾ (singular, zaʿim), who drew their authority from extensive landownership, and on the other hand by the colonial mandate authorities: the French in Lebanon and the British in Palestine. Educated in village schools, Husayn's first experience of incarceration was at eleven years old, when he was imprisoned and beaten by the British authorities in Palestine for collecting greens across the colonial border. The intercession of one of Jabal ʿAmil's leading notables, Ahmad al-Asʿad of al-Tayba, secured his release and that of his friends, further illustrating the relations between patrons and clients that characterised political representation at the time.[11]

Husayn was seventeen at the time of the 1948 Nakba, which in many ways bound the fates of southern Lebanese and Palestinians more tightly. During the 1948 war, ʿAytarun became a base for the irregulars of the Arab Rescue Army (Jaysh al-Inqadh). The experience of the war was imprinted on young Husayn, who recoiled from the Rescue Army's disorganisation, as well as their harassment and extortion of villagers. Like other ʿAmilis, he witnessed the arrival of the first Palestinian refugees expelled during the Nakba. After the loss of Palestine, ʿAytarun and Jabal ʿAmil generally experienced a rapid economic decline that began to push southern villagers to leave their villages for the slums of Beirut. Husayn was among these early urban migrants. Ahmad al-Asʿad got Husayn a job at the Beirut airport in exchange for securing his family's vote in Lebanon's notoriously corrupt 1949 election. Such internal migration continued southerners' long-term experience of comingling with Palestinians, who now worked and lived together far from home, in camps and slums in Beirut and its environs. The political and social deprivation

---

[10] He would collect camels and goods like wheat, sugar, and kerosene from northern Palestine to sell in Lebanon, and he would take cows, sheep, and other things from Lebanon to Palestine. Author interview with Husayn Baʿlbaki, 17 September 2019.

[11] Author interview with Husayn Baʿlbaki, 18 September 2019. For more on social reproduction in south Lebanon, see Munira Khayyat, *A Landscape of War: Ecologies of Resistance and Survival in South Lebanon* (Oakland, CA: University of California Press, 2022), where Abu Jubran also makes an appearance.

in this milieu, among both Lebanese and Palestinians, shaped a collective consciousness of openness to change, reform, and revolution.[12]

Baʿlbaki's long life of political activism started at the Beirut airport, in his job with the rescue team. All twelve of his co-workers were also ʿAmili peasants. Around the same time, he found intellectual inspiration in the writings of Jubran Khalil Jubran (known in English as Khalil Gibran) and Khalid Muhammad Khalid, a critical Islamic intellectual from Egypt who at the time called for a secular state, and advocated birth control, and a social democratic economy.[13] Shortly after joining the airport, a month or two at most, he asked one of his co-workers from Hula, a southern village near ʿAytarun known for its communist political leanings, if he knew where the office of the Lebanese Communist Party (LCP) was located. His friend immediately took him there, and he was introduced to two leading members of the party, Hasan Quraytim and Sawaya Sawaya. He did not read a word about communism before he joined in 1950. But from that moment, 'there wasn't anything on the face of the earth that I gave importance to in my head other than the Communist Party ... I didn't think of my children, I didn't think of anything [else].'[14] Despite his communist membership, al-Asʿad's patronage allowed him to continue in a succession of public sector jobs, which took him from the airport to the Ministry of Posts and Telegraphs, and all the way to the police force.[15] While at the Ministry of Posts and Telegraphs, he organised some sixty construction workers to join the Communist Party and take strike action in Ashrafiyya, a largely Christian and conservative quarter in eastern Beirut. A flexible and dedicated organiser, Abu Jubran focused not only on grassroots labour organisation, but he also came to take part in armed struggle. President Camille Chamoun's authoritarian pro-US alignment against Gamal Abdel Nasser's United Arab Republic (UAR) prompted Lebanon's first civil war in summer 1958. Abu Jubran left his police job, joined the 'revolution' (*thawra*), and travelled to Kuwait to retrieve more than a hundred Communist Party members – again,

---

[12] Abisaab and Abisaab, *Shi'ites of Lebanon*; Sayigh, *The Palestinians: From Peasants to Revolutionaries*.

[13] Author interview with Husayn Baʿlbaki. Specifically, Khalid Muhammad Khalid, *Min Huna...Nabda'* [From Here...We Begin] (Cairo: Maktabat Wahba, 1950).

[14] Author interview with Husayn Baʿlbaki, 17 September 2019.

[15] Abu Jubran's boss in the Lebanese police was none other than Maʿruf Saʿd, the popular Arab nationalist and labour leader from Sidon. Saʿd would later become a member of parliament, and his assassination during a labour protest in February 1975 – likely by Lebanese military intelligence – was one of the most important sparks of the civil war.

all southerners – and bring them back to join the fight in Lebanon via an arduous trek from Syria.

After 1958 and the US intervention, a generational and ideological rift developed within the LCP centring around the party's stance on the Arab national question. Heavily sympathetic to Abdel Nasser's anti-colonial, pan-Arab, national project, Abu Jubran was instrumental in forming a series of heterodox factions that sought to shake Soviet tutelage and engage more with the unfolding Arab national liberation movement. This started with the inner party faction calling itself the 'Leninist Current', which improbably married admiration for and links with the Italian Communist Party and its developing democratic line with support for the long-time Stalinist leader of the Syrian Communist Party, Khalid Bakdash.[16]

After the Leninist Current was expelled around the time of the 1968 LCP party conference, it linked up with groups of Trotskyists and students to form the Union of Communists (*Ittihad al-Shiyu'in*). At one of the Union's meetings in Zuqaq al-Blat, a neighbourhood in Beirut long-famed for its intellectual ferment, Abu Jubran explained his practical approach to ideology.[17] 'I told them that my belief is changeable, I mean it is not fixed. I gave them a simple example: that Abdel Nasser came, I left communism and marched with Abdel Nasser. Abdel Nasser exited and Fatah appeared, again I left [Nasser] and went on' with Fatah.[18] Freed from the LCP's cautious, pro-Soviet line, the Union of Communists vocally and practically supported the Palestinian revolution from its earliest days and formed part of Lebanon's 'Fatah Support Front' (*Jabhat Musanadat Fatah*). Owing to his southern pedigree, Abu Jubran assisted people crossing the border, and his house in 'Aytarun became a refuge and co-ordination point for such missions.[19] Figures such as Yasser Arafat, George Habash, and the Kuwaiti prince and Fatah member Fahd al-Sabah passed through the remote village. After the 1968 battle of Karama, Husayn was among five Union cadres, along with Isma'il Yusif of 'Aytarun and 'Ali Srur, sent to Jordan (via Syria and Iraq) to link up with the *fida'yin*.[20] Despite their small size, such experience

---

[16] Sulayman Taqi al-Din, *al-Yasar al-Lubnani wa-Tajribat al-Harb: Munazzamat al-'Amal al-Shuyu'i (al-Luhmah wa-l-Tafakkuk)* [The Lebanese Left and the Experience of War: OCAL] (Beirut: Dar al-Farabi, 2013), 23.

[17] On Zuqaq al-Blat, see particularly Jens Hanssen, *Fin de Siècle Beirut: The Making of an Ottoman Provincial Capital* (Oxford: Oxford University Press, 2005), 163–189.

[18] Author interview with Husayn Ba'lbaki, 18 September 2019.

[19] Author interview with Husayn Ba'lbaki, 18 September 2019.

[20] Author interview with Husayn Ba'lbaki, 17 September 2019.

prepared the Union of Communists to play a disproportionate role in the upswing of Lebanon's revolutionary atmosphere from the very outset, during the April 1969 uprisings in support of *fida'yin* action in Lebanon.[21] The Union's pro-*fida'yin* line soon brought them into close contact with similarly minded militant intellectuals like Muhsin Ibrahim and Fawwaz Traboulsi, who would soon be instrumental in the 1971 foundation of the Organisation of Communist Action in Lebanon (OCAL), to which most of the members of the Union of Communists soon adhered.[22]

While in the early 1970s the OCAL and LCP carried out a somewhat bitter rivalry over which party was the true vanguard of the Lebanese revolution; their ideological competition can obscure the larger context of a growing consensus around Marxism, anti-colonialism, Arab political belonging, and secular citizenship on the Lebanese left. Both organisations were at the forefront of all the major demonstrations and social struggles of the time, whether the issue was support for striking workers or *fida'yin* freedom of action. The breakout of outright war in April 1975 brought the two communist parties closer together almost immediately, along with the various strands of the Lebanese left, within the framework of the LNM. The OCAL and LCP joined with Kamal Junblat's Progressive Socialist Party (PSP) to form the backbone of the LNM, with the political leadership clearly in Junblat's hands. At the time, the LNM was united by two war aims: 1) abolishing political sectarianism and establishing a secular, democratic republic characterised by the formal political equality of all citizens; and 2) defending the Palestinian revolution from an international counter-revolutionary offensive.[23] The revolutionary upsurge peaked in spring 1976, when the Joint Forces of the LNM-PLO established control

---

[21] These demonstrations produced a crisis that ended with the signing of the November 1969 Cairo Agreement, in which the Lebanese state agreed to permit Palestinian armed units to make use of designated territories in Lebanon. While the document was signed by the Lebanese Army Commander and ratified by all members of parliament except for Raymond Eddé, the agreement became the focal point of the political polarisation in Lebanon.

[22] The OCAL was a merger of the bulk of the Lebanese branch of the Movement of Arab Nationalists under Ibrahim and the dynamic intellectuals of Socialist Lebanon aligned with Traboulsi. See Taqi al-Din, *al-Yasar al-Lubnani*; Fawwaz Tarabulsi, *Surat al-Fata bi-l-Ahmar: Ayyam fi al-silm wa-al-harb* [Portrait of the Young Man in Red: Days of Peace and War] (London: Riyad al-Rayyis, 1997); Bardawil, *Revolution and Disenchantment*.

[23] Nathaniel George, '"Our 1789": The Transitional Program of the Lebanese National Movement and the Abolition of Sectarianism, 1975–77', *Comparative Studies of South Asia, Africa and the Middle East* 42, no. 2 (2022): 470–488.

of over two-thirds of Lebanon and appeared on the verge of defeating their opponents outright and establishing a new regime. At the climactic moment in June 1976, the LNM's rivals in the counter-revolutionary Front for Freedom and Man in Lebanon were rescued from the brink of defeat by the Syrian military intervention against the Joint Forces, an intervention supported by the US and Israel, as well as a wide range of their international allies.[24] Syria's deliberate, painstaking intervention grindingly rolled back the gains of the Joint Forces. Moreover, it confounded many within the LNM-PLO ranks and their sympathisers, who previously thought of Syria as a friendly power committed to Arab national goals.

The October 1976 Riyad conference ended the first major phase in Lebanon's war by establishing a ceasefire and giving official Arab legitimation to Syrian dominance, while bringing additional minority contingents of Arab troops into the Arab Deterrent Forces (ADF). Shortly thereafter, the LNM's undisputed leader, Kamal Jumblatt, was assassinated in March 1977 – likely on Syrian orders. The tremendous crescendo of violence also fragmented Lebanese society into political and sectarian cantons, militarised politics, and dramatically reduced the space for the popular labour and student mobilisations that pushed forward progressive social demands in the late 1960s and early 1970s. The rapid recession of the revolutionary horizon led to a corresponding downturn in revolutionary morale. This conjuncture threw the previously ascendant Joint Forces onto the defensive and pressed the LNM to contract its goals from the transformation of the Lebanese regime to preserving its existence.

THE SOUTH IN THE EYE OF THE STORM

While civil violence spread to most areas of the country in 1975, the principal theatre of battle between the warring partisans was the capital, Beirut. This left the south relatively calm and unattended. The Lebanese Front took advantage of this first, and from summer 1976, with Israeli support

---

[24] See George; Fawwaz Traboulsi, *A History of Modern Lebanon* (London: Pluto, 2007); Osamah F. Khalil, 'The Radical Crescent: The United States, the Palestine Liberation Organisation, and the Lebanese Civil War, 1973–1978', *Diplomacy & Statecraft* 27, no. 3 (2016): 496–522; David M. Wight, 'Kissinger's Levantine Dilemma: The Ford Administration and the Syrian Occupation of Lebanon', *Diplomatic History* 37, no. 1 (2013): 144–177; James R. Stocker, *Spheres of Intervention: US Foreign Policy and the Collapse of Lebanon, 1967–1976* (Ithaca, NY: Cornell University Press, 2016).

and the wind in their sails after the Syrian intervention, moved to bolster their presence in the south-eastern villages and towns, such as Marj'ayun, Qlay'a, 'Ayn Ibl, Rumaysh, and Dibl.[25] Situated at sensitive points along the frontier with occupied Palestine, these locations featured predominantly Maronite Christian populations and over the previous year they became the principal bastions of scattered forces, mostly ex-army soldiers, aligned with the Lebanese Front against the Joint Forces.[26] These would soon mature into the Free Lebanon Army (FLA), a pro-Israeli militia under Lebanese army Major Sa'd Haddad. Often inaccurately described as a 'breakaway force' from the regular Lebanese military, the FLA's mission was endorsed by top postholders in the state apparatus. The commander of the Lebanese Armed Forces, General Hanna Sa'id – himself a native of Qlay'a – as well as Minister of Defence Camille Chamoun – a top leader of the Lebanese Front and a former president of Lebanon – gave the orders sending Haddad south via Israel.[27] Under Israel's 'Good Fence' policy, these villages acted as entryways for Israeli materiel, soldiers, and even development aid. Simultaneously, Lebanese workers were enticed to labour in Israel for higher wages, further consolidating the dependent relationship. However, outside these significant but limited areas, the groups of the LNM and PLO were politically ascendant, and the FLA had trouble making further headway. In an attempt to break out of these boundaries, in August 1976 the Lebanese

---

[25] Despite acknowledging that the Israeli intervention in the south via its 'Good Fence' policy came first, Theodor Hanf is quick to attribute the rise of hostilities in the south to 'the PLO' (a formulation that erases the LNM). Theodor Hanf, *Coexistence in Wartime Lebanon: Decline of a State and Rise of a Nation*, trans. John Richardson (London: I.B. Tauris, 1993), 227.

[26] Ahmad Beydoun, 'The South Lebanon Border Zone: A Local Perspective', *Journal of Palestine Studies* 21, no. 3 (1992): 40.

[27] Until at least 1977, all members of breakaway factions of the LAF continued to draw their salaries. This included the predominantly Muslim, pro-Joint Forces, Lebanese Arab Army of Lt Ahmad al-Khatib, and the predominantly Christian, pro-Lebanese Front groupings of Haddad and Antoine Barakat. However, the leftist Khatib was court martialled for rebellion in January 1977 and was detained in Syrian custody, whereas Haddad and other pro-LF formations continued to work in close co-ordination with the central state – and Israel. (During 1976, al-Sa'iqa, the pro-Syrian Ba'th Palestinian organisation, delivered the government salaries of Haddad's men from Beirut to Qlay'a.) Beate Hamizrachi, *The Emergence of the South Lebanon Security Belt: Major Saad Haddad and the Ties with Israel, 1975–1978* (New York, NY: Praeger, 1988), 73–74; Yezid Sayigh, *Armed Struggle and the Search for State: The Palestinian National Movement, 1949–1993* (Oxford: Oxford University Press, 1997), 428.

Front sent battle-hardened partisans from Beirut and Juniya to the south via Israel in order to open a new front against the Joint Forces.[28]

In reaction to these moves, as well as their defeat in Mount Lebanon and east Beirut, the Joint Forces prioritised the struggle for south Lebanon as the most strategically important and politically promising front. In the 'Red Line Agreement' negotiated by the US between Syria and Israel, the Syrian army was allowed to impose its authority in the central and northern regions of the country, while Israeli opposition to any Syrian positions near its borders prevented it from deploying in the south. Ironically, this is where the Joint Forces maintained considerable support. In reaction to the LF–Israeli gains, the LNM raised the slogan of 'protecting the Arabism of the south' ('himayat 'urubat al-janub').[29] For their part, many Palestinian organisations underwent a reassessment of their participation in the 1975–1976 war and the experience of their alliance with the LNM. For many, and in particular Fatah – the largest and most influential tendency by far – the experience redoubled their focus on anti-Zionist armed struggle as opposed to revolutionary change in Arab societies.[30] Much Palestinian armour and many personnel were thus relocated south, out of the reach of the Syrian army and within range of their principal adversary.[31]

The importance of the border villages of Jabal 'Amil thus increased to become the only openly contested front in Lebanon and the wider Arab-Israeli War. Yet the ranks of the LNM in the south were fragmented and disorganised. Muhsin Ibrahim and George Hawi, the Marxist leaders of the LNM following Jumblatt's assassination, approached Abu Jubran to become the head of the LNM's newly formed 'Popular Security' (al-amin al-sha'bi), or militia forces, along the south-eastern border. 'We can't depend on anyone other than you in this position,' Hawi and Ibrahim reportedly

---

[28] Mundhir Mahmud Jabir, al-Sharit al-Lubnani al-Muhtall: Maslalik al-Ihtilal, Masarat al-Muwajahah, Masa'ir al-Ahali [The Occupied Lebanese Border Strip: Paths of Occupation, Lines of Confrontation, and the Fate of the Population] (Beirut: Institute for Palestine Studies, 1999), 116. For an account by one Lebanese Front militiaman who made the trek, see Robert Maroun Hatem, From Israel to Damascus: The Painful Road of Blood, Betrayal, and Deception (New York, NY: Pride International Publications, 1999). See also Sayigh, Armed Struggle, 411.

[29] See, for instance, 1 October 1977, al-Watan; al-Haraka al-Wataniyya al-Lubnaniyya, Watha'iq al-Haraka al-Wataniyya al-Lubnaniyya, 1975–1981 [Documents of the LNM, 1975–1981] (Beirut, n.d.), 43–53.

[30] Sayigh, Armed Struggle, 410.

[31] Shafiq al-Ghabra, Hayat Ghayr Amina: Jil al-Ahlam wa-l-Ikhfaqat [An Insecure Life: A Generation's Dreams and Failures] (Beirut: Dar al-Saqi, 2012), 217.

told him. Abu Jubran closely trained some sixty partisans, only to find that their main preoccupation became not the FLA and Israel but policing the thuggish actions of various members of LNM parties themselves. Looking back, Abu Jubran recalled, 'there wasn't a day where I didn't record ten to fifteen incidents between the organisations.'[32] He cast doubt especially on the Arab-regime sponsored organisations, such as the Arab Liberation Front, a PLO-affiliated guerrilla organisation funded and organised by Iraq's ruling Baʿth Party.[33] His main job was to work to discipline the Joint Forces to correct the relations between the parties and the villagers. His patient work and ecumenical demeanour produced results, such as when he began making inroads into Christian villages controlled by enemy forces like ʿAyn Ibl and Rumaysh. Perhaps the sincerest tribute to his work was that the Israelis soon started focusing their fire on the LNM's Popular Security office and units, instead of attacking the positions of individual parties.[34]

This situation prevailed 'until God sent us the Student Battalions', Abu Jubran recalled.[35] Fatah's Student Battalions had played a major role in the LNM–PLO offensive in Mount Lebanon in spring 1976, holding positions on Jabal Sannin until they were dislodged by the Syrian army in October. Within a few days, they redeployed south, led by twenty-five-year-old Muʿin al-Tahir.[36] 'It changed,' Abu Jubran recalled about the arrival of the Student Battalions in the south-eastern sector. 'Even our mentality changed about all their previous actions, in their relationship with the people, with everything. They were truly responsible. I mean there was no part of any other organisation that was better, they were distinguished from all other organisations.'[37] The Student Battalions – whose members were significantly influenced by Maoism – emphasised a model of resistance inspired by the methods of people's warfare in China and Vietnam: inconspicuous guerrilla presence, high ethical standards of conduct, the establishment of close relationships with villagers via regular and frank consultations, and joint responsibility for local security. Abu Jubran, his comrade Ismaʿil Yusif, and

---

[32] Author interview with Husayn Baʿlbaki, 23 September 2019.
[33] While the long-standing animus between Communists and Baʿthists colouring such characterisations should be kept in mind in this ideologically plural environment, the indiscipline of the ALF and pro-Iraqi Baʿth in Bint Jubayl is repeated in al-Ghabra, *Hayat Ghayr Amina*, 234.
[34] Author interview with Husayn Baʿlbaki, 23 September 2019.
[35] Author interview with Husayn Baʿlbaki, 23 September 2019.
[36] al-Ghabra, *Hayat Ghayr Amina*, 220–221.
[37] Author interview with Husayn Baʿlbaki, 17 September 2019.

Ghabra all underline that this contrasted with how they experienced the practices of other *fida'yin* movements, which tended to focus on military action at the expense of dealing with the 'political, human, social, and moral environment surrounding it'.[38]

THE BATTLE FOR THE SOUTH-EAST, 1977–1978

The arrival of the Student Battalions led to an underappreciated highlight of the struggle for south Lebanon: the fight for the south-east, which culminated in the battle of Marun al-Ras in February 1978. Over the course of late 1976, FLA forces attempted to consolidate control in the area by breaking out of the Christian border villages and moving into the predominantly Shi'i central region. Haddad and his men, based along the south-eastern border in Marj'ayun and Qlay'a, attempted to link up with Major Sami al-Shidyaq's group on the southern fringe based in Dibl, 'Ayn Ibl, and Rumaysh. Shidyaq was another Christian LAF officer from the north who had been sent south via Israel by the LAF commander. A stranger to the 'Amili environment, he publicly referred to Shi'is as 'cannibals' and was reputed to be close to Lebanese Forces leader Bashir Gemayel.[39] Their major political target was the predominantly Shi'i southern market town of Bint Jbayl, which stuck out and separated the two FLA pockets 'like a thorn in the Israeli security belt'.[40] Marun al-Ras, on the other hand, was the principal military target. Situated on the summit of the highest peak in the region, with an expansive view of Galilee, whoever controlled Marun could easily impose their will on Bint Jbayl and the surrounding villages, while Israeli settlements like Avivim – built on the ruins of the Palestinian village Saliha – lay within range across the border. In the contest between the FLA and the Joint Forces, Marun had heretofore been a neutral village. The Joint Forces lacked inroads there due to the heavy presence of the Lebanese army as well as the UN Truce Supervision Organisation (UNTSO), an observer mission that was usually composed of career intelligence officers from states with strong links to Israel.[41]

---

[38] al-Ghabra, *Hayat Ghayr Amina*, 236–237.
[39] Hamizrachi, *Emergence*, 107–108.
[40] al-Ghabra, *Hayat Ghayr Amina*, 218.
[41] Jabir, *al-Sharit al-Lubnani al-Muhtall*, 199; Hamizrachi, *Emergence*, 65.

Lacking any significant consensual political prospects – or, it seems even intentions – the FLA attempted to gain control over these areas primarily through terror. Haddad's methods included shelling the weekly market at Bint Jbayl, which drew farmers, merchants, and townspeople from much of the south every Thursday. On 21 October 1976, the FLA shelled the market, killing fourteen and injuring twenty-seven. A further attack on 24 February 1977 was so quickly repelled by Fatah's Jarmaq and Central Brigades that some villagers claimed to have witnessed 'guardian angels fighting to defend them' as well as 'knights on white horses fighting alongside the *fidaʾyin*'.[42] This small victory opened a phase of warm relations between the fighters and the townspeople. This and other related battles shook the Israelis' confidence in the FLA and prompted further Israeli involvement.

Facing the structural limitations of pitting Christian against Muslim in the ʿAmili environment, in late 1977 Israel expanded its recruitment of collaborators in the Shiʿi villages such as Mays al-Jabal, Blida, ʿAytarun, and Marun al-Ras, distributing money and arms among them.[43] Employing kinship networks as leverage, the Israelis first targeted families whose political loyalties leaned toward the traditional *zuʿama* rather than the parties of the National Movement, seized upon existing family rivalries, or simply pressured the most socially marginalised with fiscal opportunities. Recognising that a solely military approach to the struggle could easily exacerbate such divisions, the Joint Forces adopted a politically oriented strategy. 'This battle,' Tahir recalls, 'was harsher and more difficult than the military battle.'[44] And within it, Tahir credits the 'great help of Abu Jubran Baʿlbaki ... and a number of others'.[45] Abu Jubran recalls that, in ʿAytarun,

> There were as many collaborators as there were patriots ... One of them, I talked to, I asked him, 'What can you offer to Israeli intelligence?' He was a peasant farmer [*fallāh*]. Really. His children and wife were sitting with us ... I talked to him until he started crying while he was sitting. I said, 'you can save yourself, I can't save you. If you can't save yourself, we can't save you.'

---

[42] Muʿin al-Tahir, *Tabagh wa Zaytun: Hikayat wa Suwwar min Zaman Muqawim* [Tobacco and Olives: Stories from the Age of Resistance] (Beirut: al-Markaz al-ʿArabi lil-Abhath wa-Dirasat al-Siyasat, 2017), 105–106; al-Ghabra, *Hayat Ghayr Amina*, 246–249.
[43] Author interview with Husayn Baʿlbaki; Hamizrachi, *Emergence*, 109–110.
[44] al-Tahir, *Tabagh wa Zaytun*, 107–108.
[45] al-Tahir, 107.

Through his local reputation and his ability to gently engage and persuade, Abu Jubran was able to disarm not only this man but also a network of collaborators in ʿAytarun. Several of them repurposed their Israeli arms towards the defence of the village alongside the Joint Forces.

The Israelis were more successful in Marun al-Ras, exploiting clan rivalries to build a network of support. In the early morning hours of 2 March 1978, Major Sami Shidyaq's battalion pushed into Marun al-Ras under the cover of darkness. Shidyaq's effort was supervised by General Mordechai Gur of the Israeli army, whose engineering corps helped clear the way for the Lebanese troops. Residents of Marun immediately began to flee while FLA snipers shot at Bint Jbayl. Without contacting the Fatah leadership in Beirut, Ghabra and Tahir quickly sprang their battalion into action, and organised co-ordinated action with the Popular Front, the Organisation of Communist Action in Lebanon, the Syrian Social Nationalist Party, the pro-Iraqi Baʿth, and even the pro-Syrian Saʾiqa.[46] Under the cover of artillery, Ghabra led a force of some eighty men directly up the mountain by foot.[47] Their midday ambush quickly and efficiently defeated Shidyaq's Israeli-backed forces, who lost eighteen men and four tanks. The Joint Forces incurred no losses and even captured a Sherman tank and three armed vehicles.[48] When Haddad learned of his comrades' astounding defeat he prepared a counterattack, but it was decisively rejected by his Israeli superior, General Gur.[49]

The FLA network in Marun collapsed completely in the wake of their defeat, with most of their followers fleeing to the Haddad-controlled areas. Israeli sources recorded that retreating Phalangist forces enacted their revenge by kidnapping local Shiʿi women, of whom they tortured, raped, and killed at least two.[50] Most of the defeated FLA soldiers hailed from Dibl, where the resulting anger at Shidyaq was so great he was forced to flee permanently to Israel.[51] Anticipating that their continued military presence in Marun would bring relentless Israeli attacks, the Joint Forces did not attempt to establish positions in the village. Abu Jubran understood the liberation of Marun al-Ras as a significant event that frustrated Israel's

---

[46] Until shortly before this, Saʾiqa had bitterly opposed the Joint Forces, in line with Syrian policy. Author interview with Husayn Baʿlbaki, 31 August 2022; al-Ghabra, *Hayat Ghayr Amina*, 283.

[47] For Ghabra's account, see al-Ghabra, 281–289.

[48] al-Tahir, *Tabagh wa Zaytun*, 111.

[49] Hamizrachi, *Emergence*, 112.

[50] Hamizrachi, 112.

[51] al-Tahir, *Tabagh wa Zaytun*, 111.

attempt to create 'a Shi'i canton' loyal to Haddad and Israel.[52] The well-executed victory also improved the relations between the Joint Forces and the surrounding villages.

DEUS EX MACHINA: ISRAEL'S 1978 INVASION

The failure of the FLA pointed to their inability to control the situation and convinced their Israeli sponsors of the need for further direct intervention. A few days after the fall of Marun al-Ras, on 11 March 1978 nineteen-year-old female Fatah commando Dalal al-Mughrabi led a group of Palestinian and Lebanese militants from Lebanon into Israel by sea to carry out the 'Kamal 'Adwan Operation', the biggest *fida'yi* operation inside Israel to date, which resulted in the death of thirty-eight Israelis and the wounding of over seventy-five more, mostly civilians.[53] The operation, planned by the Fatah leader Abu Jihad, was intended to reassert the capabilities of the resistance amidst Sadat's unprecedented settlement initiative.[54] In light of the success of the Joint Forces in repelling FLA and Israeli expansion in south Lebanon, the operation provided a suitable pretext for Israel to mount its most extensive invasion of Lebanon to date: 'Operation Litani' on 14 March 1978. Over the course of some eight days of fighting, Israel killed some 2,000 people, civilians in the vast majority, while 220,000 refugees fled north.[55]

The political deck was once again shuffled. Israel had pushed back much of the Joint Forces and increased its support for the FLA, while also inaugurating a continuous direct occupation of some ten per cent of the country. On top of this, the UN Security Council – at the behest of the US – despatched another foreign military force to the south: a multinational armed peacekeeping force, the UN Interim Force in Lebanon (UNIFIL), which remains in place today, despite its name.[56] Notwithstanding the overwhelming cost

---

[52] Interview with Abu Jubran, 31 August 2022.

[53] Kamal 'Adwan was a Fatah leader assassinated by Israel in Beirut on 11 April 1973. Israelis refer to al-Mughrabi's operation as the 'Coastal Road Massacre'.

[54] al-Ghabra, *Hayat Ghayr Amina*, 291.

[55] On the 1978 invasion, see particularly Walid Khalidi, *Conflict and Violence in Lebanon: Confrontation in the Middle East* (Cambridge, MA: Center for International Affairs, 1979), 123–143.

[56] Susann Kassem, 'Peacekeeping, Development, and Counterinsurgency: The United Nations Interim Force in Lebanon and "Quick Impact Projects"', in *The Land of Blue*

to civilians, the Joint Forces sustained minimal losses while performing far above both expectations and the historical performance of Arab regular armies.[57] The PLO in particular emerged strengthened.

THE TRIUMPH OF CONSERVATISM: THE RISE OF AMAL

On the Lebanese side, the rapidly shifting conjuncture empowered the LNM's rivals, favouring conservative political trends among 'Amili Shi'is. This turn of events encouraged the rise of the Amal Movement, founded and led by the charismatic Iranian-Lebanese cleric Seyyed Musa al-Sadr.[58] In Sadr's succinct expression 'I demand the rights of the sect', declared at a major founding rally of the movement in 1974, he did more than anyone else to mobilise the Shi'i as a sect-for-itself within the bounds of the sectarian regime.[59] Sadr's method was to cultivate a Shi'i consciousness by forcefully denouncing the inequities and neglect the community faced within the sectarian regime, while implicitly (and sometimes explicitly) opposing Shi'i identification with class or pan-Arab attachments. Sadr thereby represented a conservative alternative to the Marxist-led LNM that attracted the majority of Shi'i youth in the early 1970s.[60] In the words of Seyyed Hani Fahs, a close associate of Sadr as well as a clandestine member of Fatah, Sadr's goal was to 'remove the Left's exclusive custody of Shi'ite activism, prevent it from investing in a project that destroys the state, and preserve the Left only in the framework of a labour–social opposition that leaves the [Shi'ites'] national roots intact and remedies the branches through a realistic and rational method that makes violence unlikely'.[61] Karim Pakradouni, a leading Phalangist and close adviser of both President Elias Sarkis and

---

Helmets, eds Vijay Prashad and Karim Makdisi (Berkeley, CA: University of California Press, 2016), 460–480; Karim Makdisi, 'Reconsidering the Struggle over UNIFIL in Southern Lebanon', *Journal of Palestine Studies* 43, no. 2 (February 2014): 24–41.

[57] Khalidi, *Conflict and Violence*, 137–139.

[58] For more on Sadr, see Abisaab and Abisaab, *Shi'ites of Lebanon*; H.E. Chehabi and Majid Tafreshi, 'Musa Sadr and Iran', in *Distant Relations: Iran and Lebanon in the Last 500 Years*, ed. H.E. Chehabi (London: I.B. Tauris, 2006), 137–161; Fouad Ajami, *The Vanished Imam: Musa al Sadr and the Shia of Lebanon* (Ithaca, NY: Cornell University Press, 1986).

[59] 18 March 1974, *al-Nahar*.

[60] Norton, *Amal*, 49–50.

[61] Cited in Abisaab and Abisaab, *Shi'ites of Lebanon*, 114.

Bashir Gemayel, wrote that Sadr was 'the Khomeini of Lebanon', albeit, he qualified thereafter, 'an enlightened Khomeini'.[62]

While appreciative of Sadr's charisma and 'balance', ʿAmili Marxists such as Abu Jubran recognised his anti-communist, anti-*fida'yin* bent early on, and viewed him as an agent of the Shah.[63] Yet relations between the left and Sadr's movement were not anathematised until much later. Neither was there a neat separation between secular and religious people or ideas.[64] Being active and anchored in the same community, Abu Jubran had several interactions with Sadr and his closest associates.[65] He sent two of his sons to Sadr's ʿAmiliyya school near Tyre, where the aforementioned Sheikh Fahs was their teacher. On one occasion Fahs introduced Abu Jubran to the school's director, Mustafa Shamran. Shamran, an Iranian with a PhD in physics from Berkeley, was a key figure in the establishment of Amal, and he maintained close relations with Fatah's Jarmaq Battalion. Among his students was a young Hasan Nasrallah, who became an Amal activist.[66] Shamran was also close to Ayatollah Khomeini and would go on to serve as the Islamic Republic's first defence minister from 1979 until he was killed during the war with Iraq in 1981. When Abu Jubran entered his office, Shamran was talking to a German journalist. Abu Jubran recalled:

> When the word 'communist' came out of [the reporter's] mouth,
> I noticed, and started to listen. He [Shamran] told him in English
> 'Here, in my school, there are many students, communists.'[67]

---

[62] Karim Pakradouni, *La paix manquée: Le mandat d'Elias Sarkis, 1976–1982*, 2nd ed. (Beyrouth: Éditions FMA, 1984), 106.

[63] 31 August 2022. The Shah's government and intelligence service did maintain close contact with Sadr and his associates, though he rejected the government's material support, as shown in Abbas William Samii, 'The Shah's Lebanon Policy: The Role of SAVAK', *Middle Eastern Studies* 33, no. 1 (1997): 66–91.

[64] As Rula Jurdi and Malek Abisaab astutely argue, in the ʿAmili context, 'Marxism evidently did not entail a formulaic adherence to Marxist theory or severance of ties with religious traditions'. Abisaab and Abisaab, *Shi'ites of Lebanon*, 210.

[65] This was a continuation of the ecumenical frame identified by Ussama Makdisi, *Age of Coexistence: The Ecumenical Frame and the Making of the Modern Arab World* (Berkeley, CA: University of California Press, 2019).

[66] Amal Saad, 'Challenging the Sponsor-Proxy Model: The Iran–Hizbullah Relationship', *Global Discourse* 9, no. 4 (November 2019): 631.

[67] Author interview with Husayn Baʿlbaki, 31 August 2022.

In Abu Jubran's view, shared by many of his contemporaries, Sadr and Shamran's mission in Lebanon was to contain the rise of the left among Shiʿis, and in the south in particular. At the same time, it must be said that Sadr's movement was inchoate and combined several different tendencies. Shamran indeed took a dim view of the Lebanese and Palestinian left and pressed for a more focused Shiʿi political movement, whereas others such as Muhammad Salih al-Husayni, another Iranian active in Amal in south Lebanon, took a more expansive view of the internationalist possibilities linking the Palestinian, Lebanese, and Iranian revolutions.[68] Others such as Nabih Berri, then Amal's spokesman, steered a course distant from religious ideology that was resolutely devoted to improving the position of Shiʿi representation within the sectarian regime.

If Sadr's movement enjoyed remarkable popularity prior to the opening of the civil war, it is often forgotten that by the end of 1976 his following was seriously compromised. After initially endorsing the Palestinian resistance and then the LNM's August 1975 Transitional Programme calling for the abolition of sectarianism and the establishment of secular political equality, Sadr withdrew his support by the end of the year in accordance with Syrian initiatives. To many, this move confirmed that Sadr and Amal's defining political goal was to reform the sectarian regime to give greater weight to the Shiʿi community. This stance, coupled with Sadr's feeble response to the Lebanese Front's counter-revolutionary, anti-Muslim massacres and expulsions, as well as his further support of Syria's political and military interventions against the Joint Forces, cost him a significant amount of support among the embattled Shiʿi community.[69] Sadr continued to be harshly critical of the National Movement, and particularly its leader Kamal Jumblatt, whom he claimed had single-handedly prolonged the war beyond a two-month conflict, and was cynically willing 'to fight the Christians until the last Shiʿite'.[70] The PLO, Sadr continued, 'is not a revolution' but 'a military

---

[68] al-Ghabra, *Hayat Ghayr Amina*, 245.

[69] Especially after he negotiated the surrender and displacement of some 200,000 predominately Shiʿi residents of the Nabʿa quarter of Beirut to the Lebanese Front in August 1976. Asʿad AbuKhalil, 'Shiites and Palestinians: Underlying Causes of the Amal-Palestinian Conflict', in *Amal and the Palestinians: Understanding the Battle of the Camps*, ed. Elaine C. Hagopian, Arab World Issues 9 (Association of Arab-American University Graduates, Inc., 1985), 10.

[70] Pakradouni, *La paix manquée*, 106. While Pakradouni was an adversary of the PLO and, at certain points, of Sadr, these quotes he attributes to personal interactions with Sadr have often been repeated among wider elements hostile to the Joint Forces.

machine terrorising the Arab world'.[71] Moreover, the US embassy, through its meetings with Sadr, had been well acquainted with these stances longer than most, and appreciated Sadr's often private criticism of the *fida'yin* and 'strong anti-communist views' since 1974.[72]

By late 1978, the wind was back in Amal's sails. If the Joint Forces had performed well during the 1978 invasion, Israel's mass destruction, displacement, strengthened occupation, and increasingly aggressive ('pre-emptive') attacks severely tested the political patience of ʿAmili communities with the Joint Forces' resistance agenda, which implied long-term sacrifice amidst questionable gains for the populace. Regionally, Sadat's ongoing diplomatic manoeuvres towards a separate Egyptian–Israeli peace brokered by the US removed the largest Arab army from the confrontation and further sapped the potential of co-ordinated Arab resistance to Israeli colonialism, particularly in the frontline states. In Iran, the beginning of the popular mobilisations raised the profile of Islamic revolutionary ideologies as an alternative to the flagging energy of secular Third Worldism – and particularly among Shiʿites. Finally, the disappearance of Sadr himself while visiting Libya in August 1978 worked to resurrect his agenda by catalysing action against the Joint Forces, who were increasingly scapegoated for Lebanon's ills from a variety of angles. This turn of events markedly affected Shiʿi political mobilisations and in turn provoked serious questions for the LNM–PLO alliance, and for the LNM especially.

The LNM – and the LCP and OCAL in particular – had traditionally been heavily constituted by Shiʿi cadres due to the community's structural deprivation within the sectarian regime. Both Amal and the communists were thus fishing in the same waters for support, while at the same time proposing dramatically different aims and sensibilities. The communist and nationalist parties recognised that Amal's aims were antithetical to their own on the questions of secularisation, social reform, and foreign relations. Many within Amal sought to dramatically reduce the armed struggle in south Lebanon, if not halt it entirely, due to the extensive damage wrought by Israeli attacks, harassment, and occupation. An understanding of shared interests developed between Amal and FLA–Israeli forces in the south.[73] Tensions between Amal and LNM forces quickly escalated into bitter,

---

[71] Pakradouni, 107.

[72] 30 April 1974, Beirut 5095, 'Shi'ite Imam Musa Sadr' and 19 August 1974, Beirut 9900, 'Imam Musa as-Sadr', Access to Archival Databases (AAD).

[73] Hamizrachi, *Emergence*, 110; Norton, *Amal*, 50, 122.

violent conflicts in Jabal ʿAmil and Beirut's southern suburbs in late 1978. The battle climaxed in the summer of 1981, when Amal nearly collapsed in the face of a vigorous communist offensive infused by the zeal of young members of its own Student Brigade, whose members had returned from university studies (and for some, official military training) in the socialist bloc.[74] According to leading LCP cadre George al-Batal, a communist victory was once again prevented by the Syrian military, who occupied the suburbs with tanks and permanently shuttered the LCP's offices there. Arafat, for his part, refused to intervene out of concern not to alienate either his fragile rapprochement with Syria or the increasingly restless Shiʿi activists and their constituencies.[75] 'The Communist presence remained in the southern suburbs,' recalled the LCP leader George al-Batal, 'but the influence we had disappeared.'[76]

Relations with Amal became one of the key areas of LNM–PLO disagreement that reflected larger strategic divergences. Fatah had initially sponsored and trained Amal as the clandestine armed wing of Sadr's movement at its inception in 1975, to solidify relations with the charismatic and influential Sadr, and thereby the Shiʿi community.[77] If the Lebanese and Palestinian left was wary of Amal's motives and intentions, particularly after its 1976 defection, Fatah's mainstream behind Arafat continued to court Amal's support in the late 1970s and early 1980s. Muʿin al-Tahir recalls meeting with Mustafa Shamran, who complained about his movement's treatment at the hands of the Lebanese and Palestinian left. Shamran and Tahir decided that the only solution was to have Amal fight on the front lines to prove their credibility against the Zionist enemy and its Lebanese auxiliaries.[78] Amal units fought alongside the Jarmaq Battalion in the 1978 invasion, who continued to advocate for their inclusion in a broad national alliance in favour of the resistance through 1982.[79] 'We used to imagine that we were stronger,'

---

[74] Jurj al-Batal, *Jurj al-Batal: Ana al-Shuyuʿi al-Wahid* [George al-Batal: I am the Only Communist] (Baghdad: Dar al-Mada, 2019), 276–277.

[75] Sayigh, *Armed Struggle*, 520; Hanna Batatu, *Syria's Peasantry, the Descendants of Its Lesser Rural Notables, and Their Politics* (Princeton, NJ: Princeton University Press, 1999), 300–302.

[76] al-Batal, *Jurj al-Batal*, 277.

[77] 'Amal' is after all an acronym for the Lebanese Resistance Detachments (*Afwaj al-Muqawama al-Lubnaniyya*). On PLO sponsorship, see the comments by Abu Iyad in Rex Brynen, *Sanctuary and Survival: The PLO in Lebanon* (Boulder, CO: Westview Press, 1990), 135–136.

[78] al-Tahir, *Tabagh wa Zaytun*, 149–150.

[79] al-Tahir, 186.

recalled Ziyad Saʿb, a former military leader in the Lebanese Communist Party and the communist-led Lebanese National Resistance Front after 1982. Saʿb also recalls receiving messages sent from Arafat's representative in a 1981 meeting of the Joint Forces command in Nabatiyya, saying that 'if we don't stop fighting against Amal, they [Fatah] will stand with Amal'. The threat was repeated and strengthened again in 1982.[80]

What the Arafat wing of the PLO wanted from the LNM was a base of popular and political support for the Palestinian resistance, and not necessarily a transformation of the Lebanese political system. What the Lebanese communists wanted from the PLO was support for Lebanese political transformation. Both miscalculated. Fatah's moderation may have bought it some valuable time and goodwill among a vital component of Lebanese society, but it also misread Amal's motivations and aims. By 1985, Amal would replace the Lebanese Front groups as the primary antagonist of the Palestinian presence in Lebanon – both civilian and military – when it launched its War on the Camps.[81]

A PROLONGED DISSOLVE

This chapter argues that the very success of the Joint Forces' activities repeatedly drew the intervention of overwhelming external counterforces, while favourable international conjunctures enabled rival conservative and anti-colonial Islamist forces to make the most of these defeats and to gradually achieve hegemony in this area. The 1979 moment produced conjunctural shifts that placed the sort of secular Third Worldism advocated by the LNM–PLO alliance increasingly on the defensive. Israel's 1982 invasion of Lebanon and the expulsion of the PLO is widely recognised as a turning point in the fortunes of the Palestinian revolution's ability to resist Zionist colonialism and influence in an international scene increasingly dominated by US imperial hegemony.[82] It was also a major setback for the LNM as a secular, anti-colonial, and socialist force in Lebanese and regional politics.

[80] Dalal al-Bizri, *Yasariyun Lubnaniyun fi Zamanihim* [Lebanese Leftists in their Times] (Beirut: al-Markaz al-ʿArabi lil-Abhath wa-Dirasat al-Siyasat, 2021), 173.

[81] Sayigh, *Too Many Enemies: The Palestinian Experience in Lebanon*; Joe Stork, 'The War of the Camps, The War of the Hostages', *MERIP Reports* 133 (1985): 3–7.

[82] Ibrahim Abu-Lughod, 'The Meaning of Beirut, 1982', *Race & Class* 24, no. 4 (1983): 345–359.

The invasion, the installation of a Phalangist regime, the defeat of the Joint Forces, and the adherence of Amal to negotiations with Israel likewise inspired an acceleration of revolutionary Islamist mobilisation, sponsored by the arrival of a small but influential group of Iranian Revolutionary Guards in Lebanon.[83] However, the scope of the Joint Forces' defeat can be overstated. For a time, the invasion and occupation renewed the mission of the anti-colonial left under a new guise, marked by the formation of the Lebanese National Resistance Front in September 1982 (*Jabhat al-Muqawama al-Wataniyya al-Lubnaniyya*, popularly known by its Arabic acronym JAMUL). Between 1982 and 1985, JAMUL and the Islamic resistance were remarkably effective and forced an Israeli withdrawal from Beirut back to an expanded security belt in the south. For the first time, Arab resistance forced (1) the abrogation of an Arab–Israeli normalisation treaty, the 17 May 1983 agreement imposed by Amin Gemayel's regime, Israel, and the US; and (2) a unilateral Israeli withdrawal in 1985 from the advanced positions it took in the country in 1982 back to an expanded 'security belt'.[84]

But after the 1985 Israeli pullback, the role of the secular left, which by this time was mostly limited to the LCP, continued with diminishing results in an overwhelmingly hostile environment on local, regional, and international levels. The head of the LNM, Walid Jumblatt, declared the LNM's dissolution in 1983 as he completed a reorientation of his PSP away from the secular Third Worldism of his father Kamal into the sectarian organisation of the Lebanese Druze.[85] Deprived even of a toehold inside official national politics, Lebanese communists struggled to maintain independence and influence amidst an array of powerful adversarial forces. Moreover, their cause of anti-colonial resistance was increasingly taken up by rivals with antithetical ideologies, practices, and aims. These included the authoritarian co-optation strategies of the Iraqi and Libyan, but especially Syrian, regimes that attempted to monopolise leadership of anti-colonial action (see the introduction to this book). At the same time

---

[83] H.E. Chehabi, 'Iran and Lebanon in the Revolutionary Decade', in *Distant Relations: Iran and Lebanon in the Last 500 Years*, ed. H.E. Chehabi (London: I.B. Tauris, 2006), 201–230.

[84] Two important memoirs of this period by female resistance militants are available in English. For a communist view, see Soha Bechara, *Resistance: My Life for Lebanon*, trans. Gabriel Levine (New York, NY: Soft Skull Press, 2003); for an Islamist view, see Nawal Qasim Baidoun, *Memoirs of a Militant: My Years in the Khiam Women's Prison*, trans. Caline Nasrallah and Michelle Hartman (Northampton, MA: Olive Branch Press, 2022).

[85] Traboulsi, *History of Modern Lebanon*, 229.

the bitter rivalry between upstart Islamist forces, backed at times by Syria and Iran, and the secular forces of the LCP, which enjoyed no significant external support by the late 1980s, exploded into a deadly conflict in which most of the casualties were the communists.

Now over ninety years old, Abu Jubran continues to live in an ʿAytarun liberated from Israeli occupation. Liberation – the common goal of the national and Islamic resistances – was achieved on 25 May 2000, primarily through the efforts of Hizbollah in the final period. At the time of our interviews, Abu Jubran spent much of his time along the southern border in his field just metres away from an Israeli military outpost – which stands upon his family's usurped land. Like many of his generation, he looks back at his past with a substantial degree of bitterness about what he and his comrades were not able to achieve. A more balanced appraisal has been long overdue.

7

THE ISLAMIC REPUBLIC PARTY AND THE PALESTINIAN CAUSE, 1979–1980

A Discursive Transformation of the Third Worldist Agenda

Maryam Alemzadeh

'Brother Hani al-Hassan, representative of the Palestinian Revolution, visited the headquarters of *Jomhuri-ye Eslami* newspaper in Iran yesterday.' So opened a story on the front page of *Jomhuri-ye Eslami* (Islamic Republic), the Islamic Republic Party's official daily newspaper, on 9 October 1979.[1] '[D]uring the conversations between the paper's editor with Mr Hani al-Hassan,' the story continued, 'it was ensured that as a lively news outlet, *Jomhuri-ye Eslami* newspaper would put as much effort as possible to the rightful realisation of the Palestinian cause ... [It was declared that] Palestinian brothers could treat this newspaper as an important trench on the frontline that today extends throughout the Middle East against Israel's expansionism.'[2] In October 1979, when this news story was published, Third Worldist language of anti-imperialism[3] with the Palestinian struggle as its pinnacle

---

[1] *Jomhuri-ye Eslami* Editorial Board (JEED), 'Didar-e Hani al-Hassan az daftar-e ruznameh-ye Jomhuri-ye Eslami' [Hani al-Hassan's Visit to Jomhuri-ye Eslami Newspaper Office], *Jomhuri-ye Eslami* (JE) 79, 9 October 1979, p. 1.

[2] Ibid.

[3] I use the concept of Third Worldism in line with the theme elaborated in the introduction to this volume: the cluster of independent, anti-colonial, anti-West movements occurring in the Global South, supported by social movements in Western countries, roughly in the 1960s and 1970s.

was still very much prominent in the discursive space of Iranian politics. Adopted as the revolution had progressed in the context of liberation movements of the 1960s and early 1970s, commitment to freeing the oppressed all around the globe was a sign of genuine revolutionary character. Palestine had been a high-priority cause in the late 1960s and early 1970s in Iran,[4] and it had remained so after the revolution, for two main reasons. First, Palestinian resistance organisations, especially the secular, left-leaning Palestine Liberation Organisation (PLO), had established themselves as the pioneers of the global movement,[5] pushing Palestine up on the list of any internationalist group's agenda. Additionally, the Palestinian struggle being that of a Muslim population added to its urgency for the nascent Islamic Republic of Iran, where Islamists were gradually taking over political institutions.

In the early post-revolutionary months, various political views on domestic governance and international outreach were clashing with one another, being moulded and modified in the process. The technocratically minded interim government under Mehdi Bazargan was open to friendly relations with the PLO, which was the most widely recognised Palestinian authority at the time. A few clerical figures, most prominently Ayatollah Hossein-Ali Montazeri, saw liberating non-Iranian Muslim populations as the logical continuation of the 1979 revolution, and, as a result, sought to stay close to the PLO not as a static governing body but as a revolutionary organisation.[6] In other words, they were adamant about realising the goal of exporting the revolution. The PLO's secularist tendencies were overlooked in the light of its long-standing revolutionary agenda and experience. The majority of clerical leaders close to Khomeini and their lay associates, however, had a different agenda in mind. Constituting the majority of the Revolutionary Council and, later, the Islamic Republic Party, they preferred to shift their attention to the domestic power-play in order to pursue their emerging Islamist agenda and, accordingly, to modify the revolution's international agenda: from general solidarity with liberation movements of the world,

---

[4] Naghmeh Sohrabi, 'Remembering the Palestine Group: Global Activism, Friendship, and the Iranian Revolution', *International Journal of Middle East Studies* 51:2 (2019), 281–300.

[5] Paul Thomas Chamberlin, *The Global Offensive: The United States, the Palestine Liberation Organisation, and the Making of the Post-Cold War Order* (Oxford: Oxford University Press, 2012).

[6] Mohammad Ataie, 'Exporting the Iranian Revolution: Ecumenical Clerics in Lebanon', *International Journal of Middle East Studies* 53:4 (2021), 672–690.

most often carrying secular and leftist inclinations, to an 'Islamist Global Movement'.[7,8] Palestine's dual significance, as home to flagship leftist resistance groups and as a Muslim-majority nation in a difficult plight, presented this transformation endeavour with a dilemma. How this dilemma was dealt with is the topic of this chapter.

Upon establishment, different strands of the new Iranian government had their own reasons to embrace open, friendly relations with the PLO. In need of a new regional ally, PLO leader Yasser Arafat, a practising Muslim himself, was happy to highlight the Muslim heritage of the PLO to appease Ayatollah Khomeini and the clerics close to him.[9] During Arafat's trip to Tehran immediately after the February 1979 revolution, Israel's former embassy in Tehran was handed over to the PLO. The 'representative of the Palestinian Revolution', Hani al-Hassan, was in fact the PLO's official representative in Tehran and the embassy's incumbent officer.

At the same time, however, Islamists were naturally aware of the PLO's leftist inclination and its financial and political ties to both Sunni-majority Arab countries and the Soviet Union. While other revolutionary groups such as the Islamist–Marxist *Sazman-e mojahedin-e khalq-e Iran* (the People's Mojahedin Organisation of Iran, MEK) and small internationalist groups openly engaged with, supported, and sought assistance from the PLO, the Islamist and domestically oriented Islamic Republic Party (IRP) had to find a more nuanced approach to support the Palestinian cause while refusing to endorse the PLO's unfavourable history and connections.

How did the IRP, a strong political influence on the state and soon to be the most influential political entity in the country, deal with this dilemma, during the time when the revolutionary significance of the Third World as the hotbed for resisting both the East and the West[10] and the figure of the guerrilla liberation fighter were both gradually declining?[11] To find an answer, this chapter discusses the IRP's discursive manoeuvres around the

[7] Timothy Nunan, '"Neither East nor West," Neither Liberal nor Illiberal? Iranian Islamist Internationalism in the 1980s', *Journal of World History* 31:1 (2020), 43–77.

[8] It is in this sense that I use the term 'Islamist' to describe this group of politicians, including members of the Islamic Republic Party, admittedly in an anachronistic way. See also Ataie's chapter in this volume.

[9] Seyyed Ali Alavi, *Iran and Palestine: Past, Present, Future* (Oxford and New York: Routledge, 2020).

[10] Samantha Christiansen and Zachary Scarlett, *The Third World in the Global 1960s* (New York: Berghahn Books, 2012), 'Introduction'.

[11] Hamit Bozarslan, 'Revisiting the Middle East's 1979', *Economy and Society* 41:4 (2012), 558–567.

Palestinian cause. I study the Party's daily newspaper, *Jomhuri-ye Eslami*, from its first issue published on 30 May 1979 to 22 September 1980, when international news coverage and analysis shifted drastically to an almost-exclusive coverage of the Iran–Iraq War. Indeed, the PLO's choice to side with Iraq during the war alleviated the discursive dilemma – it became more justified for Iranian officials to dismiss the PLO openly. I treat *Jomhuri-ye Eslami* as the most comprehensive source reflecting the Party's stance, but occasionally complement my findings with the IRP's other, less regular publications, as well as with organisational publications of the MEK, for comparison. In its daily run during the period, *Jomhuri-ye Eslami* presented various discursive tools to meet the challenge of transition. Through an analysis of excerpts and publication trends in *Jomhuri-ye Eslami*, I show how the IRP's discourse Islamicised the global liberation movement when addressing its instances; downplayed the role of the PLO when covering the Israel–Palestine conflict; and focused its content on Israel as the target of criticism to avoid addressing Palestinian movement organisations altogether, when possible.

The IRP's transitional discourse provides an example of the day-to-day progressions of a more general trend: the worldwide demise of the Third Worldism of the long 1960s and its transformation into a new regional and highly sectarian politics in the Middle East. Both Iran at large and the IRP itself are rich contexts within which to study this transformation in practice. On the one hand, with large and small guerrilla organisations active on the ground for more than a decade, the Third Worldist liberation agenda had left a strong mark on pre-1979 resistance in Iran, with the global guerrilla fighter as a leading symbol.[12] On the other hand, through the discursive work of writers such as Ali Shari'ati, Third Worldist language of anti-imperialism, decolonisation, and liberation of the oppressed had been fused with and embraced by the discourse of Islam as a source of revolutionary inspiration.[13] Due to these strong influences, the Third Worldist agenda continued to make frequent appearances in the post-revolutionary discourse of the clerical leadership, even though their ultimate goal was to promote a more traditional understanding of Islam and the pre-eminence of Khomeini's

---

[12] Arash Davari, 'Covering Iran: Leftist Continuities and Discontinuities, from Propaganda to PR', *TRAFO – Blog for Transregional Research* (blog), https://trafo.hypotheses.org/19103 (accessed 9 October 2022).

[13] Siavash Saffari, 'Ali Shariati and Cosmopolitan Localism', *Comparative Studies of South Asia, Africa and the Middle East* 39:2 (2019), 282–295.

leadership. The IRP's newspaper as a large corpus representing Islamist clerics' political thinking is, therefore, a prime case for studying the challenges of leaving the Third Worldist, left-leaning guerrilla behind.[14]

The IRP's transitional discourse is also an instance of Iranian leaders' dilemmas in the first post-revolution year. In this window of time, various political groups were still fighting to prove themselves as authentic revolutionaries, and commitment to world liberation movements was still a major indicator of being one. In addition to the global pressure of committing to Third World liberation, in other words, the IRP had to live up to the discourse produced more prolifically by leftist guerrilla organisations such as the MEK. At the same time, the IRP's practical, as opposed to discursive, priority was to focus on the domestic power-play in order to establish its hold on state-building in post-revolutionary Iran. The transitional discourse emerged as IRP leaders strove to maintain engagement with world liberation movements in their discourse, while focusing attention on domestic affairs.

More importantly, the sometimes-paradoxical transitory stance was both a precursor and a facilitator of Iran's foreign policy in the years to come, as the government acquired the resources and methods to establish and support Islamist militias in Palestine and elsewhere. As I will discuss in this chapter, the IRP marginalised secular and leftist movements in Palestine and elsewhere to favour Islamist movements and Muslim populations that were not represented by strong left-leaning organisations such as the PLO. At the same time, they implicitly highlighted movements that favoured actual or potential regional allies. Both moves were precursors of the Iranian government's future foreign policy: establishing or supporting Islamist groups across the region that would promote its politico-economic interest alongside its Shi'ite-revolutionary ideology.[15] The Islamic Revolutionary Guards' extraterritorial branch (the Quds Force) and militias such as Hamas and Hezbollah were outcomes of this emerging policy.

Below, I will first demonstrate the IRP's and *Jomhuri-ye Eslami*'s troubled relationship with the PLO and by derivation the Palestinian liberation agenda, and how this relationship sat within the context of the global transformation of Third Worldism and liberation movements. I will then

---

[14] It is worth noting again that the term Islamist is being used as a shorthand expression and should not be seen as an already consolidated monolith. Editors of *Jomhuri-ye Islami*, for instance, were considered as Islamic left, while prominent IRP clerics such as Beheshti and Rafsanjani were known as moderate or even conservative Islamists.
[15] Nunan, '"Neither East nor West"'.

discuss the newspaper's discursive strategy of partial coverage of world lib-eration movements at large, which heavily prioritised Islamist movements and Muslim populations. Next, I focus on the newspaper's treatment of the PLO in particular to show how it was marginalised in the coverage of Palestinian resistance. Finally, I point out a growing focus on the Israeli side of the Israel–Palestine conflict, sidestepping the need to acknowledge the PLO as the main agent of the Palestinian liberation movement altogether.

THIRD WORLDISM, PALESTINE, AND THE ISLAMIC REPUBLIC PARTY

The Islamic Republic Party (IRP) was formed shortly after the 11 February 1979 revolution, when clerics close to Ayatollah Khomeini decided to better organise their political influence against political rivals. The Party was officially founded on 17 February 1979 under the chairmanship of Ayatollah Mohammad Beheshti, a prominent cleric and among Ayatollah Khomeini's top confidants. Given the individual prominence of the clerics in its leadership, their close ties to Ayatollah Khomeini, and their parallel membership in the Revolutionary Council (the highest de facto decision-making authority in early post-revolutionary times), the IRP was destined to become the most influential political body in the following years. On 30 May 1979, less than five months later, the first issue of the IRP's official news outlet, *Jomhuri-ye Eslami*, was published and distributed nationally. The paper soon became one of the main national news outlets, alongside long-running ones such as *Keyhan* and *Ettela'at*, and it has been published on every weekday ever since.

Jomhuri-ye Eslami was not just a news outlet, but a platform to promote the IRP's political agenda. Prior to the paper's inauguration, IRP founders had introduced Islam and Khomeini's leadership as their ultimate guiding principles. In a booklet published during its early months of activity, the Party described its 'worldview' and ideal 'social structure' alongside its 'economic policy' and 'foreign policy'.[16] The worldview, described over the first twenty pages and later elaborated by Beheshti, the IRP chairman,

---

[16] Hezb-e Jomhuri-ye Eslami, *Mavaze'-e ma* [Our Stances] (n.p., n.d.). The booklet was later reprinted in Seyyed Mohammad Hosseini, *Hezb-e Jomhuri-ye Eslami: Mavaze'-e tafsili* (Tehran: Bogh'eh, 2009), 357–486.

in a series of public talks,[17] was a Shiʿite Islamic one based on the primacy of prophets' and the Shiʿite Imams' guidance. The ideal social structure, authors pointed out, was to be built around the creed (*maktab*). It had to acknowledge the guiding role of Islamic jurists and revere the pivotal status of the Grand Jurist (*vali-ye faqih*). The Party's foremost *raison d'être*, according to Beheshti, was to serve as 'an Islamic political and social formation that is capable of co-ordinating plans, points of view, stances, and the people at work' in different government offices.[18]

The centrality of Islam in its ideology, as well as the Party's tendency to focus on the domestic power-play around state-building,[19] distanced the IRP from discursive and practical involvement with a secular Third Worldist agenda. The foreign policy guidelines laid out in the introductory booklet are a case in point: 'Removing the Islamic World from Eastern and Western military groupings and transforming them [sic] into a large and independent power', for instance, was one of the IRP's stated foreign policy goals.[20] Palestine had served as a central internationalist agenda for all revolutionary groups – 'freeing Muslims of the world and Islamic lands from outsiders' domination, especially freeing the Occupied Land of Palestine and Afghanistan' was another item on the list of the IRP's foreign policy goals.[21] The secular PLO, as a result, was a source of potential friction with the Islamist and domestic tendencies of the Party. The IRP's rivalry with and fight against domestic groups with Marxist and leftist-liberationist inclinations such as the MEK and *Sazman-e cherik-ha-ye fada'i-ye khalq* (Organisation of the People's Fada'i Guerrillas), was tied to the issue of Palestine. Palestine served both as a fertile ground for proving the Party's revolutionary fervour and authenticity and as a minefield, since secular, leftist organisations that the Party was not willing to accept as allies spearheaded its liberation cause. Dealing with this dilemma would make the IRP a piece in the global puzzle that was gradually being completed, picturing the dissolution of the Third World as the secular revolutionary centre of the globe.

[17] Hosseini, *Hezb-e Jomhuri-ye Eslami*, x.
[18] Farid Qasemi, *Yadnameh-ye shahid-e mazlum Ayatollah Doktor Seyyed Mohammad Hosseini Beheshti* [In Memory of the martyr Ayatollah Dr Mohommad Hoseyni Beheshti] (Qom: Moʾasseseh-ye Nashr-e Qods, 1982), 139.
[19] Kheyrollah Esmaʾili, *Hezb-e Jomhuri-ye Eslami* (Tehran: Markaz-e Asnad-e Enqelab-e Eslami, 2007).
[20] Hezb-e Jomhuri-ye Eslami, *Mavaze'- e ma*, 82.
[21] Ibid.

Despite the amicable relationship in the very early stages of the revolution, Khomeini himself and clerics of the IRP had qualms about the PLO. Its secular ideology, connections to the global left and the Eastern Bloc, and consequent prioritisation of guerrilla warfare over ideological adherence to Islam as the source of organisational identity did not sit well with the rising Islamist faction of Iranian politics. Even before moves that were unfavourable in the eyes of the Islamists – such as the attempt to mediate between Iran and the US to resolve the hostage crisis[22] or supporting Iraq during the Iran–Iraq War – these fundamental differences made the IRP–PLO relationship precarious and only strategically sustained.

Nevertheless, in the race for claiming the status of genuine revolutionaries where rival publications were flaunting active participation in the struggle for Palestine, the IRP could not afford to ignore the Third Worldist revolutionary agenda, and the PLO in particular. The MEK's periodical, *Mojahed*, for instance, emphasised its close relationship with the PLO and Fatah rather regularly. On 15 October 1979, *Mojahed* reprinted a letter they had received from Fatah inviting MEK representatives to visit the resistance front in southern Lebanon. The note preceding the facsimile of the letter boasted that '[t]he invitation attests to long-standing mutual interests of the two organisations. May the heroic peoples of Palestine and Iran succeed in ever strengthening their bonds.'[23] The letter containing the MEK's reverential acceptance of the invitation, addressed to the Fatah/PLO representative in Iran, Hani al-Hassan, appeared on the same page.

Following Khomeini's and the government's embrace of the PLO in the early days, the IRP and its newspaper, *Jomhuri-ye Eslami*, maintained a cordial relationship with the organisation as well. In October 1979, for instance, a few days after Hani al-Hassan's visit to the *Jomhuri-ye Eslami* office, a high-ranking PLO officer met with the Party's leadership council. Khalil al-Wazir, also known as Abu Jihad, was Arafat's top aide. During his trip to Tehran, he paid a visit to the IRP headquarters where he had a meeting with the leadership council, gave a talk, and had a conversation with Beheshti, the Party chairman, afterwards. The paper published the

---

[22] Alavi, *Iran and Palestine*, 57.
[23] Mojahed Editorial Board, 'Payam-e da'vat-e sazman-e azadibakhsh-e Felestin' [Palestine Liberation Movement's Message of Invitation], *Mojahed*, 15 October 1979, p. 12.

transcript of his talk on 16 October 1979,[24] and a long exclusive interview with him that was conducted during the visit, on 18 October.[25] Both in the talk and the interview, Abu Jihad emphasised the significance of the Iranian revolutionaries' victory for Palestinian fighters and reported on the Palestinian guerrillas' achievements and military strategies. Before presenting the content of Abu Jihad's talk,[26] the *Jomhuri-ye Eslami* editors explained the circumstances of the talk, mentioned the subsequent conversation with Beheshti, and promised readers that they would publish the content of that conversation in the next issue; but the promise was never realised.

Although IRP leaders and the newspaper editorial team had such direct encounters with the PLO, they were few and far between. The scarcity of such occasions both enabled and necessitated a more nuanced approach in the paper's daily content for reconciling the paradox of Palestine: the need to present an active internationalist profile around the struggle for Palestine while keeping a distance from the PLO and advancing the Party's Islamist mission.

ISLAMICISING THE THIRD WORLDIST AGENDA

Between its launch and the start of the Iran–Iraq War, the IRP newspaper kept an active publication profile with regard to the Third Worldist agenda. Almost every day, the paper included a 'Political [*siyasi*]' page featuring original and translated articles about ongoing power struggles around the world. Often, a significant portion of the page was dedicated to resistance movements or oppressed populations across the globe. At other times, the space was filled with analyses of the perpetrators of 'world imperialism'. These articles commonly took a general approach, as opposed to indicating any practical involvement on behalf of the Iranian side or addressing

---

[24] JEED, 'Sazman-e azadibakhsh-e Felestin as hezb-e Jomhuri-ye Eslami da'vat kard' [Palestine's Liberation Organisation Extends an Invitation to the Islamic Republic Party], *JE*, 16 October 1979, p. 2.

[25] JEED, 'Enqelab-e Iran halghe-ye mohasere-ye enqelab-e Felestin va a'rab ra az beyn bord: mosahebe-ye ekhtesasi-ye Jomhuri-ye Eslami ba Abujihad, rahbar-e amaliyati-ye Felestin' [Iran's Revolution Broke the Siege on the Revolution of Palestine and the Arabs: Jomhuri-ye Eslami's Exclusive Interview with Palestine's Operation Commander Abujihad], *JE*, 18 October 1979, p. 6.

[26] JEED, 'Sazman-e azadibakhsh-e Felestin as hezb-e Jomhuri-ye Eslami da'vat kard' [Palestine's Liberation Organisation Extends an Invitation to the Islamic Republic Party], *JE*, 16 October 1979, p. 2.

details of resistance strategies or ideology that could contradict the Party's Islamism. They introduced the movements' history and organisational structure, their present status, and how they followed the same pattern that the Iranian revolution had followed and contributed to – that of the global uprising of the oppressed against world imperialism.

At first glance, the political section presents a consistent effort on behalf of the editorial team to live up to the Third Worldist revolutionary ethos of the time. However, a closer look shows that the paper's editors put an Islamist slant on the Third Worldist agenda. In its coverage of international resistance against imperialism, the paper closely tied instances of resistance movements to what the IRP considered the main features of the Iranian revolution – Islam and Khomeini's leadership. When writing on oppressed populations and resistance movements across the globe without immediate ties to Iran, editors spotlighted Muslim groups and resistance movements much more frequently than non-Muslim ones. Between May 1979 and September 1980, for every story published on a non-Muslim entity, there were easily more than ten covering Muslim populations and organisations.

For instance, the Black Muslim movement in America, which had also been recognised as part of the Third World revolution by many activists around the world,[27] appeared frequently as a topic on this page. Despite its alleged deviation from the IRP's preferred version of Islam, the Black Muslims' cause as an instance of global resistance was uniquely compatible with the IRP's worldview and was of great assistance in the time of transition from the left to the religious. It was a Muslim uprising, mainly detached from the left, fighting against US hegemony. In fact, in addition to *Jomhuri-ye Eslami*'s frequent mentions and analyses of either the movement or African-American Muslims' conditions in the United States, the IRP published and circulated a booklet on the topic, introducing the movement's history, its different branches, and appreciating its existence while criticising its divergence from 'true' Islam due to innovative interpretations.[28]

Even when Iranian individuals or groups were involved in a story related to a liberation movement, the generalist treatment of Third Worldism and

---

[27] Christiansen and Scarlett, *The Third World in the Global 1960s*.

[28] Anonymous, *Mosalmanan-e siyahpust-e Amrika'i* [American Black Muslims] (*Hezb-e Jomhuri-ye Eslami*, 1980). I have not been able to find a record of the IRP's publications to be able to situate this among them. This booklet, published with a print run of ten thousand copies, according to the first page, is one of a handful that I was able to locate on WorldCat.

global liberation continued and sometimes even adopted a tone critical of practical involvement. As Mohammad Ataie discusses in his contribution to this volume, an experienced and strong internationalist faction was active in Iran in the early post-revolutionary months, endorsed by Ayatollah Hossein-Ali Montazeri and spearheaded by his son, Mohammad Montazeri. This internationalist faction of clerics, politicians, and young activists' ties to the PLO had led to an uneasy relationship with the IRP. Hence, the Iranian internationalists' activities were covered in *Jomhuri-ye Eslami* only when influential political figures such as Ayatollah Montazeri or interim government members – people who were politically significant enough for *Jomhuri-ye Eslami* to feature news stories around them – were involved. Even in these instances of selective coverage, aspects serving the IRP's Islamism were aggrandised to the detriment of the rest. On 17 March 1980,[29] for instance, *Jomhuri-ye Eslami* reported on a meeting between Munir Shafiq, a famed pro-Palestinian writer (whose adoption of political Islam is analysed in Sune Haugbolle's chapter in this volume), and Ayatollah Montazeri, in which they discussed the planning of a 'twenty-million-strong demonstration for the liberation of Palestine and the Quds [Jerusalem]'. The short report mentioned only in passing that Montazeri 'discussed matters related to global liberation movements', dedicating the remaining space to Shafiq's acknowledgement of Khomeini's popularity in Palestine.

More radical instances of internationalist activism were reported with heavy criticism. Ayatollah Montazeri's son, Mohammad, who was an experienced guerrilla and at the time commanded a militia independently of the state,[30] was occasionally the subject of such criticism. In an incident that was renounced even by his father, Mohammad Montazeri, a cleric himself, was involved in a brief armed encounter with authorities at Tehran's International Airport. The next time he appeared at the airport to fly out in pursuit of his liberationist agenda, airport security arrested him and his deputy. He 'was busted out' of the situation, as reported by *Jomhuri-ye Eslami*, by 'a

---

[29] JEED, 'Rahpeyma'i-ye bist milyuni bara-ye azadi-ye Felestin va "Qods"' [Twenty-million-strong demonstration for the liberation of Palestine and the Quds], *JE*, 17 March 1980, p. 2.
[30] Maryam Alemzadeh, 'Revolutionaries for Life: The IRGC and the Global Guerrilla Movement', in Arang Keshavarzian and Ali Mirsepassi (eds), *Global 1979: Geographies and Histories of the Iranian Revolution* (Cambridge: Cambridge University Press, 2021); Mohammad Ataie, 'Revolutionary Iran's 1979 Endeavor in Lebanon', *Middle East Policy* 20:2 (2013), 137–157.

number of his followers' who carried arms. Analysing the event critically, the story read:

> Once again, Mr Mohammad Montazeri has created drama. During days when people expect the cutting sword of justice to eliminate all inequalities and all class and group advantages, ... someone with [respectable] resistance background and wearing the sacred clerical suit has taken a new step to dull this sword with his and his friends' law-breaking and irresponsible actions ... It is as if Mr Montazeri and his associates have lost respect for [revolutionary] ideals and, pursuing the mirage of prosperity they have built for themselves, have taken up [arms] to destroy them all.[31]

Besides this critical engagement with the radical internationalism of some Iranian activists, the only other time the paper featured detailed, practical attention to global resistance movements was in stories involving pro-Khomeini movements and events. This is while publications such as *Mojahed*, the MEK's daily newsletter, reported on the Organisation's engagement with recognised liberationist movements of the world through mutual visits, communication, and analyses of resistance strategies.[32] In September 1979, for instance, Khomeini's representative in Bahrain, Hojjat al-Islam Modarresi, was expelled from that country and exiled to the United Arab Emirates. According to *Jomhuri-ye Eslami*, Ayatollah Montazeri sent a message to Bahraini government officials in protest, which was not well received in Bahrain. Bahraini media 'heavily criticised the move, claiming it amounted to ... meddling in Bahrain's domestic affairs'.[33] In response to the events, according to *Jomhuri-ye Eslami*, the Islamic Liberation Front of Bahrain – a nascent Shi'ite militia in that country – issued a declaration in protest against these events, which made a headline on 10 September ('Bahrain Liberation

---

[31] JEED, 'Cheguneh Mohammad Montazeri ra farari dadand' [How Mohammad Montazeri was Busted Out], *JE*, 16 September 1979, p. 2.

[32] An invitation from Polisario for a visit (*Mojahed*, 22 October 1979, p. 7); a report from a meeting with the Popular Front for the Liberation of Oman (*Mojahed*, 15 October 1979, p. 12); and an analysis of the Palestinian prisoners' strike and the necessity of engaging with the Palestinian liberation (*Mojahed*, 22 October 1979, p. 11) are a few examples among many.

[33] JEED, 'E'teraz-e shadidollahn-e jebheh-ye azadibakhsh-e Bahrain be tab'id-e namayandeh-ye emam' [Liberation Front of Bahrain's Severe Protest against the Exile of the Imam's Representative], *JE*, 10 September 1979, p. 2.

Movement Heavily Protest the Exile of the Imam's Representative') and was published in full, together with an analysis of the events, in the same issue.

Twelve days later, Modarresi was arrested in the UAE. IRP leaders issued a declaration in *Jomhuri-ye Eslami* demanding his release,[34] and the paper printed an exclusive interview with him upon his release and arrival in Iran on the next day.[35] Similarly detailed, explicative, and engaged coverage – as opposed to the general introductory treatment that liberation movements commonly received – resurfaced in relation to other pro-Khomeini figures and movements in the UAE, Kuwait, and Iraq, among other places.

Occasional deviations from *Jomhuri-ye Eslami*'s minimal engagement with liberation movements around the world and the internationalist faction in Iran show that the editorial team was aware that the minimal approach was insufficient for upholding the Party's revolutionary posture. Showing respect for the Third Worldist agenda was still essential to maintaining the claim to revolutionary commitment. On 6 January 1980, *Jomhuri-ye Eslami* printed a headline announcing that 'During an Exuberant Ceremony, World Liberation Movements Conference Was Inaugurated', and briefly reported on the events of the first day of the meeting.[36] In addition to covering the news of the conference in this report and a follow-up report about its second day, the paper ran a special twenty-issue series, starting a few days before the inauguration of the conference. The series, 'Introduction to Liberation Movements', which replaced the 'Political' page during its run, was the most consistent show of solidarity with the internationalist agenda to ever appear in *Jomhuri-ye Eslami*. Each rendition of the series, which was published daily with a few pauses in between, consisted of a full-page introduction of a liberation movement from across the world. Some movements took up more than one issue: 'Polisario', the 'Black American Muslims' Movement', and 'Iraq's Islamic Dawa Party – Iraq's Islamic Action Organisation' took up two issues each, and 'Afghanistan's Islamic Movements' spanned the

---

[34] JEED, 'Hezb-e Jomhuri-ye Eslami khastar-e azadi-ye Seyyed Hadi Modarresi shod' [The Islamic Republic Party Demands the Release of Seyyed Hadi Modarresi], *JE*, 22 September 1979, p. 1.

[35] JEED, 'Mosahebeh-ye Jomhuri-ye Eslami ba Hojjat-ol-Eslam Modarresi' [Jomhuri-ye Eslami's Interview with Hojjat-ol-Eslam Modarresi], *JE*, 23 September 1979, pp. 1–2.

[36] JEED, 'Dar yek marasem-e shurangiz, konferans-e jonbesh-ha-ye azadibakhsh-e jahan goshayesh yaft' [During an Exuberant Ceremony, World Liberation Movements Conference Was Inaugurated], *JE*, 6 January 1980, p. 1. See Ataie's contribution to this volume. One of the controversies he discusses was mentioned in passing in the paper's coverage of the Conference.

last four issues. Leftist groups such as the Popular Front for the Liberation of Oman and the Eritrean Liberation Front, among others, in addition to the Islamic Revolutionary Organisation of the Arabian Peninsula, filled the remaining issues. The list covered many organisations whose delegations were present at the World Liberation Conference.

Palestinian liberation movements at large claimed a single issue: 'Palestinian Liberation Organisation–Fatah'.[37] The single essay was exemplary of the paper's treatment of the Palestine agenda; the treatment that allowed the paper to keep Palestine at the ideological forefront despite the qualms IRP leaders had about the PLO, as I will discuss next.

PALESTINE WITHOUT THE PLO

Despite rather consistent, albeit selective, engagement with liberation movements of the world and with the question of Palestine (there were news headlines or op-eds published almost every day on either or both), the PLO (as the leading political authority in Palestine and the vanguard of the global guerrilla movement) appeared only marginally in *Jomhuri-ye Eslami*. When covering the news of the Israel–Palestine conflict or in Palestine-related op-eds, the PLO was rarely ever mentioned by name. The only exception was events in which PLO leaders and members were involved in a strict organisational capacity, at least in the eyes of *Jomhuri-ye Eslami* reporters and editors. For example, a brief report on 26 March 1980,[38] translated from the Kuwaiti newspaper *Al-Qabas*, told the story of a prisoner exchange between the PLO and Israel, where a captured Israeli spy was traded for two imprisoned PLO leaders. The report provided some detail of the activities of the Israeli agent but mentioned the PLO and its imprisoned members only in passing. In most other stories published in *Jomhuri-ye Eslami*, the Palestinian struggle was instead attributed to 'Palestinian resistance', 'Palestinian guerrillas', 'the Palestinian people', and, when it was necessary to be more specific, members of 'one of the important Palestinian groups'.[39]

---

[37] JEED, 'Sazman-e Azadibakhsh-e Felestin-Fath' [Palestine Liberation Organisation–Fatah], *JE*, 19 January 1980, p. 3.

[38] Al-Mustaqbal, 'Cheguneh jasus-e Esra'il dastgir shod' [How the Israeli Spy was Arrested], translated by Shaker Kasra'i, 26 March 1980, p. 3.

[39] See, for example, Shaker Kasra'i, 'Rastakhiz-e zedd-e sahyunisti' [The Anti-Zionist Renaissance], *JE*, 31 May 1980, p. 3.

In most of these cases, it is easily verifiable that the PLO was the unnamed point of reference.

The exclusive discussion of Fatah and the PLO in the 'Introduction to Liberation Movements' series was an aberration. In rare instances like this, the paper either adopted a neutral tone by focusing on the organisation's structure or emphasised its dedication to the Palestinian national cause to undermine its alleged ties to leftist social thought and the Eastern Bloc. The Palestine 'Introduction to Liberation Movements' series started with a general introduction to 'The Land of Palestine [*sarzamin-e Felestin*]' and 'The Palestine Problem [*mas'ale-ye Felestin*]', before moving on to an intro-duction of Fatah.[40] It praised Fatah for having 'started the real and armed revolution against Israel'. The article then incorporated a bullet-list of the organisation's goals according to its leaders and described its organisational structure [*tashkilat*]. When the writing did get more involved and evalua-tive, it was to defend the organisation against allegations of reactionary or communist/Marxist tendencies:

> Some countries considered Fatah a reactionary organisation, and some a Communist or Marxist one; while the only fundamental goal of this organisation was freeing the Palestinian land and liberating the Palestinian nation from the yoke of global Zionism, and until today it has continued its path as a liberationist, nationalist organisation.[41]

This was the only mention of the organisation's ideology. The text never referred to any leftist inspirations of Fatah, whether in its anti-imperialist and liberationist goals or its guerrilla tactics.

For a long time, the essay on Fatah and the PLO in the 'Introduction to Liberation Movements' series remained the only mention to appear in the paper. The second and last extensive treatment of Palestinian movement organisations in the timespan under study came about four months later. On 31 March 1980, the 'Political' page, which had been resumed after the end of the Liberation Movements series, featured the first part of a four-part article, 'Palestinian Revolution and Its Movements'. A telling note from the editorial team preceded the article's first paragraph:

---

[40] JEED, 'Palestine Liberation Organisation-Fatah', *JE*, 19 January 1980, p. 3.
[41] Ibid.

With our extensive thanks to dear audience members who read this page, we are happy that in response to their request, we have been able to publish some material on 'the Palestinian Revolution'. If dear readers ever have more information at hand, especially on statistical aspects of the Palestinian liberation movements, they should kindly send them to this newspaper so that they are published under their own names on this very page. We sincerely thank you for your critical notes [*tazakkorat*] on this matter and other matters of your interest.[42]

The note not only acknowledged the noticeable omission of Palestinian movement organisations from the paper's content, but also implied the editors' lack of interest in dedicating more time and space to the topic by delegating to readers the task of sending relevant material to the paper.

The four-part introduction of 'The Palestinian Revolution and Its Movements'[43] was another case of blasé and factually biased representation of Palestinian movements. Following the disengaged tone of the previous essay, which appeared in the 'Liberation Movements' series, it started to introduce eleven Palestinian liberation movements one by one, spearheaded by the PLO and Fatah. The second[44] and third[45] instalments consisted of a detailed introduction to the PLO's organisational structure and a chronological bullet-point list of decisions made in its major congressional meetings. The series then continued with a general history of the Palestinian Land before and after the British mandate and ended with statistics about the population of Palestinians in Palestine, in camps, and in other countries around the world in the fourth instalment.[46] Missing in this four-part series was any mention of the PLO's partially successful guerrilla operations over time and their close ties with and status within the global leftist guerrilla movement. Along the same lines, the occasional financial and material support that Palestinian organisations received from the Soviet Union or Arab countries in the region that Iran did not consider allies was also left out. When addressing the PLO's financial sources, for instance, the article merely stated that 'the PLO's budget is provided by its members'.[47]

---

[42] JEED, 'Enqelab-e Felestin va jonbesh-hayash' [The Palestinian Revolution and Its Movements], part 1, *JE*, 31 March 1980, p. 3.

[43] Ibid.

[44] JEED, 'The Palestinian Revolution and Its Movements, part 2', *JE*, 5 April 1980, p. 3.

[45] JEED, 'The Palestinian Revolution and Its Movements, part 3', *JE*, 6 April 1980, p. 3

[46] JEED, 'The Palestine Revolution and Its Movements, part 4', *JE*, 9 April 1980, p. 3.

[47] Ibid.

The other side of the PLO whitewashing and omission coin was an attempt to illustrate the Palestinian struggle as one with a strong Islamic and even Khomeinist identity. After the Saudi move to recognise Israel conditionally, for instance, *Jomhuri-ye Eslami* published a report on the ensuing conflict on the West Bank on 19 June 1980. The report contended that

> popular groups have formed and are resisting, similar to those in Iran during the revolution. The group [sic] considers itself a supporter of Ayatollah Khomeini and is known as *al-Khumeyniyyun*.[48]

The same story further highlighted the Islamists' rise by pointing out that an Islamist had won an unspecified university campus poll, because 'students saw how Iran's last Shah was toppled by Islam and they want to expel Israel the same way'. The article implicitly criticised Arafat and the PLO by quoting a '68-year-old lawyer from Ramallah': referring to Arafat and 'the moderate Arabs' who had switched sides to join him, he was quoted as saying, 'Israel assists Communists [i.e. the PLO] in the Occupied Lands and assigns them significance to show the USA that if a Palestinian country is established, it will be amongst the Soviet's satellites.'

The same Islamicising effort was also observable in occasional coverage of PLO-related news. On 26 August 1979, for instance, Arafat issued a plea following a new round of offensives against Palestinian camps in southern Lebanon. He condemned the 'terrorist Zionists'' violence, supported by 'American imperialism'. As reported by *Jomhuri-ye Eslami*, Arafat pleaded to 'kings and rulers of Arab countries', 'Muslim nations, [and] resisting nations of the world', and 'public conscience around the world and freedom fighters and awakened souls across the globe' to take a stance. *Jomhuri-ye Eslami*'s headline for Arafat's general plea, however, spotlighted the mention of Muslim nations: the front page headline read, 'Arafat pleads to Muslims of the world against Israel's expansive offensives'.[49]

Through such discursive strategies, *Jomhuri-ye Eslami* presented a distorted image of Palestinian resistance by downplaying leftist organisations' political and military influence and omitting their celebrated globalist and

---

[48] JEED, 'Gostaresh-e damaneh-ye mobarazat-e A'rab-e karaneh-ye gharbi-ye rood-e Ordon' [Expansion of Resistance among Arabs of Jordan River's West Bank], *JE*, 19 June 1980, p. 3.

[49] JEED, 'Arafat pleads to Muslims of the world against Israel's expansive offensives', *JE*, 27 August 1979, pp. 1, 2, 12.

leftist tendencies on the one hand, while over-emphasising Islamist threads within the Palestinian liberation movements on the other. In further service of the Islamicisation effort, the next discursive level of obliteration of leftist guerrillas was to focus news coverage and analysis on the other side of the conflict – Israel. So, I will now discuss how a focus on Israel as the common enemy kept the Palestinian cause at the forefront without the need for a detailed engagement with Palestinian resistance.

ISRAEL WITHOUT PALESTINE

Jomhuri-ye Eslami's discursive tactic of marginalising the PLO as the political authority representing Palestine culminated in one last move: foregrounding Israel as the common enemy in news coverage and op-eds to the detriment of the PLO, seen as an unfavourable ally. On 6 February 1980,[50] an op-ed was published on the 'Struggle of Palestine against the Israeli Government'. The author contended that '[w]hat makes Palestinian liberation organisations more resistant and more stubborn against the occupier state of Israel *is neither their improved armed power nor the support of neighbouring Arab countries*, rather the continued terrorist pose of Israel' (emphasis added). By seeking the root of the problem in Israel's paradoxical and problematic status as a hostile 'First World' product stuck in a 'Third World' context, the author concluded that:

> The Palestinian guerrilla is not a terrorist. Rather, the only initiators and innovators of the wave of terror that is observed in the Arab Middle East after WWII are Israel's radicals and groups associated with the international Zionist movement. The existence of Palestinian guerrilla organisations is fundamentally an outcome of the ravaging and invasion, and how can something born out of [i.e. in response to] and strengthened by violence go away when invasion and violence continues?[51]

---

[50] JEED, 'Fashism-e modern: tafsiri bar nabard-e Felestin dar moqabel-e dolat-e Esra'il' [Modern Fascism: An Interpretation of the Palestinian Fight against the Israeli State], *JE*, 6 February 1980, p. 3.
[51] Ibid.

Not only did the op-ed place Israel at the centre of analysis, it also degraded the sources of Palestinian guerrillas' unfavourable power, and implicitly justified their existence as tolerable as long as Israel existed.

Over time, there were more and more mentions of Israel in *Jomhuri-ye Eslami*'s coverage of the struggle, and fewer mentions of Palestine. A translated article in the 3 March 1980 issue is indicative of this trend.[52] The article was taken from the Lebanese Magazine *Al-Hawadith*, which at the time published prolifically on the PLO's military activities. The chosen article, tellingly, is one on 'Israel's Political and Military Games' – a geopolitical analysis of Israel's foreign policy, leaving out the Palestinian resistance altogether. Towards the end of the timeframe under study, pieces about Israel sans Palestine appeared more and more frequently in *Jomhuri-ye Eslami*. These pieces discussed various aspects of Israel's presence in the Middle East or its foreign policy and military capacity at large, such as lengthy coverage of the opening of Israel's embassy – or 'the den of espionage [*lane-ye jasusi*]' – in Cairo,[53] or reports on the Israeli government's nuclear plans and its co-operation with the apartheid regime in South Africa to help them produce nuclear arms.[54]

This gradual shift was in line with a more general trend in the newspaper: that of dedicating more space to the targets of Third Worldist movements, i.e. global forces of imperialism (and Zionism, by proxy), than the movements themselves. For instance, *Jomhuri-ye Eslami* published a five-part analysis titled 'The Beginning of a New Era of Global Imperialism',[55] a parallel to an earlier series that introduced liberation movements. It is worth noting that Islamist movements and (non-Palestinian) Muslim populations were still somewhat of an exception to this trend. For instance, starting in July 1980, the paper ran three instalments of a series titled 'Muslims Across the World [*mosalmanan dar jahan*]', covering colonial histories of the repression of Muslims in Malaysia, Iraq, and Egypt. The 'Islamic Revolution in Iraq' and

---

52 Al-Hawadith, 'Bazi-ha-ye siasi va nezami-ye Esra'il' [Israel's Political and Military Games], translated by Majid Dashtestani, *JE*, 3 March 1980, p. 3.
53 JEED, 'Goshayesh-e laneh-ye jasusi dar Qahere' [The Opening of the Den of Espionage in Cairo], *JE*, 9 March 1980, p. 3.
54 'Joz'iat-e avvalin azmayesh-e atomi-ye rejim-e eshghalgar-e Qods' [Details of the First Nuclear Experiment by the Regime Occupying Jerusalem], translated by Hassan Fathi, *JE*, 30 September 1980, p. 3.
55 JEED, 'Aghaz-e marhale-ye jadid dar asr-e amperyalism-e jahani' [The Beginning of a New Era of Global Imperialism] (5 parts), *JE*, 19–29 March 1980, p. 3.

'Islamic Movements in Iraq' also received special attention towards the end of our timeframe, as skirmishes close to the Iran–Iraq border escalated.

Even when the Israel–Palestine issue, as opposed to Israel per se, was the main subject, Israeli government plans and actions took precedence over Palestinian politics. A translated article from *Al-Mustaqbal* published on 5 October 1980,[56] for instance, commented on Israel's intention to annex the Golan Heights without a mention of the PLO as the authority on the ground. Interestingly, not even the word Palestine was mentioned in the relatively lengthy article, which addressed general 'Arab-Israeli' issues instead.

With the start of the Iran–Iraq War in September 1980, *Jomhuri-ye Eslami*'s coverage of Israel's 'Zionist and Imperialist' expansionism became even more abstract. As an op-ed on 21 October 1980 put it, Israel's policy was perceived as part of the global effort of 'repressing Islam' – an effort which now included Iraq, as its president was 'beating on the drums of war'.[57]

CONCLUSION

The first seventeen months after the February 1979 revolution in Iran, before the Iraqi invasion accelerated the monopolisation of power in the hands of Islamist clerics, was a period of uncertainties and possibilities. To remain viable as revolutionaries, it was essential for Islamist leaders of the IRP to interact with and respond to the prevalent revolutionary discourse of the time. The Palestinian liberation cause was a central talking point of the discourse and, although already weakened by political and military affronts from enemies and former allies, the PLO was still a name to conjure with. The IRP leaders needed to dissolve the PLO into their Islamist agenda in a way that would not sacrifice the Palestinian cause at large in the process.

By analysing the content of the IRP's daily newspaper, *Jomhuri-ye Eslami*, I have shown how the IRP used a series of interconnected discursive manoeuvres to achieve this goal. *Jomhuri-ye Eslami* Islamicised the global liberation movement by a skewed coverage, favouring Muslim and Islamist movements and highlighting Islamic traces in secular movements;

---

[56] Almostaghbal, 'Elhaq-e Jolan, qadam-e ba'di-ye Esra'il' [Annexing Golan, Israel's Next Move], translated by Majid Dashtestani, *JE*, 5 October 1980.
[57] Kamalinia, V., 'Chashm-e tama'-e Esra'il be Litani' [Israel's Greedy Gaze towards Litani], *JE*, 21 October 1980, p. 3.

marginalised or kept silent on the PLO when reporting on the Palestinian struggle; and focused most of its analytical attention on Israel as the target of the struggle, as opposed to Palestine as its subject.

This chapter has delved into nuances of the IRP's discursive treatment of the Palestinian cause to enrich the broader picture of the tumultuous period 1979–1982. It zooms in on the Iranian Islamists' attempt to sidestep the secular liberation fighter and instead promote what they perceived as a global Islamic awakening. The discursive tactics illustrated here provide a snapshot of the conservative Islamists' hesitant trial and error approach to the Palestinian cause before they took over state-building and found a foolproof ally in Hamas. In this sense, as the Iranian revolution of 1979 did at large, the IRP's Islamicising agenda contributed to the global demise of anti-imperialist movements and their replacement with sectarian conflicts affected by regional and global politics, domestic state-building concerns, and neoliberal reform agendas. It is therefore important to view the IRP's discursive tactics as one among many instances of hesitations, disappointments, and reassessed ambitions and hopes across the world, as new forces gradually redefined Third Worldism and took it in new directions.

PART THREE

THIRD WORLDISM AND THE NATION

8

TRANSLATION, REVOLUTIONARY PRAXIS, AND THE ENIGMA OF MANUCHEHR HEZARKHANI

Nasser Mohajer and Eskandar Sadeghi-Boroujerdi

The life, writings, and example of Iranian intellectual, translator, and political activist Manuchehr Hezarkhani, who passed away on 18 March 2022, touched the lives of a generation of Iranian students, intellectuals, and militants, including several of twentieth-century Iran's towering literati, Samad Behrangi (d.1968), Jalal Al-e Ahmad (d.1969), and Mostafa Shoʿaʿiyan (d.1976) among them. In this chapter we provide an outline and analysis of Hezarkhani's contribution to the intellectual and political life of modern Iran. We strive to do this while also confronting the manifest contradiction that exists between his critical intellect and erudition, steadfast commitment to anti-colonial liberation movements, redoubtable championing of the causes of freedom and democracy before and during the Iranian Revolution of 1978–1979, and his profoundly disconcerting alliance with the Organisation of the People's Mojahedin of Iran (*Sazman-e mojahedin-e khalq-e Iran*), following his exile to Paris in 1981.

The case of Hezarkhani provides a powerful illustration of a turbulent and deeply contradictory trajectory in the history of Third World liberation. In the course of his eventful political and intellectual career, Hezarkhani shifted positions from that of militant student opposition to the Shah's regime and populariser of anti-colonial and independent socialist literature, to active participation in revolutionary movements, and finally political defeat, when he ultimately entered into alliance with a diverse array of political forces in opposition to the Islamic Republic

Caricature of Manuchehr Hezarkhani accompanying his essay
'The Worldview of the Little Black Fish', originally published in
the literary journal Arash *in November/December 1968.*

of Iran. This alliance failed to achieve its objectives and after a few years
of activity in exile it degenerated into a front organisation dominated by
the People's Mojahedin.

Hezarkhani's intellectual and political commitments frequently shone
through in his choice of translations that were tantamount to political interventions and which sought to influence, cohere, and mobilise those political
and social forces with which he held himself to be broadly aligned. Moreover,
his translations and interjections were intimately bound up with *global*
problems and questions facing anti-colonial liberation movements around
the structure and distribution of power in the world system, the relationship
between nationalism, culture and resistance, the depredations of American
imperialism and the response to its implacable and enveloping expansion, the
dogmatism and authoritarian failings of Soviet socialism, and the possibilities

for internationalist solidarity across borders in a world of nation-states. The political efficacy of his translation work and his decisive role in introducing key texts in the history of socialism and anti-colonial thought to Persian-speaking audiences in the course of the 1960s and 1970s is beyond doubt.

The more thorny and challenging question, however, is how this translational praxis should be understood in relation to his concrete political decisions and manoeuvres, and it is this relationship and tension that we intend to explore through the medium of Hezarkhani's biography in this chapter.

EARLY YEARS

Manuchehr Hezarkhani was born on 23 May 1934 into a middle-class family in Tehran. His father, Yusef Hezarkhani, was a retired major in the Iranian army and his mother, Mahin Dokht, was a traditional homemaker. He attended both primary and secondary school in Tehran, graduating from Firuz Bahram High School, one of Iran's first modern and most prestigious educational institutions, which had been originally founded by Parsis hailing from the Indian subcontinent. Firuz Bahram counted myriad political and intellectual luminaries of Hezarkhani's generation among its graduates, including Hamid Enayat, Seyyed Hossein Nasr, Jamshid Behnam, Ezzatollah Fuladvand, and Hedayat Matin-Daftari.

As a young high school student, Hezarkhani was a follower of Khalil Maleki (1901–1969), a lifelong socialist, who had broken with the Tudeh Party of Iran (*Hezb-e tudeh-ye Iran*) in 1947–1948, in large part due to its perceived subordination to the political interests and machinations of the Soviet Union. In 1951, despite their sizeable differences, Maleki and the French-trained philosopher and seasoned rabble-rouser Mozaffar Baqa'i, who had pursued a doctorate in philosophy at the Sorbonne in the late 1930s, established the Toilers' Party of the Iranian Nation (*Hezb-e zahmatkeshan-e mellat-e Iran*). This new party and relatively short-lived experiment would rally to the cause of the oil nationalisation movement and champion the plight of Iran's exploited workers and the downtrodden. The young Hezarkhani considered himself a sympathiser and fellow traveller, though he was first and foremost a devotee and supporter of Maleki and his wing of the party.

STUDENT YEARS IN FRANCE

Upon graduating from high school in 1952, Hezarkhani left Iran for Montpellier, France, to continue his studies. He thus left Iran in the midst of the 1951–1953 oil crisis and before the fateful toppling of the Mosaddeq government on 19 August 1953. The coup, a watershed moment in the history of modern Iran and global struggles for decolonisation more broadly, was organised and financed by the Eisenhower and Churchill administrations and their respective intelligence services, and executed with the collaboration of their allies inside the Pahlavi court, army, and clergy.[1] Upon his arrival in France, he was quick to find fellow Iranian student activists and sympathisers of the National Front of Iran (*Jebheh-ye melli-ye Iran*), the broad coalition of individuals and groups which had expressed its commitment to the nationalisation of the almost universally maligned Anglo-Iranian Oil Company and support for the national movement under Mosaddeq's leadership.

After intensively studying the French language, Hezarkhani registered to continue his studies at the University of Montpellier's medical school. Meanwhile, he remained active in the nascent student movement abroad, which was spreading across Europe and the United States, and emerging as a conduit for discontent in the aftermath of the 1953 *coup d'état*, a decisive turning point in the country's history. He also continued to build close relationships with sympathisers of the now-disbanded Toilers' Party of Iran, Third Force, which had broken with Baqa'i after the latter had turned on the Mosaddeq government and allied itself with the Iranian premier's most recalcitrant opponents.[2]

Maleki, who had famously broken with the Tudeh Party in 1948 over its alleged subordination to the Soviet Union and its geopolitical interests, drew upon his considerable erudition and theoretical acumen to theorise the notion of 'Third Force in General' and 'Third Force in Particular'. This notion, which Maleki first formulated in a series of articles for Baqa'i's newspaper, *Shahed*, in 1949–1950, prefigured visions of non-alignment

---

[1] See Mark J. Gasiorowski, 'The 1953 Coup D'etat in Iran', *International Journal of Middle East Studies*, vol. 19, no. 3 (1987): 261–286; Ervand Abrahamian, *The Coup: 1953, the CIA, and the Roots of Modern U.S.-Iranian Relations* (New York & London: The New Press, 2013).

[2] See Homa Katouzian, *Mosaddeq and the Struggle for Power in Iran* (London & New York: I.B. Tauris, 1990), and *Khalil Maleki: The Human Face of Iranian Socialism* (Radical Histories of the Middle East) (London: Oneworld Academic, 2018).

proposed at Bandung in 1955 and Belgrade in 1961, by several years. While 'Third Force in General' referred to the imperative to break free of both US and Soviet domination on the global stage and the necessity of charting an independent course alongside fellow nations of the recently decolonised or decolonising world, 'Third Force in Particular' pertained to 'the specifically socialist road to social and economic development, which was independent from the Eastern Bloc and discovered by each country on the basis of its own culture and historical experience'.[3] During the 1950s and 1960s, Maleki would emerge as a staunch and unbending critic of Soviet socialism, translating Isaac Deutscher's *The Unfinished Revolution: Russia 1917–1967* under a pseudonym in the final years of his life. These intellectual and political insights made a significant impact at the time and were undoubtedly well known to Hezarkhani, who would both absorb and radicalise them in subsequent years.

Close associates of Maleki based in Europe during this time included future notable figures such as Amir Pishdad and Naser Pakdaman. Together they would publish the periodical *Nameh-ye Parsi* (Persian Letter), where Hezarkhani was a member of the editorial board. The journal, whose name was a clear allusion to Montesquieu's *Lettres persanes*, published on a range of issues from culture and literature to current affairs. Most importantly, however, it became a key forum for the advocacy of a transnational organisation bringing together Iranian students. Notably, Hezarkhani translated the 1946 Grenoble charter of the National Union of French Students, advocating it as a model for his Iranian compatriots. Moreover, it was in *Nameh-ye Parsi* that he called for the emergence of a form of 'student syndicalism', a radical proposal by the standards of the student movement at that time.[4]

With the growth of the number of Iranian students in Europe and the succession of economic and political crises confronting the Pahlavi regime, Hezarkhani threw himself fully into the blossoming student movement. In mid-April 1960, Hezarkhani was one of the organisers of the famous Heidelberg Congress, which resulted in the establishment of the Confederation of Iranian Students in Europe (*Konfederasiyun-e mohasselin va daneshjuyan-e irani dar orupa*) and was the only delegate from France to attend. It was in these years of frenetic student activism that Hezarkhani forged a deep attachment to the Algerian liberation struggle against French

---

[3] Katouzian, *Khalil Maleki*, Loc 1971.

[4] Afshin Matin-asgari, *Iranian Student Opposition to the Shah* (Cost Mesa, California: Mazda, 2002), 31.

settler colonialism, which he would discuss with friends and colleagues on a near-daily basis, and whose impact he would hearken back to decades later.[5]

It is also in these years that Hezarkhani developed a keen interest in the Palestinian liberation movement and Zionist colonialism, going on to translate pertinent interventions by Maxime Rodinson and Isaac Deutscher in 1967 (1346) and by the renowned Palestinian jurist Henry Cattan in 1971 (1350).[6] Hezarkhani's decision to translate and juxtapose texts by Rodinson and Deutscher alongside one another showed his keen interest in leftist circles and debates both in France and Britain, as an avid reader of *Les Temps Modernes* and *New Left Review*. It also evinces the sense of urgency he clearly felt regarding the need for a critical analysis for Persian-speaking audiences of Israel's historical emergence and aggression in the wake of the June 1967 Arab–Israeli War. In his preface to 'On Palestine' (*Darbareh-ye felestin*), Hezarkhani writes, '[Deutscher] analyses the issue of Palestine, in contrast to the widely held view ... He analyses it from the perspective of an Arab Middle East revolution'.[7] This concern with the Palestinian cause distinguished Hezarkhani from several other figures in the League of Socialists of the National Movement of Iran (*Jame'eh-ye sowsiyalist-ha-ye nehzat-e melli-ye Iran*), such as Maleki and Hossein Malek. Both men were to become sympathetic to Israel's Mapai (Workers' Party of the Land of Israel), seeing Israeli socialism/socialist Zionism as a promising alternative to the Soviet model, and had looked upon the welfare and agrarian policies it had pursued with considerable admiration.[8]

After completing his medical studies at Montpellier, Hezarkhani moved to Paris to pursue his specialism in pathology (*asibshenasi*) at Paris University. While living and studying in Paris, he continued to be an indefatigable member of the League of Iranian Socialists in Europe (*Jame'eh-ye sowsiyalist-ha-ye irani dar orupa*), a group composed of individuals who had at one time or another been affiliated with Maleki's Third Force. In 1962, at the age of twenty-eight, he married Shahrashub Amirshahi, a fellow student

---

[5] Manuchehr Hezarkhani, *Harvard University Iranian Oral History Project*, interview by Ziya Sedqi, 1 June 1984.

[6] Maxime Rodinson and Isaac Deutscher, *Darbareh-ye felestin*, trans. Manuchehr Hezarkhani (Tehran: Tus, 1346); Henry Cattan, *Felistin mal-e kist?* trans. Manuchehr Hezarkhani (Tehran: Nashr-e sepehr, 1350).

[7] Hezarkhani's preface to Rodinson and Deutscher, *Darbareh-ye felestin*, 8.

[8] See Eskandar Sadeghi-Boroujerdi and Yaacov Yadgar, 'Jalal's Angels of Deliverance and Destruction: Genealogies of Theo-politics, Sovereignty and Coloniality in Iran and Israel', *Modern Intellectual History*, vol. 18, no. 1 (2021): 223–247.

activist living in Paris, who had achieved fame as a communist firebrand inside Iran before the 1953 coup and who was a prominent figure in the Youth Organisation of the Tudeh Party of Iran (*Sazman-e javanan-e hezb-e tudeh-ye Iran*). Her mother, Mawlud Khanlari, was a stalwart supporter of the Iranian student movement in Paris and served as secretary of the pro-Tudeh Iranian Students' Society from 1952 to 1956.[9] During the 1960s, Khanlari also worked closely with the world-renowned French intellectual Jean-Paul Sartre, as one of his confidants and secretaries, acting as a key liaison between Sartre and the Iranian opposition to the Shah. Before coming to Paris in 1950, Khanlari was one of the first women members of the Tudeh Party of Iran. Hailing from a well-to-do family in Qazvin, Khanlari first encountered the Tudeh at an early age through her relative ʿAbd al-Samad Kambaskh, a founder and leading member of the party, known as the 'Red Prince' by virtue of his royal Qajar lineage.[10] Khanlari was eventually joined in Paris by her three daughters, Shahrashub, Mahshid, and Mashanah. Shahrashub Amirshahi and Hezarkhani had two sons, Shahin and Afshin, but separated in 1967. In that same year, Hezarkhani returned to Iran after a fifteen-year absence.

RETURN TO IRAN

Upon returning to Iran, Hezarkhani, much to his surprise, was employed as an assistant professor at the University of Tabriz. In response to a five-month student strike at the university, a new chancellor, Hushang Montaseri, a mathematician trained at the University of Strasbourg, was brought in to introduce a plethora of reforms at the university. Curiously enough, Montaseri also happened to be the nephew of Reza Radmanesh, then first secretary of the Tudeh Party of Iran, and during his youth had been a member of the Tudeh Party himself.[11] Montaseri proved far more tolerant and lenient with respect to independent student activism and hired a slew of new faculty members, Hezarkhani among them. Upon his employment by the university, Hezarkhani was interrogated three times by SAVAK,

---

[9] Matin-asgari, *Iranian Student Opposition to the Shah*, 30.

[10] Mawlud Khanlari, *Harvard University Iranian Oral History Project*, interview by Ziya Sedqi, 7 March 1984.

[11] See Hushang Montaseri and ʿAli Amiri, *Sal-ha-ye khakestari* (Nashr-e farhang-e iliya, 1394).

Iran's infamous secret police, who were thoroughly apprised of the radical student activism he had pursued during his years in France.

The University of Tabriz, however, also proved to be a veritable hotbed of leftist activism, with Hezarkhani quickly emerging as a popular and much-admired professor among the student body. It was during this time that he made the acquaintance of Behruz Dehqani and Ali-Reza Nabdel, two leading Azerbaijani researchers and intellectuals who would emerge at the very forefront of the Fada'i Guerrilla movement, and their close colleague and collaborator, the writer and folklorist Samad Behrangi. Hezarkhani and Behrangi would go hiking and mountain climbing every Friday, when they would discuss the pressing cultural and political issues of the day without the oppressive shadow of the police state looming over them. During this period and through his discussions with this younger generation of Azeri intellectuals and militants, Hezarkhani was further radicalised and came to align himself with their advocacy for a guerrilla movement in the fight against the Shah's regime.

It was on account of Hezarkhani's closeness to Samad that news of the latter's tragic and premature death at the age of twenty-nine came as a huge shock. Shortly after Behrangi's drowning in the Aras River on 31 August 1968, Hezarkhani wrote his seminal essay on what would become Behrangi's most read and beloved children's story-cum-allegorical tale, *The Little Black Fish* (*Mahi siyah-e kuchulu*), which he never lived to see published. Hezarkhani's seminal essay entitled 'The Worldview of the Little Black Fish' (*Jahanbini-ye mahi siyah-e kuchulu*), published in the literary journal *Arash* in November/December 1968 (Azar 1347), was received as a revelation and became almost as influential as the story itself. A generation of students and radicals first came to learn of the radical subtext of Behrangi's story, namely its valorisation of the revolutionary guerrilla movement and armed struggle, through Hezarkhani's much-feted essay. As Hezarkhani attests in the opening lines of his essay, 'the tale of the little black fish is a children's tale but woven into it is another adventure (*sargozasht*) and another lesson (*dars*) for adults. It is not a tale for amusement but for learning (*amukhtan*).'[12] As the little black fish swims to the surface of the sea and basks in the warm rays of the sun, he thinks to himself:

---

[12] Manuchehr Hezarkhani, *Jahanbini-ye mahi siyah-e kuchulu* (Tabriz: Nashr-e ehya, n.d.), 1.

Death could come upon me very easily now. But as long as I am able to live, I shouldn't go out to meet death. Of course, someday I should be forced to face death, as I shall; it doesn't matter. What does matter is the effect that my life or death will have on the lives of others.[13]

It was an intervention on his part which had an immense impact and popularised the *raison d'être* of the guerrilla movement in unparalleled fashion. Hezarkhani contended that

[Behrangi] creates a new 'form' [of human] whose foremost quality is courage and boldness, a revolutionary courage and boldness, not the kind of spurious courage of the knights of Alexandre Dumas's novels, or the pigheaded princes of the tales of *Malek Bahman*. This courage is the result of a creative energy which, suddenly, through self-consciousness and will, akin to the liberation of the force of the atom, bestows broader and more exalted dimensions on life.

He continued, ironically posing the question,

The greatest evolution and flourishing of humanity. Is this a false romanticism or petty-bourgeois adventurism?[14]

After the 1979 Iranian Revolution, Hezarkhani would comment directly on the subsequent mythologisation of Samad, and admitted to his part in contributing to it. In stark contrast to the image of a fearless and impervious militant, Hezarkhani emphasised Samad's profound humility, purity of heart, and guileless character.[15]

Following the publication of this article, Hezarkhani was expelled from the university in conjunction with the demise of the short-lived tenure of its reformist chancellor, Hushang Montaseri. Hezarkhani then returned to Tehran, where he continued to work closely with the most dedicated and radical supporters of Khalil Maleki's Socialist League, such as ʿAbbas

[13] Samad Behrangi, *The Little Black Fish & Other Modern Persian Stories*, trans. Eric Hoogland and Mary Hegland (Colorado Springs: Three Continents Press, 1976) [translation modified].

[14] Hezarkhani, *Jahanbini-ye mahi siyah-e kuchulu*, 5.

[15] Manuchehr Hezarkhani, *Harvard University Iranian Oral History Project*, interview by Ziya Sedqi, 1 June 1984.

'Aghilizadeh, Hossein Tahvildar, and Mir-Hossein Sarshar. To make a living, Hezarkhani took up a position as a physician at the Bu 'Ali Sina hospital in Tehran. He was arrested in 1969 (1348) for his clandestine activities, subjected to arduous interrogation and torture, and subsequently imprisoned for four and a half months.

THE REVOLUTIONARY TRANSLATOR

Hezarkhani was among the very first Iranian intellectuals to introduce black Francophone anti-colonial thought and literature to a Persian-speaking audience. His translations include Aimé Césaire's seminal *Discourse on Colonialism* (1950/1955), which he must have translated while still in France and published in Persian in 1966 (1345). Hezarkhani also translated a selection of the lectures that were delivered at the inaugural *Présence Africaine* conference convened at the Sorbonne, Paris, from 19–22 September 1956. These included the conference's opening address by the Senegalese author Alioune Diop, a leading light of the Negritude movement, the Malagasy poet and playwright Jacques Rabemananjara on 'Europe and Ourselves', and the Martiniquais psychiatrist and revolutionary Frantz Fanon on 'Racism and Culture', as well as 'Colonialism and Culture' by the aforementioned Aimé Césaire, poet, politician and Fanon's fellow Martiniquais intellectual and former teacher, with whose work Hezarkhani was intimately familiar.[16] The volume took its title, *Nezhadparasti va farhang* (Racism and Culture), from Fanon's lecture and was published in 1968 (1347). Finally, Hezarkhani translated Césaire's play *A Season in the Congo* (1966), which depicted the final months in the life of Patrice Lumumba (1925–1961), first prime minister of the Republic of the Congo, during the transition to independence from Belgian colonialism, and was published in the periodical *Ketab-e zaman* in 1968 (1367). In his introduction to the collection *Racism and Culture*, Hezarkhani takes aim at the dehumanising rhetoric and racism which undergirds imperialism and the capitalist exploitation of the Third World:

> It is a small step from debasing an 'inferior race' to debasing humankind and negating personhood and human dignity, and how quickly

---

[16] See The 1st International Conference of Negro Writers and Artists, *Presence Africaine: Cultural Journal of the Negro World*, Special Issue, no. 8–9–10, June–November 1956.

the advocates of 'freedom-equality-fraternity' take this step ... To transform the peoples of indigenous societies (*javame'-e bumi*) into the arm of labour, it was necessary that they cease to be human.[17]

Hezarkhani also holds the distinction of being the first to translate into Persian excerpts of the renowned Italian Marxist Antonio Gramsci's *Prison Notebooks* (from French). Hezarkhani's translations, published in the literary journal *Arash*, appeared between February 1968 and January 1972. These incredibly influential translations included 'The Formation of Intellectuals' (February–March 1968), 'The Different Positions of Urban and Rural-Type Intellectuals' (March–April 1968), 'The Criteria for Literary Criticism' (February–March 1969), and 'Some Preliminary Points of Reference' (January 1972). Their translation would achieve further circulation and fame as a result of the reproduction of 'The Formation of Intellectuals' in Jalal Al-e Ahmad's posthumously published volume, *On the Service and Betrayal of the Intellectuals* (*Dar khedmat va khiyanat-e rowshanfekran*), a work that would generate considerable controversy given the decisive role it assigned to the politically engaged faction of the Shi'i clergy and their depiction as exemplary 'organic intellectuals' within Iranian society.[18]

In the preface of this text, Al-e Ahmad expresses his gratitude to Hezarkhani and refers to their frequent correspondence. In the first volume, Al-e Ahmad goes so far as to cite directly from their correspondence and confesses that it was none other than Hezarkhani who corrected his misconceptions regarding the French Cold War liberal intellectual Raymond Aron, by informing him that Aron was not a man of the left or an anti-imperialist but 'one of the world's faithful defenders of capitalism and is closer to the likes of [W.W.] Rostow in the United States, whom you know. Aron's theories

---

[17] *Nezhadparasti va farhang*, quoted in Eskandar Sadeghi-Boroujerdi, '*Gharbzadegi*, colonial capitalism and the racial state in Iran', *Postcolonial Studies*, vol. 24, no. 2 (2021): 180; Alioune Diop et al., *Nezhadparasti va farhang*, trans. Manuchehr Hezarkhani, 2nd ed. (Tehran: Ketab-e zaman, 1348/1969); also see Eskandar Sadeghi-Boroujerdi, 'Who Translated Fanon's *The Wretched of the Earth* into Persian?', *Jadaliyya* (August 2020).
[18] Together with Jalal Al-e Ahmad, Hezarkhani translated the Romanian-French playwright Eugene Ionesco's *Hunger and Thirst*. The translation was published in 1971 (1352) after Al-e Ahmad's premature death from a heart attack in 1969. For a more detailed exploration of translations of Gramsci into Persian during the late 1960s and early 1970s, see Eskandar Sadeghi-Boroujerdi, 'Āl-e Ahmad's Faustian Bargain: Antonio Gramsci, the "Progressive Clergy", and the Search for Hegemony in Late Pahlavi Iran', *South Atlantic Quarterly*, forthcoming.

of industrial society are in every respect a justification of class exploitation ... The supporters of Sartre refer to him as the guard dog of capitalism.'[19]

During this time, Hezarkhani became fast friends with Mostafa Sho'a'iyan, the maverick revolutionary Marxist guerrilla, and leading critic of Leninism, including the concept of democratic centralism.[20] It was at this juncture that Hezarkhani seriously considered joining the guerrilla movement against the Shah's regime himself. After much back and forth discussion, Sho'a'iyan eventually persuaded Hezarkhani against the merits of such a decision, telling him that he was too well known and prominent a figure and that it would be nearly impossible to hide him from the surveillance and counter-intelligence networks of the SAVAK. Sho'a'iyan insisted that Hezarkhani, given his status as a public intellectual, could better serve the fight against the Shah's dictatorship if he continued his intellectual and cultural work, as well as his more public activities around the newly established Writers' Association of Iran (1968–1970), of which he was a dedicated member.

According to Hezarkhani, he and Sho'a'iyan would spend days debating and discussing a single political or theoretical issue at a time, and Sho'a'iyan would share his many, often voluminous, writings with Hezarkhani for his opinion and critical feedback.[21] Hezarkhani even penned one of Sho'a'iyan's letters in the course of his acrimonious debates with the Fada'i Guerrillas, which Sho'a'iyan merely amended and published in his own name.[22] Both men considered themselves sons of the national-popular movement and Hezarkhani himself described the latter as 'our inheritance'. It is therefore hardly a surprise that the notion of a broad revolutionary front and coalition composed of nationalists, socialists, and progressive religious forces would inspire and condition both men's thought in crucial ways. Moreover, because of Sho'a'iyan's lack of knowledge of any European language he would frequently rely on Hezarkhani for translations of key Marxist texts, such as Marx's *The German Ideology*,[23] among others. Sho'a'iyan was ultimately

---

[19] Jalal Al-e Ahmad, *Dar khedmat va khiyanat-e rawshanfekran*, vol. 1 (Tehran: Khvarazmi, 1357), 60–61.

[20] For a detailed account of Sho'a'iyan's life and thought, see Peyman Vahabzadeh, *A Rebel's Journey: Mostafa Sho'aiyan and Revolutionary Theory in Iran* (London: Oneworld Academic, 2019).

[21] Manuchehr Hezarkhani, *Harvard University Iranian Oral History Project*, interview by Ziya Sedqi, 1 June 1984.

[22] Manuchehr Hezarkhani, *Harvard University Iranian Oral History Project*, interview by Ziya Sedqi, 1 June 1984.

[23] Manuchehr Hezarkhani interview with Nasser Mohajer, 12 February 1988.

killed after being identified and shot by a police officer on the streets of central Tehran on 5 February 1976.

Hezarkhani's translations were intimately bound up with his political praxis and a desire to furnish radical movements against Mohammad-Reza Shah's autocracy with the relevant intellectual tools and concepts in light of Iran's socio-historical development and political conditions, and thereby inform and shape their struggle in turn. He would continue this dialectical practice until his final days in exile, where he continued with alacrity his vital work as a translator, translating several works by Antonio Negri and Michael Hardt, including the former's *Insurgencies: Constituent Power and the Modern State* and Hardt and Negri's co-authored work, *The Multitude: War and Democracy in the Age of Empire*, as well as Hartmut Rosa's *Social Acceleration: A New Theory of Modernity*, and Michel Serres' *Times of Crisis: What the Financial Crisis Revealed and How to Reinvent Our Lives and Future*.

THE IRANIAN REVOLUTION AND THE NATIONAL DEMOCRATIC FRONT OF IRAN

In 1977–1978, Hezarkhani was a leading advocate for human rights and a founding member of the Committee to Defend the Rights of Political Prisoners in Iran. He was also decisive to the revival and reconstitution of the Iranian Writers' Association (*Kanun-e nevisandegan-e Iran*), the chief organisation through which Iranian intellectuals and literati defended their basic rights to freedom of thought and expression and fought the constant threat of censorship and imprisonment at the hands of the SAVAK. Hezarkhani gave a stirring speech in defence of freedom of speech and expression to rapturous applause during the famous ten nights of poetry convened at the Goethe Institute in Tehran in October 1977, which for many marks the inception of the Iranian Revolution, and on whose organising committee he played a vital part. In his short speech he boldly declared:

> Our sin as members of the Iranian Writers' Association is our adherence to Voltaire's dictum that 'I am in complete disagreement with your beliefs, but as long as I have life in me, I will endeavour for you to have the right, to express them.' We have said that both the pen and thinking must be free, we have said that we recognise this freedom only in the form clearly stipulated by the Iranian Constitution and

the Universal Declaration of Human Rights. We have said that the apparatus of censorship and the inquisition into [people's beliefs], or any other pretext of which they [namely, the Pahlavi state authorities] avail themselves to justify [such actions], is in contradiction with freedom of thought and expression. We have said and say that a mature and upstanding people have no need for a ward or master and are themselves entirely capable of distinguishing truth from falsehood.[24]

On the more explicitly political front, Hezarkhani, alongside Hedayat Matin-Daftari, Mosaddeq's grandson, and the Marxist–Leninist and former high-profile political prisoner Shokrollah Paknezhad,[25] whose December 1970 trial defence and denunciation of the Shah's regime had become the stuff of legend, began to lay the groundwork for what would become the National Democratic Front of Iran (*Jebheh-ye demokratik-e melli-ye Iran*). The National Democratic Front (NDF) officially announced its establishment on 5 March 1979, the twelfth anniversary of Muhammad Mosaddeq's death. Hezarkhani, in collaboration with colleagues, took up the editorship of their newspaper *Azadi* (Freedom), which in its opening issue of 28 March 1979 (8 Farvardin 1358) posed the question, 'Why the National Democratic Front?' In this editorial the NDF uncompromisingly described itself as an 'anti-autocratic and anti-imperialist front [...which had emerged] in response to a historical necessity' and emphasised

the necessity of preserving solidarity and unity of action of the emancipatory and revolutionary forces, to preserve the achievements of the revolution, and spread them to the end of establishing a government of the masses and in pursuit of the anti-imperialist struggle.[26]

The NDF was the first organisation to boldly proclaim its opposition to the ever-encroaching domination of pro-Khomeini Islamists. Quite unlike either the Tudeh Party or the People's Mojahedin, as well as an array of secular intellectuals, the NDF, and most notably the Organisation of

---

[24] Naser Mo'azzen (ed.), *Dah shab* (Tehran: Amir Kabir, 1357), 61.
[25] For more information on the historical significance of Paknezhad's trial, see Naghmeh Sohrabi, 'Remembering the Palestine Group: Global Activism, Friendship, and the Iranian Revolution', *International Journal of Middle East Studies*, vol. 51, no. 2 (2019): 281–300.
[26] Chera jebheh-ye demokratik-e melli?, *Azadi*, 28 March 1979, 1.

the People's Fada'i Guerrillas, boycotted the national referendum on the
'Islamic Republic of Iran' held on 30–31 March 1979. The NDF and the
Fada'i Guerrillas shared the view that it was imperative to draft the post-
revolutionary order's constitution before the name of the new state was put
to a public vote (see also Elling and Mahmoudi's chapter in this volume).
In a short space of time, they also came to express their explicit opposition
to Ayatollah Khomeini and the Islamic Republic Party (*Hezb-e jomhuri-ye
eslami*), led by Khomeini's most trusted lieutenants.

The NDF unapologetically outlined an analysis of the ongoing revolutionary situation, which rejected the idea that the primary contradiction was
between imperialism and the remnants of the national bourgeoisie, now
known as the Iranian liberal bourgeoisie, or between imperialism and 'the
people', and instead firmly adhered to the idea that the real enemies of the
Iranian Revolution were none other than the Islamist clerics at the helm of
the new state. For the NDF, the struggle against imperialism could only be
achieved through the realisation of a progressive democratic settlement,
which was in direct conflict with those forces whom they regarded as the
most reactionary and retrograde at home.[27] In this endeavour they sought to
build a front composed of socialists, social democrats, independent Marxists,
progressive Muslim forces, and left-wing intellectuals, with an explicit focus
on the protection of basic civil liberties, and greater autonomy for all Iranian
ethnic groups and nationalities. In this respect we contend that the NDF took
a principled position on basic liberal and civic rights as well as democratic
participation and pluralism, seeing no fundamental contradiction or even
tension between the latter and the advance of an anti-imperialist politics.
In fact, broadly speaking, the NDF saw mass participatory democracy and
respect for basic freedoms as a precondition for the success and deepening
of anti-imperialist struggle. The overwhelming majority of their political
opponents, however, were often hostile or suspicious of such principles and
those who advocated for them, often regarding them as little more than a
vehicle of imperialist penetration and counter-revolutionary subversion.

A key moment in the brief history of the NDF was its unqualified support
for the most outspoken and independent newspaper of the time, *Ayandegan*,
when its offices were ransacked by pro-Khomeini Islamist forces, compelling
it to temporarily cease its activities in mid-May 1979. When the newspaper

---

[27] Nasir Pakdaman, *Harvard University Iranian Oral History Project*, interview by Ziya
Sidghi, 26 May 1984.

was finally banned on 12 August 1979, the NDF called for a popular demonstration in support of *Ayandegan*, denouncing the ongoing campaign of intimidation against the fast receding bastions of the free press in what only weeks earlier had been known as the 'Spring of Freedom'. At this huge demonstration of tens of thousands, impassioned chants of 'Long Live Freedom, Death to Fascism!' rang out. Soon after this demonstration, which was openly attacked by pro-Khomeini forces and so-called revolutionary committees, Hedayat Matin-Daftari went into hiding, leaving Paknezhad and Hezarkhani as the two most prominent spokesmen of the front.

Despite this succession of existential crises, Hezarkhani's translation of Roy A. Medvedev's dissident history and Marxist critique of Stalinism, *Let History Judge: The Origins and Consequences of Stalinism*, was published in 1981 (1360). Its original publication abroad in 1969 had led to Medvedev's expulsion from the Communist Party of the Soviet Union. Hezarkhani's translation, which he completed in a mere two months,[28] struck like a bolt of lightning and provoked feral debate among the Iranian left, huge swathes of which continued to toil under the influence of Stalinist bromides and ossified thinking.

During this volatile period between the proscription of *Ayandegan* and the ousting of President Abolhasan Banisadr, the NDF continued its efforts to build bridges to the Kurdish Democratic Party of Iran under the leadership of Abdulrahman Qassemlu, who had been prevented from taking up his seat in the Assembly of Experts charged with drafting the Islamic Republic's new constitution; leaders of the People's Fada'i (Minority); and the People's Mojahedin, as well as other assorted groups such as the Organisation of Communist Unity (*Sazman-e vahdat-e komunisti*). This endeavour was part and parcel of their ambition to expand and constitute a nationwide counter-power to the Khomeinists' total monopolisation of emerging state institutions.

EXILE AND THE NATIONAL RESISTANCE COUNCIL

In parallel with these developments and as the climate of hope gave way to fear and acrimony, the Mojahedin sought to build a coalition to counter Ayatollah Khomeini and the Islamic Republic Party in May 1980. It was during this time that they first began to seriously air the possibility of launching a *showra*, or

---

[28] Manuchehr Hezarkhani interview with Nasser Mohajer, 12 February 1988.

council, bringing together the steadfast opponents of the ruling theocracy into a single coalition and countervailing force. Events reached their denouement with the bloody repression of a massive peaceful protest of as many as half a million people in Tehran alone, denouncing the ousting of President Banisadr on 19 June 1981, and the mounting atmosphere of political repression. This final reckoning decisively inaugurated a period of unmitigated mass terror, with hundreds injured, arrested, and tortured, and thousands more executed in the ensuing months. Consequently, the People's Mojahedin openly called for armed struggle and the country was now on the brink of a civil war. During this time, it became impossible to operate politically in the open inside Iran, resulting in Hezarkhani as well as the Islamic Republic's first president, Banisadr, and the leader of the People's Mojahedin, Mas'ud Rajavi, escaping with their lives by fleeing into exile in Paris. Hezarkhani's colleague and co-founder of the NDF, Shokrollah Paknezhad, was apprehended by Khomeinist forces, imprisoned for several months, and finally executed in December 1981. In this dark period many thousands of dissidents and opponents of the Islamic Republic fled the country.

Back in Paris after a fourteen-year hiatus, Hezarkhani quickly got down to work, and was a driving force in the establishment of the previously envisioned National Resistance Council of Iran (NRC) (*Showra-ye melli-ye moqavemat-e Iran*), where Banisadr was announced president and Rajavi chairman and also the leader of the de facto provisional government-in-exile of the Islamic Democratic Republic of Iran. At this early juncture, the NRC encompassed a multitude of leading activists and intellectuals, ranging from Banisadr, Naser Pakdaman, Mahdi Khan Baba Tehrani, Kambiz Rusta, and Bahman Nirumand, to organisations including the People's Mojahedin to the Labour Party of Iran (Tufan), the Council for Left Union (*Showra-ye mottahed-e chap*), the NDF, one of the factions of the Fada'i Guerrillas led by Mehdi Same', and the Kurdistan Democratic Party of Iran. Many other left-wing groups, however, demurred and chose to pursue their resistance to the Islamic Republic outside of the framework of the National Resistance Council. When Hezarkhani was asked by the academic Fred Halliday in a 1982 interview why anyone should trust the People's Mojahedin to be more democratic than the Khomeinist regime, he insisted:

> I have worked very closely with them and I know them. They are democrats. But the real guarantee is that the Mojahedin cannot rule on their own. They will have to share power with other groups and

be democratic enough to respect the views of others. It is perhaps natural that all of us should have despotic tendencies in our hearts, but the Mojahedin are less despotic than others.[29]

In the first issue of the NRC's official monthly, *Showra* (Council), published in October/November 1984, Hezarkhani's article, simply titled 'Resistance', argued:

The most important cultural value of a resistance movement is resistance itself. In fact, it can be said that before anything else, and more than anything else, it is a form of cultural resistance. The confrontation of [one set of] values and ideals with the values and ideals of another ... The National Resistance Council is the manifestation of a form of resistance whose goal is to deepen the emancipatory revolution of the people and overthrow the apparatus of despotism, reaction, and dependence. The blood-thirsty regime of the Guardianship of the Jurist, whose essential character has been experienced time and again, has not left the smallest possibility for any form of disagreement, protest, and peaceful opposition. This resistance has therefore taken a fundamentally armed form upon itself. The nature of the armed resistance demonstrates that its contradiction with Khomeini's regime is irreconcilable, in other words, it [namely, Khomeini's regime] does not countenance any kind of reform and in the totality of its being repudiates it. But the negation of the Khomeini regime in its totality does not lead to regression or a revival of the previous regime, but guides the continuation and deepening of the revolution.[30]

It is crucial to contextualise the above statement with an eye to the fact that, at this time, Iran was in the midst of a devastating interstate conflict with Iraq following Saddam Hussein's decision to launch a military invasion of the country on 22 September 1980. The war with Iraq was an issue that polarised and at times paralysed the opposition inside and outside of Iran. While some advocated for the transformation of the war into an outright civil war, which, they argued, would in turn pave the way for the overthrow

---

[29] Fred Halliday and Manuchehr Hezarkhani, 'The Only Serious Obstacle Is Khomeini Himself', *Middle East Report*, 104 (March/April 1982).

[30] Manuchehr Hezarkhani, 'Moqavemat', *Showra*, Aban 1363/October–November 1984, 6.

of the Islamic Republic, others denounced the conflict as a battle between two equally repugnant capitalist dictatorships, demanding peace, and an immediate ceasefire. Others still insisted that there was no choice but to support Iran in the fight against its arch-enemy Iraq and Saddam Hussein's aggression. These stark divisions would provide crucial context and lay the groundwork for the subsequent weakening and degeneration of the NRC and its transformation into little more than a tool of the People's Mojahedin, in lieu of the genuinely democratic, broad-based, and inclusive opposition coalition that had been originally envisioned. The December 1982 Paris meeting of Rajavi and Iraqi Deputy Premier Tariq Aziz provoked the ire and consternation of many, both within and outside Iran, and was widely criticised within the opposition. The growing fractures within the NRC were further compounded by Rajavi's joint communiqué with Aziz in January 1983, and for many marked the beginning of the end of the NRC as a credible progressive alternative formation. Banisadr officially broke with the NRC in March 1983.

With the ebb of the movement and the dwindling relevance of the NRC, the personality cult around Rajavi increasingly began to tighten its grip. By 1986, the French government was eager to normalise its relations with the Islamic Republic of Iran and requested that the Mojahedin wind down its activities and cease to use Paris as its headquarters. In response, and just as the war was reaching its destructive crescendo, the Mojahedin leadership made the irreparable strategic blunder of making Iraq their new headquarters and base of operations. The disastrous effects of this decision were felt almost immediately. The People's Mojahedin, which had once arguably been among the most admired political forces in the country, found itself increasingly isolated and became instead an object of revilement and loathing. In the words of Ervand Abrahamian, the 'National Council, which had started with such high hopes, had become a mere shell'[31] and the People's Mojahedin had gone 'from mass movement to religio-political sect'.[32]

To the great dismay of many, Hezarkhani along with several other prominent figures of the NRC remained committed to a close-knit alliance with the People's Mojahedin and never looked back, leaving many of his closest friends and confidants puzzled and bewildered. In February/March 1985 Hezarkhani assumed editorship of the monthly *Showra*, which

---

[31] Ervand Abrahamian, *Radical Islam: The Iranian Mojahedin* (London: I.B. Tauris, 1989), 247.
[32] Abrahamian, *Radical Islam*, 258.

in its first years had featured contributions from a wide range of authors, including several of Iran's leading poets and engaged intellectuals, such as Gholam Hossein Saʿedi, Ahmad Shamlu, Simin Behbahani, Majid Sharif, Bahman Nirumand, and Naser Pakdaman. The quality and breadth of the contributions quickly declined, as the unrivalled dominance, bullying and intimidation tactics of the Mojahedin reverberated within the NRC and the opposition in general.

On 20 July 1988, the Islamic Republic of Iran accepted UN Resolution 598, agreeing to the ceasefire that would finally bring eight years of brutal interstate conflict to an end. With Saddam Hussein's assent and based on a shockingly misguided analysis – strenuously defended by Hezarkhani in the pages of *Showra* – the People's Mojahedin's National Liberation Army launched on 25 July 1988 an adventurous and reckless military incursion into Iran on the premise that they would be greeted as heroes and drive their way to Tehran to overthrow their bête noire and nemesis, the Islamic Republic, once and for all.[33] Little did they know that not only would they not be welcomed with open arms by their fellow countrymen and women, but the Iranian army, the Islamic Revolutionary Guard Corps (IRGC), and an array of Islamist para-military forces were prepared and waiting for them, consequently laying waste to the Mojahedin's forces and defeating the incursion with relative ease.[34] On 28 July 1988, Ayatollah Khomeini's fatwa sanctifying the mass execution of political prisoners who refused to retract their steadfast opposition to the Islamic Republic was put into effect and the massacre of some five thousand political prisoners, including members of the People's Mojahedin, as well as an array of leftists, proceeded apace in detention centres across the country.[35]

CONCLUSION

From this brief and schematic analysis of Hezarkhani's life and work, it should be clear that his contribution to the popularisation of Third World

---

[33] Manuchehr Hezarkhani, Maʿni-ye siyasi-ye 'forugh-e javidan', *Showra*, no. 43–44, Mordad/Shahrivar 1367.
[34] See Pierre Razoux, *The Iran–Iraq War*, trans. Nicholas Elliott (Cambridge, MA & London: Harvard University Press, 2015), Chapter 31.
[35] For further information, see Nasser Mohajer, *Voices of a Massacre: Untold Stories of Life and Death in Iran, 1988* (London: Oneworld, 2020).

anti-colonial and socialist literature inside Iran was immense. Hezarkhani's generative translations of Antonio Gramsci, attending to the importance of culture and hegemony and how leftist intellectuals, broadly speaking, should relate to Iran's working and rural classes, as well as his evocative translations of the luminaries of the Negritude movement, providing crucial tools for understanding the manner in which processes of racialisation, imperial domination, and capital accumulation feed into and reinforce one another, left an indelible mark on Iran's intellectual scene during the period under discussion. But he was also much more than a translator. As we have shown, Hezarkhani was someone who consistently and repeatedly sought to influence and shape political movements, events, and outcomes, often in creative and inspiring ways. It is in this regard that his record becomes more complicated and chequered and where we see intellectual and ethical principles give way to dubious political compromises in the aftermath of irreparable and devastating political defeats.

The fate of the NRC and Hezarkhani's role in the opposition leaves us with several uncomfortable questions: how could one of the most avant-garde, critical, and perspicacious intellectuals of his generation not only fail to distance himself from but also forcefully defend an authoritarian (and potentially totalitarian) cult which after 1986 had not only fought against Iranian military personnel serving on the warfront, but had also resorted to violence and engineered terror, and had even engaged, at times, in the mistreatment of its own dissident members?[36] In later years, the National Resistance Council of Iran, dominated and controlled by the People's Mojahedin, would welcome as friends and allies some of the most notorious and reactionary figures of American neoconservatism and the Trump administration, including Newt Gingrich, John Bolton, and Rudy Giuliani, while the People's Mojahedin was widely reported to have collaborated with a host of right-wing authoritarian states across the Middle East.

Although the reasons behind Hezarkhani's loyalty to the Mojahedin and the Mojahedin-dominated National Resistance Council are something of an enigma, we can discern several reasons which might explain his stance. Most superficially, he had reached the conclusion that any and all measures were warranted to free Iran of the clutches of the Islamic Republic. In his view, the Mojahedin was the only force among the opposition with a strong

---

[36] Human Rights Watch, *No Exit: Human Rights Abuses Inside the Mojahedin Khalq Camps*, May 2005, 16: https://www.hrw.org/legacy/backgrounder/mena/iran0505/iran0505.pdf.

organisation, sufficient arms, and a dedicated following, which made it capable of unseating the Islamic Republic. In short, he had adopted the ethics of pragmatic realpolitik. But that is only part of the answer.

Another clue lies in the 1982 interview with Halliday. From this interview and elsewhere, it clearly emerges that Hezarkhani held that the Mojahedin, for all its shortcomings, originated from a fundamentally different lineage than that of the Islamist Shi'i clergy, which for him were an irredeemable bastion of reaction and religious despotism. By contrast, the Mojahedin had emerged from the Liberation Movement of Iran (*Nehzat-e azadi-ye Iran*) and religious modernists like Mehdi Bazargan, Mahmud Taleqani, and 'Ezat'Allah Sahabi. According to Hezarkhani's reading any political coalition or front that aspired to be popular and lead a potential insurrection against a whole spectrum of reactionary forces had to take heed of Muslim religious forces.[37] But what separated the Mojahedin from Khomeini, in his eyes, was their 'modernist' and 'progressive' reading of Islam. Much like his friend and comrade Sho'a'iyan, Hezarkhani remained committed to the idea that any political initiative which categorically excluded such Muslim religious forces stood little chance of success in the Iranian context. Whether his assessment of the Mojahedin was indeed correct is a claim we cannot properly examine here, but it is certainly not without merit, at least until the revolution. Despite ultimately bowing to realpolitik, perhaps, in the recesses of his mind he still clung to a belief in the original *showra* and believed that he was doing his part in teaching the Mojahedin that if they were one day victorious they would have to share power with parties, groups, and individuals who were ideologically and politically very different from them. But Hezarkhani's critics would counter that this was either pure naivety or self-deception, given that the Mojahedin cannot tolerate, let alone respect, any grouping which is critical of their political line in opposition.

In the final analysis, we cannot provide a definitive or exhaustive answer to Hezarkhani's perplexing support for the Mojahedin or peer into the depths of his soul, but can only note the glaring disjuncture between that support and his lifelong defence of freedom and democratic self-rule in both the decades which preceded the revolution, as well as during the revolution itself. Until his last days, Hezarkhani continued his lifelong engagement with

---

[37] Manuchehr Hezarkhani, *Harvard University Iranian Oral History Project*, interview by Ziya Sedqi, 1 June 1984.

revolutionary thought and theory, with his translation of Negri's *Insurgencies: Constituent Power and the Modern State* being published a couple of days before his death at the age of eighty-eight. Alas, it is this irreconcilable contradiction which he has taken to his grave, even as it embodies both Hezarkhani's triumph and his tragedy.

9

THE FRONT OF OUR FRIENDS

Shu'un Filastiniyya as an Archive of Palestinian Third Worldism

Klaudia Wieser

Having survived the huge port explosion in 2020 that damaged nearly the whole of Beirut, the abandoned building that once served as the Research Centre of the Palestine Liberation Organisation (PLO) in Lebanon can still be found in Ras Beirut. Located close to Sadat Street and partly covered by a huge green construction sheet, it symbolises not only the aftershock of enduring empire and ongoing colonialism,[1] but also the history of anti-colonial knowledge production by the PLO between 1965 and 1983. Alongside the Institute for Palestine Studies,[2] founded in Beirut two years earlier (in 1963), it established Palestine Studies in the 1960s and 1970s and fulfilled the critical task of reconstructing and documenting Palestinian history[3] and presenting revolutionary developments in light of the Zionist

[1] Ann Laura Stoler, *Imperial Debris* (Durham: Duke University Press, 2016), 17.
[2] See *Celebrating 50 Years of the Journal of Palestine Studies*, Institute of Palestine Studies, 2021, https://www.palestine-studies.org/en/node/1651717; Maia Tabet, 'JPS "Hidden Gems" and "Greatest Hits": Fifty Years of Narrating Palestine', *Journal of Palestine Studies* 50, no. 1 (2021), 1–2.
[3] Hana Sleiman, 'The paper trail of a liberation movement', *Arab Studies Journal* 24, no. 1 (2017), 42–67.

invasion of Palestine,[4] the ongoing Nakba,[5] and later during the civil war in Lebanon (1975–1990).

The centre hosted a documentation section which consisted of a library and an archive for old documents, contemporary information files, documents of the various factions of the PLO, and old maps. It had its own publication section, and in line with the interests of its different directors and researchers, it developed departments such as Israel and Zionist Studies, Studies of the Palestinian People, Military Studies, and International Studies. The centre operated three main information outlets: a periodical, *The Palestinian Diary*, which was first issued in 1965; the journal *Shu'un Filastiniyya* (Palestinian Affairs), launched in March 1971; and a newsletter monitoring Israeli Radio Broadcasts, which was first published in 1973.[6] While Beirut was a hub for revolutionary knowledge production and intellectual debate at this specific juncture in time, *Shu'un Filastiniyya* was the first journal directed towards an Arab readership that focused on Palestine and provided a multiplicity of ideological debates and standpoints by various factions, political movements, and Arab/ Palestinian intellectuals on the Palestinian cause.[7]

In the editorial note of the first issue of the revolutionary magazine,[8] its director Anis Sayigh explained that the periodical would neither serve as just another journal about Palestine nor as a tool to 'preach and guide'. On the contrary, *Shu'un* would provide a space for 'conscious and free thought, multiple opinions, positions and voices', covering a broad spectrum of 'past- present- and future' Palestinian affairs. Grounded in critical thinking, careful investigations, and scientific analysis, the bimonthly publication would bring together Palestinian thinkers and writers and 'the masses of intellectuals'[9] to produce knowledge about themselves.

---

[4] Fayez A. Sayigh, *Zionist Colonialism in Palestine* (Beirut: Research Centre, Palestine Liberation Organisation, 1965), http://www.freedomarchives.org/Documents/Finder/DOC12_scans/12.zionist.colonialism.palestine.1965.pdf.

[5] Ahmad H. Sa'di and Lila Abu-Lughod, *Nakba: Palestine, 1948, and the Claims of Memory* (New York: Columbia Press, 2007).

[6] Anis Sayigh, *Anis Sayigh 'an Anis Sayigh* (Beirut: Riyad al-Rayyis il-Kutub wa-al-Nashr, 2006, 222–229), trans. by the Palestinian Revolution, 2016, 1–5, http://learnpalestine.politics.ox.ac.uk.

[7] Interview conducted by the author with Elias Khoury, Beirut, March 2018; interview conducted by the author with Sabri Jiryis, Fassuta, November 2021.

[8] Anis Sayigh, 'Palestine Affairs', *Shu'un Filastiniyya* 1 (March 1971), 4.

[9] Ibid.

Considering the manifold perspectives and transnational connections of many researchers and contributors to the journal, the strategic decision by the PLO leadership to globalise the Palestinian struggle in the sixties and early seventies can vividly be engaged with by re-reading *Shu'un Filastiniyya*. Looking at the early years of the archive, one finds multiple published articles, investigative studies, short comments, interviews, monthly columns, and travel reports that analyse the internationalisation of the Palestinian cause for an Arabic-speaking audience. Written and edited by militant writers and intellectuals,[10] these records provide insights into the dynamics of a generation that identified political entanglements with the so-called Tricontinental movement (Asia, Africa, Latin America) and beyond as essential to their anti-colonial struggle.[11]

While various attacks on the Palestine Research Centre (PRC) and the looting of the institution during the Israeli invasion of Beirut in 1982 have been documented by several scholars,[12] less attention has been given to the centre's journal and the impact of the deteriorating political situation in Lebanon on the fate of the publication. Its catalogue is an underexplored archive of intellectual labour by researchers who recount their lived experience of cultivating revolutionary knowledge not only about their enemies, but also about their friends. This distinction, anchored in a 'Cold War dynamics of antagonistic forces', enabled a 'global community of revolution'[13] and was based on the belief in the possibility of transforming colonial and imperialist world orders and humanity; actively confronting the 'rule of colonial difference'.[14]

The journal provides insights into a political and intellectual history of transnational connections of Palestinian revolutionaries that point to one of

[10] Katlyn Quenzer, 'Beyond Arab Nationalism? The PLO and its Intellectuals, 1967–1974', *Interventions* 21, no. 5 (2019), 690–707.

[11] Sune Haugbolle, 'Global History, and the Arab Left', *International Journal of Middle East Studies* 51 (2019), 1–4.

[12] See, for example, Anis Sayigh, *Anis Sayigh about Anis Sayigh* (Beirut: Riyad al-Rayyis il-Kutub wa-al-Nashr, 2006); Hana Sleiman, 'The paper trail of a liberation movement', *Arab Studies Journal* 24, no. 1 (2017), 42–67; Rona Sela, 'Seized in Beirut. The plundered archives of the Palestinian cinema institution and cultural arts section', *Anthropology of the Middle East* 12, no. 1 (2017), 83–114; Marah Khalifa, 'The Palestine Research Centre: What the Organisation left behind', *metras* (2021), shorturl.at/lEGL8.

[13] Laure Guirguis, 'The Arab New Left and May '68: Transnational Entanglements at a Time of Disruption', *Critical Historical Studies* 8, no. 1 (2021), 87–113.

[14] Partha Chatterjee, *The Nation and Its Fragments: Colonial and Postcolonial Histories* (Princeton: Princeton University Press, 1993).

'the most important features of popular liberation struggles': international solidarity.[15] In this regard, the content of *Shu'un* also mirrors the heyday and the decline of Palestinian Third Worldism. Skimming through the many pages of the journal, one can find contributions by militant intellectuals and debates by various political factions of the PLO on similarities, differences, and lessons learned from liberation movements and global revolutionary struggles from, for example, Vietnam, Cuba, Angola, and Iran, as well as on a cultural level.

Analysing micro-histories of intimate connections, I call this circle of friendships in the context of Palestine solidarity 'the front of friends'. The aim is to stress how Third Worldism was crucially made up of such intimate fronts, in addition to the strategic and military fronts of high politics. Therefore, the first part of my chapter draws on the epistemological and personal reflections on the *front of friends* based in Europe by different authors that published in *Shu'un Filastiniyya* between 1971 and 1975. Although not exhaustive, this analysis offers a glimpse into what constituted the basis for the close relationships that enabled spaces for encounters, translations of ideas, and political action among Palestinian revolutionaries, individuals, and movements. In the second part, I show that the significance of reporting on solidarity movements based in Europe shifted at the end of the 1970s. As with the divide within the Palestinian political factions, the intensification of the civil war in Lebanon and the Israeli aggression in Palestine and abroad had a drastic impact on the circulation of the *front of friends* and the decline of revolutionary solidarity.

POLITICAL FRIENDSHIPS

Third Worldist connectivity was not just facilitated by strategic interest and common dogma; it was also propelled by developing friendships in the circuits of 'travelling revolutionaries' (see the chapters by Pelle Olsen, Marral Shamshiri, and Sorcha Thomson in this volume). The concept of 'politics of friendship'[16] was coined by Jacques Derrida, who published

---

[15] As described in the educational online project *Learn the Palestinian Revolution, 2016*: 'For the Palestinian Revolution, there were five distinct areas of solidarity: Arab, Islamic, Tricontinental, Eastern bloc, and European-North American', http://learnpalestine. politics.ox.ac.uk.

[16] Jacques Derrida, *Politics of Friendship*, trans. George Collins (London: Verso, 1997).

several of his lectures on friendship defined as a relationship founded on virtue, love, and equality.[17] In contrast to friendship established on the base of kinship and fraternity, or what Aristotle termed friendship of fellow citizens, friendship in Derrida's words expanded to a political community whose command is 'to love the other as he is',[18] which allows for cultivating respect rather than exploitation. In applying Derrida's framework to the anti-colonialism of Frantz Fanon, Omar Chowdhury provides a better understanding of anti-colonial encounters guided by an 'effective refusal of colonial divisions'.[19] Moving from individual relationships to a broader framework of humanity, the author weaves Fanon's message of 'liberating all mankind from imperialism' around the 'universalist tendencies of love, equality and respect'.[20]

A similar understanding of political friendship during the time of the Palestinian revolution was brought up in an interview which I conducted[21] with Daoud Talhami, the head of the International Studies department of the PLO Research Centre in the early 1970s. Sitting outside a community centre in Ramallah, he recalled how he became engaged with the centre and *Shu'un Filastiniyya*. As a young Palestinian Marxist, Talhami started his studies at the University of Montpellier in France in the early 1960s and eventually moved to Paris to become part of the vibrant political scene of Third World student movements and radical intellectuals. During his time in the capital, he was frequently visited by Anis Sayigh, the director of the PLO Research Centre in Beirut. Sayigh encouraged the student activist to work as a correspondent for the journal, and later invited him to come to Beirut and take up a position at the centre. Sayigh was searching for 'young not yet professional knowledge-thirsty researchers',[22] and Talhami had much

---

[17] The concept of friendship in the context of Jean Genet's involvement with the Palestinian revolution has also been discussed by Arpan Roy at the *Palestine as Epistemic Site* conference at the University of Vienna in 2021.

[18] Jacques Derrida, 'Politics of Friendship', trans. by Gabriel Motzkin and Michael Syrotinski, *American Imago* 50 (1993), 359–362.

[19] Omar Chowdhoury, 'Frantz Fanon: Négritude, Decolonisation and the Politics of Friendship', *Houston Review of Books*, Part 1 (2021), https://houstonreviewofbooks. com/2021/05/03/frantz-fanon-negritude-decolonisation-and-the-politics-of-friendship-part-one/#_ftn50.

[20] Ibid.

[21] This interview is part of my dissertation research on the epistemologies of liberation that were developed by militant intellectuals working at the PLO Research Centre during the time of the Palestinian revolution.

[22] Anis Sayigh, *Anis Sayigh 'an Anis Sayigh* (Beirut: Riyad al-Rayyis il-Kutub wa-al-Nashr, 2006), 223.

to offer. As head of the General Union of Palestinian Students (GUPS) in France from 1965–1969, Talhami was well known in the intellectual circles of Paris during a time when the Palestinian cause was becoming a central issue in global solidarity networks and student mobilisation in the metropole.[23]

Talhami met Jean-Paul Sartre together with the Palestinian writer Kamal Nasir in the early preparations for the *Les Temps Modernes* issue on the Arab–Israeli conflict, which Talhami and Nasir decided to boycott[24] due to its attempt at political normalisation in the context of settler colonialism.[25] As Talhami mentions in the quote below, he regularly joined meetings at the house of his friend and mentor, the well-known Marxist intellectual Maxime Rodinson, whom he admired for his standpoint on the Palestine question.

> Maxime Rodinson was a good friend of mine. I consider him a friend, but for him I was a student at that time. We used to go to his house, I learned a lot from him. He was a workaholic, and his house was a library; you know, piles of books on the ground and the walls. But he is a great scholar and writer. One of the most courageous people before 1967, you know, defending the Palestinian question in France.[26]

As Talhami mingled with internationalist intellectuals in Paris, he also had the chance to engage with the French writer and political activist Jean Genet shortly after his trip to Jordan in 1970 and was central to organising Genet's trip to Lebanon some years later. But his plan to stay in Paris, continue his studies and support the Palestinian cause from Europe did not work out. After the Palestinian attacks on the Israeli Olympic team at the Munich Games in July 1972, the Israeli intelligence services intensified their ongoing surveillance and targeted killing of Palestinians and Arab student activists, and Talhami had to leave Paris out of fear for his life.

> We were very attracted by what is happening in France and we joined the Palestinian resistance from the outside. And that was probably known by the Israelis. That's why after the massacre in Munich I felt that there was a lot of movement around my building. People

---

[23] Yoav Di-Capua, 'Palestine Comes to Paris. The Global Sixties and the Making of a Universal Cause', *Journal of Palestine Studies* 49, no. 1 (2021).
[24] Interview conducted by the author with Daoud Talhami, Ramallah, November 2021.
[25] *Les Temps Modernes* 253 (1967).
[26] Ibid.

Cover of Shu'un Filastiniyya, *12 December 1972 (reproduced
by permission of the PRC).*

were waiting, it was not very comfortable ... I decided at the end of
September to take the trip to Beirut and leave Paris definitively. I left
everything and on 30 September I was in Beirut. Next day, I went to
the research centre to begin work there.

Talhami only stayed for two years at the research centre and did not
have enough time to fully develop the department's research capacities.
Nevertheless, his contributions to the revolutionary journal exemplify
how militant writers reflected on their experiences and transnational relations with the global New Left at this specific juncture.[27] Talhami was not
an exception, and as much as the student activist influenced intellectuals
like Maxime Rodinson, their friendship also allowed him to reflect on his
challenges, and it shaped his analysis and positions. It further propelled

---

[27] Laure Guirguis, 'The Arab New Left and May '68: Transnational Entanglements at a
Time of Disruption', *Critical Historical Studies* 8, no. 1 (2021), 87–113.

intimate political discussions, as is reflected in the interview published by Talhami and Rodinson in *Shu'un Filastiniyya* in 1971 and other contributions he published in the journal. And although Talhami's statement about the urgency to leave France points to their radically different positionalities and lived experiences of colonial violence and political persecution, I argue that this specific notion of political friendship offers a perspective on what the historian Naghmeh Sohrabi calls '*small histories* to understand revolutions nationally, regionally, and globally'. As Sohrabi further states, 'at a moment in which the global dominates historical thinking, it is crucial to conceptualise small as the mechanisms through which vastness – of ideas, movements, emotions, and events – is both made possible and experienced.'[28]

Cover of Shu'un Filastiniyya 8, April 1972 (*reproduced by permission of the PRC*).

---

[28] Naghmeh Sohrabi, 'Where the small things are: Thoughts on writing revolutions and their histories', *Jadaliyya* (2020), https://www.jadaliyya.com/Details/41154/Where-the-Small-Things-Are-Thoughts-on-Writing.

Although dynamic in their character, politically and socially forged friendships during the time of the Palestinian revolution might be considered as one of several analytical categories that allow us to go beyond analysing solidarity as a 'means to specific ends'[29] or to short-term coalitions. Rather, acts of friendship laid the groundwork for encounters that allowed 'a shared vision of liberation – a vision that extended beyond the nation-state and the transnational to the world'.[30]

The internalisation of the Palestinian cause[31], especially after 1967, was an essential part of numerous political imaginaries that understood the importance of forging solidarities 'across geographical and social divisions'[32] during a time of global entanglements reflected in *Shu'un*. As Daoud Talhami writes in his introduction to the reflection of the French intellectual and writer Jean Genet after his visit to the Palestinian camps in Jordan published in *Shu'un* in December 1972: 'some of his observations might be surprising and some of them are debatable, but ... imprinted with deep sincerity and love for the revolution and the people'.[33] Once such a sense of trust was established, a conversation – often stretching over decades – could begin between writers, revolutionaries, and whole intellectual milieus.

Leela Gandhi, in her work on British anti-colonial activists in Victorian England,[34] analyses similar encounters as grounds for 'affective communities' that enable joint visions against imperialism at home and in the colony. The understanding of the 'continuities in imperial policy across these two spaces' propelled international friendships of dissent that took joint action against 'social ills at home that necessarily extended into campaigns against social ills of colonialism abroad, and vice versa'.[35] Therefore, affective communities, according to Gandhi, define the inherent drive of radical individuals and movements to refuse to align with the ideologies of colonial regimes.

---

[29] David Featherstone, *Solidarity: Hidden Histories and Geographies of Internationalism* (London: Zed Books, 2012).

[30] Robin D.G. Kelly, 'From the river to the sea to every mountain top: Solidarity as worldmaking', *Journal of Palestine Studies* 48, no. 4 (2020), 85.

[31] Sorcha Thomson and Pelle Valentin Olsen, *Palestine in the World: International Solidarity with the Palestinian Liberation Movement* (London: I.B. Tauris, 2023).

[32] David Featherstone, *Solidarity*, 25.

[33] 'Jean Genet: Conversations about the Palestinian Revolution', *Shu'un Filastiniyya* 12 (December 1972), 5.

[34] Leela Ghandi, *Affective Communities: Anticolonial Thought, Fin-de-Siècle Radicalism, and the Politics of Friendship* (Durham: Duke University Press, 2006).

[35] Nicholas Hoare, 'Anticolonialism and the politics of friendship in New Zealand's Pacific', *History Australia* 15, no. 3 (2018), 540–558.

Pointing to the limitations and difficulties of such politics of friendship in the context of anti-colonial movements in New Zealand's Pacific, Nicholas Hoare reminds us about 'the thin line of speaking for the colonised and standing up for them'.[36] This analytical point recurs in the works of anti-colonial writers in the revolutionary periodicals of the PLO. What was central for them was the possibility of the activists and movements in Europe reflecting on their positionalities and privilege, and then – hopefully – acting on their shared belief by offering material or symbolic solidarity.

WHERE DO YOU STAND?

Recalling his time in Paris, Daoud Talhami told me that there was one contribution for *Shu'un* he kept postponing while still living in the metropole. Anis Sayigh had urged the student activist to engage in an interview with Jean-Paul Sartre for the first issue of the magazine. But like Edward Said nearly a decade later,[37] Talhami described Sartre's position on the Palestinian revolution as ambivalent. Therefore, he was not very enthusiastic about the idea of working on the interview and submitting it to the editors. The Palestine Research Centre, on the other hand, had published a book consisting of several Arabic translations of Zionist contributions to the debated *Les Temps Modernes* issue in 1968 and was keen to feature an interview with Sartre. Therefore, Talhami finally published an article about the interview with Sartre in August 1972, which vividly showed his disagreement with the French intellectual's assessment of the Palestinian question.

While the author started with a generous introduction of Sartre's work on existentialism, he did not quote much of the interviewee's responses to his questions and mostly paraphrased their conversation. Pointing to Sartre's signing of a petition in favour of Israel shortly before the outbreak of the 1967 war, Talhami – denouncing the imperialist nature of the Zionist project – stated that 'the eyes of many have been opened after the 1967 war, but Sartre became silent'.[38] He continuously highlighted the French intellectual's contradictory analysis of the Palestinian struggle in relation to his

---

[36] Ibid., 557.
[37] Edward Said, 'My encounter with Sartre', *London Review of Books* 22 (2000), https://www.lrb.co.uk/the-paper/v22/n11/edward-said/diary.
[38] Daoud Talhami, 'Sartre and the Palestinian question', *Shu'un Filastiniyya* 12 (December 1972), 69.

support of other liberation movements in Algeria and Vietnam and to his mobilisation against racism targeting Arab workers in France. Portraying an intensive debate, Talhami introduced the reader to the two main problems of – as he called it – Sartre's emotional support for the Palestinian struggle. First, Sartre's denial of the colonial nature of the Zionist project and second, its imperialist and racist ideology. While acknowledging Israel's expansionist and reactionary politics, Sartre – according to Talhami – found hope in the progressive movements within Israel and foreshadowed an alliance between proletarians and Palestinians that could lead to transformation. But as Talhami showed, this political analysis was far from what the Palestinian resistance at that moment in time defined as a future roadmap to liberation. Summarising Sartre's stand on the Palestinian question, he concluded: 'Sartre is not a fighter in the ranks of the Palestinian revolution, nor a soldier of the Zionist movement'.[39]

The Palestinian writer here foreshadowed what, according to many intellectuals sympathetic to the Palestinian cause, would characterise Sartre's position on the Palestinian question – contradictory, ambivalent, and disappointing.[40] Or as Edward Said noted upon his meeting with Sartre in 1979: 'All I do know is that as a very old man he seemed pretty much the same as he had been when somewhat younger: a bitter disappointment to every (non-Algerian) Arab who admired him'.[41]

During our conversation, Talhami and I could not hide our excitement about his sharp analysis of Sartre in the revolutionary magazine. Our discussion quickly turned to Maxime Rodinson, who influenced the student activist's time in Paris. Two months before the interview with Sartre, Talhami published an extensive conversation with his friend in *Shu'un Filastiniyya*.[42] Providing space for his analysis, the author dedicated ten pages to Rodinson's observation of the current political moment. Rodinson extensively answered questions about his position on Marxism, Judaism, and Zionism, the colonial reality of the state of Israel, the Jewish question on a global scale, and his standpoint on the political programme and representation of the Palestinian struggle. The reader could sense that this was

[39] Ibid., 72.

[40] Farouk Mardam-Bey, 'French intellectuals and the Palestine question', *Journal of Palestine Studies* 43, no. 3 (2014), 26–39.

[41] Edward Said, 'My encounter with Sartre', *London Review of Books* 22 (2000), https://www.lrb.co.uk/the-paper/v22/n11/edward-said/diary.

[42] Daoud Talhami, 'Sartre and the Palestinian question', *Shu'un Filastiniyya* 12 (December 1972), 66–73.

not the first time that the interviewee and the interviewer had engaged in deep political conversations.

The last answer provides an example of what it means to go beyond sympathising with the Palestinian cause (as mentioned in Sartre's interview) and taking a stand against Israel's colonial policies. Defining his positionality, Rodinson stated that due to their experience as a colonised people, the Palestinians are the first to define the necessary steps towards liberation. Yet he wanted to offer his personal analysis, which had always been critical. First, he questioned Arafat's aspiration to found a Palestinian state where Jews, Muslims, and Christians could live together; emphasising that the reality of Israel was not based on religion in the first place. Therefore, he suggested that two culturally different groups in historic Palestine could not solely be addressed by their religious identities.

He further emphasised that mass mobilisation and support for the Palestinian cause might have succeeded within the Palestinian community, but the Arab societies and the Europeans specifically still needed to be won over to the cause. In Europe, he doubted that the most radical left factions supporting the Palestinian cause would come to power anytime soon. Without providing ready-made solutions to the Palestinian struggle – according to Talhami[43] – Rodinson's long-standing engagement with the Palestinian question qualified him as a trustworthy friend whose analysis was considered worth contributing to the Palestinian cause. The article ends with a response by Talhami, emphasising once again that 'Professor Rodinson speaks as a friend of the Palestinian people.'[44]

So far, this chapter has dealt with the engagements of intellectuals and political figures like Sartre, Genet, and Rodinson, whose reflections on Palestine offer insights into the intimate yet critical transnational encounters between the Palestinian revolution and anti-colonial advocates in the metropole. It also points to their active engagement with – as referred to by Elling and Haugbolle in the introduction to this volume – 'a range of related ideas and ideologies connected across time and space to national liberation movements in what was then considered The Third World'. In what follows, I reflect on more informal networks of advocacy for the Palestinian cause and the authors' analysis of their impact and limitations. At a turning point in the historical trajectory of the Palestinian global outreach – from 'mass

---

[43] Interview conducted by the author with Daoud Talhami, Ramallah, November 2021.
[44] Daoud Talhami, 'Interview with Maxime Rodinson', *Shu'un Filastiniyya* 9 (May 1972), 92.

mobilisation of radical networks and their general coalescence around a worldwide politics of transformation' in the global sixties to a 'fracturing of these networks' in the global seventies[45] – these accounts allow for an analysis of the front of friends for not only the PLO leadership but also, more importantly, the Arab audience who read *Shu'un Filastiniyya*.

MOBILISING FRIENDS

The PLO Research Centre functioned as a hub of revolutionary intellectual sovereignty[46] and creativity and provided a space for students, researchers, and militants who wanted to support the Palestinian cause through their writing and research. Starting in one apartment in a residential building in Ras Beirut that hosted the office of Anis Sayigh, a big meeting room and corridors full of shelves to store the first shipments of books,[47] the centre quickly took over the whole building, occupying six floors and consisting of several offices, a big library, and a space to host the archive and its own printing equipment. Until the looting of the centre in 1982, it provided a physical space for students and researchers to access rare books in various languages and also served as a meeting place for Palestinian and foreign journalists.[48]

The Lebanese writer and researcher Elias Khoury, who joined the centre in 1972, pointed to the fact that the idea of the centre was to create a focus for Palestinian intellectual life.[49] 'That time, the whole sixties and seventies, was a very important moment for the Palestinian struggle,' he told me in an interview. 'There was conscious work and effort to reclaim the Palestinian identity and reclaim the Palestinian name.' In his memoirs, Anis Sayigh explains the aim of these institutions as follows: 'We believed in the existence of something called Palestinian knowledge and Palestinian

---

[45] Sorcha Thomson, Valentine Pelle Olsen, and Sune Haugbolle, 'Palestine Solidarity Conferences in the Global Sixties', *Journal of Palestine Studies* 51, no. 1 (2022), 43–44.

[46] Rana Barakat, 'Writing/righting Palestine studies: Settler colonialism, indigenous sovereignty and resisting the ghost(s) of history', *Settler Colonial Studies* 8, no. 3 (2017), 349–363.

[47] Interview conducted by the author with Bassam Abu Sharif, Jericho, July 2019.

[48] Interview conducted by the author with Rosemary Sayigh, Lacarna, September 2021. Interview conducted by the author with Anni Kanafani, Beirut, July 2021.

[49] For Palestinian intellectual debate after the Second World War, see Adey Almohsen, 'Arab Critical Culture and Its (Palestinian) Discontents After the Second World War', *Arab Studies Journal*, no. 1 (2021), 56–83.

scholarship. It attempted to channel into this field dozens of new arrivals who were armed with enough knowledge, exposure, and understanding so as to be trained towards closing the gap and confronting Zionist and Israeli knowledge.'[50]

Therefore, one of the recurring characteristics of *Shu'un*'s alternative archive is the question of information and knowledge about the Palestinian struggle and the intervention into what the research centre termed 'Zionist knowledge'. The anti-colonial intellectuals knew their global outreach had to counter the historical narrative of the coloniser, and their efforts to do so, together with Palestinian factions in the diaspora, to mobilise political groups and solidarity movements in Europe are vividly described throughout the many pages of *Shu'un*.

For example, in the May 1971 issue, Eugene Makhlouf reported on his media tour to Europe. On his way to the World Conference of Christians for Palestine in Paris, he visited Ireland and Belgium to advocate for the Palestinian cause. Ireland offered satisfying meetings with organised journalists, students, and intellectuals as well as an active Arab community that welcomed the revolution. He received immediate media attention and described a vibrant student movement eager to learn about the Palestinian struggle, support the resistance, and organise the import of Palestinian products to compete with Israeli goods. Although the author concluded that not many details were known in Ireland about Palestinian history, the Irish people's colonial past and experience of domination by Britain qualified them as 'friends who can pressure in favour of the cause'.[51] Yet the author's experience in Belgium represented a different scenario. Being met by individuals and not by organised groups, he faced orientalist attitudes, suspicion, and slogans supporting Israel's policies vis-à-vis the Soviet Union. At one point the author mentioned that these people came to criticise his position and not to listen to his presentation. This points to a clear understanding of power dynamics within the European left at that specific juncture, which was confirmed during Makhlouf's visit to the conference he was attending in Paris.

---

[50] Anis Sayigh, *Anis Sayigh about Anis Sayigh* (Beirut: Riyad al-Rayyis il-Kutub wa-al-Nashr, 2006), 222–229.
[51] Eugene Makhlouf, 'Impressions about a Media Tour in Europe', *Shu'un Filastiniyya* 2 (May 1971), 214.

Three years after Makhlouf's analysis, in the 1974 April issue of *Shu'un Filastiniyya*,[52] Fatima Abu al-Qasim described the radical left scene in the Federal Republic of Germany. Shedding light on their active support for the Palestinian cause, she further provided information about Palestinian student and labour unions and their efforts at mobilising with, and within, internationalist solidarity movements in the country. Identifying the attack on the Israeli Olympic team in Munich in 1972 and its aftermath as events that increased revolutionary solidarity,[53] al-Qasim pointed to the efforts of these groups in integrating the question of Palestine into their anti-imperialist support of liberation movements based in Africa. The author also highlights their internal debates in adopting a strategy to support the Palestinian struggle and the repercussions these allies faced for taking a stance on the question of Palestine. Addressing her audience, she concluded that 'the stronger and more effective the forces supporting us become, the more the fronts become clear. Not only in front of enemies but also in front of friends.'[54] Based on discussions with the Palestinian diaspora in Germany and a careful reading and translation of various sources on the situation in the Federal Republic, her analysis was of crucial importance for the evaluation of international solidarity for and reaction to the Palestinian revolution for her peers back in Beirut.

As argued by the scholar Joseph Ben Prestel,[55] engaging with the archival sources of the sixties and early seventies like *Shu'un* does not only provide an alternative historical narrative on the multi-layered and transformative stance of the European left towards the Palestinian cause, it also provides insights into the impact of the activism of Palestinian political groups in the diaspora that shaped and influenced their radical peers. Similarly, in the context of France, Laure Guirguis describes the emerging front of supporters for the Palestinian cause in the early seventies: 'The

---

[52] Fatima Abu al- Qasim, 'The Left of the Federal Republic of Germany and its Solidarity Movement with the Palestinian Reevolution', *Shu'un Filastiniyyah* 32 (April 1974), 142–149.

[53] Joseph Ben Prestel explains the 'paradox' of this short-term rise in solidarity in the aftermath of the Munich attacks by the impact of increasing deportations of Palestinians and the banning of the GUPS and GUPA in Germany. See the citation (2019) on the next page.

[54] Fatima Abu al- Qasim, 'The Left of the Federal Republic of Germany and its Solidarity Movement with the Palestinian Revolution', *Shu'un Filastiniyyah* 32 (April 1974), 149.

[55] Joseph Ben Prestel, 'Heidelberg, Beirut und die Dritte Welt. Palästinensische Gruppen in der Bundesrepublik Deutschland (1956–1972)', *Studies in Contemporary History* 16, no. 3 (2019), 442–466.

Cover of Shu'un Filastiniyya *32, April 1974 (reproduced by permission of the PRC).*

growing visibility of the Palestinian presence made it extremely difficult to regard Israel as a socialist society, and the representation of the Palestinian as a victimised refugee gave way to that of a fighter struggling against an oppressive colonial/imperialist rule, a shift that could but appeal to a radical French leftist.'[56]

The importance of the mobility of Palestinian revolutionaries to the promotion of solidarity movements abroad, which became increasingly difficult with the start of the civil war in Beirut, as well as counter-revolutionary action in the region and beyond, was described by another author in the March 1975[57] issue of *Shu'un Filastiniyya.* Reflecting on a trip to Switzerland, N.S.[58] reports that Palestine support committees were

---

[56] Laure Guirguis, 'The Arab New Left and May '68: Transnational Entanglements at a Time of Disruption', *Critical Historical Studies* 8, no. 1 (2021), 105.

[57] N.S., 'The Campaign supporting Palestine in Switzerland', *Shu'un Filastiniyya* 45 (March 1975), 201–203.

[58] The full name of the author is not known.

formed in cities such as Bern, Geneva, Zurich, Basel, and Lausanne. They highlighted the fact that the Swiss students supporting the Palestinian cause were not aware of the details of the Palestinian struggle. Hence, the Arab comrades decided to increase their numbers in these committees to co-ordinate more closely with the different solidarity structures in Switzerland and decided to support the travels of some of the Swiss members to Beirut.

The author also described the strategic decision by various groups to organise a week for Palestine, which aimed at bridging political and ideological divides within the movements. The event, which focused on Palestinian political detainees in Israeli prisons, provided information from lawyers and the International Committee of the Red Cross about Palestinian prisoners. A particular highlight in the article was the invitation of a speaker from the PLO Research Centre, who gave a presentation on the Palestinian question. This revolutionary speaker not only caught public attention but also motivated Arab students and comrades alike to join the solidarity committees. Concluding his/her thoughts on the necessary improvements to the support of the Palestinian struggle in Switzerland the author mentioned the following essential steps. First, building up and strengthening a network of solidarity organisations and committees in Switzerland to complement and co-operate with initiatives in France, Italy, and Germany. Second, speeding up translations from Arabic into French to provide more accurate and scientific information about the Palestinian struggle. And third, invitations and lectures by representatives of the revolutions, as well as organised visits for activists from Switzerland to Beirut.

The sense of urgency that we see here was to shape the Centre during the coming years during the Lebanese civil war and the ongoing colonisation of Palestine. Systematic reflections on solidarity networks and friends of the Palestinian cause in Europe slowly disappeared from the pages of *Shu'un* and were replaced by reports on the general political stances and support of Western countries and international institutions for the Zionist regime. In other words, defining the enemy became a necessary way of positioning oneself as multiple fronts opened up in Lebanon. For friends of the Palestinian revolution who used to frequently travel to Beirut or receive their peers in European capitals, this also meant that movement would become limited and transnational connections – often based on lived experiences of revolutionary praxis – would eventually thin out.[59] In light of the global decline of Third Worldism, this example also shows that political friendships, if solely based on individual encounters, had their limitations and that a shared understanding of the struggle against imperialism and colonialism had to be actively forged and built.

Cover of Shu'un Filastiniyya *43, March 1975 (reproduced by permission of the PRC).*

---

[59] Joseph Ben Prestel, 'When Treads Were Thin: The West German Radical Left and Palestinian Groups at the End of the 1970s', *Trafo*, December 2022, https://trafo. hypotheses.org/12156.

TRANSFORMATION OF THE FRONT(S)

'A photograph has two dimensions, so does a television screen; neither can be walked through'

JEAN GENET, 1983

The year 1975 marked a shift in channelling most of the resources of militant intellectuals to engage with friends and enemies of the Palestinian revolution back in Lebanon.[60] Such developments were also visible in the contents of *Shu'un* as the main focus of its writers shifted to covering unfolding massacres, negotiations on a political and strategic level, and internal debates and decisions by the different factions of the PLO. As pointed out by Sune Haugbolle, 'what is habitually referred to as the Lebanese Civil War was in fact a series of more or less related conflicts between shifting alliances of Lebanese groups and external actors, who from 1975 to 1990 destabilised the Lebanese state.'[61] As the PLO in Lebanon often changed their alliances during these years, Palestinian analysts and writers based at the PLO Research Centre were busy documenting these developments through often very personal accounts and strategic political analysis – that was closely linked to confronting the 'Zionist enemy' in the homeland – in *Shu'un Filastiniyya*. Even after the looting of the centre in 1982,[62] the journal kept on publishing, but Palestinian militant intellectuals who dedicated their life to the struggle lived under constant threat of being made a target.[63]

Already in his editorial note in the August 1972 issue of *Shu'un Filastiniyya*, Anis Sayigh told his readers that he sent his last comments on an article to Ghassan Kanafani on 7 July. The writer never received the director's comments. He was already dead. As one of the leading voices of the Palestinian revolution, he was a main target of Israeli intelligence. Sayigh concluded that his death was in a sense natural because 'his struggle is, in

---

[60] Fawwaz Traboulsi, *A History of Modern Lebanon* (London: Pluto Press, 2012), 157–246; Rex Brynen, *Sanctuary and Survival: The PLO in Lebanon* (London: Westview Press, 1990), 160–176.

[61] Sune Haugbolle, 'The Historiography and the Memory of the Lebanese Civil War', *SciencePo* 2011, https://www.sciencespo.fr/mass-violence-war-massacre-resistance/en/document/historiography-and-memory-lebanese-civil-war.html#title3.

[62] 'The Israeli Looting of the Centre is an Extermination of People and an Annihilation of Memory', *Shu'un Filastiniyya* 29/30/31 (August/September/October 1982), 38–49.

[63] Interview conducted by the author with Rose Shomali, Ramallah, July 2019. Interview conducted by the author with Sabri Jiryis, Fassouta, November 2021.

fact, his whole career. This was because he believed in it, and he believed that the work for Palestine has no limits.'[64] How dangerous research work during the Palestinian revolution could be is illustrated by another comment in the same issue by the poet Mahmoud Darwish – at that time editor of *Shu'un* – who wrote in the name of the 'family of freedom', the workers of the research centre. Here, Darwish discusses another assassination attempt, this time targeting the director, Anis Sayigh, one week after the car bomb that killed his colleague Kanafani. He received a letter bomb at his office that left him blinded in one eye and injured. During the invasion of the Israeli forces of Beirut in 1982, another car bomb exploded in front of the centre and in 1983 the institution was firebombed again, leaving eighteen people dead and ninety-five wounded.[65] But as stated by many of my interviewees, the work had to go on.[66]

During these difficult years, some of the friends of the Palestinian revolution stayed and decided to share the risk and burden[67] with their peers in Lebanon. In an interview, Faisal Hourani, head of Palestine Studies and later head of International Studies of the centre in 1979, provided testimony of his experiences of the Israeli invasion of Beirut and the looting of the centre and pointed to a friend who was of utmost importance for the revolutionary intellectual:

> Yasser Arafat notified Sabri Jiryis, who was the general director at the time, to not force any of the PRC crew to stay in Beirut and that everyone had the freedom of choice between staying or leaving. Sabri executed Arafat's demands and I helped. Sabri, I and half the crew stayed in the centre while others chose to leave. That day I was in my office drowned with work which doubled for all those who chose to stay. A colleague barged in my office saying in a shaky tone: 'the Israelis have invaded West Beirut.' I responded promptly, 'should we stop work every time a rumour comes about?' He said that it wasn't a rumour this time, but was broadcasted on Lebanese and Israeli media. We estimated it would take the army two hours

[64] Anis Sayigh, *Shu'un Filastiniyya* 12 (August 1972), 4.
[65] Laleh Khalili, *Heroes and Martyrs of Palestine: The Politics of National Commemoration* (Cambridge: Cambridge University Press, 2007), 62–63.
[66] Written interview conducted by the author with Faisal Hourani, trans. by Maya Zebdawi, Vienna, August 2019.
[67] Linda Tabar, 'From Third World Internationalism to "the Internationals": The Transformation of Solidarity with Palestine', *Third World Quarterly* 38, no. 2 (2017), 414–435.

to reach Ras Beirut coming from Rouche. We started to remove all documents which we deemed might pose a threat if in the hands of the invaders. We put all the documents in Sabri's car. As the Israelis reached Ras Beirut, we knew we had only a few minutes until they arrived. At that point, Sabri ordered everyone to split and find themselves havens in friends' homes ... Friends helped me contact the people I needed to contact, first the American journalist Janette Lee Stevenson who was pro-Palestinian resistance. I needed to contact her because she lived in a building close to both the PRC building and Commodore Hotel, and so she can update me with the occurrences over there ... Janette used to visit the Commodore Hotel where journalists of different nationalities used to reside. In the evening, Miss Janette stopped by unexpectedly and informed us that, according to sources, the looted material of the centre was shipped directly to Israel. Lebanese journalists informed the foreign journalists of another important piece of news. She said that General Ariel Sharon, the defence minister then, had taken for himself an office on the roof of Al Kuwaiti building and that he has been residing within the office since the morning. Al Kuwaiti building overlooked the Sabra area and Shatila camp.[68]

According to Faisal Hourani, a journalist in the following days also set up a meeting with the Israeli general responsible for looting the research centre and reported back to Hourani. She also supported him in reaching Sabra and Shatila shortly after the massacre took place.[69] The centre published one of the first accounts of survivors of the atrocities that took place in the Palestinian camps of Sabra and Shatila on 16–18 September 1982. One of the investigators was Hanna Shaheen, the wife of the director, Sabri Jiryis. Shaheen was later killed by the car explosion in front of the centre in 1983.[70]

---

[68] Written interview conducted by the author with Faisal Hourani, trans. by Maya Zebdawi, Vienna, August 2019.

[69] Bayan Nuwayhed al-Hout, *Sabra and Shatila, September 1982* (London: Pluto Press, 2004).

[70] A group of researchers, 'Survivors of the Massacre', *Shu'un Filastinyya* 132–133 (November/December 1982); Hanna Shaheen, 'Investigating the Massacre of Sabra and Shatila Amidst a Surge of Public Fury and Protest', *Shu'un Filastinyya* 132–133 (November/December 1982).

شؤون فلسطينية

Cover of Shu'un Filastiniyya *132–133, November–December 1982 (reproduced by permission of the PRC).*

Rosemary Sayigh, a pioneer in the oral history of Palestine,[71] was one of the eyewitnesses of the looting of the centre.[72] In a conversation about her engagement with the Palestinian cause, she remembered the huge conveyor belt used by the Israeli military to steal the books from the second and third floors of the building.[73] Asked about her work in Beirut during the 1970s, she explained: 'People were so happy to get their voice out. They actually thought that through me, you know publishing in England, they would have a megaphone to the prime minister. I thought writing a book about them that got sold in America and England was somehow helpful to the cause.'[74]

---

[71] Rosemary Sayigh, *Palestinians: From Peasants to Revolutionaries: A People's History* (London: Zed Books, 1979).
[72] Hana Sleiman, 'The paper trail of a liberation movement', *Arab Studies Journal* 24, no.1 (2017), 42–67.
[73] Interview conducted by the author with Rosemary Sayigh, Lacarna, September 2021.
[74] Ibid.

On the one hand, my research shows that the transformation of front(s) starting from the mid-1970s meant that the analysis and discussions about various circles of friends in the revolutionary magazine became less frequent. However, in my interviews with revolutionary intellectuals who have been based in Beirut, memories and short anecdotes about those remaining in solidarity and supporting the Palestinian cause during the years of the civil war in Lebanon are present and they have been discussed with much appreciation.

CONCLUSION

Documenting the atrocities committed against Palestinians and amplifying Palestinian voices during the final years of the 1970s became one of the top priorities of the remaining front of friends. As I have shown, this was a natural development from the earlier emphasis on an entangled international revolution at the beginning of the decade, when travel to and from Lebanon was easier. In the context of this edited volume's attempt to provide insights into micro-histories of the fate of Third Worldism, my chapter has sought to encourage an engagement with the archive of a generation that left behind a reservoir of liberatory knowledge production that keeps alive the memories of a global revolutionary moment. Combined with interviews with key protagonists, my chapter has offered a reading of *Shu'un Filastiniyya* as a repository of the ongoing reflection of transformations of the material and ideological conditions of Third Worldism as they were experienced from the vantage point of Palestinian Beirut.

This Palestinian Beirut was never just Palestinian. It was a transnational space, even when it became marginalised, brutalised, and eventually abandoned. During the worst of the fighting at the very end point of the Palestinian revolution, in August 1982, international comrades remained present to bear witness and provide support. One of them was Jean Genet, who had begun his engagement more than a decade earlier in the Paris of Talhami's youth. Politically and socially forged friendships with Palestinian militants and intellectuals encouraged Jean Genet to write a substantial account of his experiences of entering Sabra and Shatila camp after the massacre by Phalangist militias under the supervision of the Israeli occupying forces in Lebanon in 1982. At the end of his piece, which was published in the *Journal of Palestine Studies* a year after the event, he writes an open-ended passage on friendship and solidarity, which serves as a fitting conclusion to this chapter:

> You can select a particular community other than that of your birth, whereas you are born into a people; this selection is based on an irrational affinity, which is not to say that justice has no role, but this justice and the entire defence of this community take place because of an emotional, perhaps intuitive, sensual-attraction; I am French, but I defend the Palestinians wholeheartedly and automatically. They are in the right because I love them. But would I love them if injustice had not turned them into a wandering people.[75]

[75] Jean Genet, 'Four Hours in Shatila', *Journal of Palestine Studies* 12, no. 3 (1983), 3–22.

The author wants to thank the editors, Sune Haugbolle and Rasmus Christian Elling, for their belief in a collective process of developing this book project and their critical feedback on this chapter.

This contribution also benefited from an earlier round of feedback by Marral Shamshiri and Toufoul Abou-Hodeib. The author wants to thank Adriana Qubaiova and Noura Salahaldeen for their long-standing support and critical reading of her work and Marah Khalifa for establishing contact with the PRC in Ramallah to request copyright permission for the images used in this article. Finally, thanks to Maya Zebdawi, who supported this ongoing PhD project with her critical historical insights, outstanding translation expertise and fieldwork support in Beirut.

10

FRAGILE SOLIDARITY

The Iranian Left and the Kurdish National Question in the 1979 Revolution

Rasmus C. Elling and Jahangir Mahmoudi

While this chapter was being written, Iran was gripped by the most significant popular uprising since the revolution of 1979. The death in the custody of the state 'morality police' on 16 September 2022 of a young Kurdish woman, Jina Mahsa Amini, sparked a leaderless uprising, beginning in Saqqez in Kurdistan and continuing as a nationwide movement. Under two overall demands – the downfall of the Islamic Republic instituted after the revolution in 1979 and a radically different, democratic future for Iran – the uprising has heralded a new revolutionary culture of dissent and intersectional solidarity in a country shot through with gendered, ethno-national, and socio-economic inequalities.

However, the debates generated by the uprising also raise a thorny question in Iran's history of progressive politics: namely, what is or should be the place of the peripheralised and minoritised ethno-national groups' struggle for self-determination within or alongside a broader struggle for freedom for all Iranians? This question is often perceived as sensitive and divisive in Iranian public spheres: at once crucial and yet often avoided. This avoidance also extends to scholarship on Iran's modern history – among other things, on the role of the Kurdish movement in Iran during and after the 1979 revolution. Few scholars engage with primary sources from Kurdistan and in Kurdish; but also, we argue, there is a tendency to avoid such highly contentious issues altogether. Even the brief mentions of minorities and peripheries in the existing histories contain factual errors, sweeping assumptions or partial narratives.[1] Indeed, Iranian Studies has since the 1990s been subject to criticism for its Persian-centrist, Tehran-centric or Iranian nationalist orientations.[2] Even the bourgeoning literature on the Iranian left can be criticised for neglecting the periphery and minorities at the expense of the political-geographical centre.[3]

This chapter aims to shed light on the relationship between one of the major leftist groups and the Kurdish national liberation struggle in the context of revolution. By focusing on the *Sazman-e cherik-ha-ye fada'i-ye khalq* (Organisation of the People's Fada'i Guerrillas, henceforth FEK) in relation to events in Kurdistan in the period February 1979 to October 1980, the chapter contributes to a small but growing literature on Kurdistan in revolutionary Iran.[4] While we must limit ourselves in this chapter to a focus

---

[1] Generally, overviews of modern Iranian history contain very few and brief mentions of Kurdistan and its role in and after the revolution. See, for example, Ervand Abrahamian, *A History of Modern Iran* (Cambridge: Cambridge University Press), 169; Homa Katouzian, *The Persians. Ancient, Mediaeval and Modern Iran* (New Haven & London: Yale University Press), 330. Other works do not even mention the modern Kurdish struggle for self-determination. See, for example, Hamid Dabashi, *Iran. The Rebirth of a Nation* (New York: Palgrave Macmillan, 2016). Yet other works display partisan views when it comes to the subject matter of this chapter, exemplified in Abbas Amanat's description of the FEK's support for autonomy for ethnic minorities – or, in Amanat's view, 'dormant cessation tendencies' – as 'mostly in the realm of imagination' and yet 'politically dangerous' and 'ominous'. See Abbas Amanat, *Iran: A Modern History* (New Haven: Yale University Press), 810. Even histories concerned directly with the revolution tend to heavily reduce the complexities and the intensity of the conflict in Kurdistan. See, for example, Michael Axworthy, *Revolutionary Iran: A History of the Islamic Republic* (Oxford: Oxford University Press), 154–155; Said Amir Arjomand, *The Turban for the Crown. The Islamic Revolution in Iran* (New York and Oxford: Oxford University Press), 136.
[2] Mehrzad Boroujerdi, 'Contesting nationalist constructions of Iranian identity', *Critique: Journal for Critical Studies of the Middle East* 7, no. 12 (1998): 43–55; Rasmus Elling, *Minorities in Iran: Nationalism and Ethnicity after Khomeini* (New York: Palgrave, 2013); Kamran Matin, 'Decolonising Iran: A tentative note on inter-subaltern colonialism', *Current Anthropology*, 63, no. 2 (2022): 1–4; Kamal Soleimani and Ahmad Mohammadpour. 'Can non-Persians speak? The sovereign's narration of "Iranian identity"', *Ethnicities* 19, no. 5 (2019): 925–947.
[3] As an example, in his magisterial work on the FEK, Ali Rahnema only mentions ethnic minorities and geographical peripheries in brief passages. Ali Rahnema, *Call to Arms: Iran's Marxist Revolutionaries. Formation and Evolution of the Fada'is, 1964–1976* (London: Oneworld Academic, 2021).
[4] See, for example, Marouf Cabi, 'The roots and the consequences of the 1979 Iranian revolution: A Kurdish perspective', *Middle Eastern Studies* 56, no. 3 (2020): 339–358; Marouf Cabi, 'The armed struggle of the 1980s in Iranian Kurdistan: a space

on the FEK, we also hope the research contributes to a more comprehensive and nuanced historiography of the Iranian left.

Drawing on Persian- and Kurdish-language party documents and publications, published eyewitness accounts, and new oral history interviews, the chapter makes the following argument: that the conundrum of the national question in Marxist–Leninist theory, coupled with Persian-centric and nation-state-centric views entrenched on the left, came into direct clash with the Third Worldist ideal of solidarity with oppressed peoples in the case of Kurdistan in Iran after the revolution. This clash, we will argue, contributed to the failure of a leftist alternative to the emerging Islamic Republic. Zooming out, we further argue that this clash is an important but understudied component of the story about the fate of Third Worldism in the Middle East.

The chapter is structured as follows: first, we provide a background of the Kurdish national struggle and the views of the FEK on the question of ethno-national minorities during 'the long 1960s'; then we outline key events and actors in Kurdistan during the Iranian Revolution; then we analyse key contradictions in FEK's Kurdistan discourse and policy; and, finally, we discuss our findings.

CENTRE, PERIPHERY, AND EMANCIPATORY STRUGGLE

The 1960s and early 1970s was a period of radical change in the Kurdish national liberation movement in Iran. These changes were connected to political developments at home and abroad, including the wave of repression following the 1953 coup and the 1963 Qom uprising in Iran, the tensions between US-backed Iran and Soviet-backed Iraq from 1958 onwards, the land reforms of the Shah's White Revolution from 1963 onwards, and the emergence of Maoism as an alternative to Soviet communism for anti-imperialist and national liberation movements around the world.

---

for survival', *British Journal of Middle Eastern Studies*, ahead of print, https://doi.org/10.1080/13530194.2022.2057280 (2022): 1–21; Ali Ezzatyar, *Last Mufti of Iranian Kurdistan* (New York: Palgrave Macmillan, 2016); Allan Hassaniyan, *Kurdish Politics in Iran* (Cambridge: Cambridge University Press, 2021); Kamran Matin, 'The Iranian left, radical change, and the national question', *Abdou Filali-Ansary Occasional Paper Series, Aga Khan University* 1 (2019): 12–16; Abbas Vali, *The Forgotten Years of Kurdish Nationalism* (New York: Palgrave Macmillan, 2019).

While the Kurdistan Democratic Party (KDP) of Iran from 1953 to 1966 was dominated by conservative ethno-nationalism – and while the Iraq-based Kurdistan Democratic Party led by Mulla Mustafa Barzani suppressed the former to obtain Iran's support against the Iraqi state – a radical wing of leftist Kurdish student activists broke away to launch a new movement. On 14 September 1966, they established the 'Kurdistan Democratic Party – The Revolutionary Committee' (KDP-RC).[5] Under strong influence from Maoism,[6] the KDP-RC elected to engage in 'armed propaganda', justified in the Third Worldist terms that 'the only way to liberate all subordinated and colonised nations is the revolt and guerrilla struggle of the toiling peoples'.[7] After eighteen months of armed guerrilla insurgency, the KDP-RC uprising – which had seen almost no support from the rest of Iran's opposition[8] – was crushed by the Pahlavi state. While it failed to achieve its goal, the uprising was in fact the first revolutionary leftist armed insurgency in post-Second World War Iran – three years before the FEK launched its watershed Siahkal guerrilla attack in 1971.

In the meantime, the Ba'thist coup in Iraq in 1968 provided temporary respite for the Kurds and hence an opportunity for the KDP to reinvent itself. Over conferences and congresses in 1969, 1971, and 1973, the organisation moved gradually left,[9] and in 1976 the party settled on the name KDPI.[10] The Kurdish national question, which had been framed as Third Worldist anti-imperialism by the KDP-RC, became nested instead in a Leninist anti-imperialism with the key demand of 'autonomy for Kurdistan within the framework of a democratic Iran'.[11] In addition, a radical Maoist tendency

---

[5] Saeed Kave, *Awrek le besarhati xom u rodawekani naw Hezbi Demokrati Kordestani Eran* (n.p., Stockholm, 1996), 151–154; Smael Bazyar, *Karigeri Biri Chep le ser Bizafi Siasi Rojhelati Kurdistan, Hizbi Demokrati Kurdistan wek Nemone (1945–1991)* (Hawler: Rojhelat, 2020), 248.

[6] Bazyar, *Karigeri*, 248.

[7] Esmail Sharifzadeh 1967 cited in Karim Hisami, *Le bireweriyekanem, bergi sehem 1965–1970* (Stockholm: Self-published, 1988), 130.

[8] The only exception was the so-called Tudeh Party of Iran – Revolutionary Organisation (TPI-RO). See Tudeh, *Shomare-ye vizheh darbare-ye mobareze-ye mosalahane-ye Kurdestan-e Iran,* 1969.

[9] Cf. *Kurdistan*, no. 12, January 1972; no. 16, May 1972; no. 20, October 1972; KDP(I), *Tikoshir* (internal pamphlet), no. 3, 1972; KDP(I), *Documents on Third Congress of KDP(I)* (n.p., September 1973).

[10] Cf. *Kurdistan*, no. 8 (September 1971) with no. 44 (December 1976). On this period, see also: Bazyar, *Karigeri...*, 248. Mullah Rasoul Pishnamaz, *Sarborday Jianim* (Selimani: Shivan, 2012), 247.

[11] KDP(I), Documents on Third Congress of KDP(I), September 1973, 15.

took shape in 1968 among Kurdish students in Tehran under the name *Tashkilat* (The Organisation). This network wanted to distance itself from other leftist currents, above all the pro-Moscow line of the Tudeh Party of Iran (TPI) but also guerrilla movements such as the FEK.[12] Following the 1979 revolution, *Tashkilat* would become the Revolutionary Organisation of Iranian Kurdistan's Toilers (KSZKI) or *Komala*.

In other words, there was a strong current of radical and leftist mobilisation around the national question among the Kurds, which arguably impacted on or even shaped the FEK's outlook in the years leading up to the revolution. Although this influence was rarely explicitly acknowledged, it was nonetheless evident from personal relations and intellectual exchanges such as those between the prominent KDP-RC leader Ismail Sharifzadeh and the Tabriz-based proto-FEK circle of activists.[13]

Pre-revolutionary FEK itself was heavily urban-centric[14] and arguably marked in its outlook by the fact that most cadres came from Persian, Shi'ite-majority backgrounds. There were nonetheless important early voices pointing to the revolutionary potential of Iran's minoritised groups. While minorities were mostly mentioned in the FEK literature as subordinate components of broader historical analyses of Iran's socio-economic composition, they were nonetheless treated in terms of *khalq-ha* ('peoples') or, sometimes, as *mellal* ('nations')[15] – with Iran occasionally termed *kasir-ol-melleh* or 'multi-national'.[16] This pluralisation – in contrast to the singular 'people' in the organisation's name – foreshadowed a significant discursive

---

[12] On the roots of *Komala* in *Tashkilat*, see, for example, Rashad Mostafa-Soltani, *Kak Foad, rebar, siyasetmedar u zanayeki siyasi* (Selimani: Rojhalat, 2007); Bahman Saeydi, *Penj sal le gal Abdullah Mohtadi* (Zarqwez: KSZKI, 2010); Bahman Saeydi, Ibrahim Alizadeh, *Se sal le gal Ibrahim Alizadeh* (Ketab-e Arzan, 2010); Hossain Morad-Beigi, *Tarikh-e zendeh: Kordestan, chap va nasiyonalism* (Stockholm: Nasim, 2004).

[13] See Hamid Momeni, *Darbare-ye mobarezat-e Kordestan* (Tehran: Shabahang, 1979), 54.

[14] See Rasmus Elling, 'In a Forest of Humans: The Urban Cartographies of Theory and Action in 1970s Iranian Revolutionary Socialism', in *Global 1979: Geographies and Histories of the Iranian Revolution*, eds Arang Keshavarzian and Ali Mirsepassi (Cambridge: Cambridge University Press), 141–177.

[15] See, for example, Ali-Akbar Safa'i-Farahani, *Anche yek enqelabi bayad bedanad* (n.p., 1349/1970; online version republished by The Organisation for the Unity of the People's Fada'iyan of Iran, Mordad 1381/July–August 2004), 17. Note that Rahnema (*Call to Arms*, 124–126) has convincingly argued that this booklet was in fact penned by Jazani, not Safa'i-Farahani.

[16] See, for example, Mohammad Chupanzadeh Group, *Mas'ale-ye melli va tarh-e an dar mobarezat-e raha'i-bakhsh-e Iran* (n.p., 1355/1976–1977, 2nd ed., Ordibehesht 1358/April–May 1979), 8.

change away from the mainstream majority-nationalist conceptualisation of Iranians as *one*. We will return to the limits of this change, but it suffices here to state that while there were scattered references to Iran's minorities as 'nations' and 'peoples' with a right to self-determination in communist discourse as far back as the 1920s, it was with the FEK that these issues were thoroughly and radically re-conceptualised as a national question.

The FEK generally used the concept of 'national oppression' (*setam-e melli*) to describe the situation of non-majority peoples and further elaborated this by introducing 'double oppression' (*setam-e moza'ef*), for instance in the seminal 1973 pamphlet *How is armed struggle popularised?*:

> Our homeland is made up of numerous peoples. While some of these peoples are themselves subject to imperialist oppression as a whole, they [also suffer from] the double oppression of minority peoples facilitated by the ruling class and its representative regime. It is natural that the toiling masses of these peoples are in contradiction [*tazad*] with each other. The contradictions that exist in this case sometimes lead to conflict [*ta'aroz*]; this is a contradiction between the collectivity of a minority people and the ruling regime, which is mainly formed from the majority people.[17]

The pamphlet explained that while the Azeris, Iran's biggest minority, suffered 'cultural oppression', other groups suffered overlapping layers of economic, political, *and* cultural oppression – namely the Kurds, Baluch, and Arabs. While some oppression stemmed from 'remnant feudalism' and conservatism internal to these communities, it was clear that the state enacted the brunt of oppression through the capitalist class of a (Persian) majority briefly mentioned here as 'the ruling people' (*khalq-e hakem*).[18] This included keeping minority regions underdeveloped and economically marginalised; giving them little or no political representation; and suppressing their languages, cultures, and religious beliefs.[19]

---

[17] FEK, *Cheguneh mobareze-ye mosallahaneh tudeh'i mishavad?* (n.p., 1352/autumn 1973; re-published in FEK, *19-e Bahman-e te'orik*, no. 2, 2nd print, *Tir* 1355/June–July 1976), 97, available at https://www.iran-archive.com/sites/default/files/2021-08/bijan-jazani-mobarezeye-mosallahne-tudei.pdf (accessed 9 June 2023).

[18] FEK, *Cheguneh*, 97.

[19] FEK, *Cheguneh*, 97–98.

As Marxists, the FEK believed that the cultural dimension was directly rooted in the socio-economic conditions created by economic exploitation and imperialism, whether under feudalism or capitalism. However, according to the pamphlet, the intersection of all these injustices in 'national oppression' could be dated specifically to the rise of Reza Shah in the early 1920s, when minorities and nomadic societies were violently subjugated. In Kurdistan, this development generated 'a field of national struggles', first in tribal rebellions and soon also in minority uprisings that had 'a progressive colour'.[20]

A slightly different historical periodisation could be found in the writings of the FEK activist, poet, and teacher Alireza Nabdel, who pointed out that relative to his own native Azeris, the Kurds had suffered a much harsher repression that dated all the way back to the Safavid Empire (1501–1736).[21] However, Nabdel too argued that 'national awakening and consciousness' had grown exponentially during Reza Pahlavi's dictatorship.

Indeed, the case of Kurdistan provided FEK with an important example of a revolutionary potential in ethnic diversity. First, the Kurdish struggle was presented, in pamphlets such as the one mentioned above, as truly 'popular':[22] their movement already *had* mass support and did not, like the Persian-speaking centre, depend on a mobilising vanguard. Second, due to its transborder nature, the Kurdish movement even enjoyed support outside of Iran, which could potentially help drain the Iranian state's repressive resources. Third, since it was directed simultaneously at the ruling elites of Iran, Iraq, and Turkey – all of which were 'imperialist-dependent regimes' – the Kurdish struggle was hence '*automatically* anti-imperialist'.[23]

This framing turned the old left's argument against movements such as the Kurdish as being 'bourgeois' proponents of regressive nationalism on its head. It aligned FEK's views on Kurdistan with a Third Worldist understanding of national liberation as tied directly to the anti-imperialist struggle. To FEK foundational thinker, Masud Ahmadzadeh:

The struggle of the Kurdish people – subject to the most severe oppression – is now reaching new heights. How can we assist it?

---

[20] FEK, *Cheguneh*, 99.
[21] Alireza Nabdel, *Azerbaijan va mas'ale-ye melli* (n.p., 1977), 28.
[22] FEK, *Cheguneh*, 93.
[23] FEK, *Cheguneh*, 100–101. Italics ours.

How can the struggle of the Kurdish people perform its proper role in the anti-imperialist struggle of all the peoples of Iran?[24]

Indeed, as early as 1973, the FEK argued for a broad, united front to push back against 'any kind of bourgeois and petty bourgeois narrowmindedness in regard to the national question'[25] and to put an end 'to this fratricide by accepting the right to autonomy for the Kurdish people'.[26]

As much as these statements appeared to outline arguably the first, unequivocal Iranian leftist programme for supporting minority struggles, they were at the same time counterbalanced by two facts. Firstly, while they identified culture, language, history, and a shared sense of belonging as key traits of oppressed minorities, the FEK rarely if ever specified what 'the right to self-determination' should entail in terms of political and territorial realities. In the words of foundational FEK ideologue Bizhan Jazani:

> Kurdistan possesses its own special characteristics. Kurds can obtain the right to autonomy through public plebiscite [*ezhar-nazar-e 'omumi*] at first opportunity. Even if racial or linguistic ties renders autonomous governance unnecessary, it is up to Kurds to refute or verify this necessity.[27]

Phrasings such as this left more questions than answers. While particular cultural traits were framed as the basis for claims to national self-determination there was also a simultaneous, ritualistic emphasis on 'a common history, a common culture, a common fate ... with which to protect Iran's unity in the future'.[28] Indeed, all such discussions came with a clear red line drawn against 'separatism' – a phenomenon that the FEK deemed to be limited to 'reactionaries' and 'dependent bourgeoisie' elements pursuing financial gain from aligning future breakaway countries with Western imperialist powers. As we shall see later, these limits imposed on the discourse of self-determination would be a constant source of ambiguity and hesitancy.

---

[24] Masoud Ahmadzadeh, *Mobareze-ye mosallahaneh. Ham esteratezhi, ham taktik* (n.p.: 1970; republished by FEK), 57, available at https://www.iran-archive.com/sites/default/files/2021-08/masud-ahmadzade-stratezhi-taktik.pdf (accessed 9 June 2023).

[25] FEK, *Cheguneh*, 101.

[26] FEK, *Cheguneh*, 100.

[27] Safa'i-Farahani, *Anche*, 17.

[28] Safa'i-Farahani, *Anche*, 17.

In contrast, the overall actionable point when discussing minorities in the pre-revolution FEK literature was unambiguous: identifying tactics and strategies to mobilise minorities against the Pahlavi state. Hence, the FEK ideologues called on cadres to travel to minority regions – and indeed rural Iran generally – and study local conditions in detail.[29]

FROM REVOLUTION TO WAR IN KURDISTAN

Despite the severe securitisation following the 1968 Kurdish uprising, including the mass imprisonment of political leaders,[30] the political scene in Kurdistan around the time of the revolution was marked by a plurality of actors, both traditional and new. The KDPI had been largely incapacitated by repression under the Shah, and it was only after the return of Khomeini on 1 February 1979 that it could spring into open action again – now, for the first time ever, as an official political party. In the meantime, the above-mentioned *Tashkilat* established itself with clandestine activities in the early autumn of 1978, and then from February 1979 as a party (KSZKI) that would later become known under its shorthand name, *Komala*.[31] Apart from these parties, two Sunni Muslim religious leaders played a crucial role during the revolution: the left-leaning Sheikh Ezzeddin Hosseini ('Mamosta') in Baneh and the Islamist-oriented Ahmad Moftizadeh and his *Maktab-e Qor'an* ('Koran School') in Sanandaj.[32] In addition to these, the arguably most powerful actors in revolutionary Kurdistan were a range of *jam'iyyat*s ('societies'), political organisations founded mostly

---

[29] See, for example, FEK, *Cheguneh*, 87. A notable example of this was the Tabriz-born activist Behzad Karimi, who travelled with the Literacy Corps to Baneh in Kurdistan under the Shah and later became a key FEK-KB actor.

[30] Jalil Gadani, *50 sal Khebat, korteyek le mejoyi Hizbi Democrati Kurdistani Iran, vol. I* (Dhok: Khani, 2008), 124, 202–205; Karim Hussami, *Le birewereyekanim (1957–1965)*, vol. II (Stockholm: self-published, 1987); Karim Hisami, *Peda Chunew*, vol. 2 (Stockholm: Ketab-e Arzan, 1997), 256–263; Amir Qazi, *Le bireweriye siasiyekanem* (Stockholm: Apec, 2010), 39–40. On proto-*Komala*, see: Malaka Mostafa-Soltani and Said Watandoost (eds), *Mabahes-e kongre-ye avval-e Komala* (Ribaz-i Komala: 2015), 123–125. Cf. Ahmad Eskandari, 'First interview', interview by Rasmus Elling and Jahangir Mahmoudi, 30 June 2022, audio, 19:20–20:24.

[31] Mostafa-Soltani and Watandoost, *Mabahes*, 374–406.

[32] Ali Ezzatyar, *The Last Mufti of Iranian Kurdistan: Ethnic and Religious Implications in the Greater Middle East* (New York: Palgrave, 2016), 109.

in the early months of 1979 that in some cases were covers for *Komala* but mostly represented new grassroots networks of students, peasants, teachers, women, and workers. Almost all of the *jam'iyyat*s championed strongly leftist viewpoints[33] and were key in radicalising Kurdish politics, reinvigorating civil society, and establishing momentary de facto autonomy in several towns.

The outburst in political activity was concomitant with an outburst of cultural and educational activity.[34] Previously banned and new books were published and translated while the Kurdish language and history were taught openly at all levels. Eyewitnesses speak of a groundswell of knowledge dissemination and consciousness-raising activities.[35] *Komala* also turned its attention to rural Kurdistan. Prior to the revolution, its activists had concluded that the 'main contradiction/conflict' (*tazad-e 'omdeh*) was between peasants and feudalism/government.[36] After the revolution, *Komala* saw its analysis confirmed by a rising class consciousness and sporadic peasant uprisings against former landowners.[37]

Apart from Moftizadeh's soon-to-be-marginalised faction,[38] revolutionary Kurdistan's political field and public sphere remained singularly secular and left-wing in nature. This was evident when Kurdish leaders joined forces in the so-called '8-Points Declaration of Mahabad' on 19 February 1979, during a visit by an interim government delegation.[39] The declaration centred the revolutionary agency of 'toilers and workers and peasants' in

---

[33] Golrokh Qobadi, *Shaqayeq-ha bar sanglakh. Zendegi va zamane-ye yek zan az Kordestan-e Iran* (n.p.: self-published, 2015), 113–120; Eskandari, 'First interview', 40:57–41:40, 55:00–56:05.

[34] Qobadi, *Shaqayeq-ha*, 129–130.

[35] See, for example, Eskandari, 'First interview', 30:01–31:40; see also Cabi, 'The roots and the consequences'.

[36] Mostafa-Soltani and Watandoost, *Mabahes*, 374–406.

[37] Cf. KSZKI, *Set Up Peasants Unions to Wipe Out Derebegayeti (Feudalism)*, March–April 1979 (tr. and published in Uppsala: Esmail Sharifzade Publications, February 1981); KSZKI, *The Trial of a Mischievous Landowner in the People's Tribunal*, February 1980 (tr. and published in Uppsala: Esmail Sharifzade Publications, November 1980); Foad Mostafa-Soltani, *Speech in Mahabad about 'the Experience of Mariwan Peasants' Union'* on 12/7/1979, reproduced in Rashad Mostafa-Soltani, *Kak Foad*, 325–326.

[38] Cf. Ezzatyar, *The Last Mufti*.

[39] For an in-depth study of this, see Ahmad Eskandari, 'Qat'-name-ye 8–made'i-ye Mahabad, qiyade-ye movaqqat va Kordestan-e Iran'. Published on *'Asr-e now* website, 3 March 2015: https://asre-nou.net/php/view.php?objnr=33905 (accessed 31 January 2023).

a demand for an end to 'national oppression' (*setam-e melli*) and respect for 'the right to self-determination' (*haqq-e ta'yin-e sarnevesht-e khod*). Specifically, the leaders demanded 'a federal [*federativ*]' solution 'within the framework of the country of Iran',[40] while they categorically rejected 'any accusation of separatism'. They further demanded socio-economic development for Kurdistan, control over local military bases, and the punishment of security forces guilty of killing locals.[41] These demands were rejected, among other things, with the justification that the declaration operated with a definition of 'Kurdistan' geographically broader than the new regime could accept. The interim government instead offered cultural autonomy, language rights, and the inclusion of Kurds in local governance – but even this was vetoed by Khomeini.[42]

On 2 March 1979, during a mass rally in Mahabad, KDPI leader Abdulrahman Qassemlu announced KDPI's official activity in Kurdistan after thirty-two years of illegality in Iran. While the KDPI had framed social justice and the national question as mutually determining factors, and therefore not given precedence to one or the other, the demand for autonomy surged during spring and became a key popular demand by the summer of 1979. At the same time, Khomeini's new Islamist state in Tehran/Qom made its resistance to any kind of actual autonomy clear. That the new political centre deployed not the police or the regular army but the ideologically driven Revolutionary Guard[43] arguably underscored that it had inherited the *ancien régime* idea of Kurdistan as a security threat. Hence, while key Kurdish actors had declared their support for Khomeini, and some religious leaders also their conditional support for an Islamic Republic,[44] the growing tensions divided the Kurdish political landscape between supporters of the emerging regime and those hesitant or hostile towards it. Among the former were the so-called *Qiyade-ye movaqqat* (Temporary Leadership,

---

[40] As reproduced in Eskandari, 'Matn-e qat'name-ye'.

[41] The declaration placed Sheikh Ezzeddin as a representative of all Kurds in negotiations with the central government while, interestingly, it specifically rejected Mostafa Barzani and his organisation, labelling them agents of the CIA and SAVAK. Soon, Barzani would enter the fray on the side of the Islamic Republic.

[42] David McDowall, *A Modern History of the Kurds*, 3rd ed. (London and New York: I.B. Tauris, 2005), 262.

[43] See Maryam Alemzadeh, 'The attraction of direct action: the making of the Islamic Revolutionary Guards Corps in the Iranian Kurdish conflict', *British Journal of Middle Eastern Studies*, ahead of print, https://doi.org/10.1080/13530194.2021.1990013 (2021).

[44] See, for example, Sheikh Ezzeddin and Moftizadeh. Cf. *Kayhan*, 9 *esfand* 1357/28 February 1979.

henceforth QM): the remnants of the KDP-Iraq under the leadership of Masoud Barzani, the son of Mustafa Barzani, who, following defeat in Iraq in 1975 had fled to Iran where he developed a close working relationship with Islamist forces.

Pro-government Islamists exploited tensions in the city of Sanandaj to violently attack Kurdish and leftist organisations from 18 to 21 March. During this so-called Bloody Nowruz, some two hundred people were killed, many by the government's helicopter gunships. By the end of March, all major Kurdish factions boycotted a referendum that only gave Iranians the opportunity to say 'Yes' or 'No' to a so-called 'Islamic Republic'. Regime forces again attacked Kurdish groups in Sanandaj during a battle for control over the Radio and TV Centre in mid-April, followed by violent clashes in Naqqadeh on 21–26 April. On 11 July 1979, left-leaning forces in Mariwan demonstrated against the town's Radio and TV Centre, which had been spreading distorted news about Kurdistan. As a reaction to threats from the military and its local allies, the historic Mariwan Protest Exodus saw thousands of citizens vacating the city in protest. Over fifteen days, the exodus brought attention and solidarity from across Kurdistan and from leftists across Iran.[45]

While the interim PM claimed that Kurds 'didn't simply want autonomy, they wanted to be separate from Iran',[46] Qassemlu, as a representative of the Kurdish people, was denied access to the constitutional draft committee tasked over summer with developing a new political framework for Iran. Another peace treaty attempt, spearheaded by Sheikh Ezzeddin in early August, was futile as already on 14 August severe clashes had broken out in Paweh. On 19 August, Khomeini in effect pronounced a jihad against the Kurds, leading to what became known as the First Kurdistan War. Following severe casualties and a stalemate, the war officially concluded with a ceasefire on 6 September 1979. But soon thereafter, renewed fighting broke out as the central government attempted to retake key positions in Kurdistan, while Kurdish *peshmergas* or guerrillas staged ambushes on the Revolutionary Guards. In an effort to unite the ideologically divided Kurdish forces, a Kurdish People's Representative Committee was established in November 1979, demanding that autonomy be enshrined in the constitution. When

---

[45] Hossein Morad-Beigi, *Tarikh-e zendeh...*, 159; *Pishraw*, no. 2, Appendix: 3, 1981.
[46] Mehdi Bazargan quoted in McDowall, *The Modern History*, 269.

the new constitution did not even mention the Kurds, all Kurdish factions rejected the legitimacy of the ratification plebiscite on 2–3 December.[47]

Although the government made some half-hearted suggestions for meeting the Kurdish popular demand for autonomy, violence continued in the new year. In April 1980, the government launched another major military attack on Kurdistan, leading to the so-called Second Kurdistan War. As fighting continued for another year, the number of Kurdish casualties reached ten thousand. Repression, bombing of civilian areas, forced internal exile, and mass imprisonment and execution of political activists became the order of the day.

ENTRY OF THE FEK

Despite a measure of sustained attention to Iran's geographical periphery, it was only *after* the revolution – and, importantly, on the grassroots initiatives of local supporters – that the FEK gained a practical presence in regions such as Kurdistan. Indeed, the establishment of the FEK-Kurdistan Branch (henceforth FEK-KB) in Mahabad on 16 February 1979 was, according to founding member Said Shams, 'by coincidence': supporters had found each other during a trip to Azerbaijan to greet a released comrade and spontaneously decided to organise.[48] According to Shams, the FEK central committee simply 'did not have any interest in Kurdistan at all'.[49]

However, Kurdistan had an interest in the FEK. Following the revolution, and despite an already crowded field of political organisations, the FEK-KB by all accounts gained a significant following among urban and educated Kurds and to some extent also beyond that class. Among its activities, cadres engaged in so-called Peasants' Unions, which, among other things, settled land disputes in favour of farmers exploited by the Pahlavi landowning class. The FEK organised cultural activities, including a month-long celebration of 'Iran's peoples' with Turkmen, Azeri, Baluch, and Arab representatives touring Kurdistan. Cadres also carried out research on the socio-economic structure of Kurdish society and published *Rigayi Gel* (The Peoples' Way[50]),

[47] McDowall, *The Modern History*, 263.
[48] Said Shams, 'First interview', interview by Rasmus Elling and Jahangir Mahmoudi, 13 July 2022, audio, 01:40–04:25.
[49] Shams, 'First interview', 06:07–07:05.
[50] Not to be confused with a journal of similar name published from 1980. Unfortunately, we have not been able to locate this valuable first series of the journal.

a theoretical journal focused on Leninist discussions of the national question. According to the memoirs of another activist, Bahram Farshi, who may somewhat overestimate the impact of the FEK-KB, cadres also engaged in significant social work, providing education and medical services, helping in agriculture, and establishing rural libraries, etc.[51]

The very fact that the FEK-KB had working relations with a range of key Kurdish organisations is further testament to its importance. However, there were also differences if not divisions inside the FEK-KB. While the Mahabad office had close relations with the KDPI, the Sanandaj office instead worked closely with *Komala*.[52] Nevertheless, both offices were trotting the party line directly under central committee control, and according to Shams, FEK-KB activities were not always supported by the leadership. For example, the central committee forced the FEK-KB to shut down its journal after only three issues.[53]

The FEK-KB and its supporters played an indisputably important role in the defence of Kurdistan against regime forces up to and during the First Kurdistan War – this is testified by numerous accounts about martyred cadres from the region.[54] The FEK-KB was also the first of the fighting forces to return from the mountains to the towns after that war, which further bolstered their image. Additionally, the FEK-KB participated in the Kurdish People's Representative Committee in November 1979, which committed the branch fully to obtaining autonomy for Kurdistan.[55] However, according to Shams, the FEK-KB understood autonomy as a 'completely classed concept' (*yek mafhum-e kamelan tabaqati*)[56]; in other words, the demand for autonomy in its most prevalent form at the time was primarily a middle-class concern. This indicated only a tactical commitment of the FEK-KB to autonomy. Nonetheless, as the Kurdish demand for autonomy grew, the FEK-KB too had to adopt it as the solution to the otherwise Leninist 'national question' – 'even to the point of secession', as Shams puts it.[57] Still, such an adoption did not spell an end to diverging opinions inside the FEK, among cadres, and between various factions. In fact, all

[51] Bahram Farshi, *Kordestan: sarzamin-e ranj-ha va tajrobe-ha* (n.p.: self-published, 2006), 57.

[52] Shams, 'First interview', 35:20–39:15.

[53] Shams, 'First interview', 31:31–31:50.

[54] See, for example, Farshi, *Kordestan*.

[55] See FEK-KB statement quoted in Farshi, *Kordestan*, 61.

[56] Shams, 'First interview', 48:50–49:12.

[57] Said Shams, 'Second interview', interview by Rasmus Elling and Jahangir Mahmoudi, 17 August 2022, audio, 04:00–05:38.

the groups active in Kurdistan, including *Komala*, experienced significant internal disagreement. Hence, while autonomy emerged as a hegemonic idea, it was nonetheless formulated in different and competing ways.

CHAMPIONING THE DOWNTRODDEN

Minority regions were crucial to the FEK's tactical positioning vis-à-vis the myriad actors of the revolution. Ideologically, the FEK perceived its primary role as connecting the Kurdish movement with the broader movement of 'toilers' (*zahmatkeshan*) across the country. As a publication put it, the FEK's presence in Kurdistan was considered to play

> a very, very important role in ... establishing an organic, rational connection between the Kurdish people's national movement and the democratic movement, between the class struggle of Kurdistan's toilers and the class struggle across Iran, at the forefront of which is the working class.[58]

The FEK's mobilisation was hence legitimised by framing the Kurdish movement as an indispensable part of a broader class struggle. Indeed, support for the Kurdish 'national struggle' was justified by claiming that this struggle 'in itself, naturally, serves the advancement of the mass mobilisation of Kurdistan's toilers'.[59]

The FEK also tasked itself with enlightening the rest of Iran about the plight of Kurds through publications, including the official organ *Kar* ('Labour'), which ran several special themes and appendixes focused on national rights, rural populations, and minorities.[60] Apart from that, the FEK also published a broad range of pamphlets and manifestos addressing particular events in Kurdistan. Sometimes, the FEK used

---

[58] Pishgam-Tabriz (n.d.): 'Mosahebe-ye daneshjuyan-e pishgam-e Tabriz ba Sheikh Ezz-od-din Hosseini, doktor Abdulrahman Qassemlu va Sazman-e cherik-ha-ye fada'i-ye khalq-e Iran – shakhe-ye Kordestan', pamphlet, 48.

[59] Pishgam-Tabriz, 'Mosahebe-ye', 48.

[60] From the period under examination, see, for example, *Kar* no. 13 (10 *khordad* 1358/31 May 1979, appendix); *Kar*, 'Vizhe-ye Kordestan' (18 *tir* 1358/9 July 1978); *Kar*, 'Vizhe-ye khalq-ha' (11 *mordad* 1358/2 August 1979); *Kar*, 'Vizhe-ye Kordestan' (14 *ordibehesht* 1359/4 May 1980).

its media to convey solidarity between these groups[61] while it organised and participated in events, notably the so-called *Conference for Solidarity Between Peoples of Iran* in Tehran, 18–20 July 1979, which resulted in a resolution demanding autonomy for Iran's different 'peoples'.[62] Arab, Kurdish, Turkmen, and Baluch representatives participated. According to *Kar* – and couched in the same Third Worldist language used for solidarity messages sent abroad – the main conference finding was that 'oppressed peoples'' struggle for autonomy inside Iran aligned directly with a broader anti-imperialist struggle.[63]

As tensions turned to violence, the FEK continually used its publications to raise awareness about Kurdistan – and to criticise the new regime. Already in April 1979, the FEK-KB concluded that violent events in Sanandaj showed that in its treatment of non-majority peoples, this regime was mired in the same 'extreme nationalism' as the Pahlavis.[64] The revolutionary state, the FEK-KB argued, had been compromised by the penetration (*rekneh*) of imperialism, namely, through Khomeini's local allies, who had manufactured a crisis over what was in fact rivalry between two Islamist groups – and then used this as an excuse to repress their ideological rivals.

The FEK denounced the draft constitution that was drawn up over the summer of 1979 by a clergy-dominated board with no minority representative and which omitted any mention of the right to self-determination.[65] The FEK concluded that in replicating the *ancien régime*'s repressive policy against minorities, the new regime's policy 'in practice serves imperialism'.[66] From the summer of 1979 onwards, the FEK routinely linked the failure to adopt a democratic stance on the national question to a continued presence of bourgeois nationalism and even imperialism inside the state. The FEK linked the new ruling elite's penchant for centralisation and anti-minority policy to its 'class nature' – a problem that resulted, according to the FEK,

---

[61] See, for example, reports about solidarity with the Kurdish struggle from the people of Baluchistan (p. 3) and Anzali (p. 5) in *Kar* vol. 1, no. 34, 7 *aban* 1358/29 October 1979.

[62] *Kar*, 'Dar konferans-e hambastegi-ye khalq-ha-ye Iran', no. 21 (1 *mordad* 1358/23 July 1979), 1–2.

[63] *Kar*, 'Dar konferans-e', 2. The plan was for the National Democratic Front to organise a follow-up, large-scale conference in Mahabad on 25 August. However, due to the war, this never materialised.

[64] City Council – Sanandaj: *Jang-e khunin-e Sanandaj va dastavard-e an* (Sanandaj: Office of Supporters of the Organisation of Fada'i Guerrillas of Iran, 1979).

[65] See *Kar*, 'Chera Sazman-e cherik-ha-ye fada'i-ye khalq dar entekhabat-e majles-e khobregan sherkat nemikonad?', no. 21 (1 *mordad* 1358/23 July 1979), 1, 5.

[66] *Kar*, 'Vizhe-name-ye khalq-ha' (11 *mordad* 1358/2 August 1979), 1.

in 'anti-imperialism interrupted halfway on its path'.[67] Indeed, the military attack on Kurdistan in August and September was deemed 'a conspiracy of imperialism and reaction'.[68]

Kurdistan thus became a key issue on which the FEK could articulate its primary concern, anti-imperialism, in ways clearly distinct from the anti-imperialism of the Khomeinists. Furthermore, the FEK positioned itself against other political forces on the left such as the Tudeh Party and various Maoists who were castigated as 'social imperialists' for fully supporting Khomeini, even during the war in Kurdistan. Following the ceasefire in September, the FEK lambasted Tudeh as 'right-wing opportunists' who had sacrificed minorities in their blind support of the regime.[69]

The leftist appeasing of Khomeini on the issue of Kurdistan, the FEK warned, had serious consequences. The 'fate of the Kurdistan movement is deeply intertwined with the fate of the progressive movement of all of Iran's peoples', the FEK stated during a conference in early September 1979. In fact, the statement predicted that if the regime succeeded in Kurdistan, it would pave the way for the elimination of all revolutionary forces, 'even liberals and conservatives', on the road towards the establishment of '*velayat-e faqih*', or theocratic rule, 'and fascist dictatorship'.[70]

THE NATIONAL CONUNDRUM

FEK was arguably the only one of the countrywide and non-minority-specific political organisations to elevate the issue of minority rights clearly and routinely to *a national question*. This is testified by numerous statements and publications throughout the period of focus in this article. However, this framing was shot through with contradictions and ambiguity. An example is found in the article 'Kurdistan and the National Question' in *Kar* from May 1979.

The article began with a classical conceptualisation of nation (*mellat*) and nationality or nationhood (*melliyyat*) in primordial, cultural-territorial

---

[67] *Kar*, 'Bayaniye-ye Sazman-e cherik-ha-ye fada'i-ye khalq-e Iran darbare-ye Kordestan', 1, no. 30 (12 *shahrivar* 1358/3 September 1979), 4.

[68] *Kar*, 'Bayaniye-ye sazman-e', 4.

[69] *Kar*, 'Sar-maqaleh: ma va jonbesh-e moqavemat-e khalq-e kord', 1, no. 36 (5 *azar* 1358/26 November 1979), 1.

[70] *Kar*, 'Konferans-e vahdat ba mowze'-giri-ye siyasi-ye khod dar Kordestan ba erteja'-tarin jenah-e hay'at-e hakemeh hamseda shodeh ast', 1, no. 32 (19 *shahrivar* 1358/10 September 1979), 7.

terms. Indeed, 'national rights' were presented as the right of a people (*khalq*) to live in a particular geographical territory, speak its mother tongue, protect traditions and customs, and 'choose its preferred economic and political way of life'.[71] This seemed to indicate that any 'people' could in fact be a 'nation' with rights anchored in deep history. However, the argument then morphed into economism when the FEK argued that national oppression (*setam-e melli*), 'like all other injustices', was historically rooted in the emergence of class inequality in modern times. Specifically, national oppression 'intensified' in the age of imperialism, where it became a tool of dominance, namely in the Pahlavi state's policy of dividing and antagonising ethnic groups against each other.

This essentially Marxist, modernist reading is found throughout FEK writings: the emergence of the nation was tied to the growth of the bourgeoisie and as such, 'rooted in capitalism's need for expanding the relations of commodity exchange within the framework of solidified geographical borders'.[72] Hence, nation and 'nationalism, as an ideology of capitalism, which is geared to defend the motherland, the expanse of which must secure the needs of capitalists', were seen as phenomena shaped in the transitional phase from feudalism to capitalism.[73] Specifically, imperialism – with its dependent or comprador bourgeoisies in the Third World – nurtured a nationalism that demanded a homogenous nation-state in order to function as a 'national market unit'.[74] This homogeneity was only possible through the oppression of non-dominant identities.[75]

In short, imperialism was singled out as the main culprit behind the 'annihilation of national minorities' and the development of national oppression as a form of class exploitation. Put differently, the effects of the centralising nature of capital accumulation would spill over into the cultural-political domain. This materialist analysis was obviously limited to modern political economy as opposed to a culturalist interpretation of deep history: even if its primary manifestation was in identity-related and cultural spheres, national oppression in Iran was rooted in the modern intrusion of Western

---

[71] *Kar*, 'Kordestan va mas'ale-ye melli' in appendix to no. 13 (10 *khordad* 1358/31 May 1979), 4.

[72] *Kar*, 'Dar pish-nevis-e qanun-e asasi: haqq-e khalq-ha dar ta'yin-e sarnevesht-e khod nadideh gerefteh shodeh ast'', 1, no. 21 (1 *mordad* 1358/23 July 1979), 5.

[73] *Kar*, 'Dar pish-nevis-e', 5.

[74] *Kar*, 'Dar pish-nevis-e', 5.

[75] *Kar*, 'Dar pish-nevis-e', 5.

capitalism.[76] It is however telling that while the FEK in this fashion sub-scribed to a pure Leninist analysis of the national question, the organisation constantly shifted to talk of 'peoples' in a fashion more reminiscent of the idea of national-cultural autonomy of Austrian Marxist Otto Bauer. This vacillation between economistic and culturalist conceptualisations of the national question left the FEK with an inconsistent prescription for the national question, which both demanded the continued subordination of 'peoples' to one national territorial unit *and* the possibility of a pluri-national democratic state.

A further possible explanation for this incongruity can be found in the persistence of Iranian majority-nationalist sentiments – despite the FEK's stated resistance to such a bourgeois ideology. For example, in the above-mentioned article on 'Kurdistan and the National Question', the FEK first claimed that nations were not historically well-defined and homogeneous units. However, at the same time, the FEK argued that Iran was in fact historically united by a shared heritage.[77] Here, the authors defaulted to a standard trope of Iranian nationalism: that Iran was exceptional in its ancient inter-ethnic unity, exemplified in the shared tradition of celebrating Nowruz and of reading the tenth century epic *Shahnameh* and the twelfth-century poetry of Hafez. While the different peoples were now united by a common enemy in imperialism, their unity was a transhistorical fact separate from politics and economy. This analytical drift back from modernist to primordialist, from economistic to culturalist, was semantically mirrored in the shift, within one sentence, from talk of 'peoples' (*khalq-ha*) of Iran and *the* Iranian people (*khalq*) in the singular.

Tellingly, there was little reference in the FEK literature to the dominant majority, namely the Persians. One of the few exceptions was in the FEK critique of the draft constitution in July 1979. In the course of a historical discussion, the author(s) identified Iran as a 'pluri-national country' (*keshvari kasir-ol-melleh*) in which 'global imperialism has striven to imprison Iran's peoples through the capitalism of the ruling nation (Persians [*fars*])', leading to 'deprivation and economic and cultural underdevelopment of areas inhabited by national minorities in our homeland'.[78]

---

[76] *Kar*, 'Dar pish-nevis-e', 5. For the same interpretation but published by FEK-KB, see, City Council, *Jang-e khunin-e*, 3–4.

[77] *Kar*, 'Kordestan va mas'ale-ye', 4.

[78] *Kar*, 'Dar pish-nevis-e', 5.

This was, however, one of few exceptions[79] to the rule. Generally, Persians were simply not treated in discussions of ethnic diversity. Furthermore, this omission – characteristic of the majority-nationalist tendency to hide Persians by equating this 'elusive majority' with the essence of what it means to be Iranian, i.e. Persian-speaking Shi'ite from the geographical centre[80] – was not an anomaly in the FEK discourse. Indeed, majority-nationalist concerns tended to override minority-national concerns in certain important respects. For example, the adjective *sarasari* ('[nation]-wide')[81] and the construction *dar pahne-ye Iran* ('across Iran')[82] were used discursively to contrast the struggles of peripheralised peoples as 'local'. These 'local' struggles, in other words, were to be seen as smaller pieces of a larger struggle.

Importantly, the FEK never justified this subsumption in overtly majority-nationalist terms. The greater struggle was two-fold: on the one hand, an anti-imperialist struggle that pitted Iran as a single nation-state against the imperialist powers of the West, and, on the other hand, an anti-capitalist struggle that pitted the toiling classes against the capitalists. Yet the effect was arguably the same. Instead of confronting the general problem of Persian-centrism in Iranian politics, the FEK relegated discrimination and marginalisation to the specific political circumstances of the Pahlavi regime, as an entity dependent upon Western imperialism. Avoiding this confrontation arguably became a problem of both theory and practice in a tumultuous context where the FEK promised a roadmap for a pluri-national democratic future.

THE COMPASS OF DIALECTICS

Navigating between defensible and indefensible types of national struggle demanded a compass, and the FEK found it in the concept of 'dialectics

---

[79] Another exception is found, unsurprisingly, in the works of Nabdel, who finished his essay on 'Azerbaijan and the National Question' with the following slogan or poem:

> May the revolutionary unity of the world proletariat roar
> May the Marxist movement of Iran's proletariat blossom
> May imperialism and its Iranian dogs be obliterated
> Death to Persian [fars] chauvinism
> Shame on regionalists
> May the emancipatory movement of Iran's people be victorious

[80] Cf. Rasmus Elling, *Minorities in Iran: Nationalism and Ethnicity after Khomeini*, Ch. 1 (New York: Palgrave Macmillan, 2013).

[81] See, for example, *Kar*, 1, no. 36 (5 *azar* 1358/26 November 1979), 1, 11.

[82] See, for example, *Kar*, 'Kordestan va mas'ale-ye', 4.

of unity'. Accordingly, the 'point with unity is not that everyone should necessarily speak the same language or have the same preferences'; rather, 'unity is when everyone speaks their own language, but says the same; when everyone follows their penchant and preference, but with one common goal'.[83] Since 'unity is nothing else but the voluntary alliance of forces that are equal and equally bestowed in rights', the FEK argued that 'autonomy within the framework of a democratic Iran' actually *strengthened* 'the indissoluble integrity of our homeland'.[84] The dialectical balancing act, however, demanded a struggle both internally and externally: 'the toiling masses of oppressed peoples must fight just as much against the ruling nation's nationalism as they must against its own narrow-minded and reactionary capitalist nationalism'.[85]

Hence, the dialectics, the FEK argued, could discern correct from wrong national demands – and, specifically, it could separate justifiable demands for *autonomy* from unjustifiable demands for *separatism*. These two were again differentiated based on a Marxist reading: since each nation was composed of many different socio-economic layers, its members did not view the national question uniformly. When a national demand arose from the ruling class, it was, by definition, *not* a 'progressive' demand, but rather geared towards monopolising power and 'exploiting indigenous people'.[86] Here, the national question was distorted into separatism. As an example, the FEK repeatedly pointed to the views and actions of 'feudalists', 'tribal leaders', and Barzani's forces.[87] The new regime's continued support for the latter was lambasted and used as evidence of its insufficient anti-imperialism.[88]

A different but overlapping type of nationalism was associated with the petit bourgeois and merchant capitalists, for whom the primary goal was not democracy but the opportunity to expand economic exploitation. If bourgeois nationalism resulted in outright separatism, the FEK warned, imperialist powers would recalibrate their strategy and turn these breakaway nation-states into new dependent units in the global market economy.

In contrast to these two kinds of imperialism-serving bourgeois nationalisms stood the righteous nationalism of toilers and the progressives who

---

[83] *Kar*, 'Kordestan va mas'ale-ye', 4.

[84] *Kar*, 'Kordestan va mas'ale-ye', 4.

[85] *Kar*, 'Dar pish-nevis-e', 5.

[86] *Kar*, 'Kordestan va mas'ale-ye', 4.

[87] See, for example, City Council – Sanandaj, *Jang-e khunin-e*, 2 and 5.

[88] See, for example, *Kar*, 'Vizheh-nameh-ye khalq-ha' (11 *mordad* 1358/2 August 1979), 2.

'view the national question from a standpoint of the right to self-determination and the eradication of economic, political and national oppression'.[89] While the protagonists were the working class and its progressive vanguard, support for toilers in places like Kurdistan appeared conditional: 'the struggle for securing peoples' national rights in countries under domination is inextricably linked to the anti-imperialist struggle and the eradication of any kind of class oppression', the FEK argued.[90] Indeed, 'oppressed peoples should allow themselves no illusions that they can be completely freed from their double-oppression of nation and class without destroying the dominance of imperialism and eradicating exploitive classes'.[91] Any attempt at political independence *before* and *without* the destruction of imperialism and capitalism was repeatedly castigated by the FEK as 'bourgeois nationalism' that would weaken the anti-imperialist front.

Furthermore, the political demand for autonomy was often reduced to a question of identity-based claims and 'cultural domination'. Hence, while *Komala* and the KDPI – at least up until the Second Congress in the case of the former, and up until the First Kurdistan War in the case of the latter – argued that anti-imperialism, democracy, and autonomy were three mutually reinforcing struggles, the FEK chose to give the first precedence over the two others. It did so by criticising not just the reactionaries but also their progressive allies for postponing the anti-imperialist struggle with parochial concerns about autonomy. This policing of how and when autonomy demands were framed arguably made the FEK unable to accommodate the surge in demands from the Kurdish national movement after the revolution.

Throughout the summer of 1979, the FEK criticised Barzani's militia as 'the bludgeon of imperialism and reaction', indeed as an agent of US, Turkish, and Israeli interests in Kurdistan – an accusation that served to remind the public of the Barzani family's history of tactical ties to the CIA and the Shah's regime.[92] Similarly, during the Mariwan Exodus, the FEK attached to their statement of support a reminder that 'until imperialism and its domestic allies have been uprooted, any talk of the right to self-determination and obtaining autonomy can be no more than an illusion'.[93]

---

[89] City Council – Sanandaj, *Jang-e khunin-e*, 34–35.
[90] *Kar*, 'Dar pish-nevis-e', 5.
[91] *Kar*, 'Dar pish-nevis-e', 5.
[92] FEK-KB, *Qiyadeh-ye movaqat, chomaq-e amperiyalism va erteja' dar Kordestan* (n.p., *mordad* 1358/July–August 1979).
[93] FEK-Sanandaj, *Siyasat-e dowlat dar Mariwan*, pamphlet (n.p., n.d.), 12.

This line became ever more pronounced during the First Kurdistan War in August. To position itself, the FEK insisted that the war was in fact a pre-text for moving focus away from proletarian towards nationalist concerns. As the FEK put it, 'the effort to prioritise the national issue and, under its guise, to embrace a class compromise is a completely bourgeois policy' that ran counter to the communist movement and in fact boosted the 'liberal-ist' KDPI.[94] Hence, as it strove to gain hegemony in the working class, the FEK increasingly portrayed nationalism as a sign of weakness or a deficit in Kurdish class consciousness.[95]

By autumn 1979, it was clear that the FEK's support for Kurdish aspira-tions was contingent on these aspirations aligning with the broader aim of 'enacting the power of the masses' and 'preparing a democratic revolution of the peoples'.[96] Specifically, the support was conditional on 'whether the Kurdish people's movement connect[ed] to the [nation]wide (*sarasari*) working-class movement'.[97] In this quote, the three variables we argue influenced the FEK policy vis-à-vis Kurdistan – namely, lingering Iranian nationalism, class-centrism, and the anti-imperialist primacy – came into play. This was semantically represented with *sarasari*, '(nation-)wide' or '(country-)wide': without explicitly naming Iran as the space covered, the implication was that the class struggle was broader than, and therefore over-ruled, any local struggles. The latter were *parts* of the former – subordinate and ultimately expendable. In contrast to the slogan of the 'dialectics of unity', such statements underscored that the oppressed minorities simply had to fall into line with a larger purpose dictated by the central committee.

LIMITS TO NATION

After three months of fighting in Kurdistan, the FEK-KB announced in November 1979 that in the interest of 'the struggling masses' it supported a 'just peace' if it involved all forces in Kurdistan.[98] Hinting at the Khomeinists' occupation of the American embassy in Tehran, the FEK-KB deemed this

---

[94] *Kar*, 1, no. 33 (9 *mehr* 1358/1 October 1979), 6–7.
[95] *Kar*, 1, no. 33 (9 *mehr* 1358/1 October 1979), 6.
[96] *Kar*, 'Sar-maqaleh: ma va jonbesh-e', 1.
[97] *Kar*, 'Sar-maqaleh: ma va jonbesh-e', 1.
[98] FEK-KB's proposal (dated 18 *aban* 1358/9 November 1979), printed in: *Kar*, 'Tarh-e Sazman-e cherik-ha-ye fada'i-ye khalq-e Iran 'shakheh-ye Kordestan' bara-ye solh-e 'adelaneh dar Kordestan', 1, no. 36 (5 *azar* 1358/26 November 1979), 12–13.

'a historic moment' for solving the national question in Iran in accordance with the Leninist principle for self-determination. However, the FEK-KB demanded that Kurdish autonomy should be established 'within the framework of Iran's [territorial] integrity' and be governed through 'peoples' councils'[99] – implying an alternative leadership to those of both Khomeini and the Kurdish nationalist organisations.

In these and similar statements,[100] the FEK now walked a careful line between condemning forces deemed too radical in their demands for Kurdistan, while at the same time upholding their own claim to fight for minorities; and between criticising Khomeini but staying within the anti-imperialist front. However, the FEK itself was increasingly threatened on all fronts. In February 1980, another FEK-supported minority rebellion by Sunni Turkmen in Torkamansahra, north-eastern Iran, was crushed. In late March 1980, the Second Kurdistan War broke out. The FEK once again sided with the Kurds and criticised the government and its army[101] but could not or would not muster the same defence as in the previous war. As an 'imposed war', the FEK argued, the attack on Kurdistan had in effect led 'the people's anti-imperialist struggles astray'.[102] In turn, Khomeini's IRGC and the army released a statement on 1 May 1980 condemning FEK, *Komala*, and KDPI as 'deviants' and 'armed infidels'.[103] This religious wording betrayed a point of no return for the Islamic Republic after which it became impossible to imagine the acceptance and accommodation of either secular leftists or nationalist Kurds.

The FEK was also threatened from within. A division that had been brewing inside the organisation since the spring of 1979 crystallised by autumn into a clash between a Majority that accepted Khomeini's leadership of the anti-imperialist struggle and a Minority that rejected it.[104] While outside

---

[99] *Kar*, 'Tarh-e sazman-e cherik-ha-ye', 12–13.

[100] See, for example, *Kar*, 'Duy rebendan (salruz-e ta'sis-e jomhuri-ye khodmokhtar-e Kordestan), tajrobe'i ke az an bayad amukht', 1, no. 44 (10 *bahman* 1358/30 January 1980), 4; FEK-KB, 'Ashraf Dehqani: bazmande'i az dowran-e kudaki! darbare-ye sokhanrani-ye Ashraf Dehqani dar Mahabad', appendix to *Rigayi Gel*, no. 6 (2 *esfand* 1358/21 February 1980), 19.

[101] *Kar*, 'Vizhe-ye Kordestan' (Kurdistan Special no. 3), 2, no. 57 (14 *ordibehesht* 1359/4 May 1980), 1–2.

[102] *Kar*, 'Solh dar Kordestan be naf'-e zahmatkeshan', 2, no. 57 (17 *ordibehesht* 1359/7 May 1980), 16.

[103] Statement from the army and the Revolutionary Guard quoted from *Jomhuri-ye eslami*, no. 244 (10 *ordibehesht* 1359/1 May 1980), reprinted in *Kar*, 'Vizhe-ye Kordestan' (Kurdistan Special no. 3), 3.

[104] For a summary, see Maziar Behrooz, *Rebels with a Cause: The Failure of the Left in Iran* (London: I.B. Tauris, 1999), 109–113.

the scope of this chapter, the split was above all concerned with divergent interpretations of two issues – namely, the organisation's past strategy of armed struggle and the class nature of the new regime – and with the central committee's undemocratic way of dealing with disagreement over these topics. While scholars tend to highlight the issue of Kurdistan as a third source of divergence,[105] it could also be argued that the issue of Kurdistan was in fact subordinate to and derivative of the two above-mentioned issues. The disagreement would lead to a formal split in June 1980.

Already by the end of May 1980, there was a noticeable discursive change in FEK publications such as *Kar*, which was now under FEK-Majority control. While previously the Kurdish struggle and its actors were presented as essential components of the anti-imperialist struggle, they were now accused of 'left opportunism' and 'warmongering'.[106] For example, in its 21 May 1980 editorial, *Kar* stated that 'the reality is that Ayatollah Khomeini is still the leader of the struggle against US imperialism'; hence, even though the government was criticised for its 'fratricidal war in Kurdistan and Gonbad [i.e. Torkamansahra]', it was nonetheless exonerated with the claim that 'it has not been and is not a dependent government'.[107] Henceforth, key FEK-Majority organs would castigate anyone opposed to the Islamic Republic as 'leftist deviations', 'liberals' and those 'inclined to anarchist actions and slogans for the overthrow [of government]'.[108]

These discursive manoeuvres heralded the FEK-Majority's 'tactical and conditional unity' policy, in which the central committee acquiesced to the Islamic Republic and eventually retreated from Kurdistan over the summer of 1980. The FEK-Minority would continue to fight against Khomeini's forces in Kurdistan for several years to come but only as part of a broader attempt to discredit the Islamic Republic for being insufficiently anti-imperialist and antithetical to the proletariat. Kurdistan still was, in other words, an obstacle to be tackled on the road to a democratic mass revolution in Iran.[109]

---

[105] Cf. Peyman Vahabzadeh, 'FADĀʾIĀN-E ḴALQ', *Encyclopædia Iranica*, online edition, 2015, available at http://www.iranicaonline.org/articles/fadaian-e-khalq (accessed on 31 January 2023); Behrooz, *Rebels*, 108, 110.

[106] Cf. *Kar*, 2, nos. 59 through 61.

[107] *Kar*, 'Bara-ye moqabeleh ba amperiyalism-e amrika, ettehad-e hame-ye zahmatkeshan yek zaruri-ye tarikhi ast', 2, no. 59 (31 *ordibehesht* 1359/21 May 1980), 1.

[108] *Kar*, 'Bara-ye moqabeleh', 2.

[109] Cf. *Kar* (Minority), no. 67 (24 *tir* 1359/15 July 1980); no. 68 (31 *tir* 1359/22 July 1980); no. 69 (7 *mordad* 1359/29 July 1980).

The decision to retreat from Kurdistan was made without conferring with Kurdish FEK members[110] and as a sign of disagreement with the decision the FEK-KB called for a conference in Bukan in October 1980.[111] It appears that the central committee of FEK-Majority was able to cement the decision to evacuate with reference to the Iran–Iraq War, which had started a month earlier with Saddam Hussein's attack on Iran. Henceforth, anyone opposing Khomeini would essentially be seen as supporting Saddam. FEK-KB was disbanded and most of the cadres who complied were ordered to resettle in other regions of Iran. In a recent interview, a key FEK-KB member called this evacuation 'one of the most tragic moments in the political life of the [FEK] movement'.[112]

Whereas the FEK-Minority faction again sought shelter in Kurdistan in 1981, the FEK-Majority instead aided the regime's clampdown on the Kurdish national movement. While the Islamic Republic used the war with Iraq to push Kurdish *peshmerga*s and civilians into refugee camps and across the border, ideological tensions and factional rivalries among the Kurdish parties eventually led to intra-Kurdish war (1983–1988). Various FEK factions also turned their weapons against erstwhile leftist allies and eventually against each other.[113]

Just as the FEK had predicted, losing the fight in Kurdistan paved the way for the Islamic Republic's eradication of all other revolutionary forces in the name of theocratic dictatorship. By 1983, not even the FEK-Majority or the Tudeh Party were safe. Most FEK members who had not already escaped from Iran were arrested, imprisoned, tortured, and eventually wiped out in the massacre of political prisoners in 1988.

CONCLUSION

What were the possibilities and limits for Third Worldist solidarity between Iranian revolutionary leftists, exemplified by the FEK, and the Kurdish national liberation movement during a revolution such as that in Iran in 1979?

---

[110] Farshi, *Kordestan*, 64.

[111] Shams, 'Second interview'; cf. Farshi, *Kordestan*, 66–67.

[112] Behzad Karimi, 'Kordestan dar behbuhe-ye enqelab-e Iran. Yadvare'i az yek anternasiyonalist', interview on Turkmensahra Media (7 *dey* 1400/28 December 2021), reproduced by *Asr-e Nou* website: https://asre-nou.net/php/view_print_version. php?objnr=54999

[113] On fratricidal fighting between leftists, see, for example, Farshi, *Kordestan*, 62.

We have explained in this chapter how the FEK clearly identified a 'national question' in the plight of Iran's minorities. Through the FEK-KB and similar branches in Torkamansahra, the FEK was arguably the only one of the major, Iran-wide political organisations to have an active local presence as a militant opponent of the emerging anti-minority policy of the new regime. In adopting a Third Worldist position that was attuned to the oppression of minorities – even when these minorities were placed inside a nation seen to be oppressed by imperialist powers – the FEK championed an understanding of inequality that in today's terms would be called intersectional. As the recent *Woman, Life, Freedom* movement has amply testified, there is a continued demand for such multi-layered interpretations of oppression and inequality in Iran today.

At the same time, we have identified some of the limits to the FEK's theory and practice vis-à-vis the peripheralised and minoritised people of Iran. We have argued that the FEK discourse – and hence not just its rhetoric but its actual policy, as testified in the case of Kurdistan – was shot through with contradictions and tension. The tension can, at least partly, be explained by a Marxist–Leninist reliance on ideological doctrine to dictate policy and strategy over and above anything else – specifically class-centrism and the privileging of the anti-imperialist struggle against the US. Or it can be at least partly explained by a lingering Iranian majority-nationalism, i.e. a reluctance to interrogate the nature of the power of the largely Persian-speaking dominant core population; or by conflating this dominant majority with the subjugated minorities by reference to a transhistorical, cultural essentialism that directly contradicted the otherwise modernist, Marxist mode of explanation about the national question. Above all, it should be remembered that despite its pioneering ability to encompass the national question in a vision for a democratic Iran – an ability that in many ways placed it ahead of its time – the FEK was limited by the same practical realities as the rest of the political landscape.

The tension between what was envisioned and what became possible becomes particularly evident when seen in light of the Third Worldist discourse within which the idea of minorities-as-nations was couched: the same ideological imaginary that had shaped the FEK vocabulary on the national question generated a conundrum in its post-revolution context. *The* national liberation (of Iran against imperialism) was potentially undermined by *another* national liberation (of Kurdistan in Iran) – at least this was the conclusion drawn by FEK-Majority when it sacrificed the Kurdish right to self-determination for the sake of what was seen as *the* national liberation struggle. In other words, the fact that the overriding Third Worldist concern, in the situation of Iran in 1979, was that of an existing nation-state fighting Western imperialism and capitalism meant that the Kurdish national question was always in danger of being degraded to a 'local' concern, reduced to 'cultural' issues, or dismissed as 'separatism'.

Hence, while the so-called 'anti-imperialist consensus' forged by Khomeini up to and during the US embassy hostage-taking was certainly an important factor behind the FEK-Majority's choice to abandon Kurdistan, it was not necessarily the *decisive* factor. Even when rejecting the Khomeinist line (that Kurdistan was being exploited by Western powers), the FEK still had other qualms about accepting the broad demand for autonomy. These qualms should be located in a rigid understanding of how a mass popular democratic revolution led by the working class would establish socialism. Due to this understanding, the actual Kurdish demand for anything more than cultural autonomy came to be seen as a nuisance or, to the FEK-Majority, even a distortion of the struggle.

In other words, the national question was difficult if not impossible to solve for the rigid, top-down leadership of a Marxist–Leninist organisation, when developments in places such as Kurdistan simply did not follow the trajectories envisioned by the Leninist textbook. The FEK could not claim leadership at a time when the national question manifested itself as the most important issue in Kurdistan. This role instead fell to Kurdish organisations. At the same time, the FEK became entangled in prolonged battles elsewhere. Like Torkamansahra, the Kurdistan issue had the potential of dragging all FEK resources into an unwinnable war that was understood to potentially derail the socialist revolution. The nail in the coffin was the September 1980 Iraqi invasion of Iran.

The FEK, as the prime example of the Iranian revolutionary Third Worldist left, faced a serious challenge when it came to peripheralised, minoritised people – *especially* when these were treated in terms of a national question and the right to self-determination. In a situation of post-revolution turmoil, and with its available ideological prescriptions, the FEK could not solve the issue of how to balance, on the one hand, an anti-imperialist struggle inevitably pitting an existing nation-state against Western powers with, on the other hand, small and non-dominant nations' struggle for the right to self-determination. Just as the potential of the FEK line on minorities contains important lessons for progressives in Iran today, so does the story of the limits to this line.

THE 'ENDS' OF THE PALESTINIAN REVOLUTION IN THE FAKHANI REPUBLIC

Sune Haugbolle

The Palestinian condition today is a tortured set of separations and contra-dictions, between the inside (*al-dakhil*) and the diaspora (*al-shatat*), Gaza and the West Bank, Hamas and Fatah, and between hopes of liberation and a reality of domination. These dualisms centre on the experience of revolution that in the twists and turns of the past century became resist-ance. Before there was revolution, there was also resistance. All the dif-ferent registers of resistance that we see today link to the earliest forms of resistance that took shape in the 1930s. Resistance was born from the onslaught of colonial domination, and gradually turned into a revolution-ary mobilisation between the birth of Fatah in 1959 and the PLO and associated institutions and movements in the mid- to late 1960s. It involved broad mobilisation and institutionalisation, state-building, and elements of class transformation. Like Syria and Yemen in the 2010s, Palestine in the 1960s and 1970s witnessed a revolution, even if it failed to achieve its goals.[1] The Palestinian revolution drew inspiration from, and intersected with, revolutionary and liberation movements in the rest of the world. At its high point in the early 1970s, when Palestinian populations embraced the idea of general mobilisation and global support for the Palestinian cause skyrocketed, Palestinian revolutionaries claimed to be leading an uprising

---

[1] See the website The Palestinian Revolution, https://learnpalestine.politics.ox.ac.uk. For a discussion of the perceived failure of revolutions, see Sune Haugbolle and Andreas Bandak, 'The Ends of Revolution: Rethinking Ideology and Time in the Arab Uprisings', *Middle East Critique* 26 (3) 2017: 191–204.

against conservative regimes in the Arab world and a national liberation of the Palestinian people, while also playing an increasingly iconic role in a global socialist, anti-imperialist revolution.

The relationship between these three aspects of the Palestinian revolution – the national, the regional and the global – and the temporal continuum on which they developed from revolution to resistance between 1967 and 1982, is complicated. In this chapter, I employ a social-historical approach to analyse stages, actors, and themes in the transformation. In line with the themes of this book, I argue that the 1970s laid the foundation for the great landmark changes of 1979 and the early 1980s. By scrutinising these years when the Palestinian revolution unfolded in Lebanon, I examine how the relative unity of the revolutionary heyday in the early 1970s gave way to fragmentation, doubt, and internal contradictions. My particular focus is the Palestinian left, where discussions about strategic and historical direction led to polarisation towards the end of the decade.

This development is well known and has been shown already by Palestinian historians like Yezid Sayigh (1997). Sayigh's magisterial study mostly looks at institutions, diplomacy, and the military. By turning a sociological gaze onto the way social and ideological transformation was experienced by militants and thinkers on the left, the chapter shines light on more intimate dimensions of the internal contradictions that Sayigh analyses at the political level. Rethinking the 'ends' of the Palestinian revolution in this way can help us reconsider the ends – in the dual sense of endings and ambitions – of Third Worldism. What did its actors hope to achieve, how did their idea of a revolution change under the influence of state-building and military struggle in Lebanon, and what effect did these transformations have on Palestine's place in global revolutionary Third Worldism? And most importantly, how can we conceptualise an ending of something so large-scale as a global ideology and a revolution?

THEORISING ENDINGS

Recent historiography of the Palestinian revolution has been mostly interested in the early years of revolutionary mobilisation, from the very early beginnings after the 1948 Nakba to the June 1967 war with Israel that sped up the emergence of the guerrilla movements. Another body of work examines the proliferation of solidarity movements in the late 1960s and early 1970s.[2] This focus is quite typical for revolution studies. Until quite recently, historians and sociologists of revolutions tended to focus on beginnings rather than endings.[3] Perhaps it goes for all social phenomena: we are more drawn to the potentiality of mobilisation that makes social transformation possible than to the muddled end stage when projects collapse or change irreversibly. The defeat of revolutionary armies or the collapse of governments, such as the end of communism in Eastern Europe, attracts more attention than the slow grind of internal contradictions. Classic *longue durée* and comparative studies of world revolutions by the likes of Tilly and Skocpol compare and theorise the outcomes of revolutions, but not the ending as a period when internal dynamics cause movements to either stall, be defeated, or change. Recent studies – sometimes dubbed a fourth school of revolution studies – that focus on culture and ideology rather than causal variables in political organisation provide a toolbox for moving towards a better understanding of endings.

This book belongs to the fourth generation of revolution scholarship that was initiated in the late 1990s, taking inspiration from global history, micro-histories, and the anthropology of revolutions. It is also influenced by historiographic and conceptual currents in the past decade of uprisings and revolutions. These events have been occasions to study and experience revolutions as they unfolded – and often collapsed. New ethnographies of revolutionary situations, such as Egypt, Yemen, and Syria, draw from the experience of revolutionaries.[4] The sociologist Bjørn Thomassen has even suggested that this work could be considered a fifth school of revolution scholarship, offering an approach that incorporates insights from all the previous generations but moves definitively beyond structuralist dichotomies of structure/agency, materialism/idealism, and content/form, opening the way for comparative reflection.[5] If there is indeed a fifth generation of scholars, the questions they ask today often highlight temporality instead. They ask how revolutionary time is experienced, what the relationship is between different historical revolutionary moments, and how revolutionaries learn from past experiences.

---

[2] S. Thomson and P. Olsen (eds), *Palestine in the World: International Solidarity with the Palestinian Liberation Movement* (London: I.B. Tauris, 2023).
[3] See, for example, Alice Wilson, *Afterlives of Revolution: Everyday Counterhistories in Southern Oman* (Berkeley: Stanford University Press, 2023).
[4] See Haugbolle and Bandak 2017, 198.
[5] Bjørn Thomassen, 'Wandering the Wilderness or Entering the Promised Land?' *Middle East Critique* 26 (3) 2017: 297–307.

Asking such large questions invites an engagement with the lifeworld of revolutionaries past and present. So, in this chapter, I examine different lived experiences of those who participated in the Palestinian revolution towards and just after its supposed end in 1982. The Palestinian revolution does not have a '1979 moment' similar to Iran, particularly since resistance continues today. But if it did, the fall of the so-called Fakhani Republic in Lebanon in 1982 would be an appropriate event to mark the transition from revolution (back) to resistance. It accentuated changes that were on their way; first, in the early 1970s, from guerrilla warfare to state formation project, and then after 1982 from anti-colonial state-in-exile to the (stymied, perverted, and unfinished) postcolonial 'statelet' in the West Bank. To show how these changes were experienced and contested, I analyse the autobiography of a mid-ranking militiaman and the life and writings of a Maoist Fatah militant turned Islamist, as well as his engagement with solidarity movements. Paired with secondary literature on the period, these sources help reconstruct the 'structure of feeling' inside the Fakhani Republic and how it foreshadowed the institutional, ideological, and social transformations that became ubiquitous after 1982. I start the chapter with a discussion of how we might think of August 1982, not just as a turning point but as a vector for analysing the gradual material and ideational transformations that changed the Palestinian revolution – a change that for many Palestinians feels like a protracted end today.

THE END OF REVOLUTION IN 1982?

Only the most hackneyed historian would say that the Palestinian revolution *definitely* ended in August 1982. If we ask the leading Palestinian political movements, PLO, Fatah, PFLP, DFLP, and Hamas, they will say that *al-thawra mustamirra*, the revolution continues.[6] That is of course rhetoric that denies the obvious material defeats and, more importantly, the existential 'stuckedness' that most Palestinians experience and have experienced since the early 2000s, or even longer. The Lebanese-Australian thinker Ghassan Hage defines stuckedness as an affective state related to imaginary mobility, the idea that one is going somewhere physically, socially, mentally,

---

[6] Somdeep Sen, *Decolonizing Palestine: Hamas between the Anticolonial and the Postcolonial* (Ithaca: Cornell University Press, 2020), 120–130.

economically, or, indeed, as a political collective.[7] In a situation of continued occupation that restricts movement, and where the ossified leadership has failed to push a political process forward, stuckedness also has a temporal dimension. It is linked to a knowledge of defeat – itself linked to memories of revolution. The Palestinian historian Karma Nabulsi has described the defeat as 'the fragmentation of the body politic – externally engineered, and increasingly internally driven'.[8] Palestinians (of this critical persuasion) then disagree on when the fragmentation began. Some date it back to Black September in Jordan in 1970 when the PLO was expelled from its bases, ending the first heady period of guerrilla organisation; others claim that it ended in 1975 when Palestinian groups became embroiled in the Lebanese civil war.

However, the war also provided an opportunity to develop what Yezid Sayigh calls Arafat's state-in-exile, the Fakhani Republic.[9] It was destroyed by Israel's invasion in 1982, which initiated a period of further exile for the leadership before the Oslo process, the first Intifada (1987–1993), Arafat's return to Gaza and the West Bank (1994), and the gradual, grinding destruction and deception of occupation and domination – and internal corruption – that has followed since. As Nabulsi notes, the communiqués and declarations issued during the first Intifada were expressed in the language of revolution, 'but everyone except perhaps the Fatah leadership agrees that it was all over by 1991, when the Madrid peace process was accepted on unequal terms'.[10]

Of course, it can be discussed whether the revolution was really over by 1991; whether the Fakhani Republic is an accurate term for Palestinian relative sovereignty in Lebanon; and whether this entity in fact resembled a state, as Sayigh suggests. I am aware that the expression 'Fakhani Republic' sometimes connotes placing blame for the Lebanese civil war primarily with the Palestinian leadership. By using the term in this article, I do not embrace that interpretation. Rather, I follow Sayigh and other Palestinian historians who use the term in a more value-free sense to describe the

---

[7] Ghassan Hage, 'Waiting Out the Crisis: On Stuckedness and Governmentality', *Anthropological Theory* 5 (1) 2009: 463–475.

[8] Karma Nabulsi, 'Lament for the Revolution', *London Review of Books* 32 (20): 2010.

[9] It's worth noting that the idea of a 'state in exile' promoted by Sayigh, Rashid Khalidi, and others is contested among Palestinian historians and revolutionaries, some of whom never saw the PLO as a state in exile, at least not until 1988 and the lead-up to the Oslo process.

[10] Ibid.

Palestinian entity in Lebanon from 1969 to 1982. The aim is to anchor my analysis of divergent imaginaries of revolutionary time and 'ends' in a concrete historical experience. They reflect competing understandings of what constituted the core of the revolutionary project.

For some, it was the state-in-exile; for others it was national unity; the connection to international support and the 'world revolution'; or the ability to mobilise and organise broadly. In that sense, resistance has not ended. Revolution continues as resistance, and those who participate in resistance (in the *dakhil*, the *shatat*, or international solidarity) dream nostalgically, tragically, and wistfully of *zaman al-thawra*, the era of revolution. Memories of those who lived in this time conjure up a compressed, hectic, and focused time of revolutionary work.[11] International solidarity activists who encountered the Palestinian revolution remember the same experience of living in a compressed time – the liminal moment – where historical change is possible. They convened in Jordan between 1967 and 1970 and then in Lebanon between 1970 and 1982. These spaces became revolutionary hubs where ideas and alliances were developed. Some came prepared by contacts they had made with Palestinians in their home countries, while others sought out liaisons in the offices and international co-ordination units of Fatah, the PFLP, and the DFLP. Work in this space 'buzzed with energy' as one Danish solidarity activist recalled it to me.[12] All actions seemed imbued with purpose and telos that drew on the energies of liberation movements and various other forms of resistance against domination and ossified power structures around the world in 'the long 1960s'. The telos of liberating oneself from these overlapping orders of domination and creating a new society structured not just the political project but also provided a spirit of camaraderie and a feverish energy to struggle. People got a lot done in a small amount of time. The Palestinian author Ghassan Kanafani published more than thirty books and thousands of articles before his assassination at the age of thirty-five, and the founder of the PLO Research Centre, Fayez Sayigh, put out more than fifty volumes in five years (see the chapter by Klaudia Wieser in this volume), to name just two prominent Palestinian revolutionary intellectuals. At a time when travelling was expensive and difficult, networks of Palestinian militants managed to set up and inspire solidarity movements across the whole world. The movement drew on

---

[11] Zeina Maasri, *Cosmopolitan Radicalism: The Visual Politics of Beirut's Global Sixties* (Cambridge: Cambridge University Press, 2020), 140–152.
[12] Interview with Niels Stockmarr, Copenhagen, 22 October 2019.

its own energy and achievements to push forward, expand, connect, and consolidate. The will to transform society, resist, and achieve liberation was electrifying and infectious.

In my interviews with solidarity activists from this era, a recurrent memory that they want to share is the sense of unity in the Palestinian movement. They often stress this in response to my questions about the splits and disagreements that set in from the mid-1970s onwards. The splits were related to Cold War politics and Sino-Soviet competition, which Palestinian groups also had to navigate. In Norway, as in many other places, members of the initially unified Palestine Committee (founded in 1970) split in 1976 into a new more pro-Soviet group, The Palestine Front. They did so with active support from the PLO representative in Stockholm. At this point, Arafat – under Soviet pressure – had moved Fatah and the PLO towards a diplomatic solution based on two states, and implicitly based on the acceptance of American brokerage, creating a split between the left – mainly PFLP and DFLP – and Fatah. From an organisational and military perspective, Yezid Sayigh has written the most elaborate analysis of the implications of this move and how it may explain the transformation of the Palestinian revolution. Writing shortly after 1982, Sayigh concluded that Palestinian forces in Lebanon had lost the 'guerrilla's advantages of mobility, flexibility, and relative invisibility', but at the same time had not gained the advantages of a regular army. He called this a 'functional dualism' for the Palestinians as the leadership in Fakhani faced an external Israeli enemy and several internal Lebanese enemies.[13] For quite a few years before 1982, they anticipated an Israeli assault and speculated whether the landing would come in Khalde, in Damour or some other locality, but according to Sayigh they made no efficient contingency plans, which became evident when the invasion began. Neither an army nor a guerrilla force, the Palestinian forces had become trapped in an organisational no-man's land, despite the obvious success of creating a state-in-exile in Lebanon.[14]

In his 1997 landmark study *Armed Struggle and the Search for State*, Sayigh expands on this analysis. He highlights the statist ambitions that were present

---

[13] Yezid Sayigh, 'Palestinian Military Performance in the 1982 War', *Journal of Palestine Studies* 12 (4) 1983: 3.

[14] This is a contested version among some Palestinians who participated in the fighting, according to whom there were contingency plans, but they were foiled in the south by the scale of the invasion, whereas in Beirut they mostly succeeded from a military perspective.

from the very foundation of the PLO as the main telos of the revolution, even inside the guerrilla movement.[15] While the core of the revolution may be remembered fondly as the daily activities of grassroots organisation, mobilisation, and networking, or the heroics of military combat, it also involved a diplomatic offensive to achieve recognition. Arafat took charge of this process, while having to deal with a backlash from the rejection front led by the PFLP. This contestation happened relatively democratically – that is to say, without sweeping arrests and military clashes, and with the continued close contact and presence of the left.

This new 'political arena' was centred on Palestinian spaces in Lebanon.[16] The militarisation of Palestinian refugees in Lebanon began in 1969 and escalated with the arrival of the PLO leadership in September 1970, following its confrontation with the Jordanian state.[17] Palestinians were settled in densely populated refugee camps around Beirut and in the south near the Israel–Lebanon border. Based in the camps of Burj al-Barajneh and Shatila in south-west Beirut, the leadership of the PLO as well as various groups expanded into the adjacent neighbourhood of al-Fakhani, which in the early 1970s began to be known as the operational centre for Palestinian activities. At the same time, this part of south-west Beirut became the main space where outside solidarity activists visiting – and sometimes training with – Palestinian groups would convene, where solidarity art exhibitions would be staged, and where Lebanese political leaders would come to meet and confer with the political leadership, not least PLO and Fatah leader Yasser Arafat. While south Lebanon, where Palestinian commandos carried out raids into Israel and clashed with the Lebanese army, was often referred to as 'Fatah-land', the Fakhani Republic became the catch-all for all Palestinian territorial control and presence.

At the same time, Fakhani was also a particular physical space in west Beirut where the Palestinians for the first time attempted something akin to constructing a state-in-exile. Military support from Arab states before, but particularly after, the outbreak of war in Lebanon in 1975, gave the PLO heavier weapons with which to protect their territorial independence. The statist project gained steam after the 1978 Israeli–Egyptian peace treaty,

---

[15] While I lean on Sayigh's analysis in this chapter, I recognise that other historians contest his understanding of Arafat's statist ambitions in Lebanon. See https://learnpalestine. politics.ox.ac.uk and a forthcoming work by Abed Takriti.

[16] Yezid Sayigh, *Armed Struggle and the Search for State: The Palestinian National Movement 1949–1993* (Oxford: Oxford University Press, 1997), 669.

[17] Ibid., 156.

which pushed Yasser Arafat to pursue state-building in lieu of a direct nego-
tiation with the US. In the early 1970s, Arafat banked on secure support
from a relatively united Arab front and the Soviet Union. With the Arab
countries divided, and support for the so-called 'rejection front' (named
after Palestinian factions who rejected the Ten Point Programme adopted
by the PLO in its Twelfth Palestinian National Congress session in 1974)
forthcoming from states like Syria and Libya, Arafat now felt he had to
solidify control and build a 'state in the state' – or rather, a 'state-in-exile'
– to achieve control over Palestinian diplomacy and a strong position from
which to negotiate internationally.[18]

As the Lebanese civil war broke out in April 1975, the PLO was, in
the words of Sayigh, in the 'transition from the period of revolutionary
ascendancy in 1967–1970 to a typically post-revolutionary phase of (in
this case neo-patrimonial) state-building'.[19] This patrimonialism, backed
by a cash influx from Arab states, made the PLO further attractive for various allies and even more of a menace for Israeli leaders, who believed that
they could control the revolutionary assault but feared state-building in
exile and the international legitimacy, and ensuing territorial claims, that it
threatened to bestow on the Palestinian leadership. These fears were somewhat justified by the PLO's successes in the UN, first with Arafat's 'olive
branch speech' in 1974 and then with the adoption by the UN's General
Assembly of Resolution 3379 in 1975 that equated Zionism with racism.
These were major achievements that established Arafat as the representative of the Palestinian cause to the outside world. Internally, however, the
rifts ran deep. Daily life in the Fakhani Republic reflected these tensions. It
is to this reality that the chapter now turns.

FRAGMENTED IN FAKHANI

In this part of the article, I will contrast Sayigh's structural analysis with
inside accounts from the period. They can be found in memoirs, interviews,
ethnography, and – in more interpretive and imaginative form – in literature.

In Palestinian and Lebanese literature, the period has been covered
in many novels and short stories. As cultural products, they are of course

---

[18] Ibid., 447.
[19] Ibid., 463.

reflexive rather than documentary sources, but they still give a good sense of the experience of this crucial period for the Palestinian revolution. In contrast to more official sources, they present a wealth of voices and perspectives of women, militants, children, and non-Palestinians. The inclusion of marginal voices and counter-narratives with political discourse was, however, also a product of the crises of the revolution through the 1970s, which was in turn – as I shall argue later in this chapter – linked to the crisis of Third Worldism. The literary critic Joseph Farag has noted that in the early period of the Palestinian revolution between 1969 and 1975, 'committed' writers mainly supported the optimistic, militant approach of the political institutions, as for example in the later (post-1967) work of PFLP leader and writer Ghassan Kanafani.[20]

When the war began in Lebanon, a new more sceptical, sometimes even sardonic, literature appeared. The change in revolutionary subjectivity is visible here in changing aesthetics and poetics, as well as thematic and narrative strategies. The writers of the late 1970s increasingly left behind the heroic voice and rather sought to reflect the duress of revolutionary life and not least the confusing reality of living through a civil war. In this period, literature became one of the arenas to express perspectives and experiences that differed from the official political narratives.

Examples of this new multi-vocalic realism are the short stories of Yahya Yakhlif that portray Palestinian militiamen caught in a war that they have increasingly little appetite for, even if they understand the necessity of the struggle. In the story that lends its name to his 1976 collection *Nurma and the Snowman*, we follow the newly arrived conscript Saeed who is stationed with a group of *fida'yin* on top of a mountain during the first phase of the civil war.[21] He descends periodically to visit his fellow fighters at the encampment below and see his lover, Nurma. The story gives space to the different, often sardonic, voices of the militiamen as they reflect on life during the battle. In subtle ways, the text allows for critique of the Palestinian elite through the development of characters and their discourse. The Lebanese writer Elias Khoury's 1977 novel *Little Mountain* – set during the very same battle on Mount Hermon in 1976 as *Nurma and the Snowman* – creates a similar register where inner dialogues of militiamen struggling with

---

[20] Joseph Farag, *Politics and Palestinian Literature in Exile: Gender, Aesthetics and Resistance in the Short Story* (London: I.B. Tauris, 2016), 45.
[21] Yahya Yakhlif, *Nurma wa rajul al-thalj* [Nurma and the Snowman] (Amman: Dar al-Karmal lil-Nashr wal-Tawzi', 1977).

their predicament in a confusing war relay the gradual disappearance of revolutionary conviction.[22] The literary techniques employed by Khoury and Yakhlif contrast with the didactic storylines of committed literature of the late 1960s and early 1970s that sits closer to political propaganda. Multivocality relays doubt, ponderance, but also a multiplicity of actual existing perspectives and opinions, and as such is an arguably more democratic form of representation.

Another focus of cultural production during this period is the terrible massacres committed against Palestinian camps. The Sabra and Shatila massacre in September 1982 elicited many literary works, mainly written years later and concerned with the memory and post-memory of this traumatic event. Even more so than the 1976 siege of the Palestinian refugee camp Tall al-Za'atar, which was heavily covered in the press and documented by Lebanese, Palestinian and international filmmakers,[23] Sabra and Shatila was the 'Palestinian Guernica' – the archetypical atrocity – that has been interpreted and reinterpreted as the marker of Israeli and Falangist cruelty towards and dehumanisation of Palestinians, but also as the moment when the dominant trope representing the Palestinian revolution turned decisively from revolutionary heroism to emasculated victimisation and martyrdom.[24] This moment coincided with the departure of the PLO from Beirut and has been documented and treated in landmark cultural productions like Mai Masri and Jean Chamoun's 1982 documentary *Under the Rubble*, Elias Khoury's 1998 novel *Gate of the Sun*, and not least Mahmoud Darwish's poem *Memory for Forgetfulness*, first published in Arabic in 1986 as *The Time: Beirut/The Place: August*.

These literary and cinematic accounts reflect the brutal end point of the Palestinian revolution in Lebanon. Their tragic cry of despair contrasts with earlier renditions of dynamism and hope, but also shows the social transformation taking place within the Fakhani Republic. Many such accounts remain relatively hidden in small-circulation genres such as autobiographies by militants. Here, I will focus on two accounts from members of the Palestinian left, who had a particular affiliation with Third Worldist ideas. I do not read their accounts merely to extract their ideological reflections

---

[22] Elias Khoury, *Little Mountain* (London: Picador, 2007).

[23] Nadia Yaqub, *Palestinian Cinema in the Days of Revolution* (Austin: Texas University Press, 2018), 162–194.

[24] Laleh Khalili, *Heroes and Martyrs of Palestine* (Cambridge: Cambridge University Press, 2009).

and developments, but rather – following the general methodology in this book – to relate their experience of everyday life to the transformation of political ideas.

The first text is a 2012 autobiography by Samih Shabib, a former member of the PFLP-GC (General Command).[25] This group was led by one of the original members of the Arab Nationalist Movement, Ahmed Jibril, and belonged to the so-called rejection front inside Fakhani. Jibril allied himself closely with Syria and resided in Damascus after the end of the civil war and until his death in 2021. Shabib was one of the movement's early members in Syria. After an education as a primary school teacher, he was assigned to help the construction of the party's branch in Lebanon. In 1973, Jibril sent him to Burj al-Barajneh and later to Fakhani itself, where he worked in the Central Media Committee and the Research Centre of the PLO and edited several Palestinian publications including *Falastin al-thawra* (which some members of the 'rejection front' sarcastically referred to as *Falastin al-dawla* [the state] because of its close connection to the PLO leadership), *al-Summud*, and *al-Qa'ida*. The aim of the book is, as he writes, to show the 'inner factional life' of the PFLP-GC and daily life in what he calls the 'resistance society' of Fakhani.[26]

Shabib's perspective straddles several social layers in Palestinian society. As a lower-level militant and journalist before the war, he describes the cramped offices and living spaces of low-ranking revolutionaries like himself, the internal fights between Palestinian factions, and the bad sanitation in the area. Later, as the war breaks out, he rises in the ranks and makes himself a useful stringer for Beirut-based newspapers like *al-Nahar* that previously rejected him. His description of relations with *al-Nahar* journalists is telling of cultural hierarchies but also the fluidity of ideological positions in wartime Lebanon. He dreams of writing for *al-Nahar*, despite its centre-right politics. Likewise, he edits the PLO publication *Falastin al-thawra* despite his association with the rejection front. His acquaintance at *al-Nahar*'s editorial office looks down on the quality of Palestinian publications like *al-Summud*. But when the war in downtown Beirut breaks out, *al-Nahar* begins to depend

[25] Samih Shabib, *Tada'iyat 'ala hamish tuwajid al-fasa'il al-musalaha fi lubnan 1973–1983* [On the sidelines of the presence of Palestinian armed factions in Lebanon 1973 – 1983] (Ramallah: East Press Studies, 2012).

[26] Ibid., 10.

on Shabib's direct access to information and sources. He is invited to work with them, which he describes as a major career advancement.[27]

That a revolutionary Syrian Palestinian would aim for, and be accepted into, the circles of a bourgeois Lebanese newspaper often associated with the Christian right in the war, may seem surprising. But it is revealing of the often counterintuitive links and connections in Lebanese society that survived, and sometimes even thrived, during the war. This ideological and cultural syncretism rubbed off on Palestinians in Lebanon (and vice versa, the transnationalism of Palestinians made its mark on Lebanon). Links across the Green Line that separated east and west Beirut during the war, but also outside of Lebanon, were a common part of people's war experience. As he rises in the ranks of his movement, Shabib is afforded the opportunity to travel as a political representative. This part of the memoir reveals the internationalist dimension of the Fakhani Republic.

Before the war, he joins the Palestinian delegation to the 1973 World Youth Conference in East Berlin, where he witnesses the iconic Vietnamese leader Võ Nguyên Giáp, nicknamed the Red Napoleon, speaking to the crowd and passing a symbolic banner to Yasser Arafat, in an enactment of Palestinian artist Ibrahim Shattout's famous 1972 poster that was used for Palestinian propaganda globally, where a Vietnamese FLN soldier passes the torch of the revolution to a saluting *fida'yi*. At a later point back in Fakhani, he describes the visit of six blonde Trotskyist Italian girls in 1976, whose sudden presence in Fakhani causes a lot of confusion and unwarranted excitement. He acts as their protector and has them shipped off to a base in the south, where they can do solidarity work in the more protected environment of health clinics – by then a regular feature of international solidarity work (see the chapter in this book by Pelle Olsen as well as that of Marral Shamshiri). His international work also extends to military intelligence. He is sent on a mission to solicit weapons from Bulgaria, which are to be sent by plane to Cyprus and then shipped to Sidon. Although he succeeds, the weapon transport ship is intercepted by the Israelis.

These episodes paint a picture of Fakhani as a small but extremely connected space, open to Western solidarity activists and eastern European and Arab radical regimes. Participants in the struggle travelled freely and

---

[27] Ibid., 35–46.

extensively to these countries and continuously sought to maximise benefit from their Third Worldist connections.[28]

INFIGHTS AND BACKLASH IN THE LEAD-UP TO 1982

Shabib's memoirs paint a picture of an internationalist, connected, and somewhat protected Palestinian movement. Just like Yezid Sayigh, however, Shabib finds that the heavy interference of Libya, Iraq, and Syria had very negative consequences, as Yasser Arafat tried to steer the PLO through the labyrinthine twists and turns of the civil war and its Byzantine fratricides and alliances while being increasingly more cornered by US and Israeli diplomacy. Palestinian factions coexisting inside Fakhani found frequent reason to wage war against each other, urged on by their external backers, and the inhabitants of the area consequently suffered.

Shabib describes how he was sitting on his balcony in the autumn of 1977, a few hundred metres from Arafat's headquarters, watching the battles take place on the street below him. Writing in hindsight and at a time when he has abandoned the struggle, Shabib remembers 1977 through a lens of defeat and mistakes of the past that is undoubtedly influenced by his present (2012) context. At this stage, he muses, 'there was no scientific basis for our struggle any more'.[29] From a Marxist–Leninist perspective, the internal contradictions had exceeded the social and geopolitical contradictions that the struggle was meant to resolve. In terms of the delicate relationship between Palestinians and Lebanese, he describes how many Lebanese (in late 1976) had now begun to view Palestinians as 'colonisers' who must be eliminated. The irony of this is not lost on Shabib and his friend as they discuss it in downtown Beirut, among the rubble of the destroyed hotel district. One of his friends, who is 'constantly drunk', takes a sip of his bottle and remarks ruefully: 'Imagine, all our lives we lived as colonised, and here we are, colonising!'[30]

In these sections, Shabib's memoir unintentionally comes close to reifying a Lebanese right-wing narrative of the war suggesting ultimate Palestinian culpability, but also a Syrian regime narrative whereby the PLO got too involved in the civil war and therefore distracted from the more important

---

[28] Ibid., 39–49.
[29] Ibid., 52.
[30] Ibid., 66.

task of liberating Palestine. As someone close to the Syrian regime, Shabib probably remembers a conversation that did or did not take place refracted through these contextual lenses. The aim is to highlight the growing feeling that the Palestinians were not welcome any more, which in the book becomes the prelude to the 1982 invasion. During the Israeli bombardments of west Beirut in July 1982, Shabib writes that 'the Palestinians acted as if Beirut was their capital, and the Secretary-General of the PFLP, Dr George Habash, announced that the resistance would make Beirut another Hanoi. This angered the Lebanese, even the National Movement [the Lebanese leftist alliance fighting with the Palestinians in the civil war]. The Lebanese National Movement had glorified the Palestinian heroic *summud* (steadfastness), but these slogans were undermined by the Israeli war machine.'[31]

The severed or at least damaged link, as Shabib describes it, between the Palestinian and Lebanese resistance, had severe consequences for the Palestinian presence in the country. In Shabib's historical analysis, the 'ghetto mentality' that had existed in the camps prior to the arrival of the Palestinian revolution in 1969 had been replaced with an internationalist revolutionary outlook that gave them hope and expanded their horizon. He concedes that 'the Palestinian presence in Lebanon has had a direct impact on its political entity, as the Palestinian armed parties became part of Lebanese conflicts, and Palestinians have benefited from Lebanon, both as a media and military platform.'[32] The direct consequence of 'this dependence on armed military presence for the integration of Palestinians into Lebanon'[33] was a campaign of discrimination, violence, and expulsion of Palestinians after 1982. The era of the Lebanese rejection of the nationalisation of Palestinians and the effective suppression of Palestinian rights, called *rafd al-tawteen*, effectively began on 22 August 1982, as Palestinian leaders bid their heroic farewell to Beirut from the deck of the ships taking them on their new exodus.

FROM THE MAOIST INTERNATIONAL TO PALESTINIAN ISLAMISM

Fighting alongside Elias Khoury and possibly Saeed the *fida'yi* from *Nurma and the Snowman* on Mount Hermon in 1976 was a small group of

---

[31] Ibid., 79.
[32] Ibid., 86.
[33] Ibid., 87.

Maoist-influenced fighters, the so-called *katiba tullabiyya* (student battalion) that contained Palestinian, Lebanese, and other Arab intellectuals who had joined the military struggle in 1975. The *katiba* included several intellectuals who later became prominent writers and cultural producers, including Khoury, the playwright Roger Assaf, the sociologist Saud al-Mawla, and the writer Naji 'Alloush (who was not strictly a member but had a strong influence on the group and later became one of its chroniclers). It also contained militants who later became Islamist leaders, like Imad Moughniya, Hizbollah's head of international operations who was killed in Damascus in 2008, and Tarad Hamade, Hizbollah politician and government minister (2005–2008), as well as several Palestinian Maoists who became members of Palestinian Islamic Jihad after 1981.

This diverse group had come together in 1974 as a meeting between a small number of Fatah members, who from the beginning in the late 1960s had defended a Maoist interpretation of the revolution, and a splinter group of Marxist intellectuals from the Organisation of Communist Action in Lebanon. Before it formed a militia in 1976, the group had already been known as the *katiba* inside Fatah. One of its leaders, Munir Shafiq, has recounted how he did not primarily see the group as Maoist but as a revolutionary force inside Fatah that sought to maintain 'the original 1960s Fatah spirit' and not the increasingly pro-Soviet and accommodationist Fatah of Arafat.[34] Ideologically, they took certain aspects of Mao's thoughts, particularly the notions of a 'people's war' and the 'mass line' – the idea that popular struggle had to engage peasants directly and learn from them. In addition, learning revolution from a non-Western source – from Mao as much as from Marx – appealed to their thirst for full cultural and political independence.

The *katiba* was composed of Palestinians and Lebanese from different confessional and regional backgrounds, but also counted Iraqi communists, Maoists, and revolutionaries with a strong Islamic orientation, who had found refuge in Lebanon, as well as Iranians who had joined Fatah to train militarily and fight. These Iranian volunteers came from the Marxist group *Sazman-e cherik-ha-ye fada'i-ye khalq* (the Organisation of the People's Fada'i Guerrillas; see Elling and Mahmoudi's chapter in this book) as well as from the Islamo-Marxist counterpart *Sazman-e mojahedin-e khalq-e Iran*

---

[34] Manfred Sing, 'Brothers in Arms: How Palestinian Maoists Turned Jihadists', *Die Welt des Islams* 51 (1) 2008: 1–41, 17.

(the People's Mojahedin Organisation of Iran).[35] The *katiba* embraced the ideological syncretism of these groups. More broadly, one could say that Fatah as a nationalist movement, and Fakhani as a revolutionary space, were very open to all kinds of revolutionary groups of the left, regionally and internationally. Maoism may not have been the largest tendency in the *katiba*, but its followers were devoted and internationalist in orientation.

Another of its leading members, Naji 'Alloush, had a complex background as a Palestinian who had been a member of the Ba'th Party and various leftist revolutionary groups since the late 1950s. In Beirut, he was approached by Fatah in 1967 because of his writings about the need for a people's war at the leftist publishing house Dar al-Ta'lia, where he worked. In the decade that followed, he moved up the ranks in Fatah as a close associate of the leader, Abu Nidal, and led several missions to Cuba. He wrote influential books about China and Vietnam and translated the works of Third Worldist intellectuals like Stokely Carmichael, Giáp, and Rodinson into Arabic. In 1970, he became a member of Fatah's Revolutionary Council, which illustrates the central position and internationalist orientation of *katiba* members inside Fatah.[36]

In the late 1960s and early 1970s, the Maoist approach to mobilisation appealed to all those who rejected a Western model of revolution and development. For the main leadership in Fatah, Maoism was just as over-intellectualising as they found Marxist–Leninist theory of the Soviet strain (and both were present in the PFLP and the DFLP). Arafat and his deputy Salah Khalaf (Abu Iyad) advocated a broad patriotic front for the liberation struggle, even if Khalaf had a more leftist leaning. Although Arafat often appealed to anti-imperialist internationalism, he eschewed intellectualisation. Arafat had his own 'mass line', and it was much simpler and aligned with a pragmatism that gradually, after 1972, became quite devoid of Chinese romanticism. At the same time, revolution remained important

---

[35] Mu'in al-Tahir, *Tibgh wa zaytun: hikayat wa suwar min zaman muqawam* [Tobacco and olives: stories and images from the time of resistance] (Beirut: Markaz al-'arabi lil-bahath wa dirasat al-siyasat, 2017).

[36] Interview with Naji 'Alloush conducted by his son Ibrahim 'Alloush, published 1 May 2015 on the *la'iha al-qawmi al-'arabi* [Slate of the Arab Nationalist] website. Retrieved 11 January 2023 from http://qawmi-jathri.net/2015/05/01/%D8%B7% D9%84%D9%82%D8%A9-%D8%AA%D9%86%D9%88%D9%8A%D8%B115- %D9%86%D8%A7%D8%AC%D9%8A-%D8%B9%D9%84%D9%88%D8%B4- %D9%85%D9%84%D9%81-%D9%88%D9%85%D8%B0%D9%83%D8%B1%D8%A 7%D8%AA. Unfortunately, this richly detailed interview does not touch directly on 'Alloush's experience in the *katiba*.

for Arafat, who maintained his Third Worldist alliances even though his political engagements gradually shifted. In contrast, Maoism offered a more uncompromising worldview that fully rejected Western models of societal transformation and instead sought political and emotional visions in Asian revolutionary philosophy and experience. This (very modernist) rejection of Western modernity opened the door to political Islam when it began its ascendance during the last part of the 1970s.

For the international solidarity movement, speaking a common language (that of Marxism–Leninism, and that of English, mastered by the more intellectual and educated on the left more so than regular Fatah members) was a major attraction. They admired the sophistication of the likes of Ghassan Kanafani and found much to learn from practitioners of revolution. Quite a few of them leaned towards Maoism. To give an example of how these Third Worldist meetings took place in and around Fakhani, we can take the example of Peder-Martin Lysestøl, a Norwegian Maoist and one of the founders of the Palestine Committee in Norway (see also the chapter by Pelle Olsen).

As a representative of the Norwegian left student movement, Lysestøl spent time in Yugoslavia and Cairo in the late 1960s and encountered fellow Maoists and members of Fatah. These encounters pushed him towards membership of the Norwegian Maoist group AKP (m-l). One of his contacts in Cairo in 1968 was a key member of the later *katiba tullabiya*, Munir Shafiq. Shafiq helped procure Fatah material for the Norwegians and inspired them to organise a solidarity movement. In May 1970, Lysestøl and his comrades invited Shafiq to speak in Oslo in a landmark visit that mobilised a large part of the left-wing Norwegian student movement for the Palestinian cause. He became one of the main members responsible inside Fatah for creating such links to the European left as part of its foreign committee. Despite their ideological differences, Shafiq advised Arafat and attempted to keep him from forming a close alliance with the Soviet Union. The Norwegians approved of this line and communicated it to the Norwegian public in their magazine *Fritt Palestina*. Lysestøl stayed in contact with Shafiq and exchanged ideas over the years, even to this day.[37] Several times in 1970 and 1971, he visited Shafiq and other Palestinians in Jordan and Beirut, conducting long meetings to co-ordinate their understanding of the revolution.

---

[37] Interview with Peder Martin Lysestøl, Trondheim, 10 March 2020.

As a Palestinian communist intellectual with a West Bank Christian background who had been a long-term resident of Lebanon, Shafiq has a rather singular but interesting trajectory that is relevant to our analysis. First, he was one of the liaisons (there were many others, like Naji 'Alloush) between the Palestinian revolution and what they called the 'world revolution' in the guise of New Left groups, student groups, solidarity groups, and liberation movements and governments across the world.[38] Second, Shafiq has produced a significant body of memoirs and reflections on the period that we can draw on to analyse his changing positions.[39] And finally, Shafiq became one of the pioneers of an Islamist interpretation of the struggle which was to become one of the major factors in the fragmentation and 'end' of the Palestinian revolution.

The general climate in mid-1970s Lebanon produced doubts about the Third Worldist project. Shafiq has described how doubts began to set in inside the *katiba* around the time the two-year war (1975–1976) had ended. This is the same aftermath in which Elias Khoury wrote his retrospective novel *Little Mountain* and which caused many leftists to rethink their engagement. Syria – a socialist power in the region supported by the Soviets – had intervened to put a halt to the PLO and the Lebanese left. Shortly afterwards, in 1977, Mao Zedong died, and the new leadership prosecuted hardline Maoists in the trial of 'the gang of the four'. In Munir Shafiq's rendition of this period, the Maoists of the *katiba tullabiya* began to realise that the Cultural Revolution had failed.[40]

These events foreshadowed the transformation of Third Worldism often associated with 1979. In Lebanon, Third Worldist combatants lived and felt the contradictions a few years earlier than this. The infighting between regional powers and local militias generated questions about their creed. Perhaps Marxism–Leninism was failing as the universalising ideology that explained their predicament and its solution, in Lebanon, in Palestine and in the region as a whole. Perhaps it did not, after all, contain the supreme social, historical, ideological, and methodological knowledge that they had thought. And perhaps this was because Marxism–Leninism was in fact not a

---

[38] Sorcha Thomson, Pelle Olsen, and Sune Haugbolle, 'Palestine Solidarity Conferences in the Global Sixties', *Journal of Palestine Studies* 51 (1) 2021: 27–49.

[39] I draw on Manfred Sing's comprehensive analysis of Shafiq's oeuvre, Sing, 'Brothers in Arms: How Palestinian Maoists Turned Jihadists'.

[40] Munir Shafiq, *Shuhada' wa masira. Abu Ḥasan wa-Ḥamadi wa-ikhwanuhuma* (Beirut: Mu'assasat al-Wafa', 1994), 45–62.

universal ideology but one that mainly reflected European modernity. While some Arab Marxists like the Lebanese Communist Party thinker Hassan Hamdan (known as Mahdi Amil) continued to defend a possible accommodation of Marxist theory and the Arab context, others were moved by the events of the war to question the universality of Marxism, including its Third Worldist (contextualised) versions.[41] As Shafiq describes this change of heart, he and his comrades came to attribute the failure of the Cultural Revolution in China to the 'European [sic!] mentality', namely the 'European idea' of a 'total break with the past' – the classic Marxist understanding of modernity as a force where 'everything that is solid melts into air.'[42]

The defeats and transformations that followed the two-year war and the assassination of leftist leader Kamal Jumblatt and the death of Mao in 1977 occasioned a major rethinking about the cultural specificity of a revolution (as opposed to its historical materialist universality) and about how to win over the masses. When protests began in Iran in 1977 and escalated in 1978, the Maoists in Lebanon were struck by the masses streaming into the streets of Tehran shouting *Allahu Akbar* and *la illaha illallah* ('God is great' and 'there is no God but God'). At this point, Shafiq recounts, most of his comrades concluded that Marxism had proven to be impractical compared to Islamic principles that served directly as instruments for a revolution of the Palestinian and Arab masses. They knew that many of their comrades lacked knowledge and conviction, and they wondered if this was also the case for the masses. As for his own comrades in groups like the Organisation for Communist Action in Lebanon and the PFLP, Shafiq concludes that their study of Marxism at Western universities had made them unreceptive to the inner transformation that was necessary to embrace Islam – an embrace that Shafiq now saw as strategically necessary. What the masses needed, he believed, was a comprehensive Islamisation of society, led by a vanguard party (that later became the Palestinian Islamic Jihad movement). It would operate on fertile soil as the cultural roots of society were, so he now firmly thought, essentially Islamic.

These radical conclusions foreshadow the belief in *'asala* (cultural roots) as the ideological core became a general trend among Arab intellectuals

---

[41] See Samer Frangie, 'Theorizing from the Periphery: The Intellectual Project of Mahdi 'Amil', *International Journal of Middle East Studies* 44 (3) 2012: 465–482.

[42] All three citations from Munir Shafiq, *Shuhada' wa masira. Abu Ḥasan wa-Ḥamadi wa-ikhwanuhuma*, 52–53.

and leftist thinkers during the 1980s.[43] After intense studies and discussions between late 1976 and 1979, the Maoists in the *katiba* had concluded that its 'pivotal axis' – mass mobilisation through Islam – was without any value or even unreliable if they had no deeper understanding of the core creed of Islam. The idea that there could be no revolution without belief eventually forced many of them to pull away from historical materialism.[44]

The conversion of Palestinian Maoists to political Islam is significant because it was a direct reason – if not the only one – for the emergence of Palestinian Islamist movements and the further fragmentation of the Palestinian liberation movement that it produced. But it is also important for the changing political language of resistance that it created. A recurrent comment in my conversations with solidarity activists, when I ask them about the first meetings with Palestinian militants in the late 1960s and early 1970s, is their joy of discovering a common language of dissent and revolution, which was essentially the language of Marxism–Leninism. There is no question that the arrival of political Islam as a central force also left a mark on Fatah's vocabulary. As a case in point, take Arafat's televised speech on the occasion of his first visit to Khomeini's Iran:

> Khomeini is our Imam, our leader, the leader of all mojahedin, we are two peoples in one, two revolutions in one and every fida'i, every mojahed, every revolutionary Iranian will be ambassador of Palestine in Iran. We [sic] have liberated Iran, we will liberate Palestine. We will continue our efforts until the moment we have defeated imperialism and Zionism; the struggle of Iranians against the Shah is identical with the struggle of Palestinians against Israel.[45]

The tone of this speech reflected the occasion more than a wholesale abandonment of secular nationalism. Nonetheless, the full embrace by Palestinian leaders – including PFLP's George Habash – of the Iranian revolution marked a historical shift. For Shafiq, it was not so much the Iranian people's reaction to Khomeini that struck him. Rather, it was the way the Lebanese and Palestinian masses instinctively endorsed the Imam that convinced

---

[43] Michaelle Browers, *Democracy and Civil Society in Arab Political Thought: Transcultural Possibilities* (Syracuse: Syracuse University Press, 2006).

[44] Sing, 'Brothers in Arms: How Palestinian Maoists Turned Jihadists', 32.

[45] Retrieved from the Yasser Arafat Foundation's webpage, 11 January 2023. https://yaf.ps/page-581-ar.html.

him that the *katiba*'s gradual 'conversion' to (their form of) political Islam was not just vindicated but destined. Charisma was more important than ideology because it relayed a direct link to the masses. A 'mobilised and unanimous people' would, finally, provide the iron fist of popular backing that was needed to reclaim Palestine. A new political vocabulary, amalgamated from Koranic language and Ibn Khaldun's historical sociology, would replace Marx and Mao to produce a truly indigenous revolutionary script.[46]

CONCLUSION

This chapter has suggested that Palestinian interpretations of Third Worldism underwent a fundamental transformation starting in 1975, culminating in the embrace of the Islamic Revolution in Iran and the formation of the Palestinian Islamic Jihad in 1981. I have focused on the Palestinian left, but the conclusions may extend further to Fatah, as seen in Arafat's Tehran speech. From a rather firm belief in the Third Worldist project of liberation and solidarity, many moved to question the historical direction of their revolution and its ideological underpinnings. I have pointed to three reasons for this shift.

The first was related to a fundamental conflict inside the movement between nationalist and Marxist tendencies, which from 1973–1974 translated into a full-blown conflict over strategic direction. The second reason was the lived experience of the civil war and in particular the conditions inside the Fakhani Republic. The hardship of battles and the syncretism of alliances inside Lebanon occasioned a more sceptical attitude to transnational unity and the historical direction of the revolution. The third shift was the Islamic Revolution in Iran, which I have analysed here through a small circle of Maoist radicals. However, the revolution reverberated broadly in Palestinian society and political culture. It foreshadowed a new international order where Islamist and authoritarian states would take the lead in resisting American hegemony. As a result of these shifts, the object of solidarity changed gradually from being the Palestinian political movements as such to the Palestinian people on the ground. After all, most Europeans could identify with a *fida'yi* but had a hard time identifying with a *mojahed*. Revolution became resistance.

---

[46] Sing, 'Brothers in Arms: How Palestinian Maoists Turned Jihadists', 35–36.

AFTERWORD

Towards a Praxis-Centred Historiography of Middle East Third Worldism

Toufoul Abou-Hodeib and Naghmeh Sohrabi

The words 'Third Worldism' carry not just the meaning laid out succinctly in the introduction to this volume but also, strangely perhaps, evoke an era and a feeling that seem to have fiercely lived and then firmly died. Rasmus Elling and Sune Haugbolle, the volume's editors, tell us that 'Third Worldism was the idea that revolutionary, anti-imperialist militancy in what we today term the Global South, buttressed by international solidarity, would not only lead to national liberation of oppressed peoples but also to universal emancipation.' Conventional wisdom tells us that this 'anti-imperial militancy' in the Middle East, which was in the service of both national and universal liberties, was dealt a debilitating blow by the 1979 revolution in Iran and then killed off completely by the 1982 invasion of Lebanon by Israel. The fact that 'Third Worldism' brings to mind only the past, a past tinted with either romanticism or fear depending on one's political inclination, but never the present and never the future, seems to only prove this conventional wisdom.

This impression of 'Third Worldism' in the Middle East is partly born out of how both Third World activists at the time and later observers defined the success of the project on a state level, that is, by the effects that Third Worldism as an idea and movement exerted on various states throughout the region. As such, in a historiography that sees the Islamic Republic of

Iran as the immediate result of the 1979 revolution and the destruction of the PLO in Lebanon as the absolute result of the 1982 invasion, it stands to reason that the death knell for this broad amorphous concept has been rung definitively. This volume sketches a different – and much needed – story by bringing new geographies and spaces into conversation with each other and by, even more importantly, shedding a bright light onto the period between 1979 and 1982. Taken together, this three-dimensional observation of Third Worldism in the Middle East allows us to acknowledge the fact that something did 'end' by the 1980s. But not everything that ends vanishes into thin air.

The essays in this volume are part of a welcome trend in the historiography of the Global South that gives primacy to a broad notion of social history. While intellectual and political history have traditionally informed the bulk of scholars' attempts to study transnational movements in the period (and in the region), these essays highlight the centrality of praxis to social movements and transform the image of Third Worldism from one of ideological frontlines to that of a world shaped by a myriad of practices in service to Third Worldism's varied and crisscrossing political concerns.[1] In what follows, we would like to focus on two crucial aspects of Third Worldism in the Middle East that emerge from this volume's centring of social groups and social movements in its assessment of the fate of Third Worldism.

The first aspect concerns how the periodisations of both 1979 and 1982 have worked hand-in-hand, resulting in the interplay of Third Worldism and Islamism, and specifically the ways in which the left fed into and even sometimes became Islamist. The second aspect concerns the shapes and spaces of the praxis of Third Worldism, which continued far past the phenomenon's endpoints. This praxis encompasses different types of networks located in expected and unexpected spaces such as conferences, publications, obituaries, and particularly friendships, which in precarious times form the core of networks of trust.

---

[1] For examples of the intellectual and political history of Third Worldism, see the introduction to this volume, which provides a comprehensive view of the dominant historiography.

THE TIME IN BETWEEN: 1979 AND 1982

In scholarship, the year 1979 has interpretive and analytical power as a watershed moment. Even at the time, observers flocked to Iran to witness the revolution unfold over the course of several portentous months in 1978–1979, most famously Michel Foucault, who recorded his observations for *Corriere della Sera* in the fall of 1978.[2] With the passage of time, 1979 acquired an interpretative power that guided much of the political and intellectual historiography of that period. In historians' terms, it became truly an event, 'a conceptual vehicle by means of which historians construct or analyse the contingency and temporal fatefulness of social life'.[3] With the Iranian Revolution, the Egyptian–Israeli peace treaty, the Soviet invasion of Afghanistan, the seizure of the Grand Mosque in Saudi Arabia, and other events outlined by Elling and Haugbolle in the introduction, 1979 became 'the year that shaped the Middle East', with all the violent connotations this entails.[4] Its significance seeped into a wider interpretation of shifts in the region, including an intellectual and ideological shift from the radical left to radical Islam.[5]

For outside observers, the 1980s witnessed a 'disenchantment' and 'the decline of great revolutionary hopes' for the Third World.[6] The Iranian Revolution seemed to embody this and mark the limits of affirmative revolutionary change, 'where the third world failed to emulate the spirit of the Enlightenment'.[7] From the point of view of the global New Left, 1979 seemed to mark the limits of solidarity, and the shrinking back from an internationalist vision to the particularities of Islamism and identitarianism. In the eyes of many Western activists at the time, the politics

---

[2] See Behrooz Ghamari-Tabrizi, *Foucault in Iran: Islamic Revolution after the Enlightenment* (Minneapolis: University of Minnesota Press, 2016).

[3] William H. Sewell Jr., *Logics of History: Social Theory and Social Transformation* (Chicago: University of Chicago Press, 2005), 8.

[4] David W. Lesch, *1979: The Year That Shaped the Modern Middle East* (New York: Routledge, 1991).

[5] Manfred Sing, 'Brothers in Arms: How Palestinian Maoists Turned Jihadists', *Die Welt des Islams* 51, no. 1 (2011): 1–44.

[6] Jean-Pierre Garnier and Ronald Lew, 'From the Wretched of the Earth to the Defence of the West: An Essay on Left Disenchantment in France', trans. David Macey, *Socialist Register* 21 (1984): 299–323; Paul-Marie de la Gorce, 'Le Recul des grandes espérances révolutionnaires', *Le Monde diplomatique*, May 1984.

[7] Elleni Centime Zeleke and Arash Davari, 'Introduction', in 'Third World Historical: Rethinking Revolution from Ethiopia to Iran', *Comparative Studies of South Asia, Africa and the Middle East* 42, no. 2 (2020), 423.

of the Middle East were abruptly transformed into a distant, foreign, and unrecognisable object.

The contributions in this book complicate the picture around 1979 in two important ways. First, they shed light on how informal networks stretched out on both sides of the 1979 divide. Second, and in relation to that, they complicate the conceptualisation of the relationship between, on the one hand, the leftism that characterised Third Worldism in the 1960s and 1970s, and, on the other hand, Islamism. The relationship between the two cannot be understood either as a linear development or as a clean break. Between Iran and Palestine, there were ideological currents and activist networks that persisted after the Iranian Revolution, even as they transformed in the process. The period stretching up until 1982 saw a balancing act and a set of tensions between two political visions that co-existed on the political scene in the Middle East and had reverberations that extended beyond their nationalist descriptives: the Iranian Revolution and the Palestinian liberation movement. The first was increasingly Islamist, the other remained leftist and secularist in orientation. Yet, while they seem irreconcilable on the level of big politics, the histories traced out in this volume shed light on the tensions as well as the dynamics between the two.

Placed chronologically, several chapters in this volume trace this interplay between Third Worldism and Islamism across state borders. During the 1970s, there were already transnational points of contact and arenas of interaction between the two. In the context of the Lebanese civil war, these tensions sometimes seemed irreconcilable, as George's contribution shows in the case of Amal. At the same time, there were arenas of contact between the PLO and members of the Islamic regime in Iran, such as Abbas Zamani, who had worked with the PLO in Lebanon and Syria for years before 1979. Concomitantly, Palestinian Maoists were beginning to look to Islamist thought as an alternative to the fragmentation and internal contradictions that characterised the Palestinian scene in the late 1970s, as becomes evident in Haugbolle's contribution. Ataie's chapter deftly illustrates how such Third Worldist networks were crucial for convening the first conference of liberation movements in post-revolutionary Iran. Further, Fuchs shows how the Islamic regime sought to build on and extend these networks by attempting to export the Islamic revolution to the Global South in the early 1980s.

By the time the revolution in Iran was proclaimed victorious, the Palestinian cause had become a poster child of liberation movements globally, including in Iran. The Iranian regime could simply not ignore it. The Iranian regime and the PLO might have had a working relationship, but, as becomes evident in the contributions to this volume, it was often an uneasy one, subject to the vicissitudes of geopolitical priorities and ideological considerations. Nevertheless, both in terms of discourse as well as in terms of networking, Palestine remained high on the Iranian agenda after 1979, even as it complicated the Islamic Republic Party's (IRP) attempt to steer the revolution's international agenda away from secular and leftist inclinations into a transnational Islamist one, as Alemzadeh argues in her contribution. The revolutionary promises of Third Worldism, it seems, did not simply vanish after 1979, even if they began to look unrecognisable from what they were before.

The question then is, if there were so many crisscrossing currents beyond 1979 and one cannot rely on the year itself as a point of analysis, when and how did the eclipse of Third World leftism take place? Although there cannot be one simple answer, part of it lies in another significant year: 1982. The wider effects of the violence that the Israeli invasion of Lebanon wreaked upon the country and the Palestinians living in it should not be underestimated. The results of the Israeli military campaign were not restricted to the loss of more than 30,000 lives and extensive physical destruction. They also included the dismantling of an entire infrastructure that the PLO had built in Lebanon. In addition to the military, the infrastructure included many institutions that were meant to be the embryo of a future Palestinian state. This included health services, research, industry, media, and culture, just to name the most significant.

From the point of view of the social movements that this volume advocates, the violence of 1982 extended beyond its larger political, military, and diplomatic significance. It also took out everyday places of praxis in and around the Palestinian refugee camps that nurtured transnational activism and solidarity. From health projects to cultural activities, the PLO's institutions had become regional and transnational meeting points for an ideologically complex project that had its established place in Third Worldism and on the left.[8] In a very material sense, 1982 eliminated spaces

---

[8] In addition to Olsen's contribution to this volume, see Toufoul Abou-Hodeib, 'The Traveling Scarf and Other Stories: Art Networks, Politics, and Friendships between Palestine and Norway', in *Art and Solidarity Reader: Radical Actions, Politics and Friendships*, ed. Katya García-Antón (Amsterdam: Valiz, 2022), 181–188; Kristine Khuri and Rasha Salti, eds, *Past Disquiet: Artists, International Solidarity and Museums in*

of gathering, networking, and consolidating that constituted the practices of the Palestinian internationalist option at the time. Thus, Iran and Palestine – and by extension 1979 and 1982 – become more than two case studies in this volume. They are two events that punctuate a transformative process that is often summarised by the year 1979.

PRAXIS: FROM SOLIDARITY TO SUPPORT

Even from a surface viewpoint, Third Worldism in some shape or form is associated with the Bandung conference.[9] Be it in histories that trace the genealogy of Third Worldism or in relation to what is termed as the 'Bandung spirit', the conference in 1955 convened in Indonesia figures prominently in histories of Third Worldism. This is not surprising. Not only for obvious reasons but also as an implicit recognition of the importance of the idea of 'praxis' at a time when ideological discourses on anti-imperialism and leftist solidarity had material and inseparable corollaries in action. In other words, the fact that we trace the origins of Third Worldism to a conference of nations and people where not just ideas but also forms of solidarity-in-action were centred is emblematic of the crucial characteristic of Third Worldism as praxis.

Conferences and gatherings play a central role in many of the essays in this volume. While Ataie and Thomson's contributions place conferences at the centre of their analyses, almost all of the other essays here at some point highlight the gathering of Third Worldist activists in the pre and post 1979 era in their narratives. What stands out in this volume is the proliferation of other such spaces, many of which intersected, such as obituaries (Shamshiri), professional associations (Olsen), journal editorial boards (Wieser), and friendship circles (Fuchs). Many of these spaces and places were bottom-up experiments, literal 'praxis', and were understood by the actors as being on a par with theoretical and intellectual discourses. In this way, the essays in this volume reflect the spirit of Third Worldism in highlighting the porous

---

Exile (Warsaw: Museum of Modern Art in Warsaw, 2018); Zeina Maasri, *Cosmopolitan Radicalism: The Visual Politics of Beirut's Global Sixties* (Cambridge: Cambridge University Press, 2020), esp. chaps 5 and 6.

[9] See, for example, Hee-Yeon Co and Kuan-Hsing Chen, 'Bandung/third Worldism' and other articles in *Inter-Asia Cultural Studies* 6, no. 2 (2005): 473–475.

lines between intellectual work and political work,[10] and the purposeful collapsing of theorising and action during that era.[11]

This proliferation of interest in previously ignored or taken-for-granted formal networks of activism such as professional organisations, transnational routes of ideas such as publications, and informal networks such as friendship networks created an important yet rarely commented on distinction between the practice of solidarity versus that of support. Both of these shaped Third Worldism historically even as some of the more material forms of support such as Cuba as a space of Third Worldist gathering or medical organisations supporting the PLO have died out. As such, taken together the essays in this volume raise the question of how we can take the praxis of Third Worldism to conceptualise both the various meanings and work of solidarity, and the ways in which the meanings of 'support' shaped the form of struggle. This distinction comes out of simple questions: Why did so many people travel so far to express their solidarity when issuing declarations and pamphlets was a common practice? Why organise conferences? Why gather? Was the solidarity of words in this historical context not the same as support even as later scholars seemed to have conflated the two?

The support/solidarity interplay that runs through many of the chapters in this volume sheds light on the centrality of the materiality of transnational linkages at the time. Material support as a different historical experience and analytical category from ties of solidarity had real impact on the history of the period and the fate of Third Worldism within it. One place where, for example, conceptualising the actuality of support had an effect is how PLO camps borrowed from and were shaped by Cuban camps. We know that for many Middle East groups that turned to armed struggle, the PLO camps in Jordan, Iraq, and Lebanon were important places where they trained (both Islamists and leftists as several chapters of this volume mention) and

---

[10] This is a distinction raised by David Scott as quoted by Naghmeh Sohrabi, 'Writing Revolution as if Women Mattered', *Comparative Studies of South Asia, Africa and the Middle East* 42, no. 2 (2022): 546.

[11] For other works that similarly reflect spaces of praxis, in addition to works cited throughout this volume, see Christopher J. Lee and Anne Garland Mahler, 'The Bandung Era, Non-alignment and the Third-Way Literary Imagination', in *The Palgrave Handbook of Cold War Literature*, ed. Andrew Hammond (New York: Palgrave Macmillan, 2020), 183–202, and Paraska Tolan, *Maghreb Noir: The Militant-Artists of North Africa and the Struggle for a Pan-African, Postcolonial Future* (Palo Alto: Stanford University Press, 2023).

there is evidence that these camps differed experientially from the Cuban camps. Would a rethinking about PLO/Cuba as both 'praxis of reciprocal anti-imperial solidarity' and material support allow us to take our understanding of these ties beyond the imaginary of Third Worldism and into the experience and practice of it?

Networks of support and solidarity both relied on trust. Underlying several of the chapters in this volume is a concern with how friendship and kinship enabled the creation of transnational networks for Third Worldist activism. These informal ties stood out from formal networks even as they undergirded more formal actions. This volume suggests how a focus on informal networks alongside a distinction between solidarity and support can and should be leveraged to theorise and conceptualise another overarching framework that often dominates our writings about Third Worldism, namely the notion of failure/end/defeat. While the formal networks that enabled a particular type of transnational support ended through the powerful events of 1979 and 1982, it stands to reason that the informal ties of trust and solidarity that maintained them had an afterlife and trajectory that went past these two events. As some of the chapters in this volume show, the informal networks were not shattered by the ostensible rupture of 1979/1982 but were transformed. These transformations enabled the interplay of leftism and Islamism that is key to the shape of the revolutionary praxis that emerged in the time (and in the space) between the Iranian Revolution and the end of the Palestinian presence in Lebanon.

BEYOND THIRD WORLDISM

Activism in the 1960s and 1970s was characterised by short horizons. Change was to come in their time, so the revolutionaries believed. Today, activism often works with longer timeframes. Be it against the structural nature of racism or the environmental impact of humankind, the expected fruits of activism exist beyond the foreseeable future. At the same time, the historiography of activism in contexts outside the Middle East illuminates how solidarity transformed over time. For example, looking across the span of several decades, it traces how the New Left fed into the anti-nuclear movement, which, in turn, constituted the beginnings of environmentalist activism.[12] We have still no such understanding of the transformation of social movements in the Middle East, where historical change is understood more in terms of violent ruptures and periodisation consists of punctuating time with wars and revolutions. As a result, our questions themselves remain stuck in binaries of success/defeat or life/death of movements with long histories and that merely reflect the surface of the movements' historical realities.

Focusing on the practices and materialities that constituted social movements in the Middle East, it becomes evident that while violent ruptures did play a transformative role, treating them as absolutes obscures a process of change over time, even across social movements that are ideologically at odds with each other. The overreliance on violent ruptures to do the periodisation for us makes it difficult to think creatively beyond them. Conceptualising 1979/1982 as a tool for problematising such a periodisation can only be a starting point. As the 1980s and 1990s become the objects of historical studies, the perspectives, approaches, and ensuing questions from this volume can lead the way towards a praxis-centred historiography, one where the questions we pose of social movements are not of life or death but rather how ideas and practices transformed and fed into other types of movements.

---

[12] For example, Francesca Polletta, *Freedom Is an Endless Meeting: Democracy in American Social Movements* (Chicago: University of Chicago Press, 2002); Kyle Harvey, *American Anti-Nuclear Activism, 1975–1990: The Challenges of Peace* (London: Palgrave Macmillan, 2014); Frank Zelko, *Make It a Green Peace!: The Rise of a Countercultural Environmentalism* (Oxford: Oxford University Press, 2013); Astrid Mignon Kirchhof and Jan-Henrik Meyer, 'Global Protest against Nuclear Power: Transfer and Transnational Exchange in the 1970s and 1980s', *Historical Social Research/Historische Sozialforschung* 39, no. 1 (2014): 165–190.

Index

References to images are in *italics*; references to notes are indicated by n.